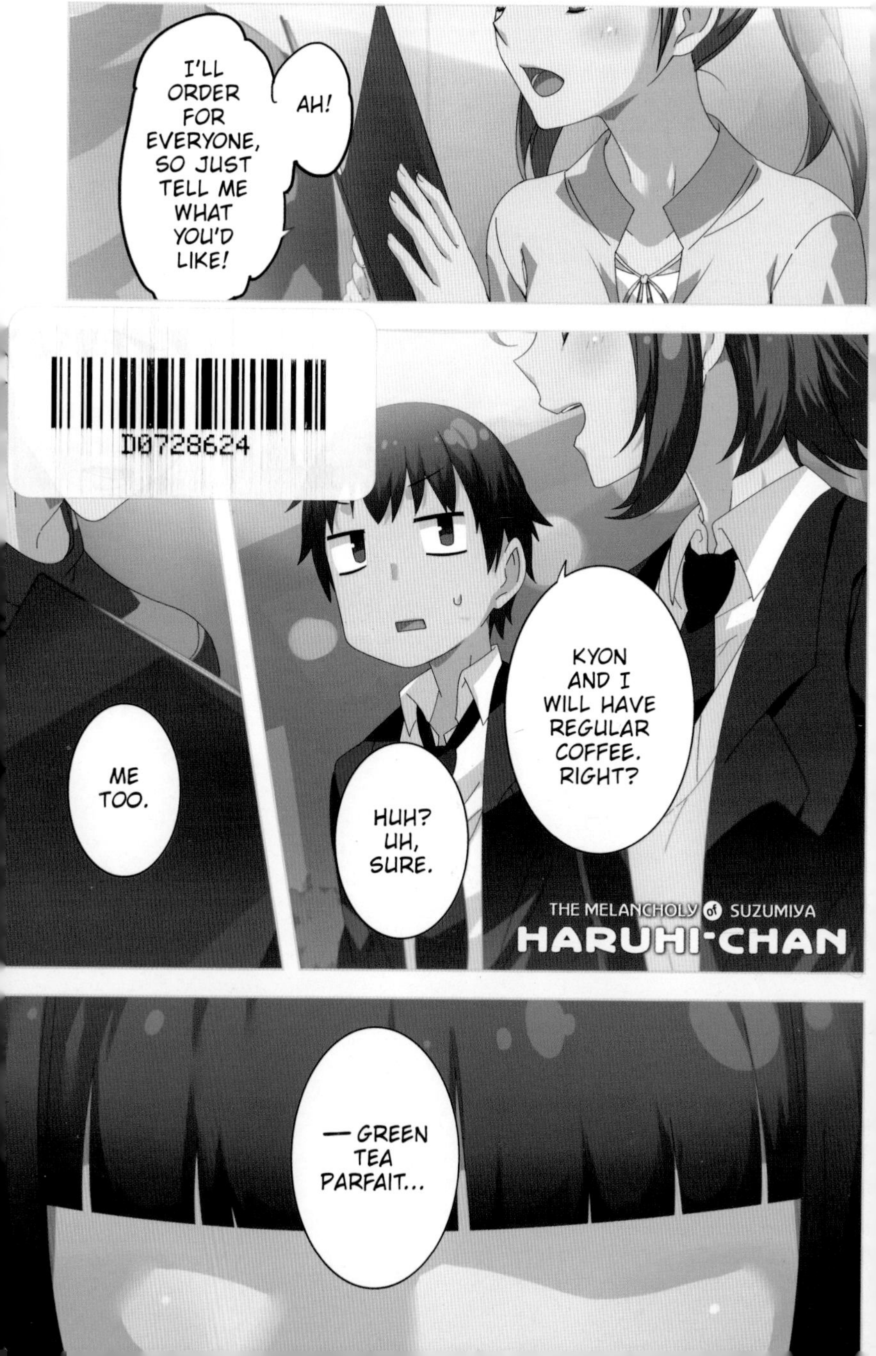
AH!
I'LL ORDER FOR EVERYONE, SO JUST TELL ME WHAT YOU'D LIKE!
KYON AND I WILL HAVE REGULAR COFFEE. RIGHT?
HUH? UH, SURE.
ME TOO.
THE MELANCHOLY of SUZUMIYA HARUHI-CHAN
— GREEN TEA PARFAIT...

THE MELANCHOLY of SUZUMIYA HARUHI-CHAN

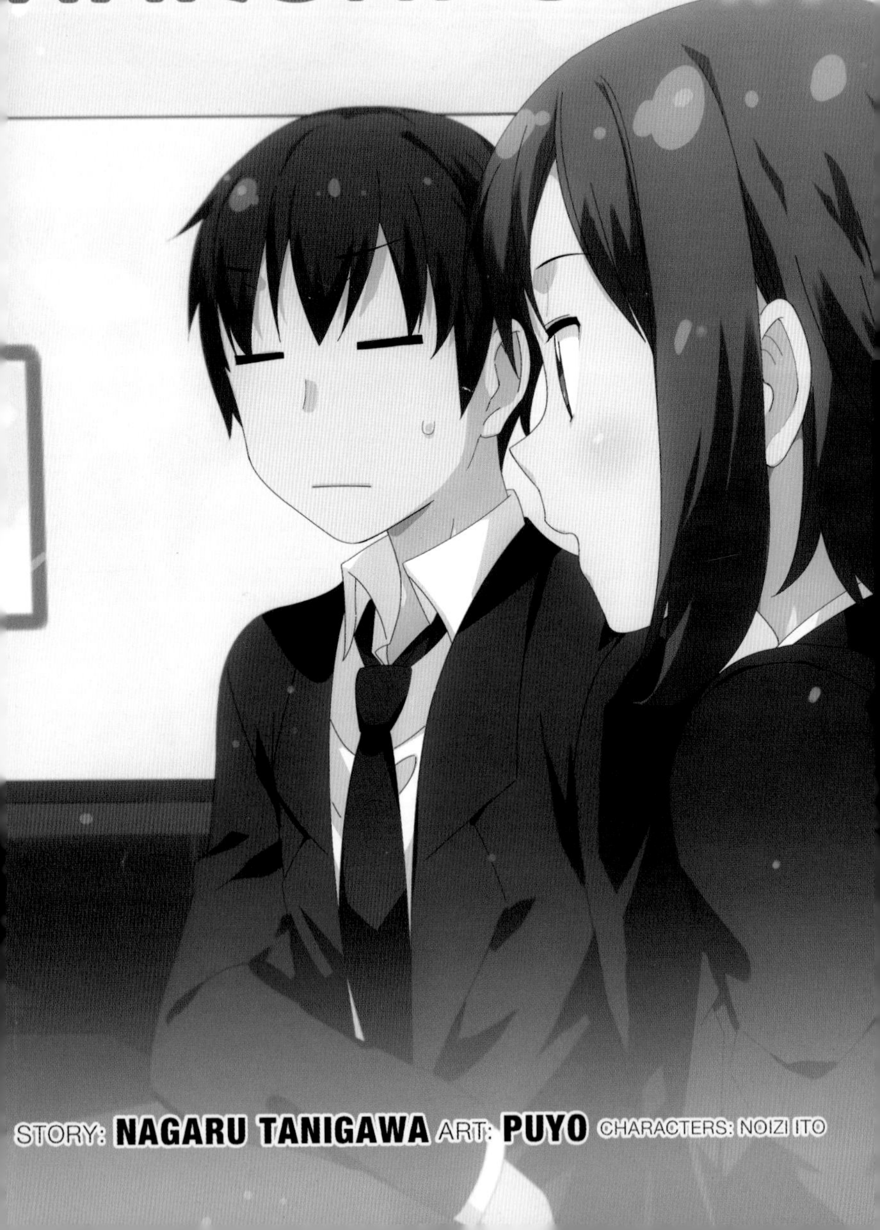

STORY: **NAGARU TANIGAWA** ART: **PUYO** CHARACTERS: NOIZI ITO

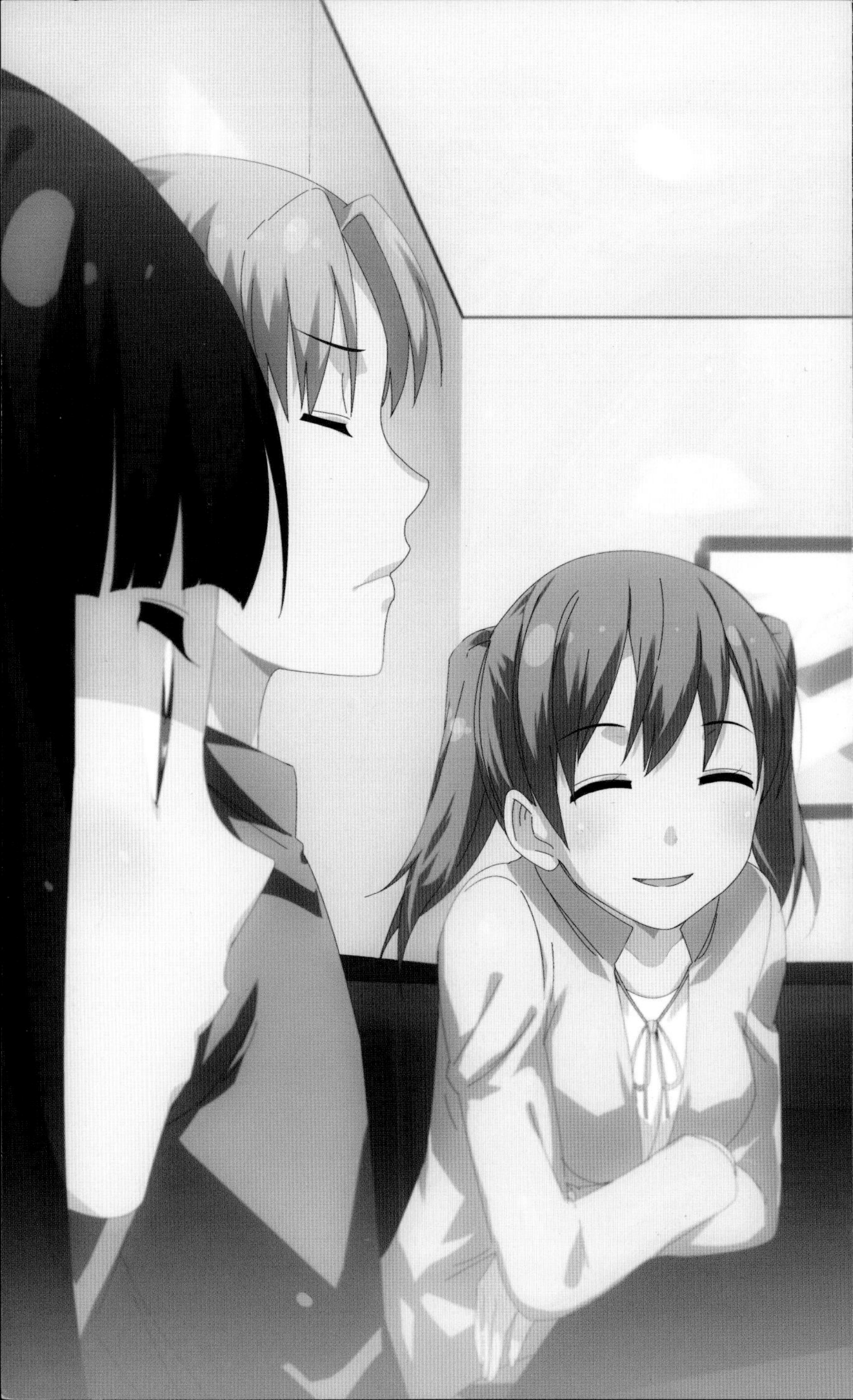

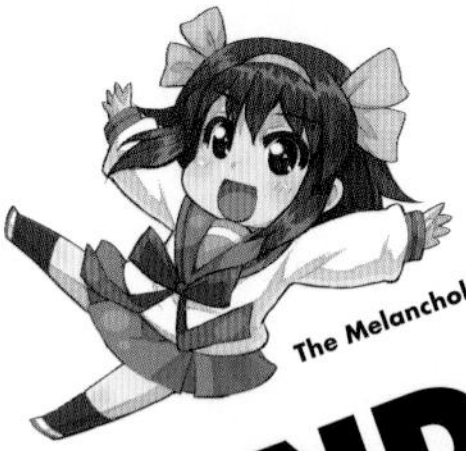

The Melancholy of Suzumiya Haruhi-chan 08

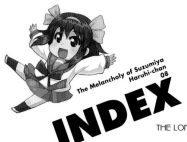

INDEX

THE MELANCHOLY OF SUZUMIYA

HARUHI-CHAN

The Untold Adventures of the SOS Brigade

THIS IS FICTION

STORY: **NAGARU TANIGAWA** ART: **PUYO** CHARACTERS: NOIZI ITO

GIVING HER
HAIR MORE
VOLUME
IS PRETTY
TOUGH.

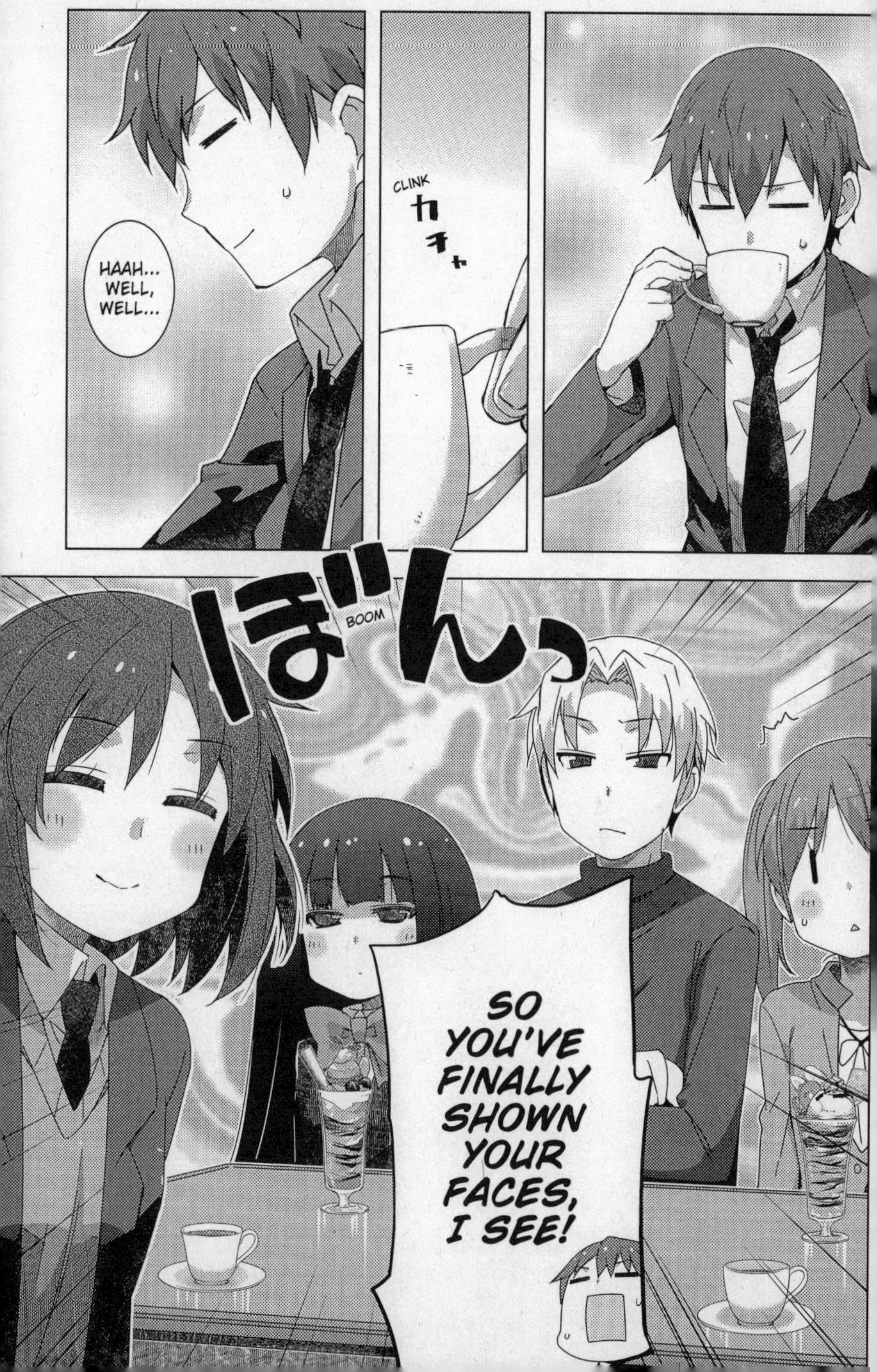
CLINK
カチャ
HAAH... WELL, WELL...
ぼんっ
BOOM
SO YOU'VE FINALLY SHOWN YOUR FACES, I SEE!

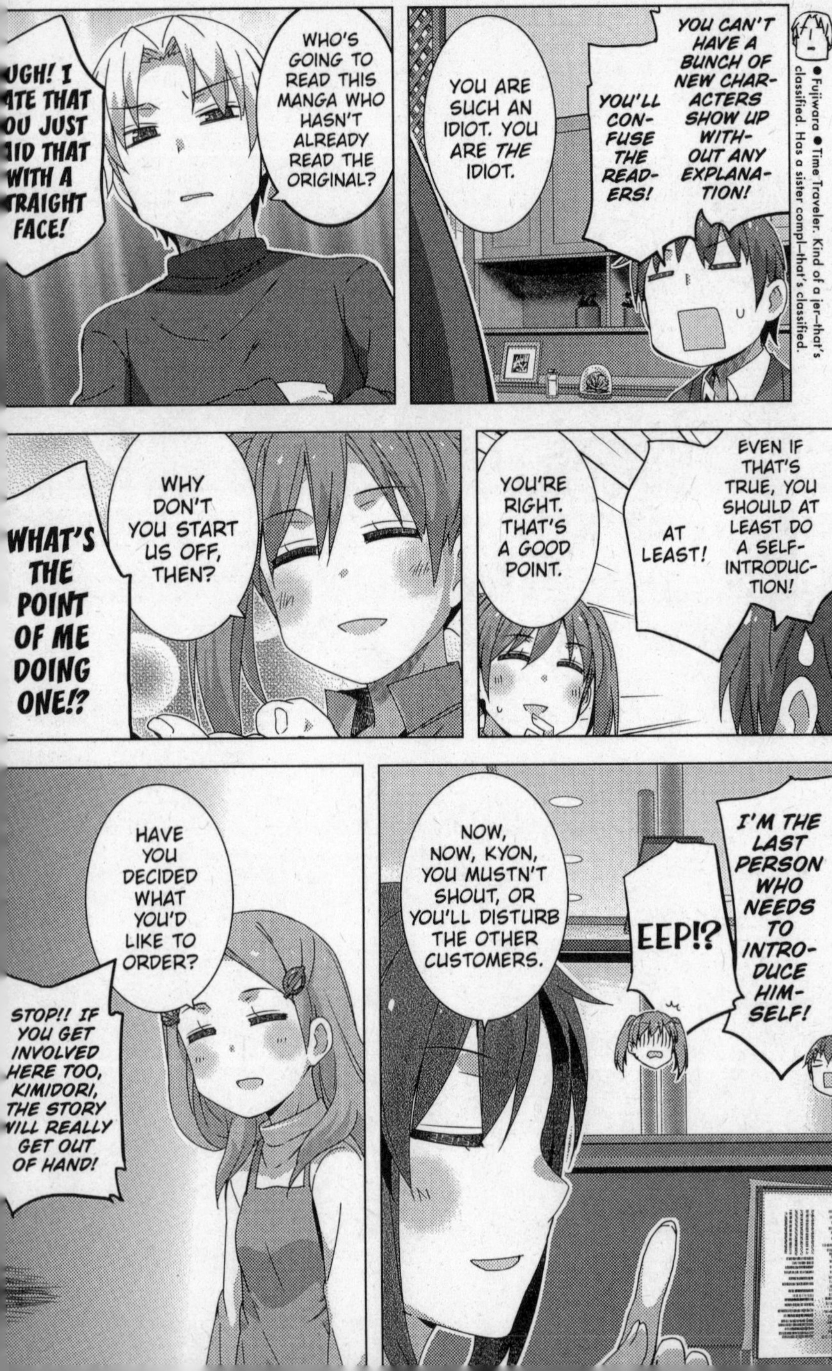
●Fujiwara ●Time Traveler. Kind of a jer—that's classified. Has a sister compl—that's classified.
YOU CAN'T HAVE A BUNCH OF NEW CHARACTERS SHOW UP WITHOUT ANY EXPLANATION!
YOU'LL CONFUSE THE READERS!
YOU ARE SUCH AN IDIOT. YOU ARE *THE* IDIOT.
WHO'S GOING TO READ THIS MANGA WHO HASN'T ALREADY READ THE ORIGINAL?
UGH! I ATE THAT OU JUST AID THAT WITH A TRAIGHT FACE!
EVEN IF THAT'S TRUE, YOU SHOULD AT LEAST DO A SELF-INTRODUCTION!
AT LEAST!
YOU'RE RIGHT. THAT'S A GOOD POINT.
WHY DON'T YOU START US OFF, THEN?
WHAT'S THE POINT OF ME DOING ONE!?
I'M THE LAST PERSON WHO NEEDS TO INTRODUCE HIMSELF!
EEP!?
NOW, NOW, KYON, YOU MUSTN'T SHOUT, OR YOU'LL DISTURB THE OTHER CUSTOMERS.
HAVE YOU DECIDED WHAT YOU'D LIKE TO ORDER?
STOP!! IF YOU GET INVOLVED HERE TOO, KIMIDORI, THE STORY WILL REALLY GET OUT OF HAND!

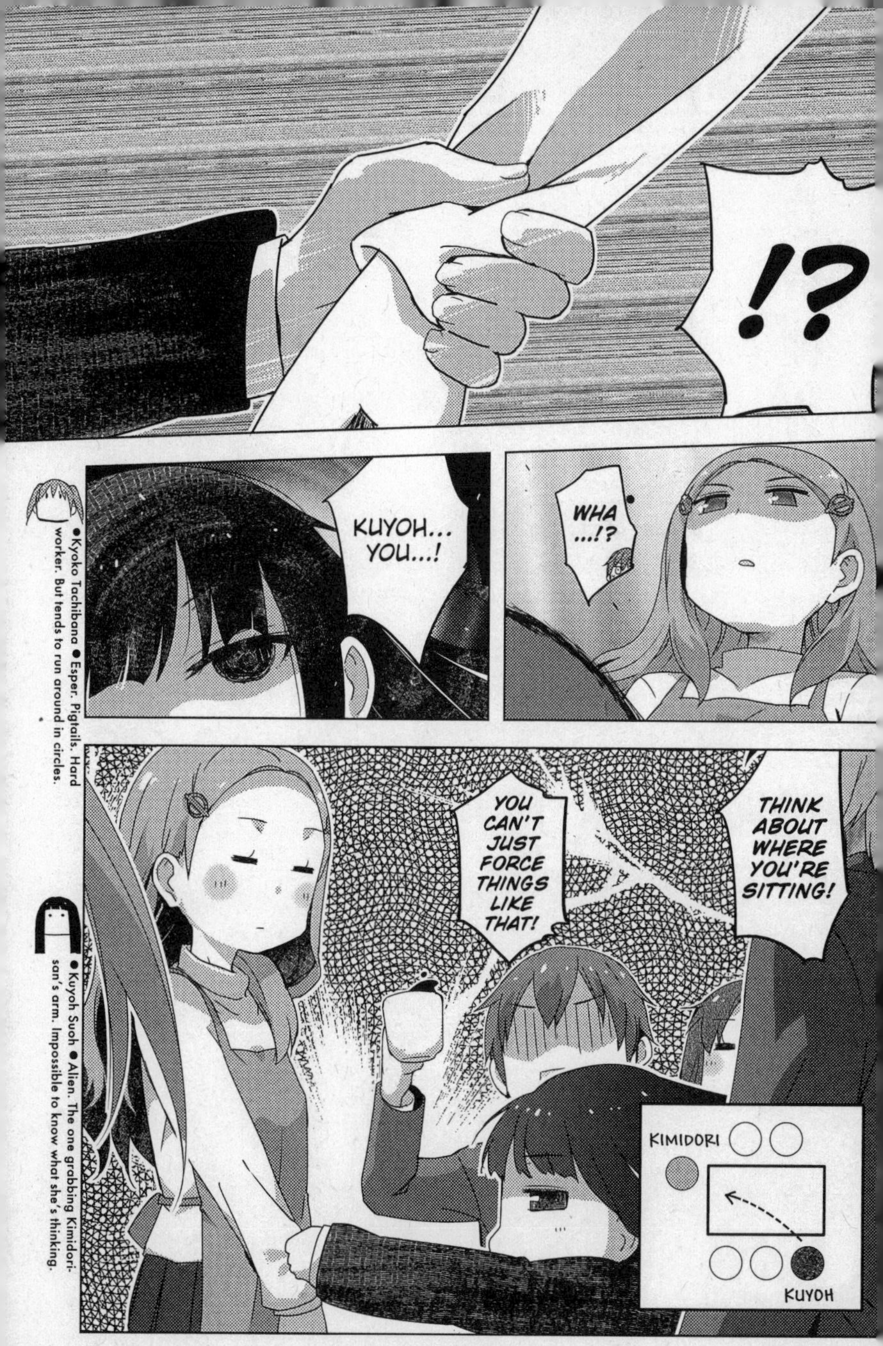
!?
WHA ...!?
KUYOH... YOU...!
THINK ABOUT WHERE YOU'RE SITTING!
YOU CAN'T JUST FORCE THINGS LIKE THAT!
KIMIDORI
KUYOH

●Kyoko Tachibana ●Esper. Pigtails. Hard worker. But tends to run around in circles.

●Kuyoh Suoh ●Alien. The one grabbing Kimidori-san's arm. Impossible to know what she's thinking.

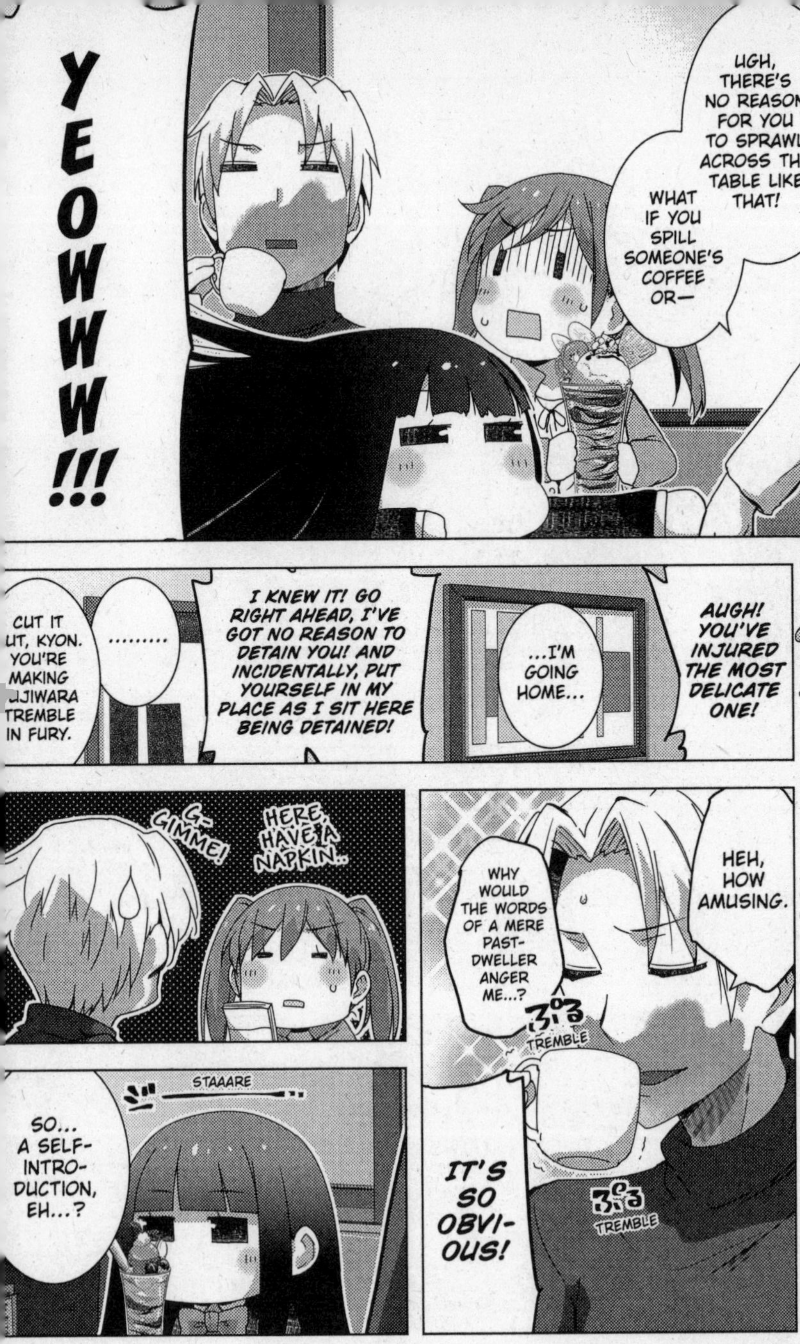
UGH, THERE'S NO REASON FOR YOU TO SPRAWL ACROSS THE TABLE LIKE THAT!
WHAT IF YOU SPILL SOMEONE'S COFFEE OR—
YEOWWW!!!
AUGH! YOU'VE INJURED THE MOST DELICATE ONE!
...I'M GOING HOME...
I KNEW IT! GO RIGHT AHEAD, I'VE GOT NO REASON TO DETAIN YOU! AND INCIDENTALLY, PUT YOURSELF IN MY PLACE AS I SIT HERE BEING DETAINED!
....
CUT IT UT, KYON. YOU'RE MAKING UJIWARA TREMBLE IN FURY.
HEH, HOW AMUSING.
WHY WOULD THE WORDS OF A MERE PAST-DWELLER ANGER ME...?
ぷる TREMBLE
ぷる TREMBLE
IT'S SO OBVIOUS!
HERE, HAVE A NAPKIN..
G-GIMME!
STAAARE
SO... A SELF-INTRODUCTION, EH...?

● Kimidori-san ● Alien. Unauthorized part-timer. Kuyoh often grabs her arm when she's not paying attention.

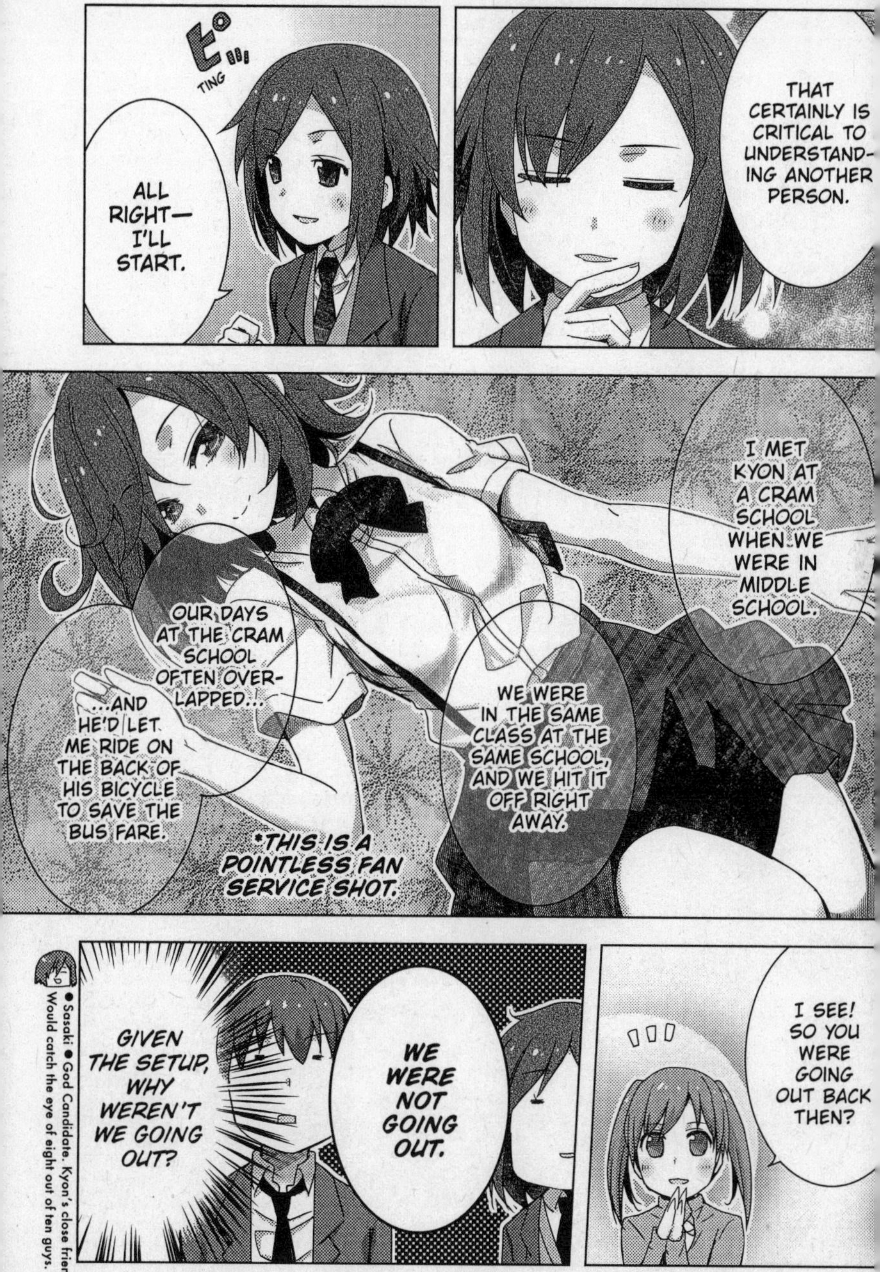
THAT CERTAINLY IS CRITICAL TO UNDERSTANDING ANOTHER PERSON.
TING
ALL RIGHT— I'LL START.
I MET KYON AT A CRAM SCHOOL WHEN WE WERE IN MIDDLE SCHOOL.
WE WERE IN THE SAME CLASS AT THE SAME SCHOOL, AND WE HIT IT OFF RIGHT AWAY.
OUR DAYS AT THE CRAM SCHOOL OFTEN OVERLAPPED...
...AND HE'D LET ME RIDE ON THE BACK OF HIS BICYCLE TO SAVE THE BUS FARE.
*THIS IS A POINTLESS FAN SERVICE SHOT.
I SEE! SO YOU WERE GOING OUT BACK THEN?
WE WERE NOT GOING OUT.
GIVEN THE SETUP, WHY WEREN'T WE GOING OUT?

● Sasaki ● God Candidate. Kyon's close friend. Would catch the eye of eight out of ten guys.

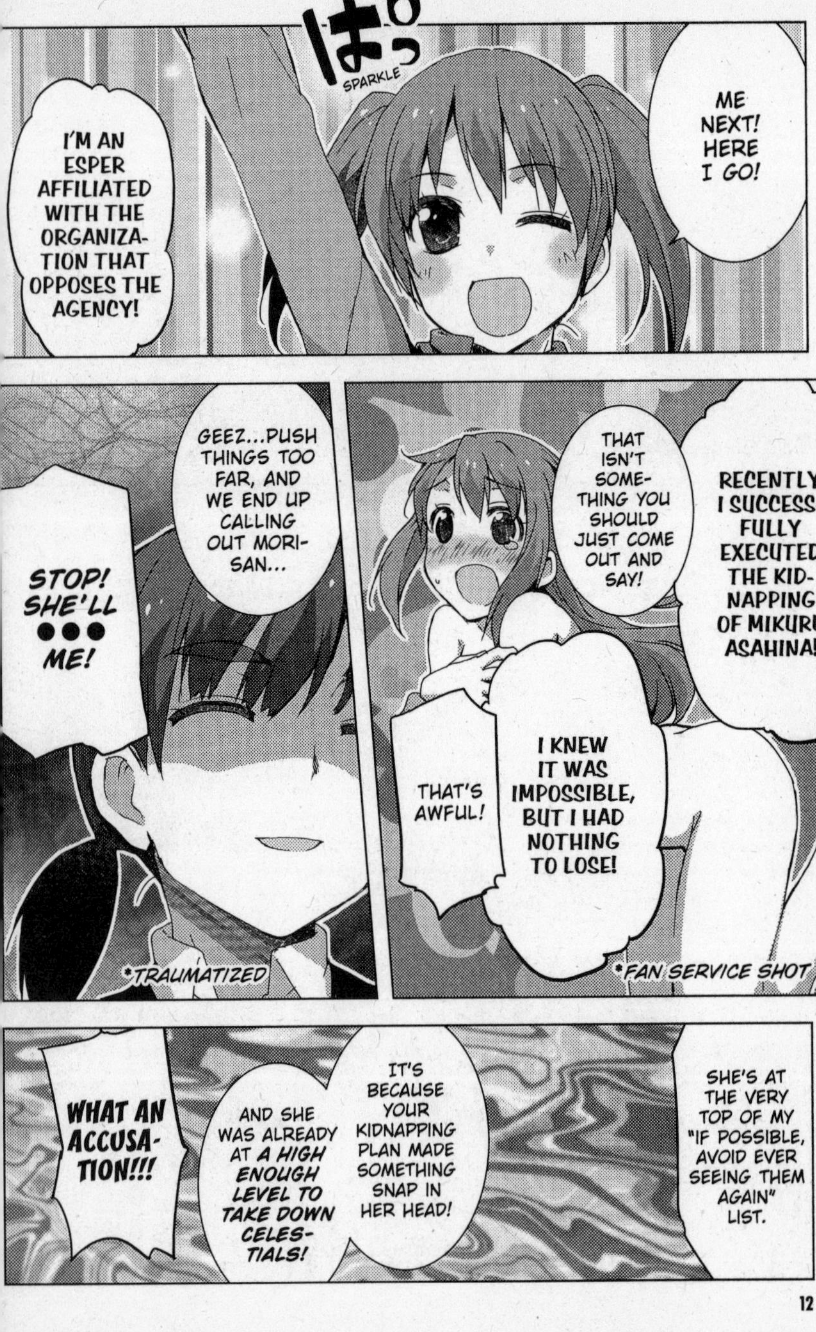
ぱっ
SPARKLE
ME NEXT! HERE I GO!
I'M AN ESPER AFFILIATED WITH THE ORGANIZATION THAT OPPOSES THE AGENCY!
RECENTLY I SUCCESSFULLY EXECUTED THE KIDNAPPING OF MIKURU ASAHINA!
THAT ISN'T SOMETHING YOU SHOULD JUST COME OUT AND SAY!
I KNEW IT WAS IMPOSSIBLE, BUT I HAD NOTHING TO LOSE!
THAT'S AWFUL!
*FAN SERVICE SHOT
GEEZ...PUSH THINGS TOO FAR, AND WE END UP CALLING OUT MORI-SAN...
STOP! SHE'LL ●●● ME!
*TRAUMATIZED
SHE'S AT THE VERY TOP OF MY "IF POSSIBLE, AVOID EVER SEEING THEM AGAIN" LIST.
IT'S BECAUSE YOUR KIDNAPPING PLAN MADE SOMETHING SNAP IN HER HEAD!
AND SHE WAS ALREADY AT A HIGH ENOUGH LEVEL TO TAKE DOWN CELESTIALS!
WHAT AN ACCUSATION!!!

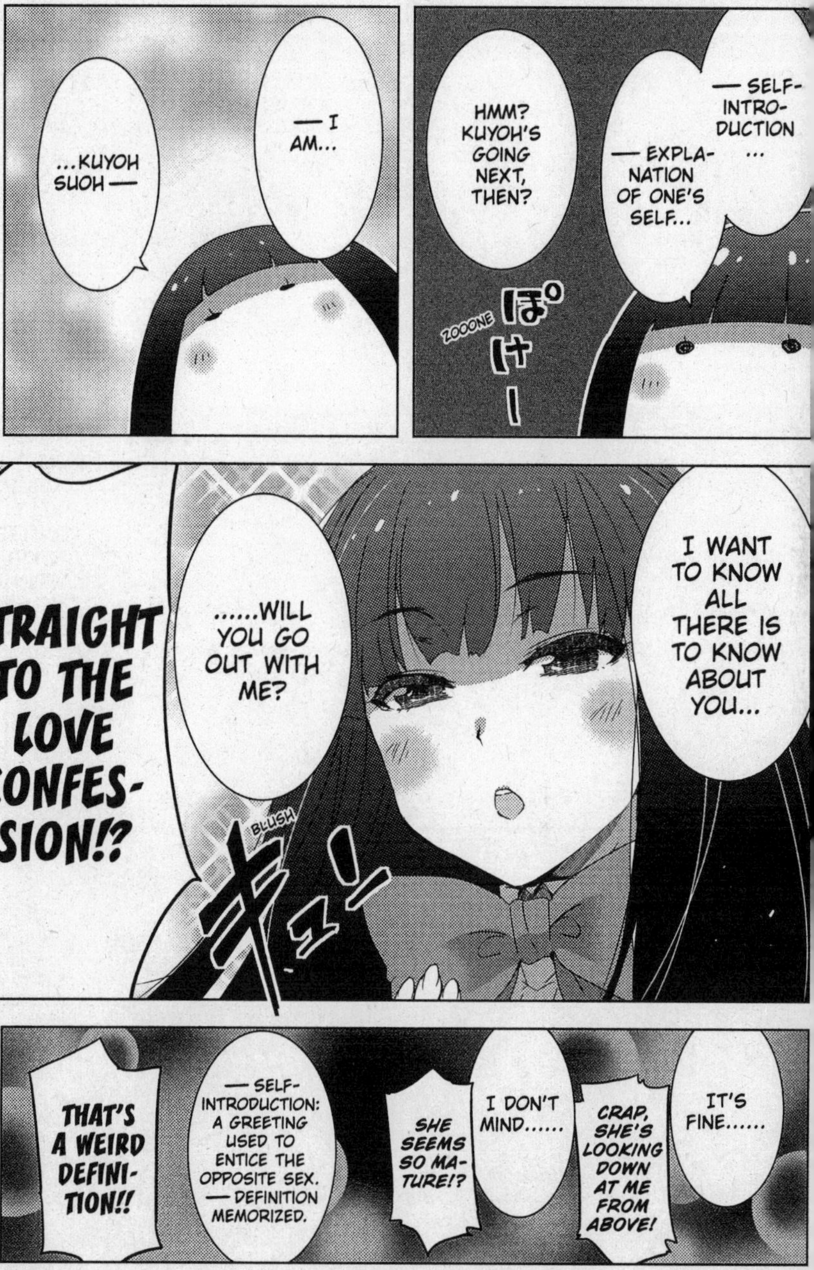
— SELF-INTRODUCTION ...
— EXPLANATION OF ONE'S SELF...
HMM? KUYOH'S GOING NEXT, THEN?
ZOOONE
ぽけー
— I AM...
...KUYOH SUOH —
I WANT TO KNOW ALL THERE IS TO KNOW ABOUT YOU...
......WILL YOU GO OUT WITH ME?
STRAIGHT TO THE LOVE CONFESSION!?
BLUSH
キュン
IT'S FINE......
CRAP, SHE'S LOOKING DOWN AT ME FROM ABOVE!
I DON'T MIND......
SHE SEEMS SO MATURE!?
— SELF-INTRODUCTION: A GREETING USED TO ENTICE THE OPPOSITE SEX. — DEFINITION MEMORIZED.
THAT'S A WEIRD DEFINITION!!

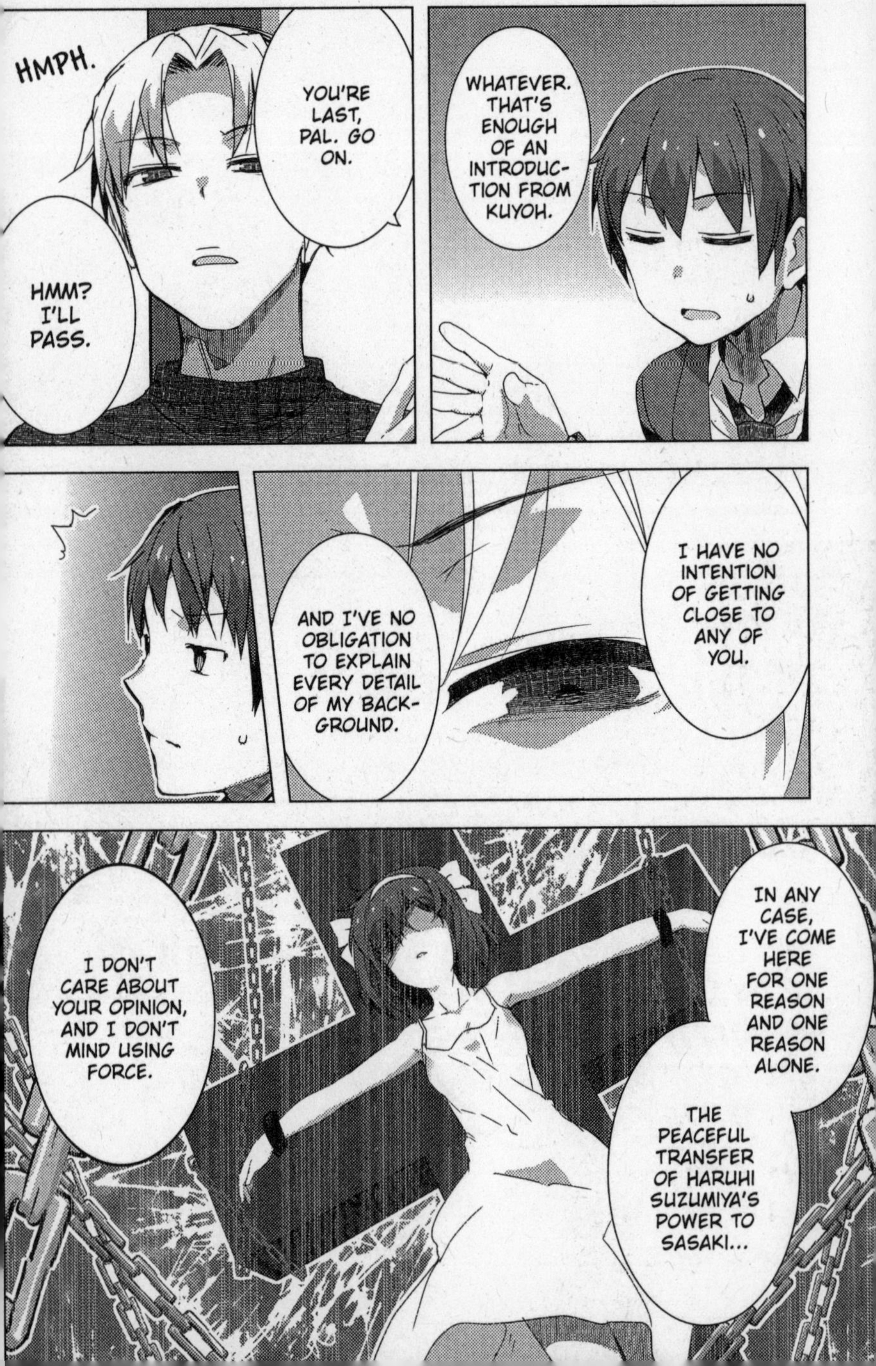
WHATEVER. THAT'S ENOUGH OF AN INTRODUCTION FROM KUYOH.
YOU'RE LAST, PAL. GO ON.
HMPH.
HMM? I'LL PASS.
I HAVE NO INTENTION OF GETTING CLOSE TO ANY OF YOU.
AND I'VE NO OBLIGATION TO EXPLAIN EVERY DETAIL OF MY BACKGROUND.
IN ANY CASE, I'VE COME HERE FOR ONE REASON AND ONE REASON ALONE.
THE PEACEFUL TRANSFER OF HARUHI SUZUMIYA'S POWER TO SASAKI...
I DON'T CARE ABOUT YOUR OPINION, AND I DON'T MIND USING FORCE.

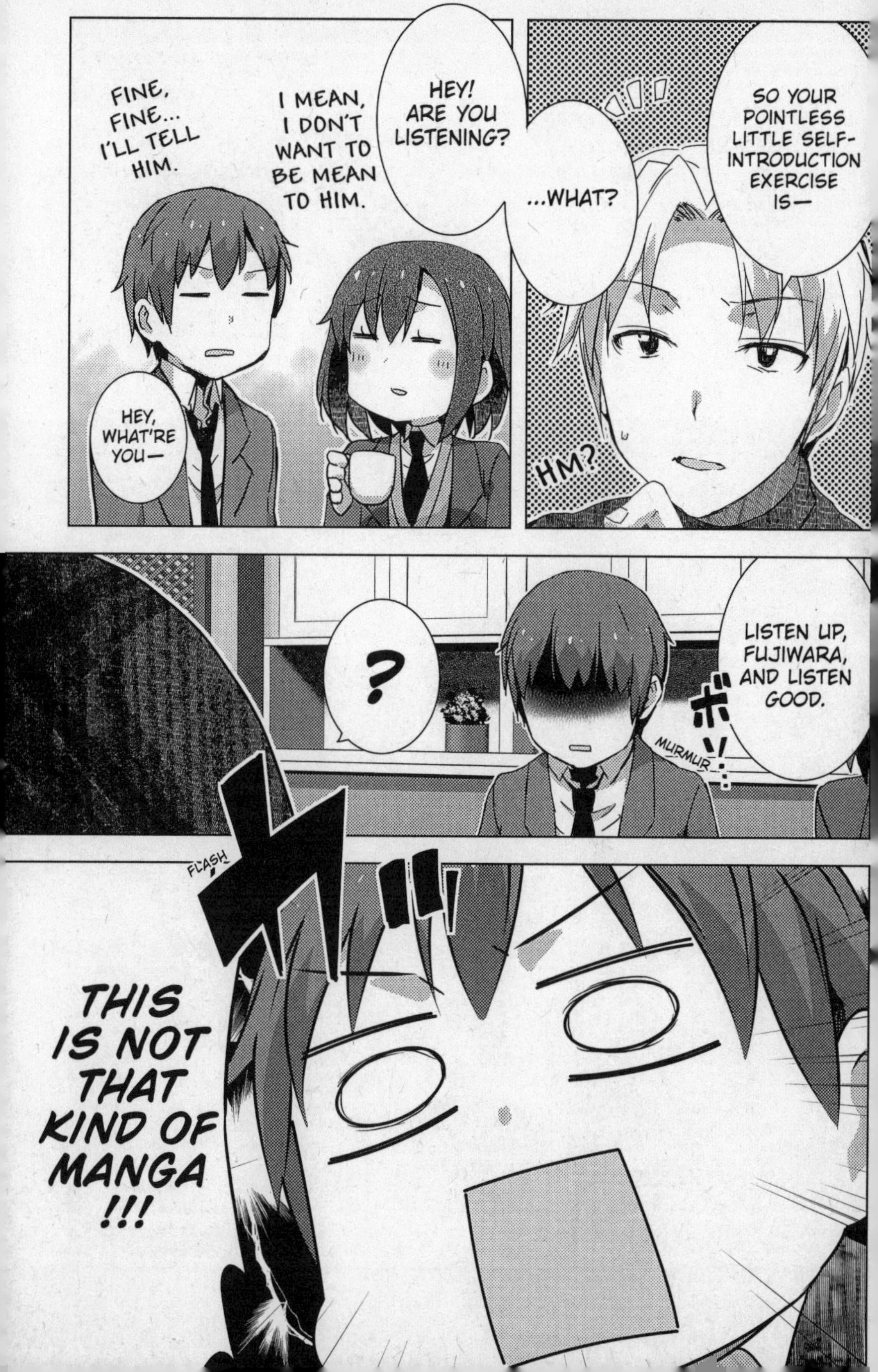
SO YOUR POINTLESS LITTLE SELF-INTRODUCTION EXERCISE IS—
...WHAT?
HM?
HEY! ARE YOU LISTENING?
I MEAN, I DON'T WANT TO BE MEAN TO HIM.
FINE, FINE... I'LL TELL HIM.
HEY, WHAT'RE YOU—
LISTEN UP, FUJIWARA, AND LISTEN GOOD.
ボッ!
MURMUR
?
FLASH
THIS IS NOT THAT KIND OF MANGA!!!

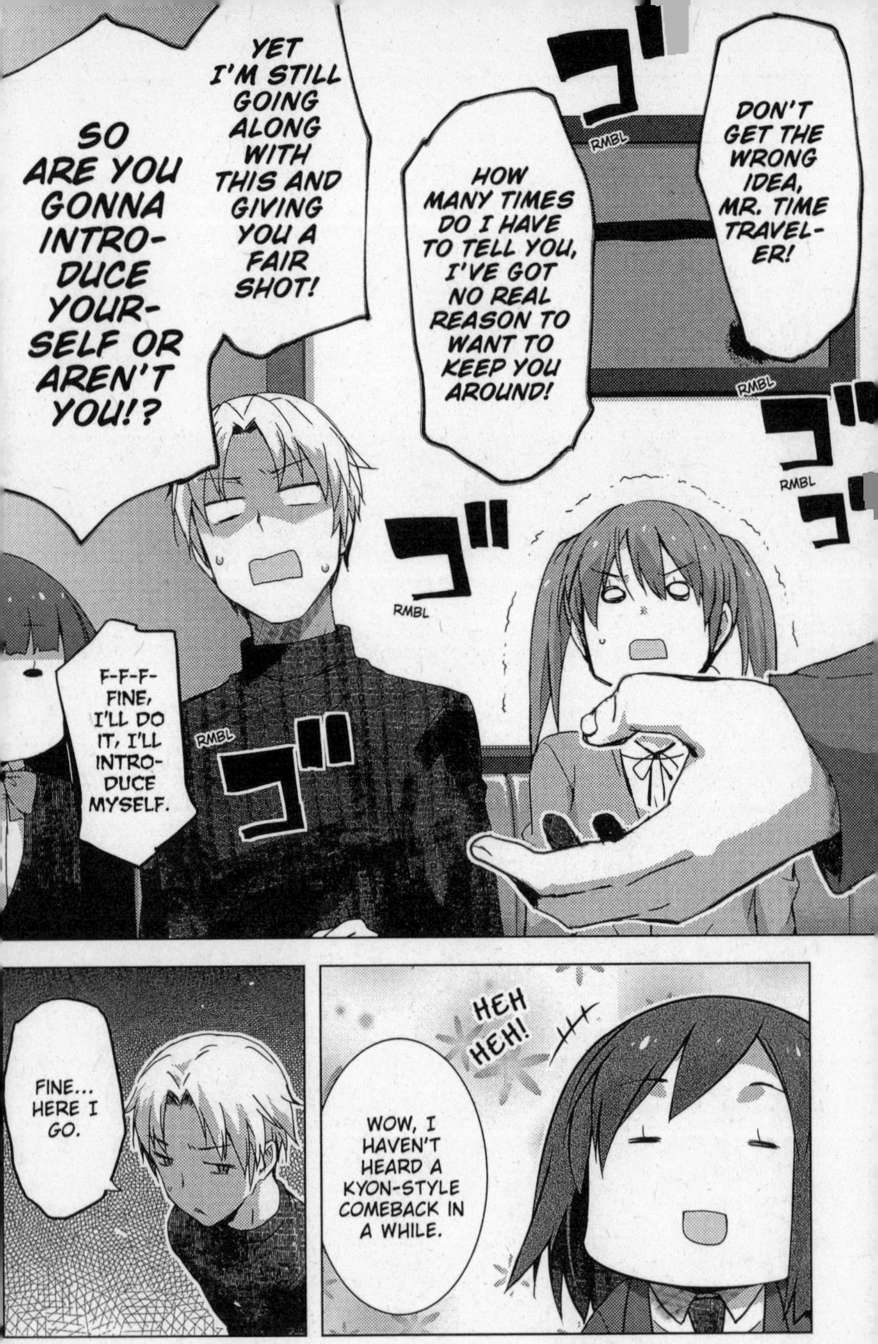
DON'T GET THE WRONG IDEA, MR. TIME TRAVELER!
RMBL
HOW MANY TIMES DO I HAVE TO TELL YOU, I'VE GOT NO REAL REASON TO WANT TO KEEP YOU AROUND!
YET I'M STILL GOING ALONG WITH THIS AND GIVING YOU A FAIR SHOT!
SO ARE YOU GONNA INTRODUCE YOURSELF OR AREN'T YOU!?
RMBL
RMBL
RMBL
RMBL
F-F-F-FINE, I'LL DO IT, I'LL INTRODUCE MYSELF.
HEH HEH!
WOW, I HAVEN'T HEARD A KYON-STYLE COMEBACK IN A WHILE.
FINE... HERE I GO.

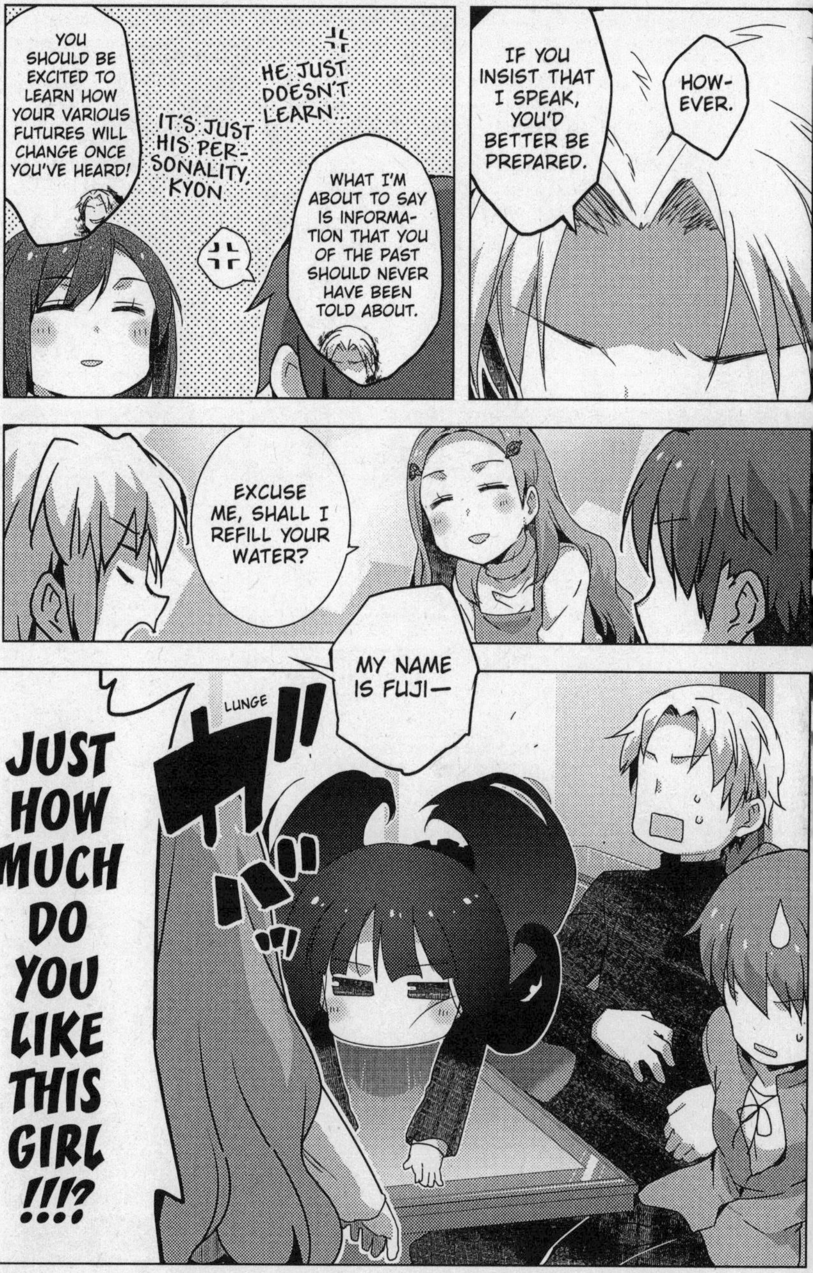
HOW-EVER.
IF YOU INSIST THAT I SPEAK, YOU'D BETTER BE PREPARED.
WHAT I'M ABOUT TO SAY IS INFORMATION THAT YOU OF THE PAST SHOULD NEVER HAVE BEEN TOLD ABOUT.
YOU SHOULD BE EXCITED TO LEARN HOW YOUR VARIOUS FUTURES WILL CHANGE ONCE YOU'VE HEARD!
HE JUST DOESN'T LEARN.
IT'S JUST HIS PERSONALITY, KYON.
EXCUSE ME, SHALL I REFILL YOUR WATER?
MY NAME IS FUJI—
LUNGE
JUST HOW MUCH DO YOU LIKE THIS GIRL!!!?

END

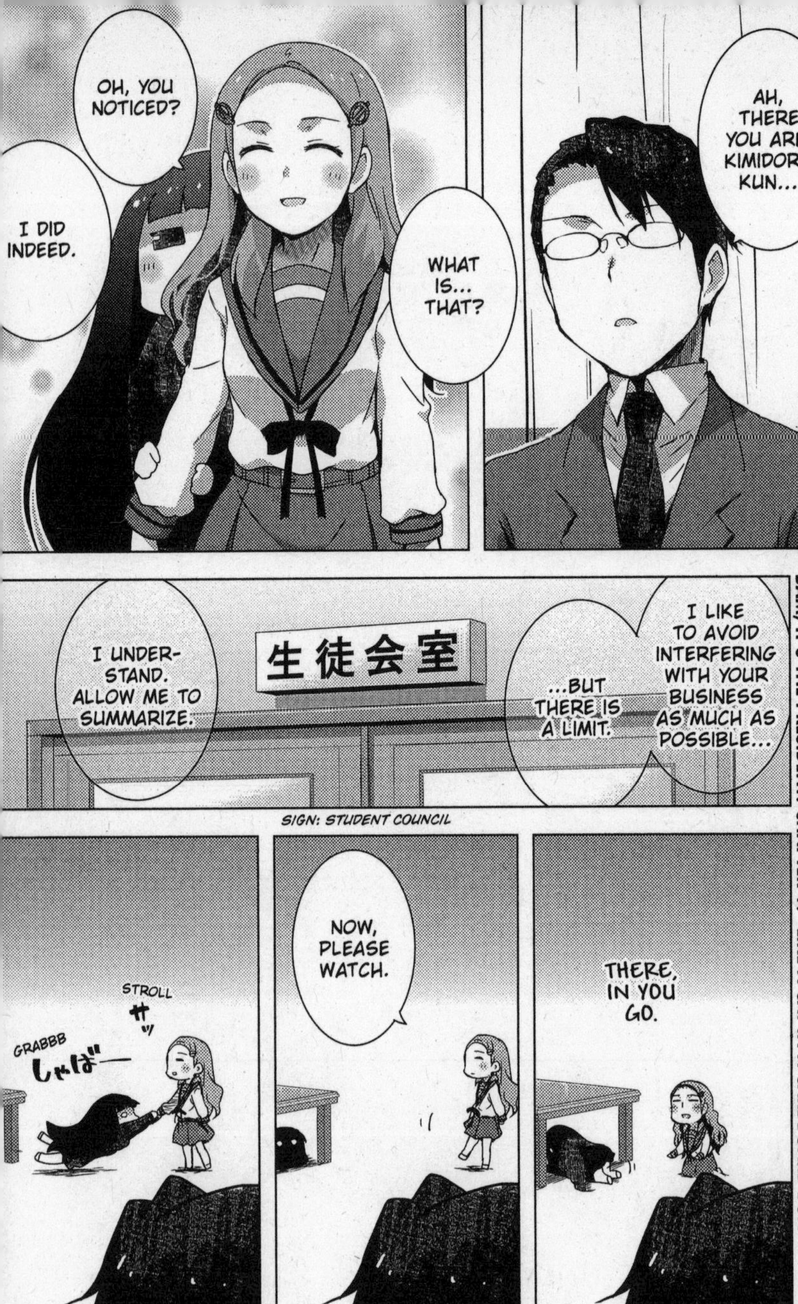
AH, THERE YOU ARE, KIMIDORI-KUN...
WHAT IS... THAT?
OH, YOU NOTICED?
I DID INDEED.
I LIKE TO AVOID INTERFERING WITH YOUR BUSINESS AS MUCH AS POSSIBLE...
...BUT THERE IS A LIMIT.
生徒会室
I UNDER-STAND. ALLOW ME TO SUMMARIZE.
SIGN: STUDENT COUNCIL
THERE, IN YOU GO.
NOW, PLEASE WATCH.
STROLL
サッ
GRABBB
しゃばー

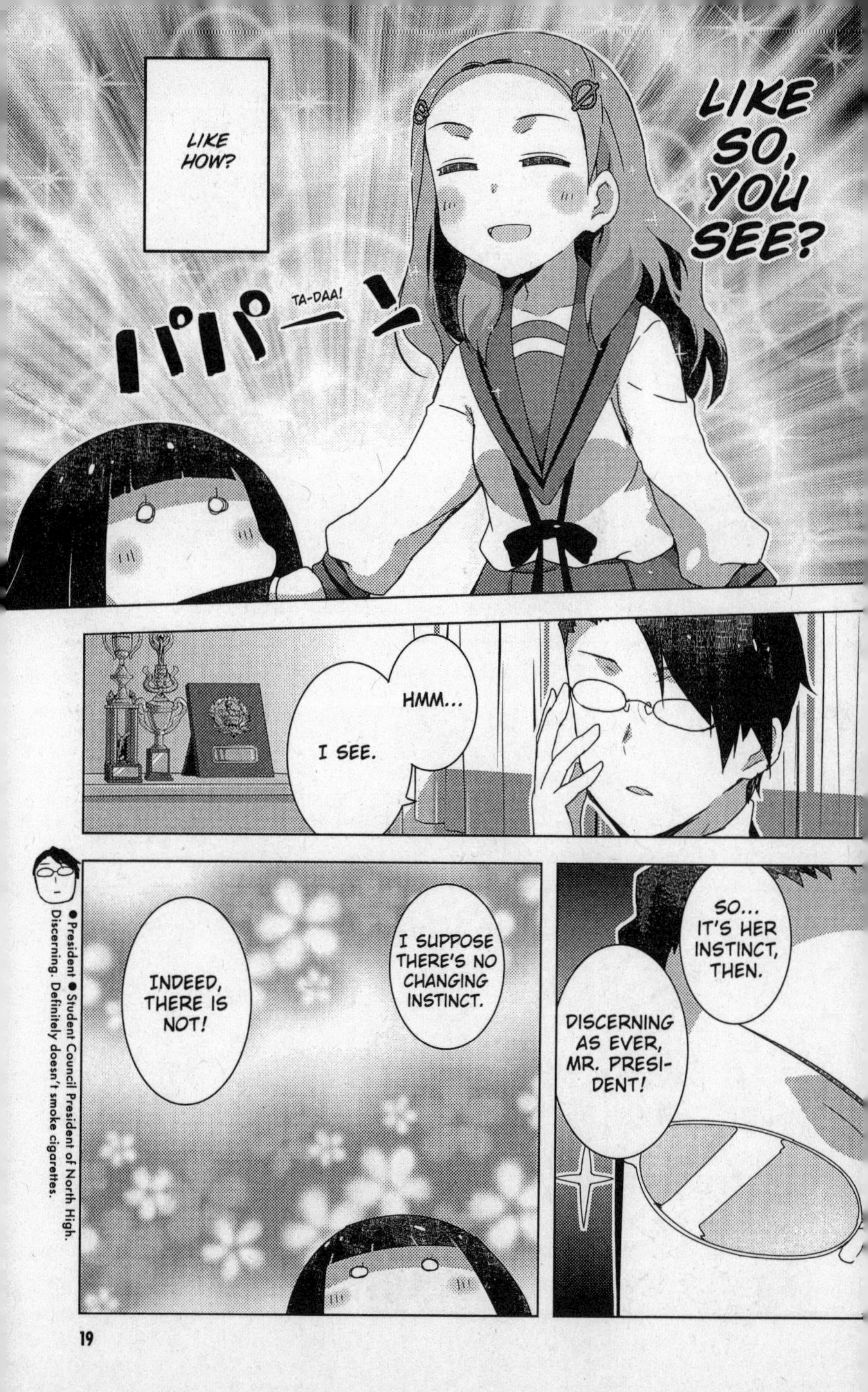
LIKE SO, YOU SEE?
TA-DAA!
LIKE HOW?
HMM...
I SEE.
SO... IT'S HER INSTINCT, THEN.
DISCERNING AS EVER, MR. PRESIDENT!
I SUPPOSE THERE'S NO CHANGING INSTINCT.
INDEED, THERE IS NOT!

●President ●Student Council President of North High. Discerning. Definitely doesn't smoke cigarettes.

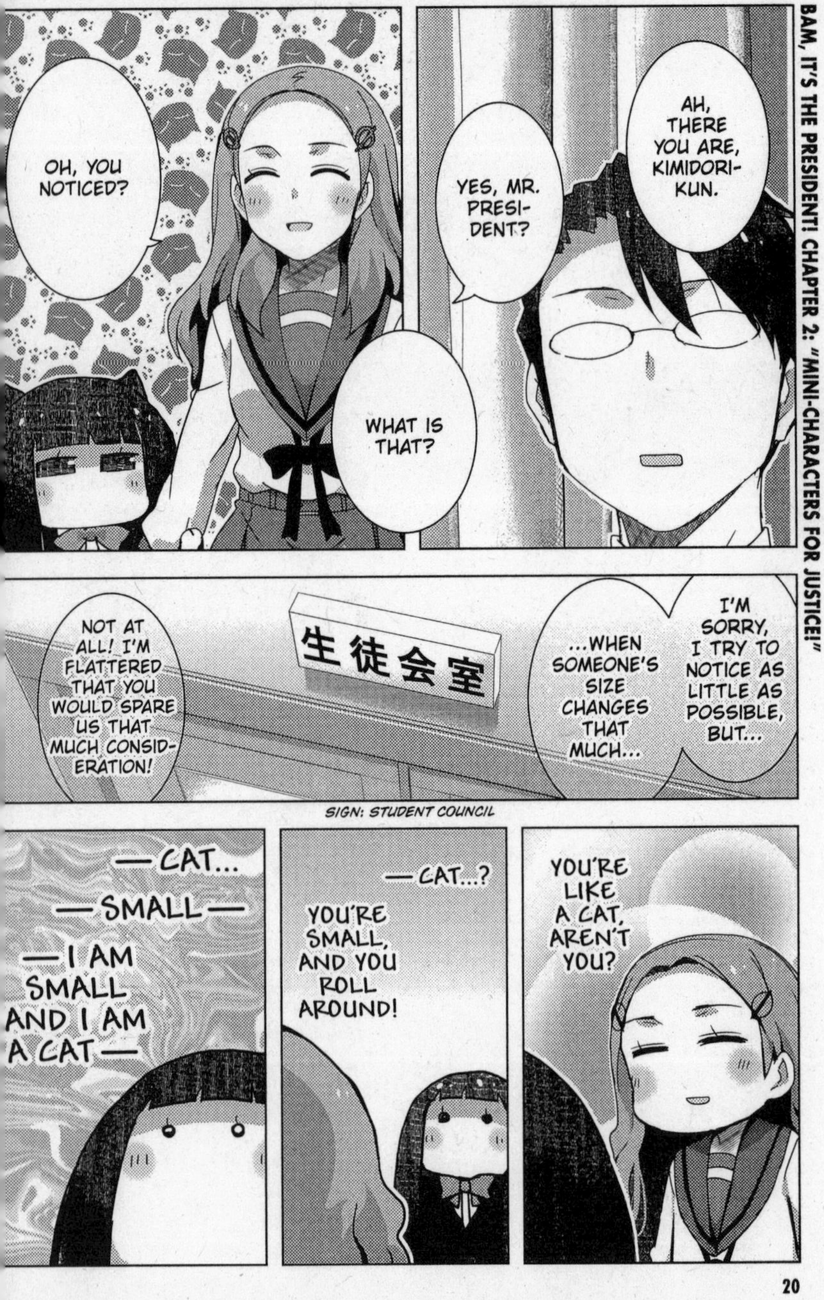
AH, THERE YOU ARE, KIMIDORI-KUN.
YES, MR. PRESIDENT?
WHAT IS THAT?
OH, YOU NOTICED?
I'M SORRY, I TRY TO NOTICE AS LITTLE AS POSSIBLE, BUT...
...WHEN SOMEONE'S SIZE CHANGES THAT MUCH...
生徒会室
NOT AT ALL! I'M FLATTERED THAT YOU WOULD SPARE US THAT MUCH CONSIDERATION!
YOU'RE LIKE A CAT, AREN'T YOU?
—CAT...?
YOU'RE SMALL, AND YOU ROLL AROUND!
—CAT...
—SMALL—
—I AM SMALL AND I AM A CAT—
SIGN: STUDENT COUNCIL

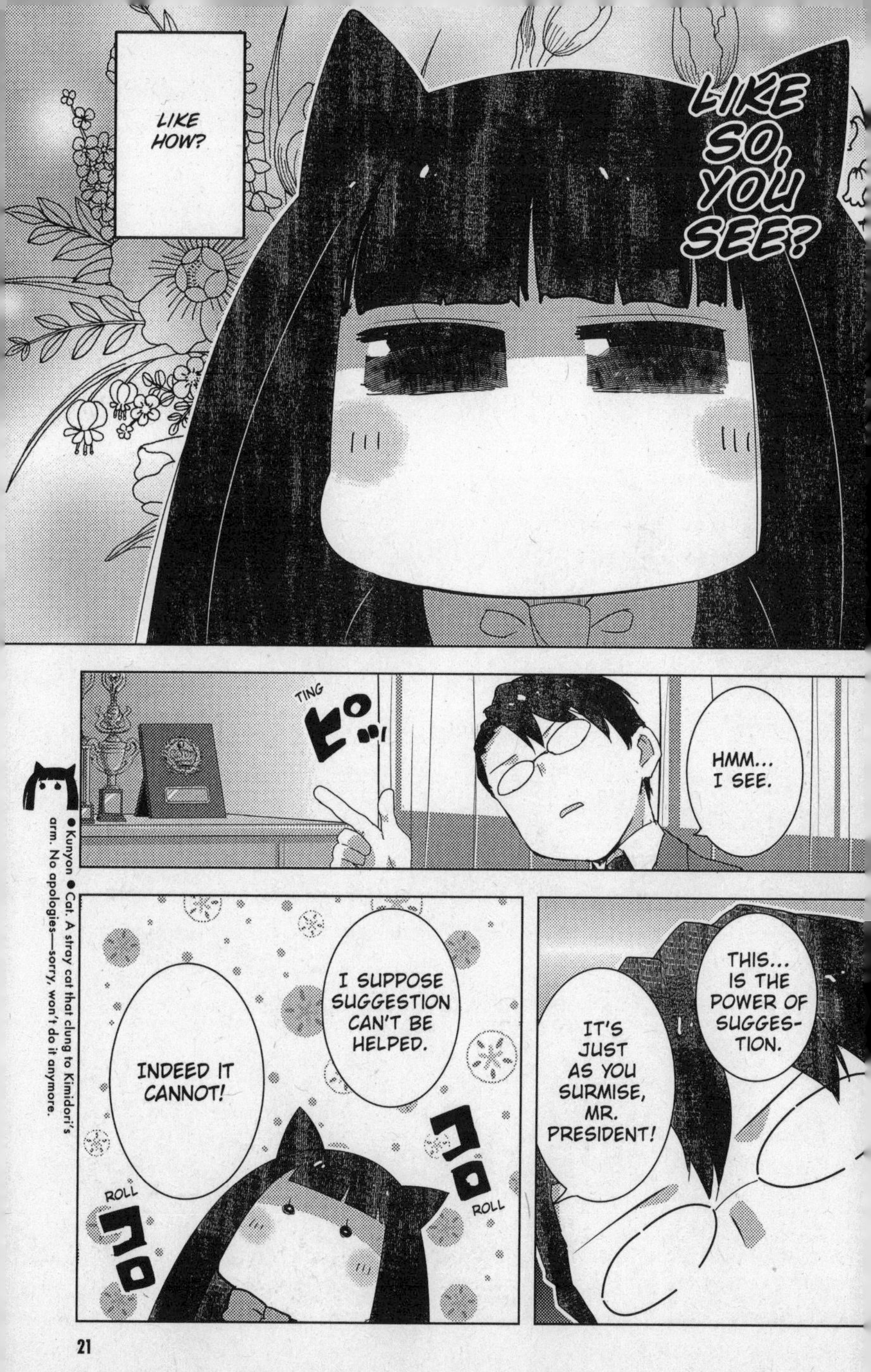
LIKE HOW?
LIKE SO, YOU SEE?
HMM... I SEE.
TING
THIS... IS THE POWER OF SUGGES-TION.
IT'S JUST AS YOU SURMISE, MR. PRESIDENT!
I SUPPOSE SUGGESTION CAN'T BE HELPED.
INDEED IT CANNOT!
ROLL
ROLL

● Kunyon ● Cat. A stray cat that clung to Kimidori's arm. No apologies—sorry, won't do it anymore.

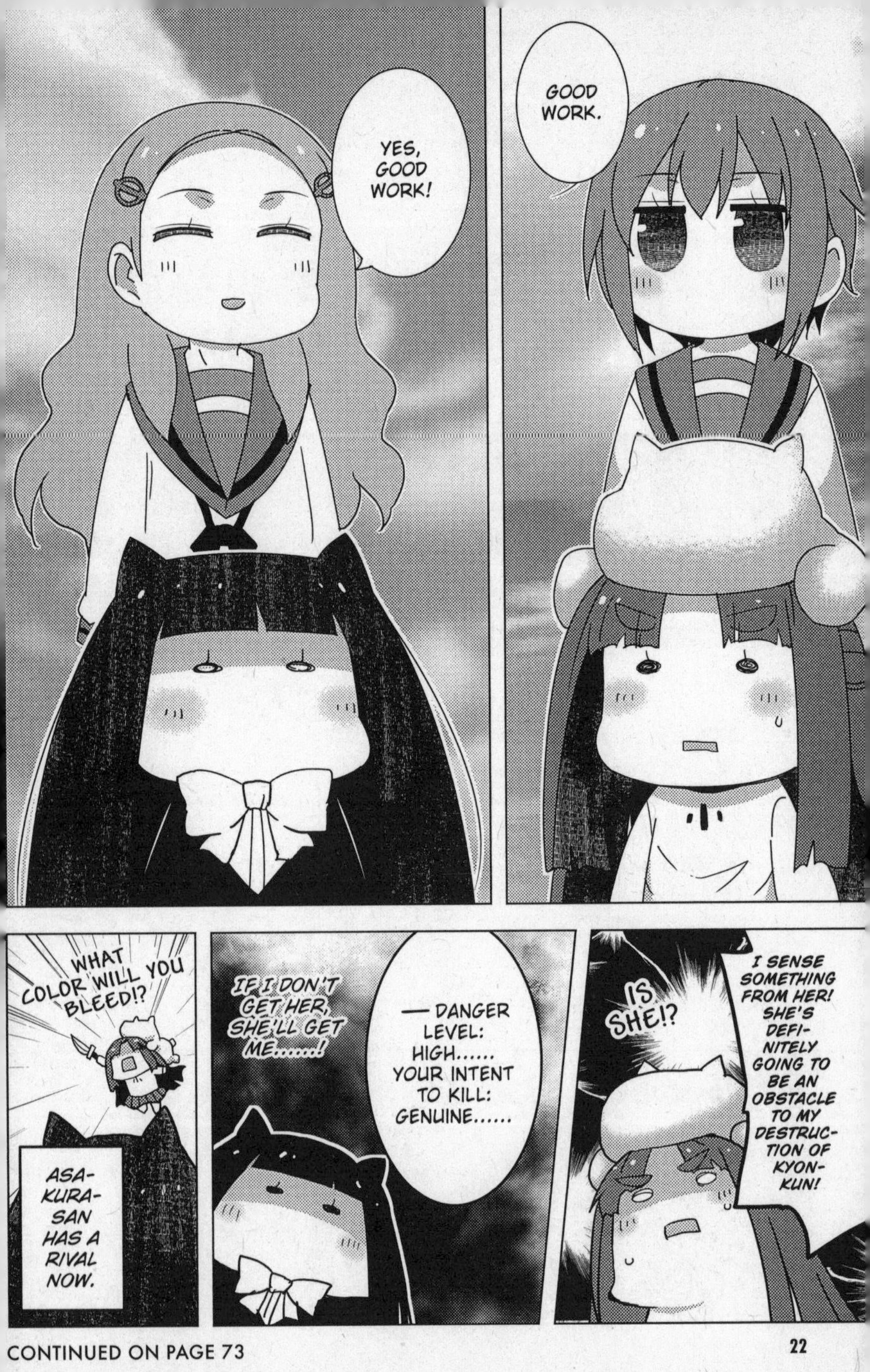
GOOD WORK.
YES, GOOD WORK!
I SENSE SOMETHING FROM HER! SHE'S DEFI-NITELY GOING TO BE AN OBSTACLE TO MY DESTRUC-TION OF KYON-KUN!
IS SHE!?
— DANGER LEVEL: HIGH...... YOUR INTENT TO KILL: GENUINE......
IF I DON'T GET HER, SHE'LL GET ME......!
WHAT COLOR WILL YOU BLEED!?
ASA-KURA-SAN HAS A RIVAL NOW.

CONTINUED ON PAGE 73

THE
FAVORITE.

A MORE
WAIFISH
VERSION.

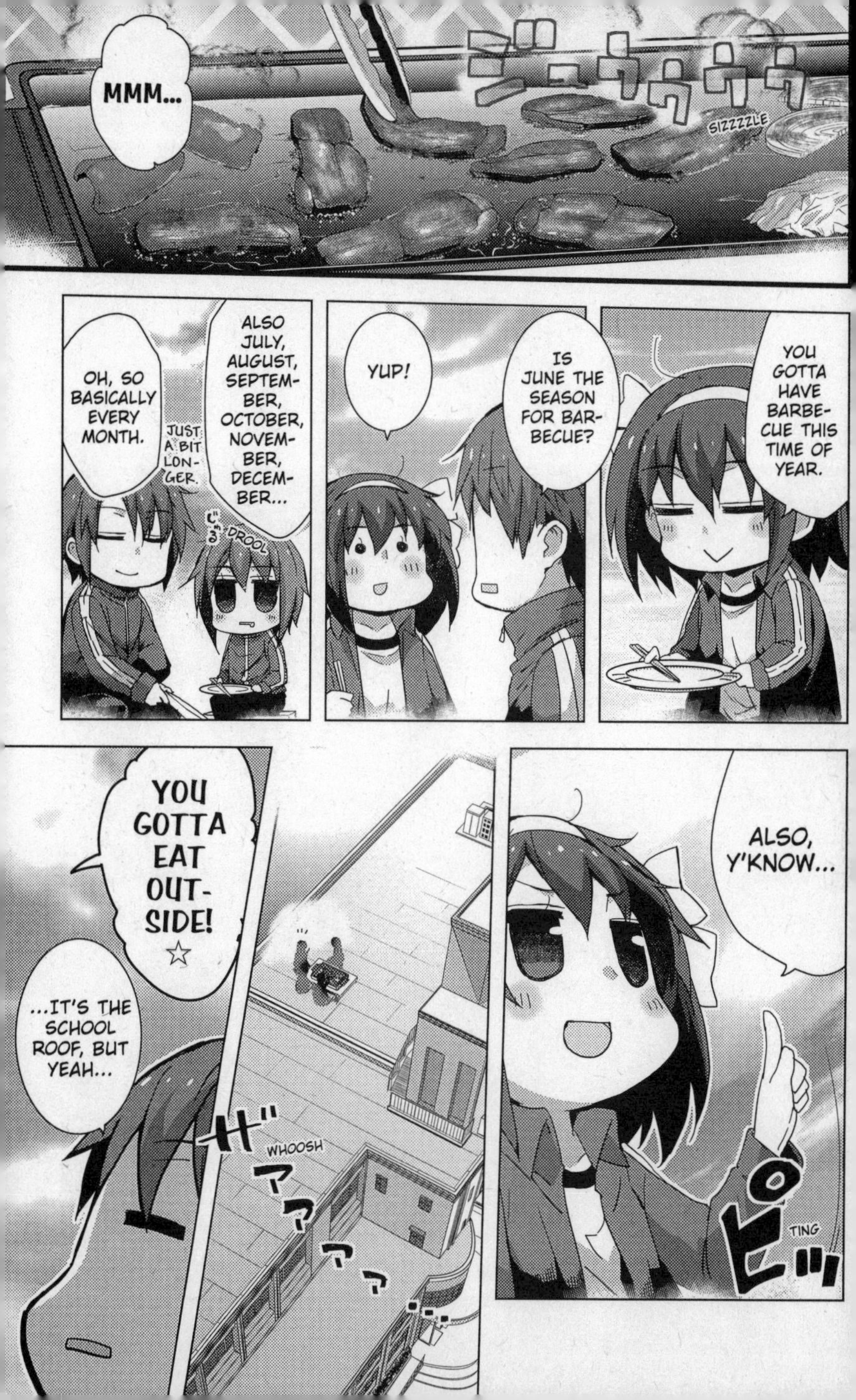
MMM...
SIZZZZLE
YOU GOTTA HAVE BARBECUE THIS TIME OF YEAR.
IS JUNE THE SEASON FOR BARBECUE?
YUP!
ALSO JULY, AUGUST, SEPTEMBER, OCTOBER, NOVEMBER, DECEMBER...
OH, SO BASICALLY EVERY MONTH.
JUST A BIT LONGER.
DROOL
ALSO, Y'KNOW...
TING
YOU GOTTA EAT OUTSIDE! ☆
...IT'S THE SCHOOL ROOF, BUT YEAH...
WHOOSH

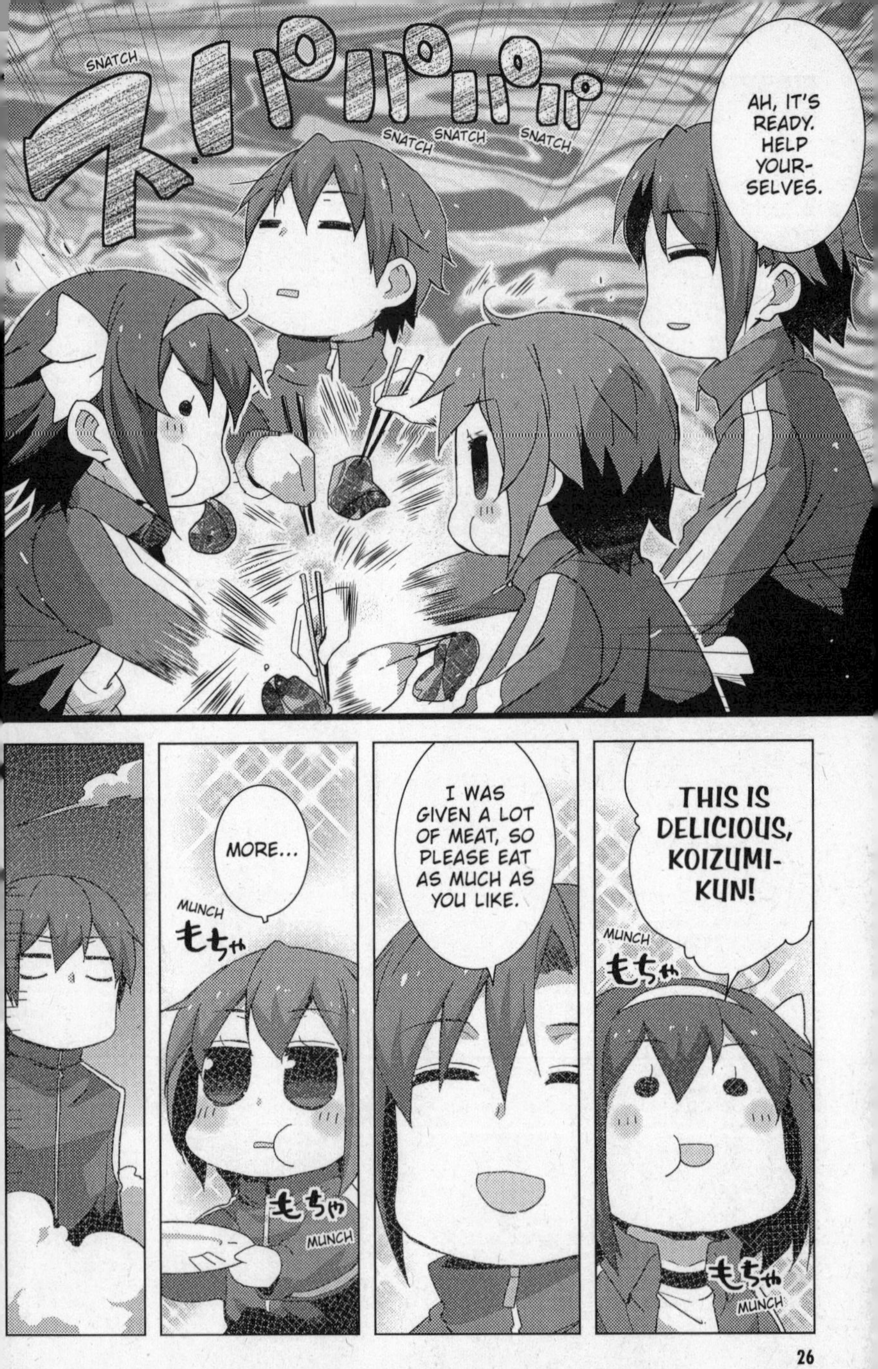
AH, IT'S READY. HELP YOURSELVES.
SNATCH
SNATCH
SNATCH
SNATCH
THIS IS DELICIOUS, KOIZUMI-KUN!
MUNCH
もちゃ
もちゃ
MUNCH
I WAS GIVEN A LOT OF MEAT, SO PLEASE EAT AS MUCH AS YOU LIKE.
MORE...
MUNCH
もちゃ
もちゃ
MUNCH

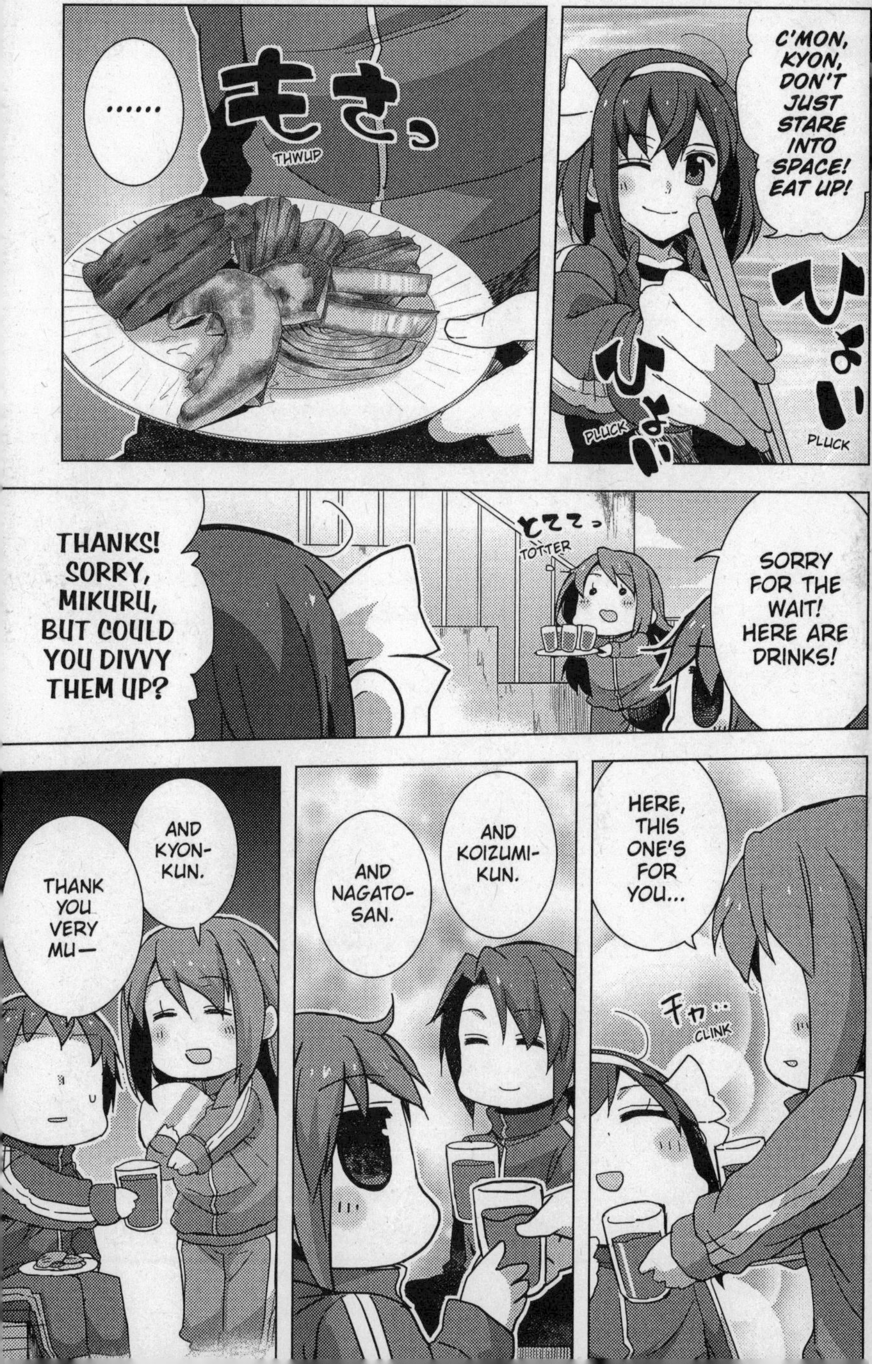
C'MON, KYON, DON'T JUST STARE INTO SPACE! EAT UP!
ぴょい
PLUCK
PLUCK
もさっ
THWUP
......
SORRY FOR THE WAIT! HERE ARE DRINKS!
とててっ
TOTTER
THANKS! SORRY, MIKURU, BUT COULD YOU DIVVY THEM UP?
HERE, THIS ONE'S FOR YOU...
チャ..
CLINK
AND KOIZUMI-KUN.
AND NAGATO-SAN.
AND KYON-KUN.
THANK YOU VERY MU—

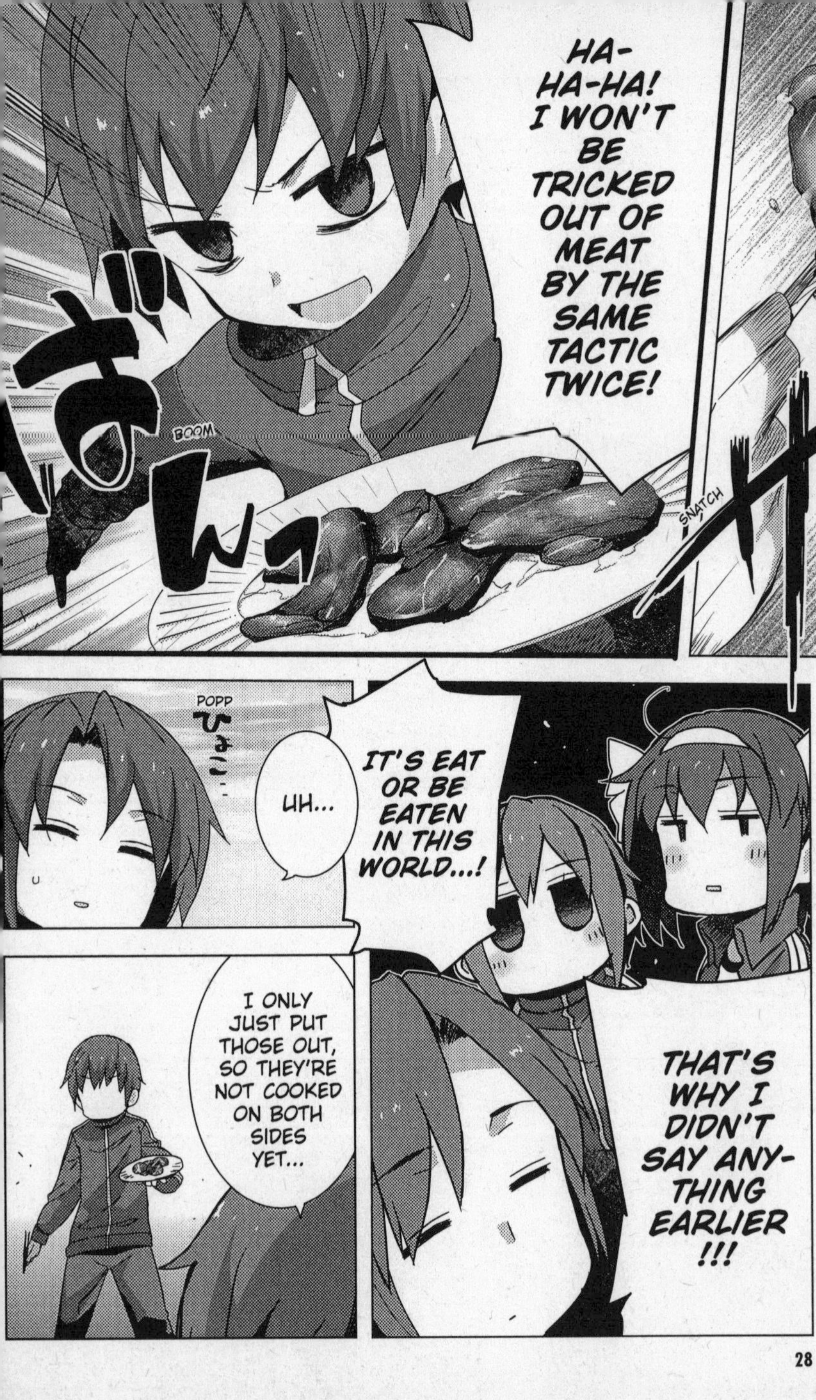

HA-HA-HA! I WON'T BE TRICKED OUT OF MEAT BY THE SAME TACTIC TWICE!
BOOM
SNATCH
IT'S EAT OR BE EATEN IN THIS WORLD...!
THAT'S WHY I DIDN'T SAY ANY-THING EARLIER!!!
POPP
UH...
I ONLY JUST PUT THOSE OUT, SO THEY'RE NOT COOKED ON BOTH SIDES YET...

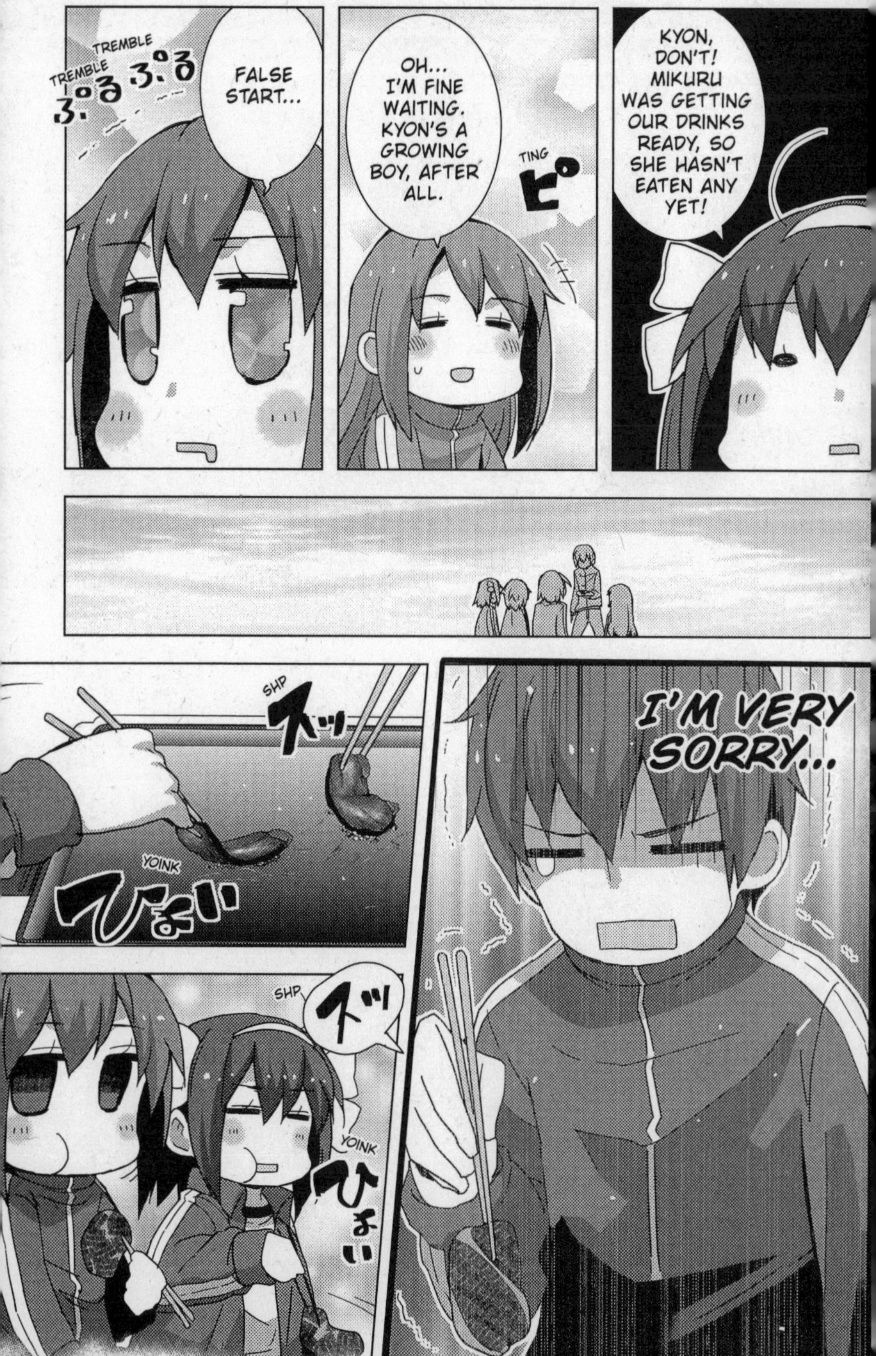
KYON, DON'T! MIKURU WAS GETTING OUR DRINKS READY, SO SHE HASN'T EATEN ANY YET!
TING
ピ
OH... I'M FINE WAITING. KYON'S A GROWING BOY, AFTER ALL.
TREMBLE TREMBLE
ぷるぷる
FALSE START...
I'M VERY SORRY...
SHP
スッ
YOINK
ひょい
SHP
スッ
YOINK
ひょい

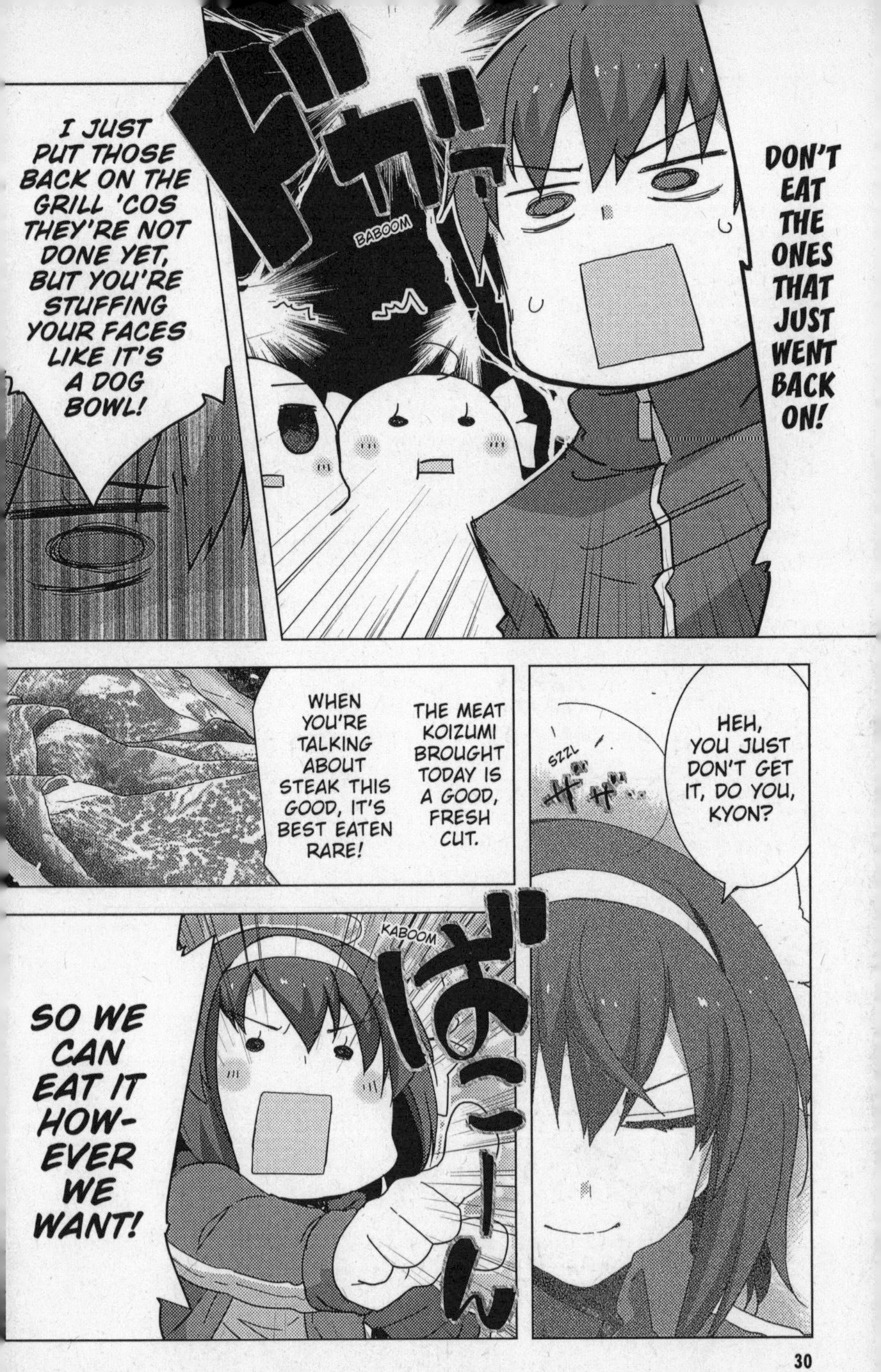
DON'T EAT THE ONES THAT JUST WENT BACK ON!
BABOOM
I JUST PUT THOSE BACK ON THE GRILL 'COS THEY'RE NOT DONE YET, BUT YOU'RE STUFFING YOUR FACES LIKE IT'S A DOG BOWL!
HEH, YOU JUST DON'T GET IT, DO YOU, KYON?
SZZL
THE MEAT KOIZUMI BROUGHT TODAY IS A GOOD, FRESH CUT.
WHEN YOU'RE TALKING ABOUT STEAK THIS GOOD, IT'S BEST EATEN RARE!
KABOOM
SO WE CAN EAT IT HOW-EVER WE WANT!

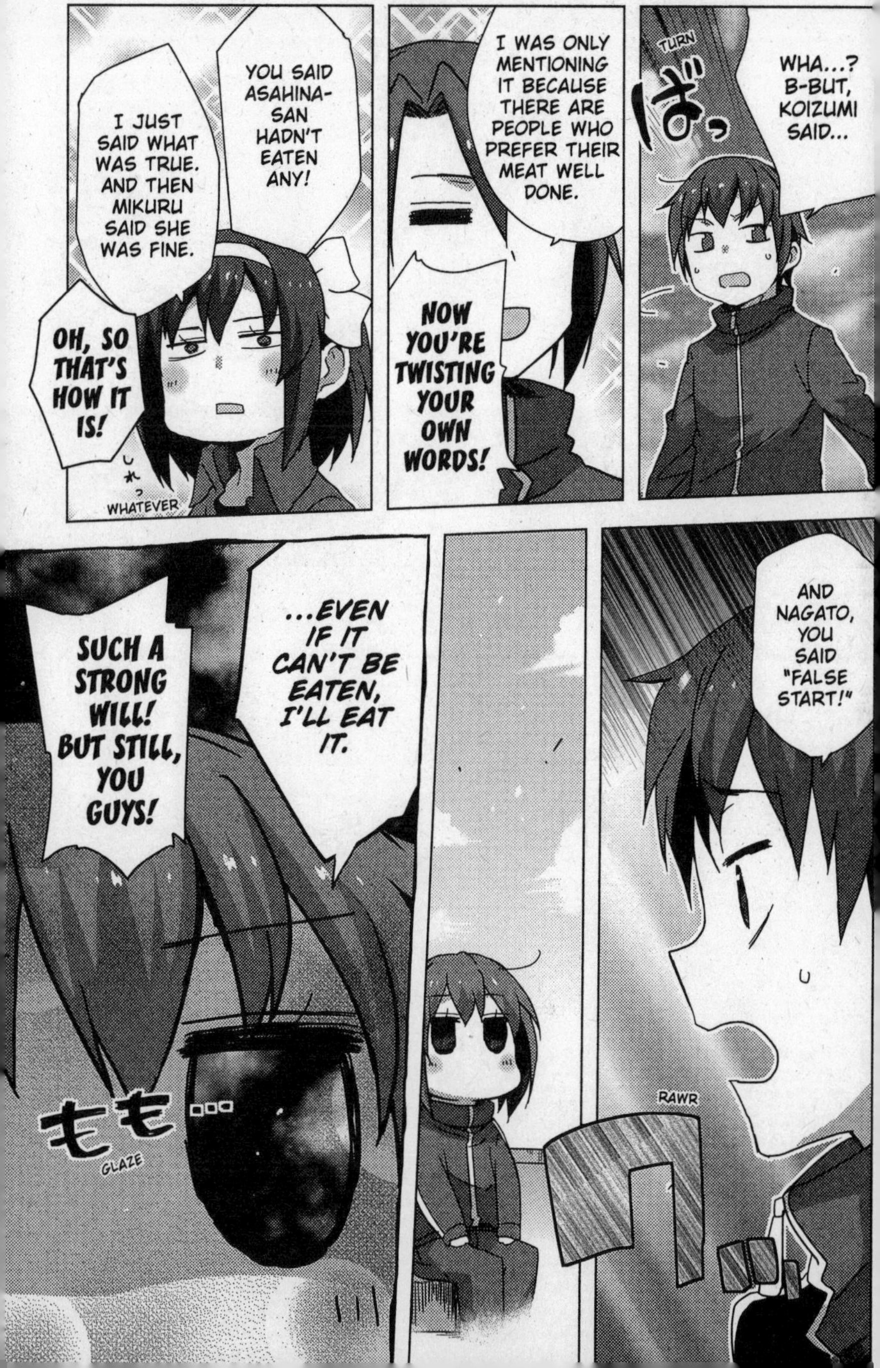

TURN
ばっ
WHA...? B-BUT, KOIZUMI SAID...
I WAS ONLY MENTIONING IT BECAUSE THERE ARE PEOPLE WHO PREFER THEIR MEAT WELL DONE.
NOW YOU'RE TWISTING YOUR OWN WORDS!
YOU SAID ASAHINA-SAN HADN'T EATEN ANY!
I JUST SAID WHAT WAS TRUE. AND THEN MIKURU SAID SHE WAS FINE.
OH, SO THAT'S HOW IT IS!
しれっ
WHATEVER
AND NAGATO, YOU SAID "FALSE START!"
RAWR
...EVEN IF IT CAN'T BE EATEN, I'LL EAT IT.
SUCH A STRONG WILL! BUT STILL, YOU GUYS!
もも...
GLAZE

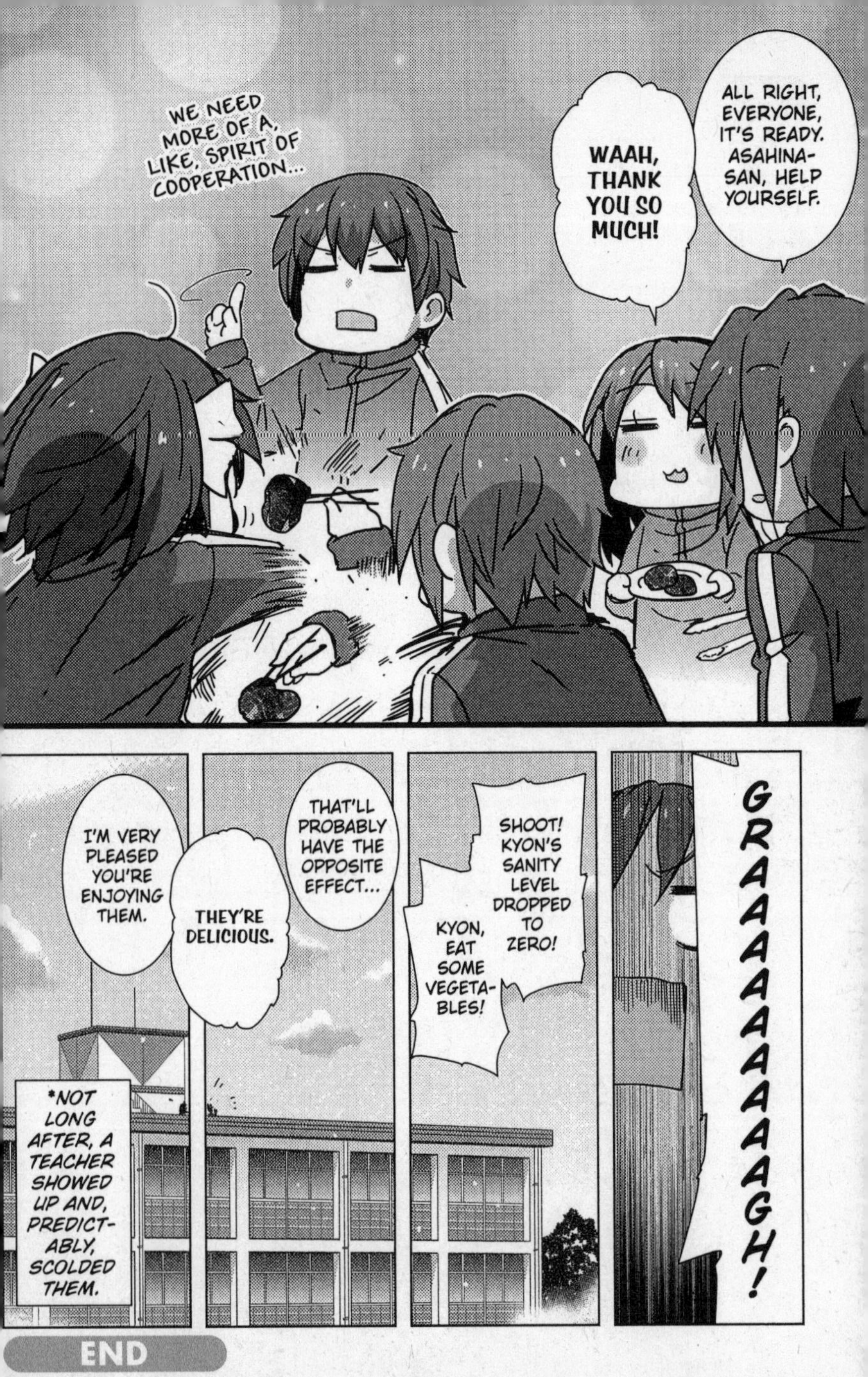
ALL RIGHT, EVERYONE, IT'S READY. ASAHINA-SAN, HELP YOURSELF.
WAAH, THANK YOU SO MUCH!
WE NEED MORE OF A, LIKE, SPIRIT OF COOPERATION...
GRAAAAAAAAAGH!
SHOOT! KYON'S SANITY LEVEL DROPPED TO ZERO!
KYON, EAT SOME VEGETA-BLES!
THAT'LL PROBABLY HAVE THE OPPOSITE EFFECT...
I'M VERY PLEASED YOU'RE ENJOYING THEM.
THEY'RE DELICIOUS.
*NOT LONG AFTER, A TEACHER SHOWED UP AND, PREDICT-ABLY, SCOLDED THEM.
END

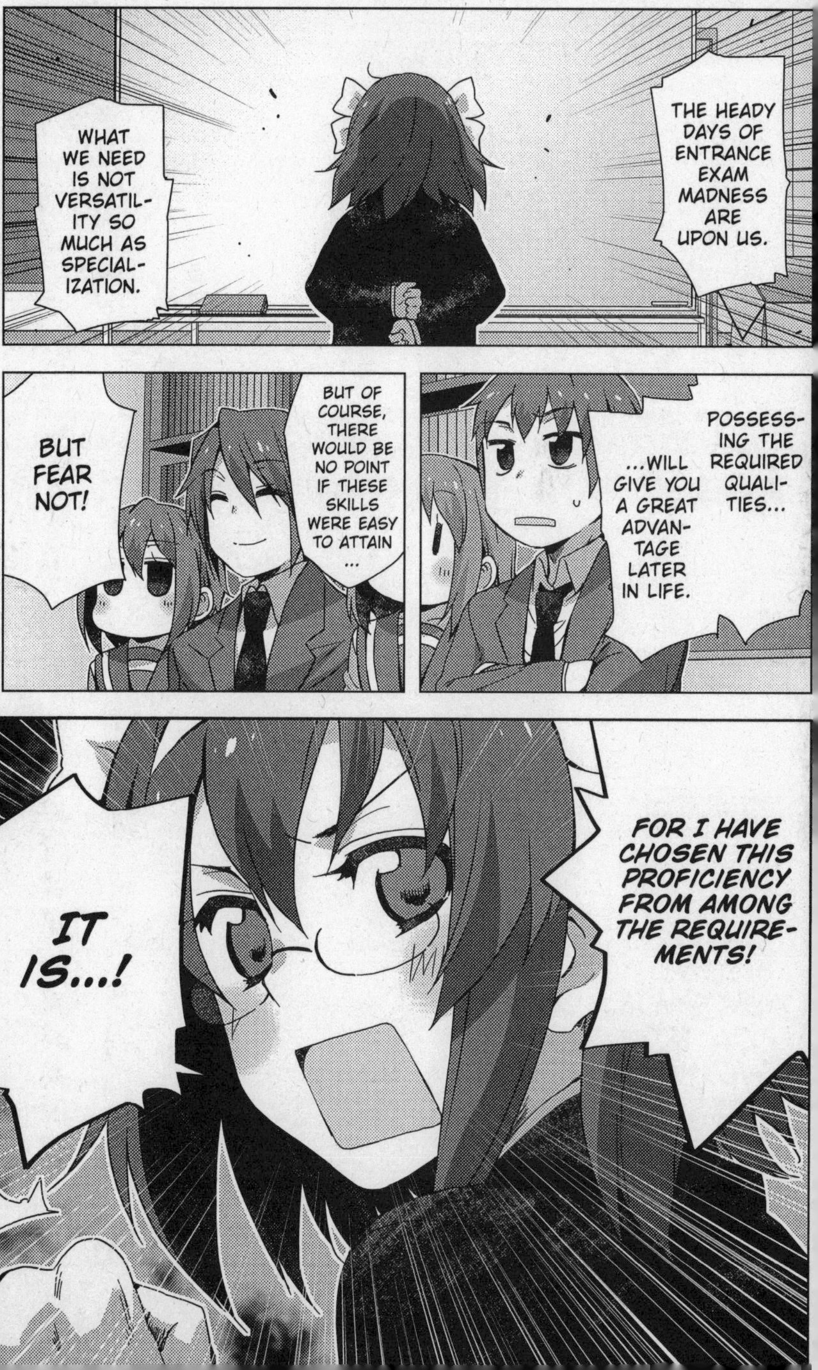
THE HEADY DAYS OF ENTRANCE EXAM MADNESS ARE UPON US.
WHAT WE NEED IS NOT VERSATILITY SO MUCH AS SPECIALIZATION.
POSSESSING THE REQUIRED QUALITIES...
...WILL GIVE YOU A GREAT ADVANTAGE LATER IN LIFE.
BUT OF COURSE, THERE WOULD BE NO POINT IF THESE SKILLS WERE EASY TO ATTAIN...
BUT FEAR NOT!
FOR I HAVE CHOSEN THIS PROFICIENCY FROM AMONG THE REQUIREMENTS!
IT IS...!

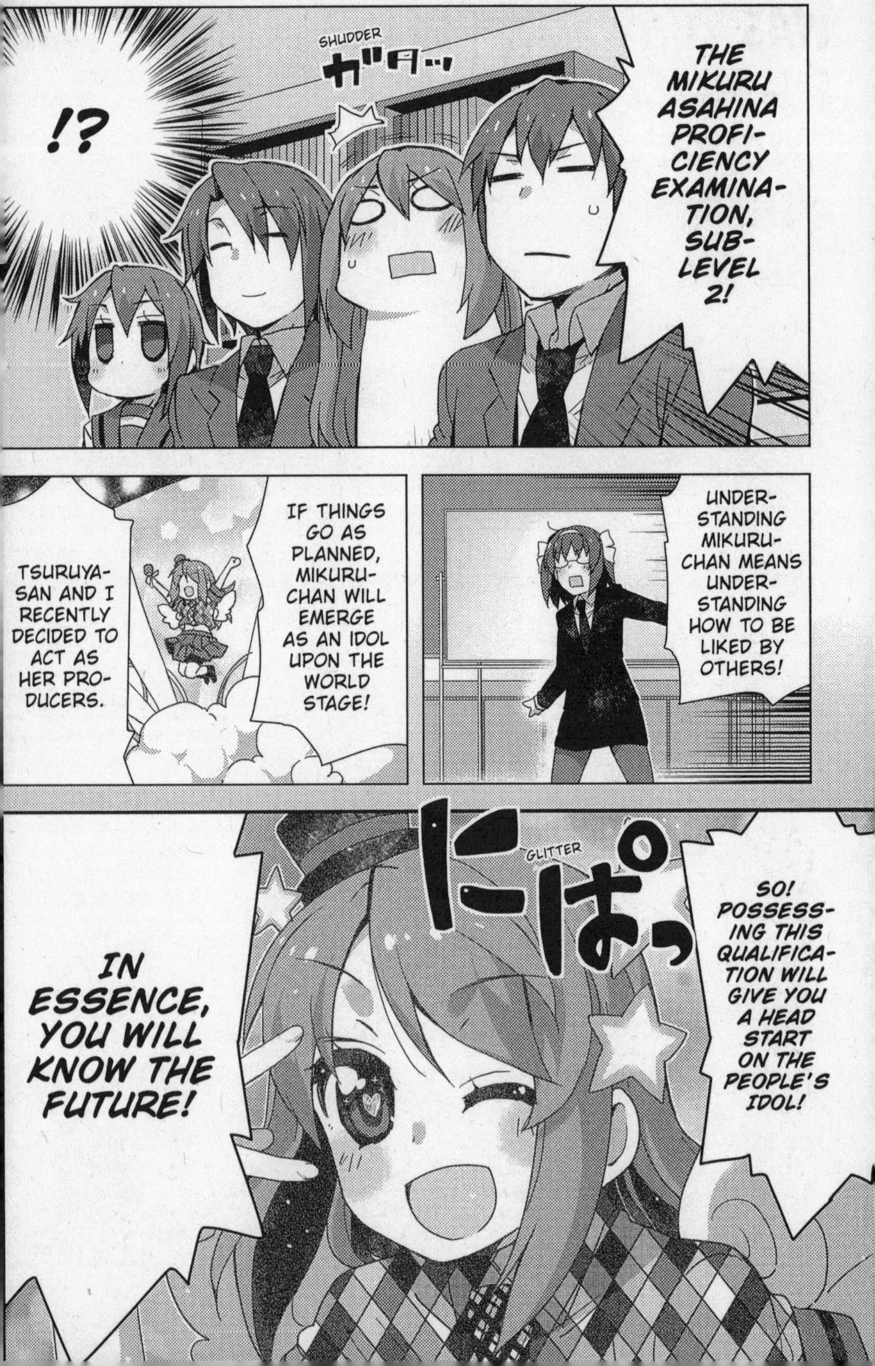
THE MIKURU ASAHINA PROFICIENCY EXAMINATION, SUB-LEVEL 2!
SHUDDER
ガタッ
!?
UNDERSTANDING MIKURU-CHAN MEANS UNDERSTANDING HOW TO BE LIKED BY OTHERS!
IF THINGS GO AS PLANNED, MIKURU-CHAN WILL EMERGE AS AN IDOL UPON THE WORLD STAGE!
TSURUYA-SAN AND I RECENTLY DECIDED TO ACT AS HER PRODUCERS.
GLITTER
にぱっ
SO! POSSESSING THIS QUALIFICATION WILL GIVE YOU A HEAD START ON THE PEOPLE'S IDOL!
IN ESSENCE, YOU WILL KNOW THE FUTURE!

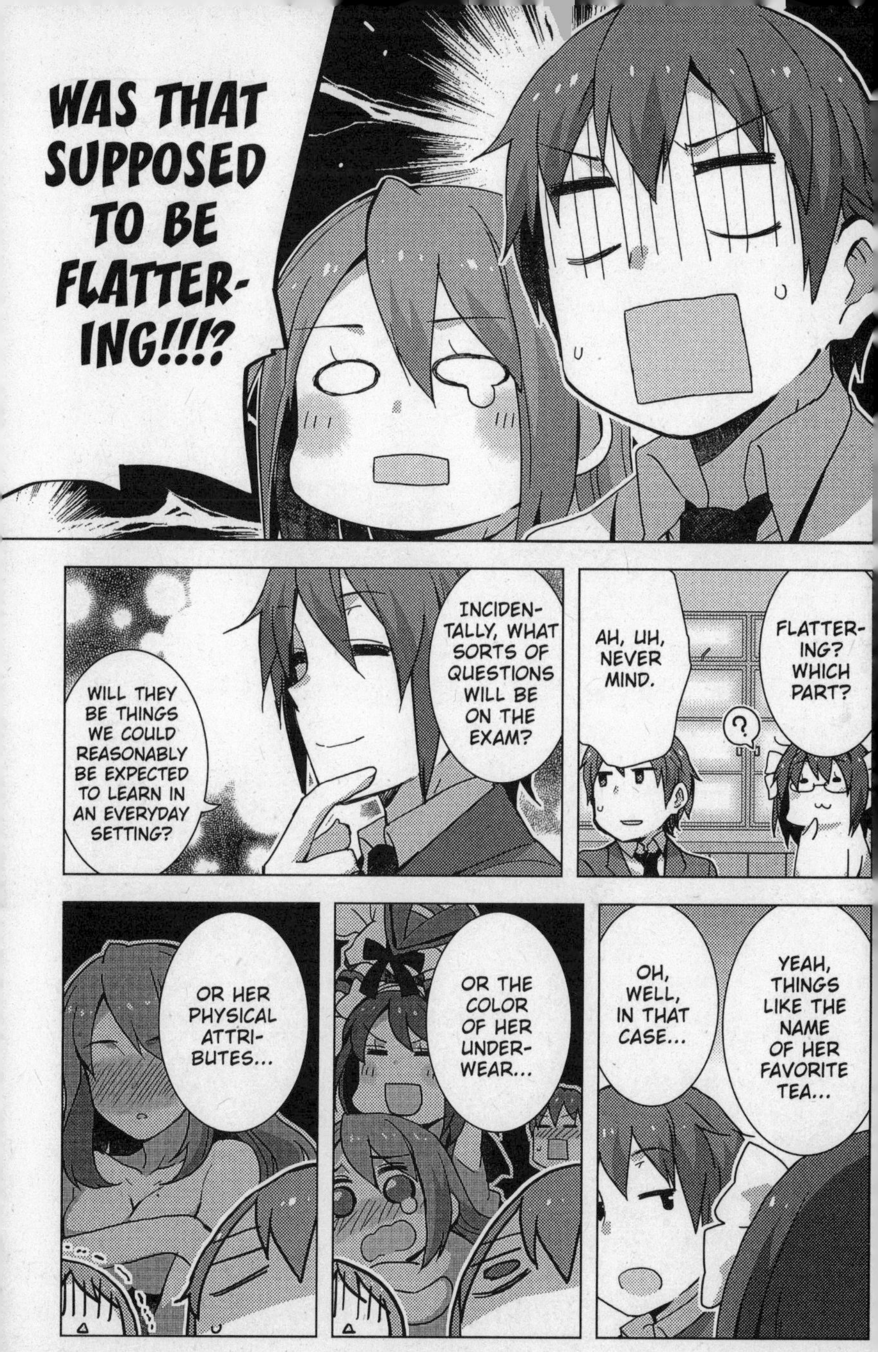
WAS THAT SUPPOSED TO BE FLATTER-ING!!!?
FLATTER-ING? WHICH PART?
?
AH, UH, NEVER MIND.
INCIDEN-TALLY, WHAT SORTS OF QUESTIONS WILL BE ON THE EXAM?
WILL THEY BE THINGS WE COULD REASONABLY BE EXPECTED TO LEARN IN AN EVERYDAY SETTING?
YEAH, THINGS LIKE THE NAME OF HER FAVORITE TEA...
OH, WELL, IN THAT CASE...
OR THE COLOR OF HER UNDER-WEAR...
OR HER PHYSICAL ATTRI-BUTES...

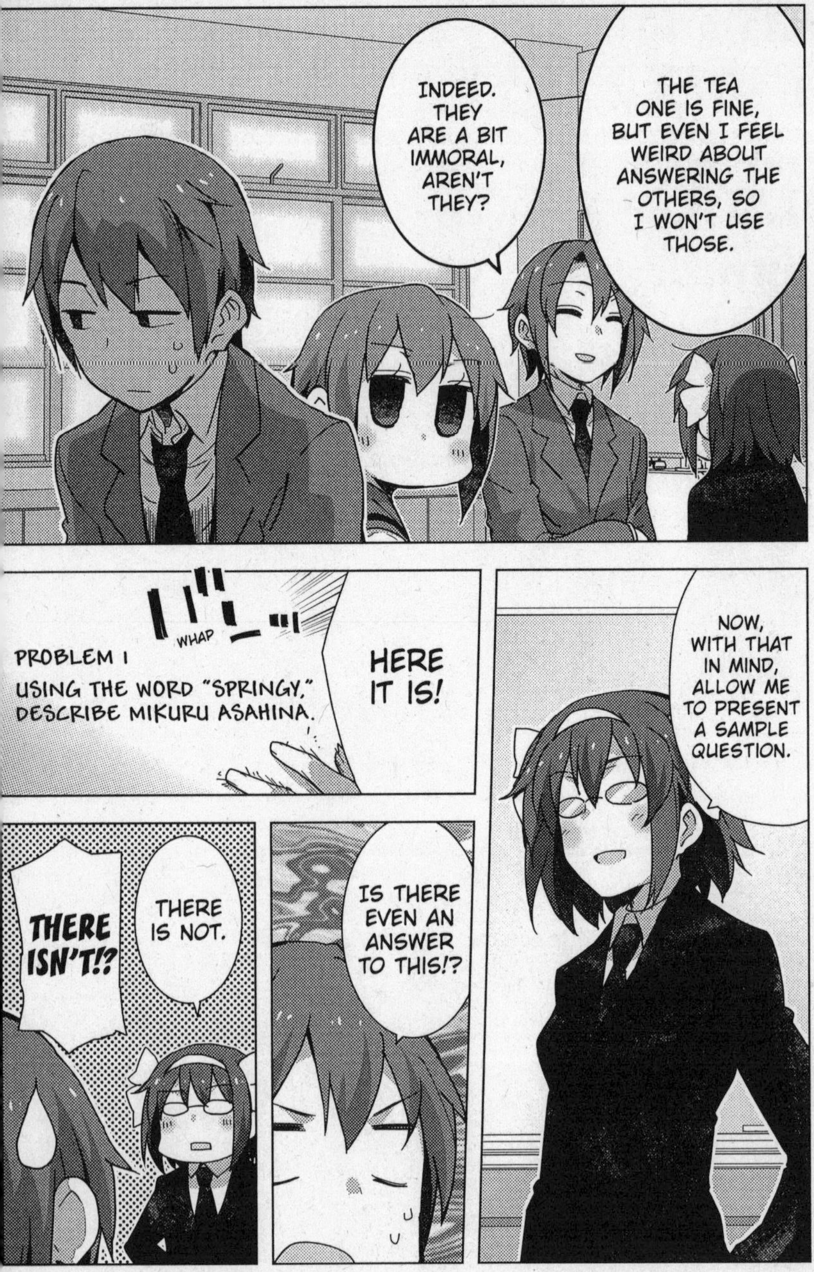
THE TEA ONE IS FINE, BUT EVEN I FEEL WEIRD ABOUT ANSWERING THE OTHERS, SO I WON'T USE THOSE.
INDEED. THEY ARE A BIT IMMORAL, AREN'T THEY?
NOW, WITH THAT IN MIND, ALLOW ME TO PRESENT A SAMPLE QUESTION.
HERE IT IS!
WHAP
PROBLEM 1
USING THE WORD "SPRINGY," DESCRIBE MIKURU ASAHINA.
IS THERE EVEN AN ANSWER TO THIS!?
THERE IS NOT.
THERE ISN'T!?

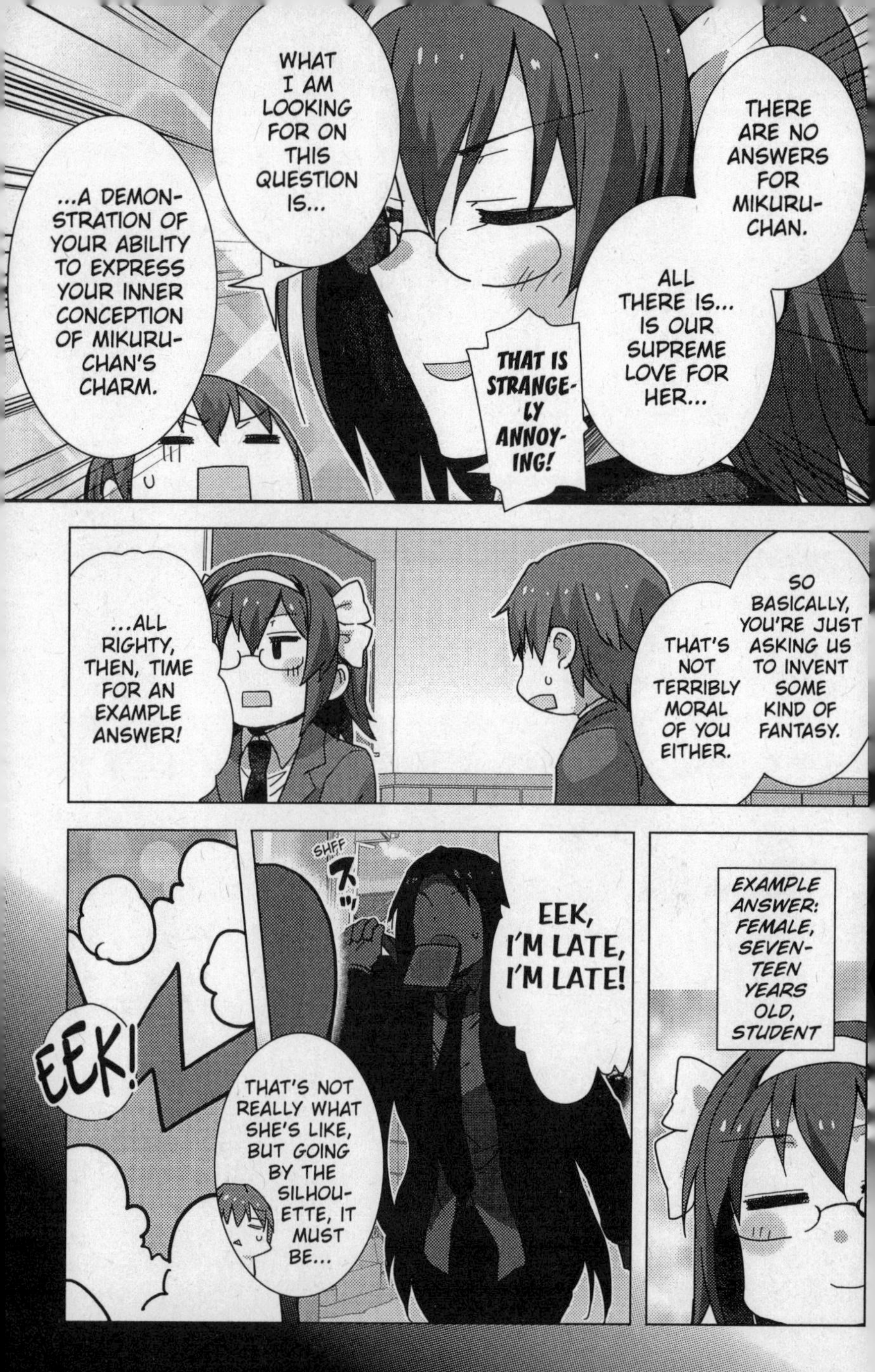
THERE ARE NO ANSWERS FOR MIKURU-CHAN.
ALL THERE IS... IS OUR SUPREME LOVE FOR HER...
WHAT I AM LOOKING FOR ON THIS QUESTION IS...
...A DEMON-STRATION OF YOUR ABILITY TO EXPRESS YOUR INNER CONCEPTION OF MIKURU-CHAN'S CHARM.
THAT IS STRANGE-LY ANNOY-ING!
SO BASICALLY, YOU'RE JUST ASKING US TO INVENT SOME KIND OF FANTASY.
THAT'S NOT TERRIBLY MORAL OF YOU EITHER.
...ALL RIGHTY, THEN, TIME FOR AN EXAMPLE ANSWER!
EXAMPLE ANSWER: FEMALE, SEVEN-TEEN YEARS OLD, STUDENT
EEK, I'M LATE, I'M LATE!
SHFF
THAT'S NOT REALLY WHAT SHE'S LIKE, BUT GOING BY THE SILHOU-ETTE, IT MUST BE...
EEK!

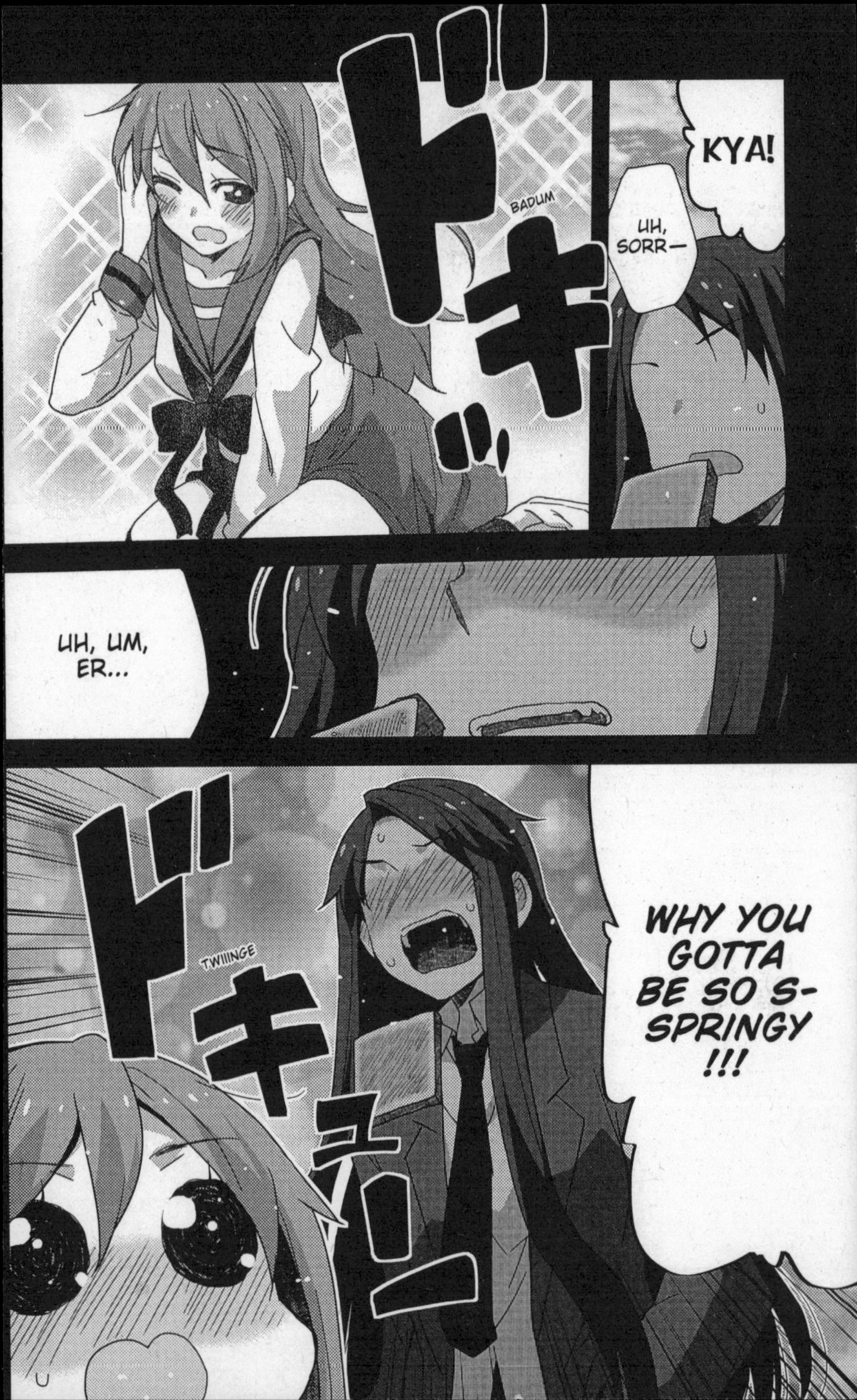
KYA!
UH, SORR—
BADUM
ドキッ
UH, UM, ER...
WHY YOU GOTTA BE SO S-SPRINGY !!!
TWIIINGE
ドキューン

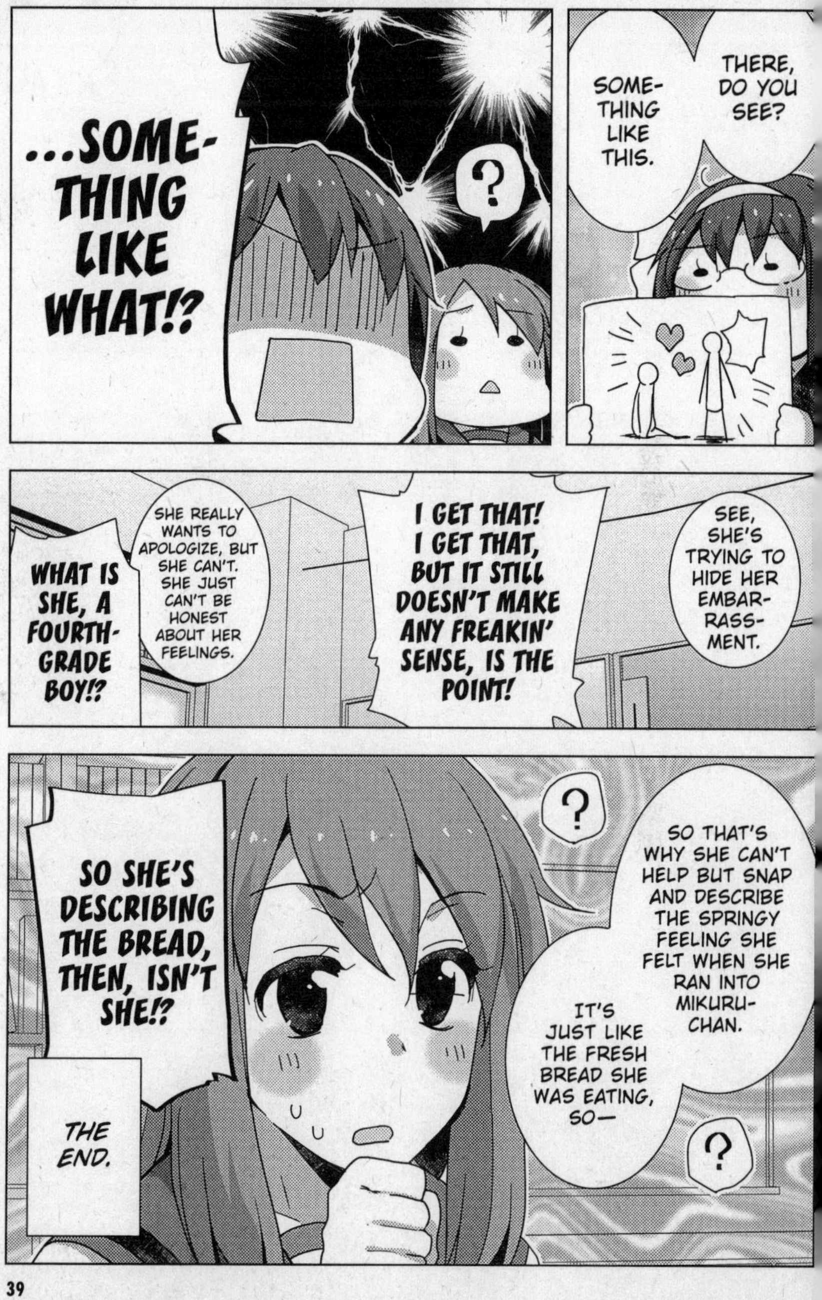
THERE, DO YOU SEE?
SOME-THING LIKE THIS.
?
...SOME-THING LIKE WHAT!?
SEE, SHE'S TRYING TO HIDE HER EMBAR-RASS-MENT.
I GET THAT! I GET THAT, BUT IT STILL DOESN'T MAKE ANY FREAKIN' SENSE, IS THE POINT!
SHE REALLY WANTS TO APOLOGIZE, BUT SHE CAN'T. SHE JUST CAN'T BE HONEST ABOUT HER FEELINGS.
WHAT IS SHE, A FOURTH-GRADE BOY!?
SO THAT'S WHY SHE CAN'T HELP BUT SNAP AND DESCRIBE THE SPRINGY FEELING SHE FELT WHEN SHE RAN INTO MIKURU-CHAN.
IT'S JUST LIKE THE FRESH BREAD SHE WAS EATING, SO—
?
?
SO SHE'S DESCRIBING THE BREAD, THEN, ISN'T SHE!?
THE END.

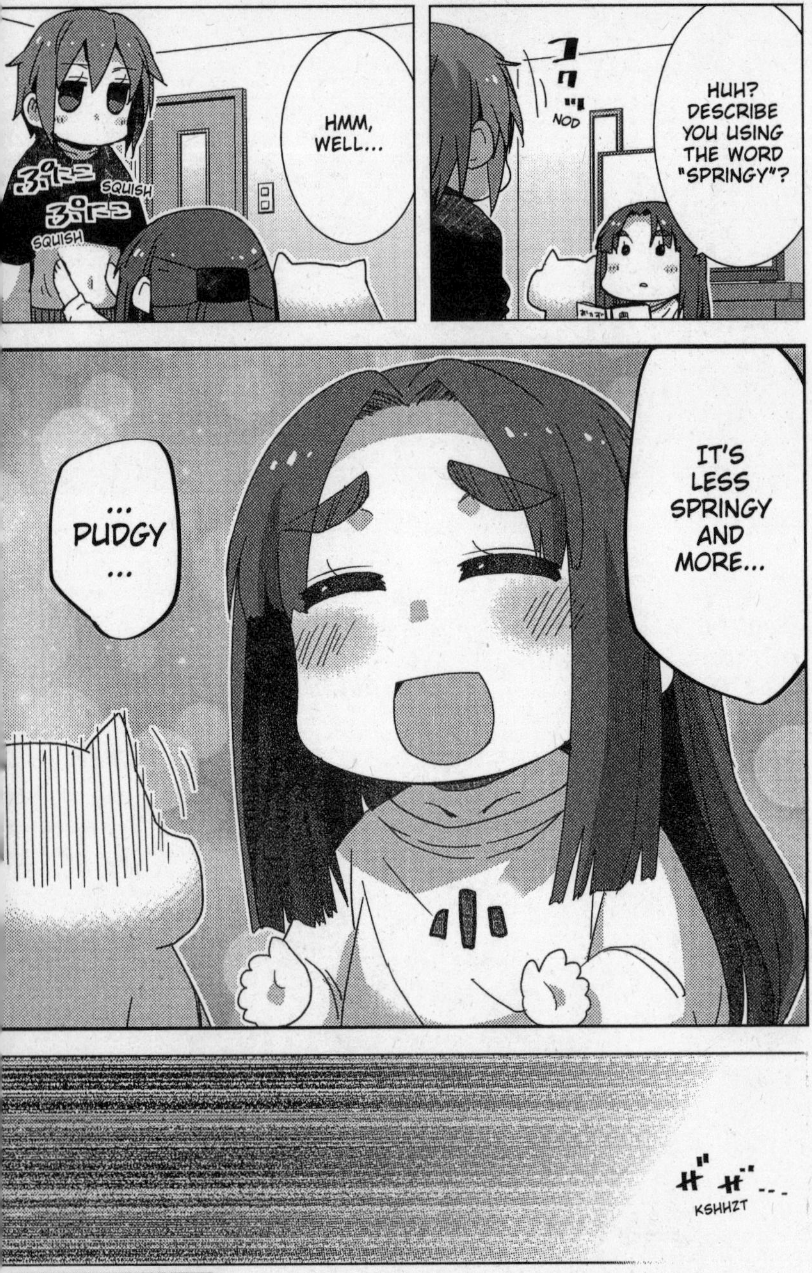
HUH? DESCRIBE YOU USING THE WORD "SPRINGY"?
コクッ
NOD
HMM, WELL...
ぷにぷに
SQUISH
ぷにぷに
SQUISH
IT'S LESS SPRINGY AND MORE...
... PUDGY ...
KSHHZT

END

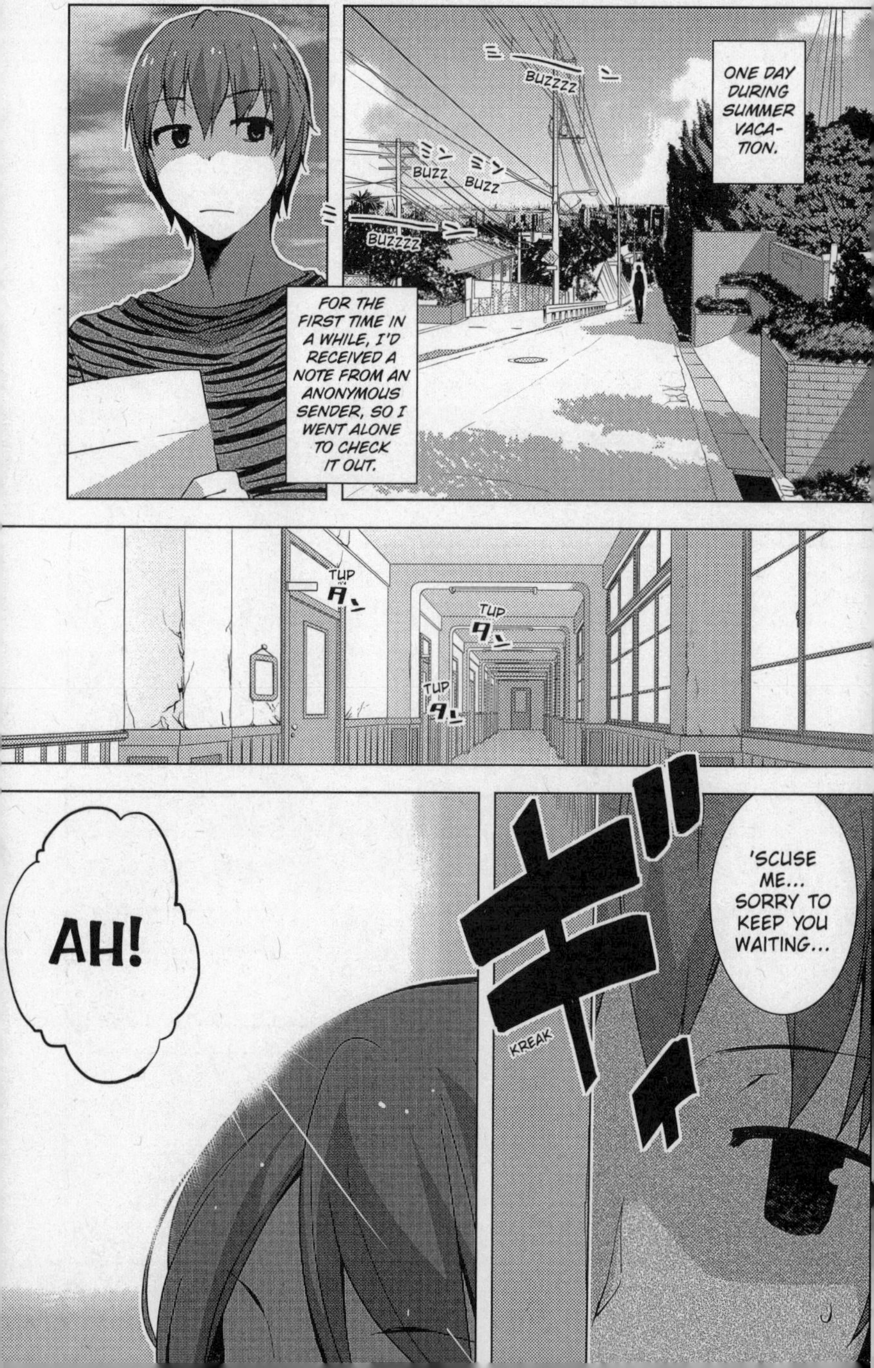
ONE DAY DURING SUMMER VACATION.
BUZZZZ
BUZZ
BUZZ
BUZZZZ
FOR THE FIRST TIME IN A WHILE, I'D RECEIVED A NOTE FROM AN ANONYMOUS SENDER, SO I WENT ALONE TO CHECK IT OUT.
TUP
TUP
TUP
'SCUSE ME... SORRY TO KEEP YOU WAITING...
KREAK
AH!

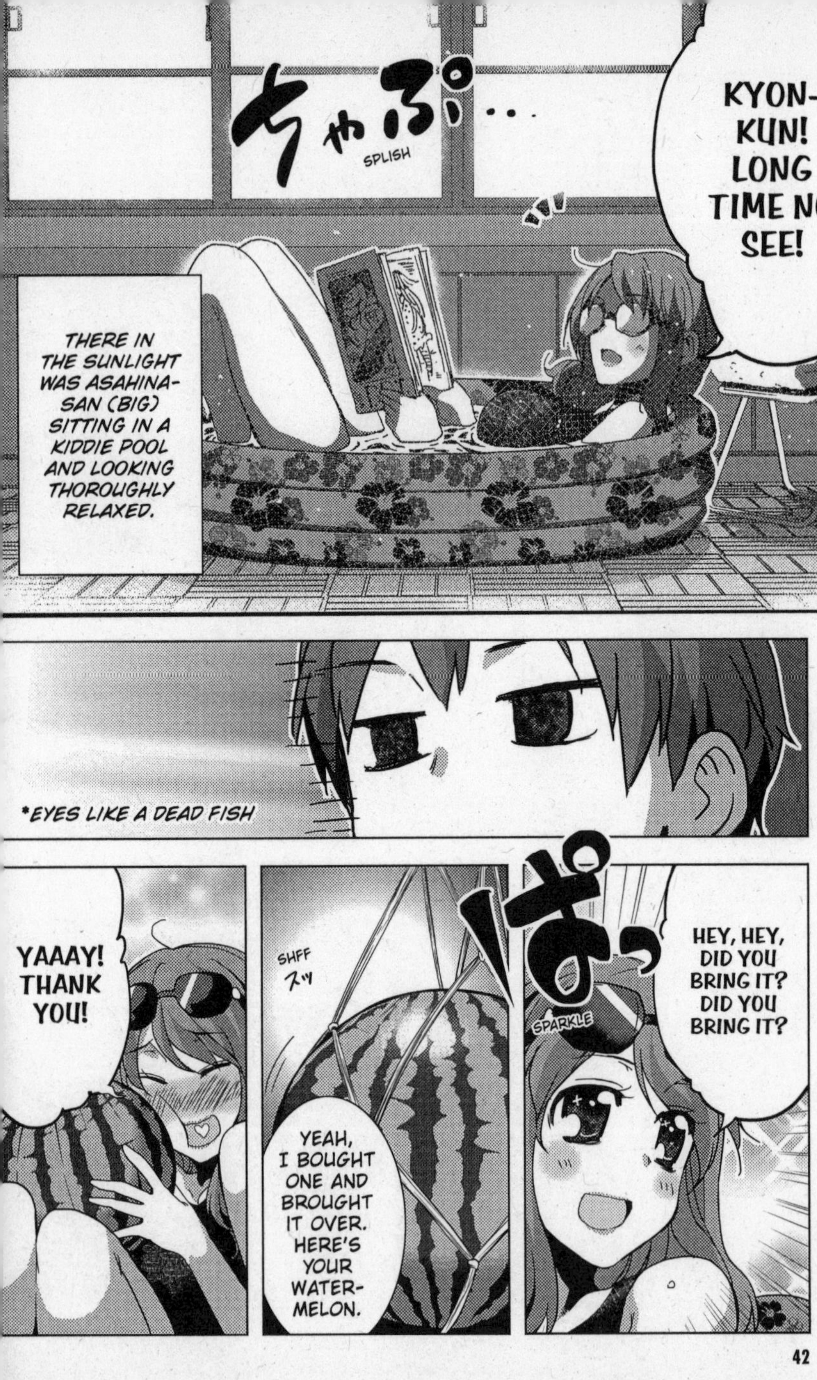
KYON-KUN! LONG TIME NO SEE!
ちゃぷ…
SPLISH
THERE IN THE SUNLIGHT WAS ASAHINA-SAN (BIG) SITTING IN A KIDDIE POOL AND LOOKING THOROUGHLY RELAXED.
*EYES LIKE A DEAD FISH
HEY, HEY, DID YOU BRING IT? DID YOU BRING IT?
ぱっ
SPARKLE
SHFF
スッ
YEAH, I BOUGHT ONE AND BROUGHT IT OVER. HERE'S YOUR WATER-MELON.
YAAAY! THANK YOU!

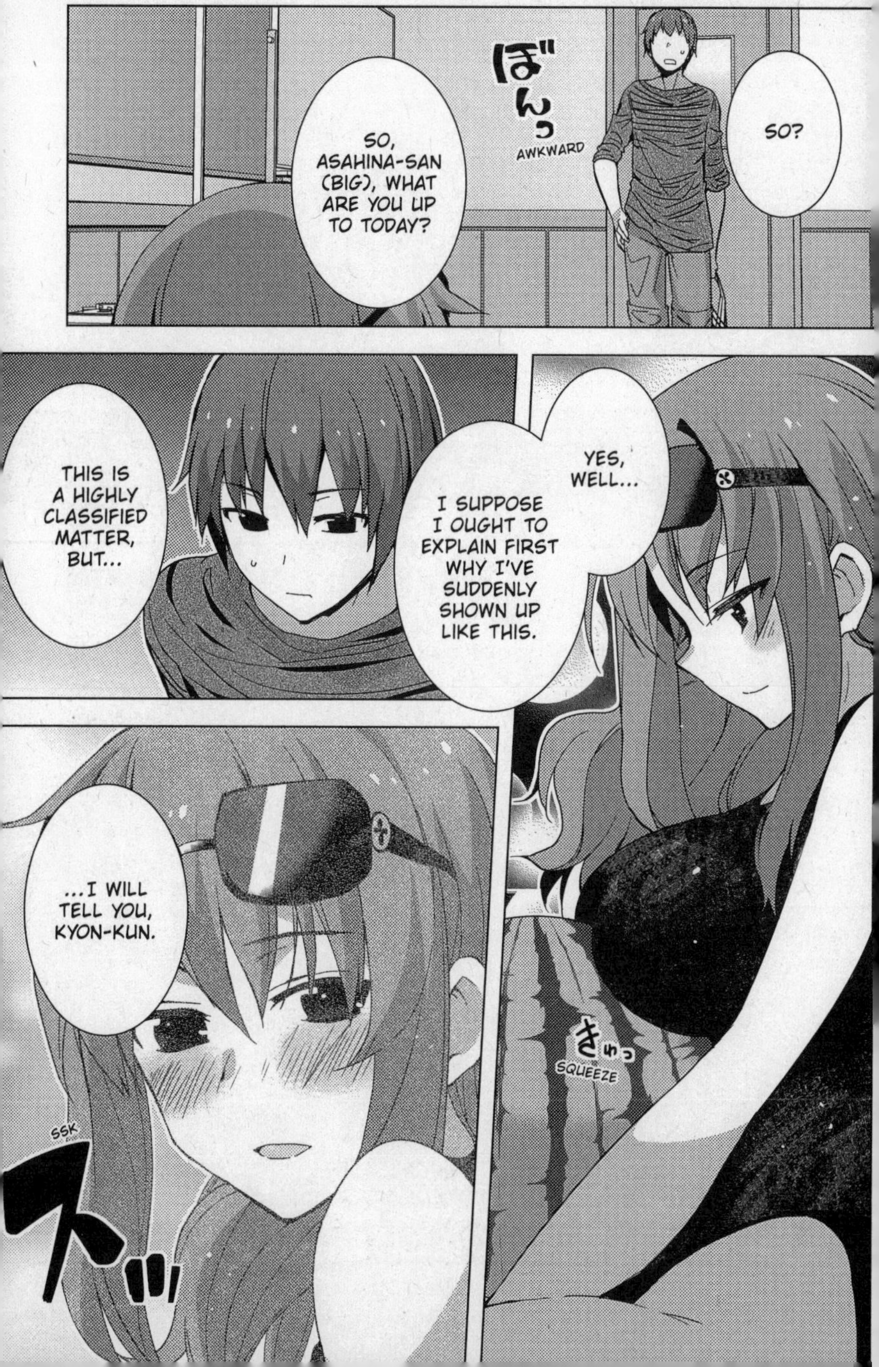
SO?
ぼんっ
AWKWARD
SO, ASAHINA-SAN (BIG), WHAT ARE YOU UP TO TODAY?
YES, WELL...
I SUPPOSE I OUGHT TO EXPLAIN FIRST WHY I'VE SUDDENLY SHOWN UP LIKE THIS.
きゅっ
SQUEEZE
THIS IS A HIGHLY CLASSIFIED MATTER, BUT...
...I WILL TELL YOU, KYON-KUN.
SSK
スッ

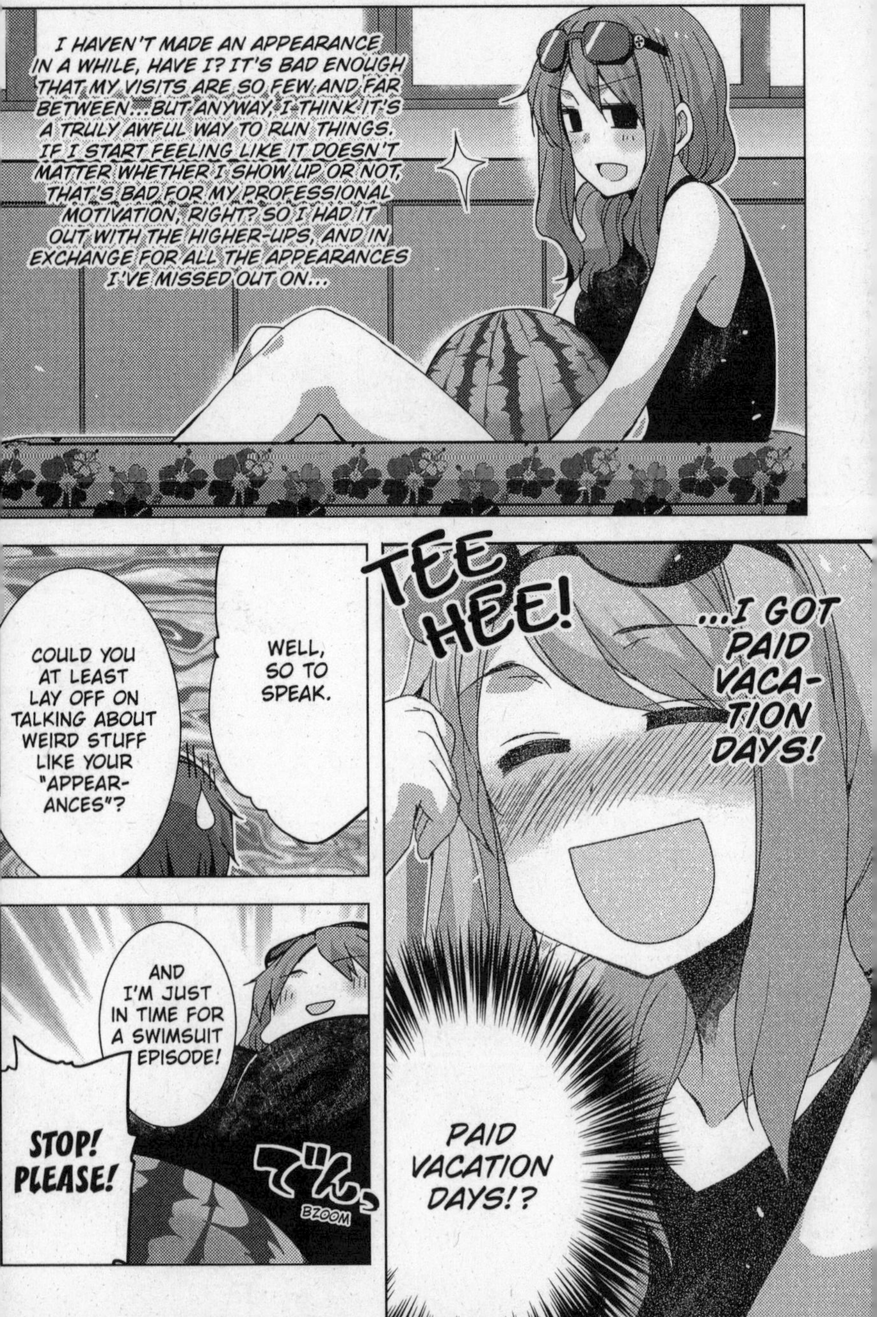
I HAVEN'T MADE AN APPEARANCE IN A WHILE, HAVE I? IT'S BAD ENOUGH THAT MY VISITS ARE SO FEW AND FAR BETWEEN...BUT ANYWAY, I THINK IT'S A TRULY AWFUL WAY TO RUN THINGS. IF I START FEELING LIKE IT DOESN'T MATTER WHETHER I SHOW UP OR NOT, THAT'S BAD FOR MY PROFESSIONAL MOTIVATION, RIGHT? SO I HAD IT OUT WITH THE HIGHER-UPS, AND IN EXCHANGE FOR ALL THE APPEARANCES I'VE MISSED OUT ON...
TEE HEE!
...I GOT PAID VACATION DAYS!
PAID VACATION DAYS!?
WELL, SO TO SPEAK.
COULD YOU AT LEAST LAY OFF ON TALKING ABOUT WEIRD STUFF LIKE YOUR "APPEARANCES"?
AND I'M JUST IN TIME FOR A SWIMSUIT EPISODE!
でんっ
BZOOM
STOP! PLEASE!

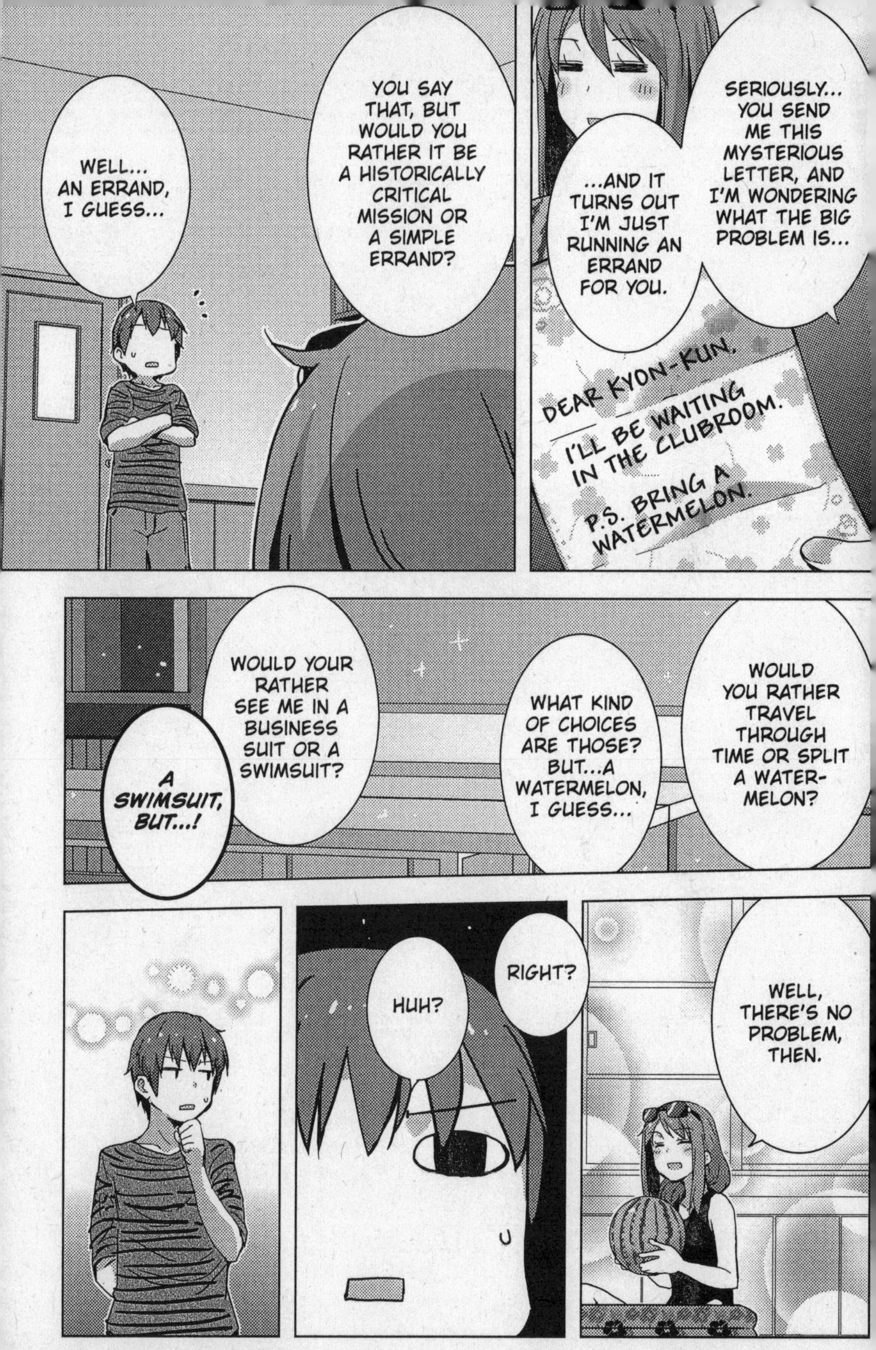
SERIOUSLY... YOU SEND ME THIS MYSTERIOUS LETTER, AND I'M WONDERING WHAT THE BIG PROBLEM IS...
...AND IT TURNS OUT I'M JUST RUNNING AN ERRAND FOR YOU.
DEAR KYON-KUN,
I'LL BE WAITING IN THE CLUBROOM.
P.S. BRING A WATERMELON.
YOU SAY THAT, BUT WOULD YOU RATHER IT BE A HISTORICALLY CRITICAL MISSION OR A SIMPLE ERRAND?
WELL... AN ERRAND, I GUESS...
WOULD YOU RATHER TRAVEL THROUGH TIME OR SPLIT A WATER-MELON?
WHAT KIND OF CHOICES ARE THOSE? BUT...A WATERMELON, I GUESS...
WOULD YOUR RATHER SEE ME IN A BUSINESS SUIT OR A SWIMSUIT?
A SWIMSUIT, BUT...!
WELL, THERE'S NO PROBLEM, THEN.
RIGHT?
HUH?

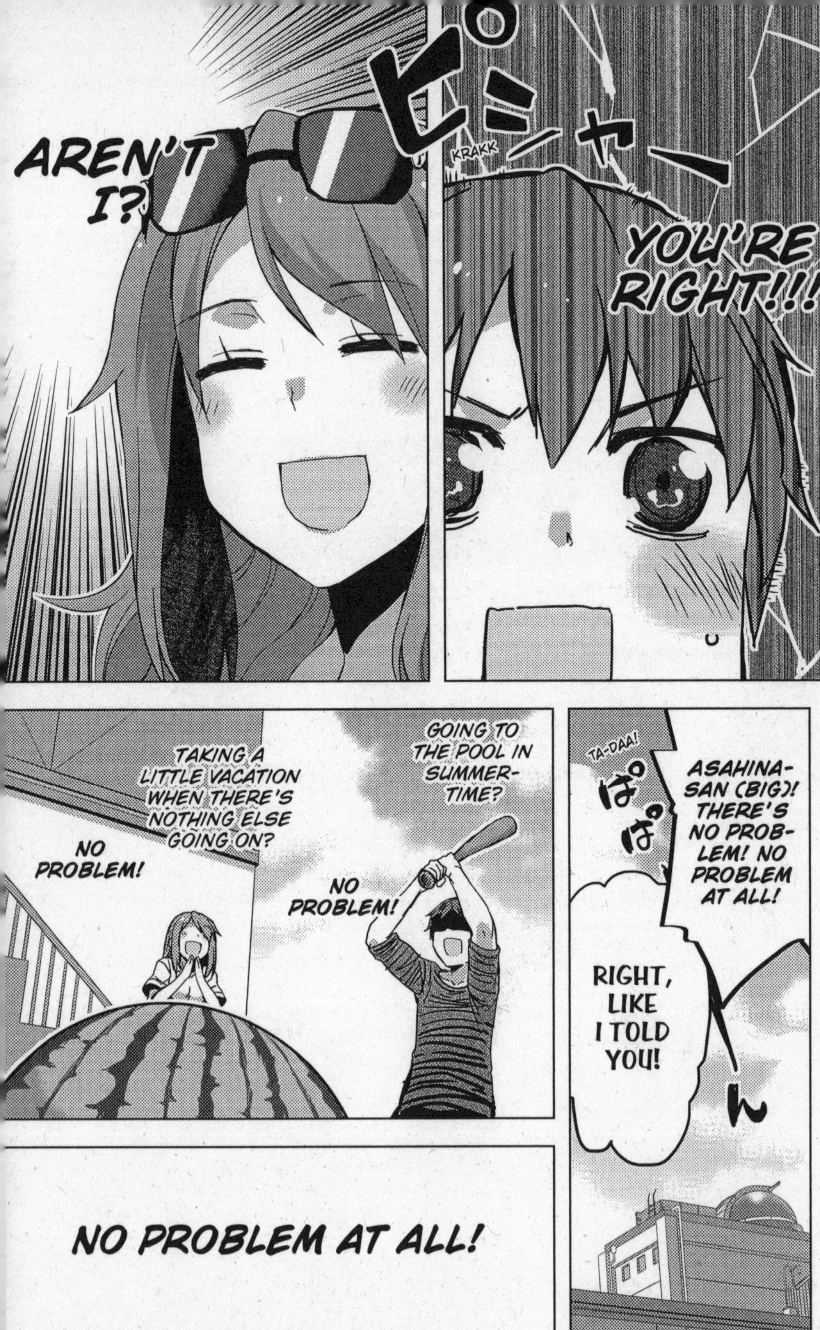

ピシャー
KRAKK
YOU'RE RIGHT!!!
AREN'T I?
TA-DAA!
ぱぱ
ASAHINA-SAN (BIG)! THERE'S NO PROBLEM! NO PROBLEM AT ALL!
RIGHT, LIKE I TOLD YOU!
ん
GOING TO THE POOL IN SUMMERTIME?
NO PROBLEM!
TAKING A LITTLE VACATION WHEN THERE'S NOTHING ELSE GOING ON?
NO PROBLEM!
NO PROBLEM AT ALL!

ASAKURA-SAN TODAY

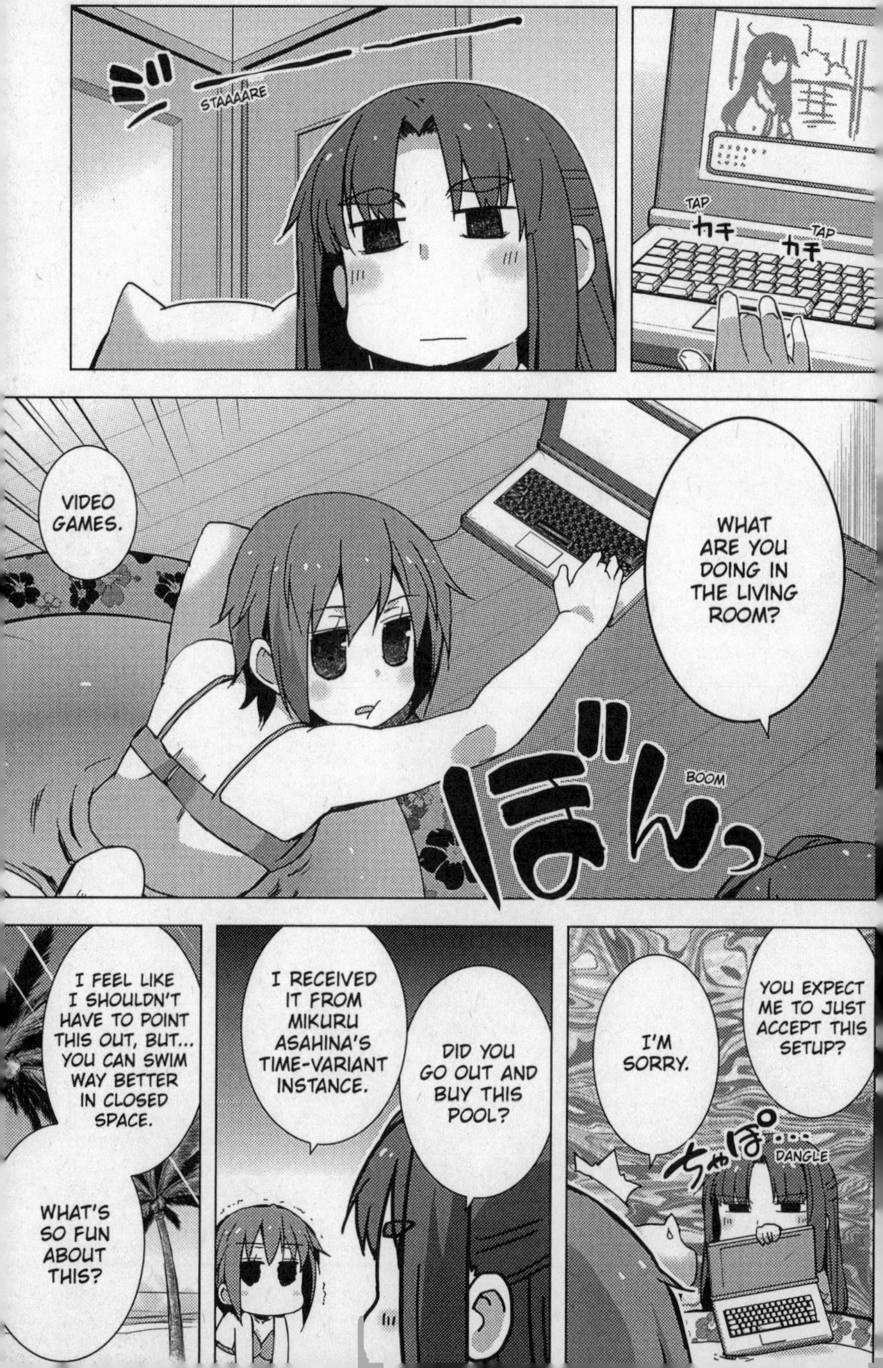

TAP
カチ
TAP
カチ
ジーー
STAAAARE
WHAT ARE YOU DOING IN THE LIVING ROOM?
ぼんっ
BOOM
VIDEO GAMES.
YOU EXPECT ME TO JUST ACCEPT THIS SETUP?
I'M SORRY.
ちゃぽ…
DANGLE
DID YOU GO OUT AND BUY THIS POOL?
I RECEIVED IT FROM MIKURU ASAHINA'S TIME-VARIANT INSTANCE.
I FEEL LIKE I SHOULDN'T HAVE TO POINT THIS OUT, BUT... YOU CAN SWIM WAY BETTER IN CLOSED SPACE.
WHAT'S SO FUN ABOUT THIS?

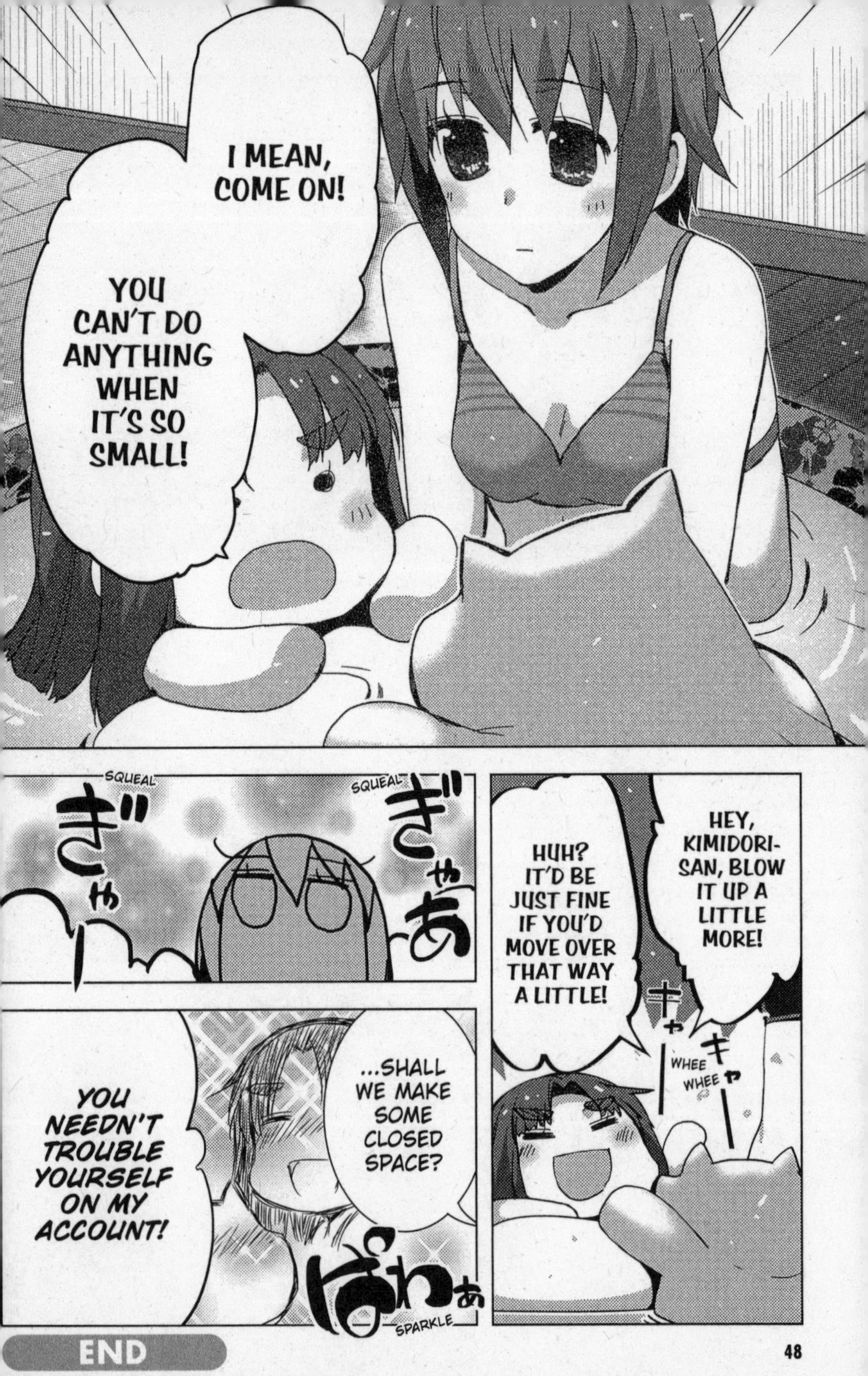
I MEAN, COME ON!
YOU CAN'T DO ANYTHING WHEN IT'S SO SMALL!
HEY, KIMIDORI-SAN, BLOW IT UP A LITTLE MORE!
HUH? IT'D BE JUST FINE IF YOU'D MOVE OVER THAT WAY A LITTLE!
キャー
WHEE
キャー
WHEE
ぎゃあ
SQUEAL
ぎゃー
SQUEAL
...SHALL WE MAKE SOME CLOSED SPACE?
YOU NEEDN'T TROUBLE YOURSELF ON MY ACCOUNT!
ぱわぁ
SPARKLE
END

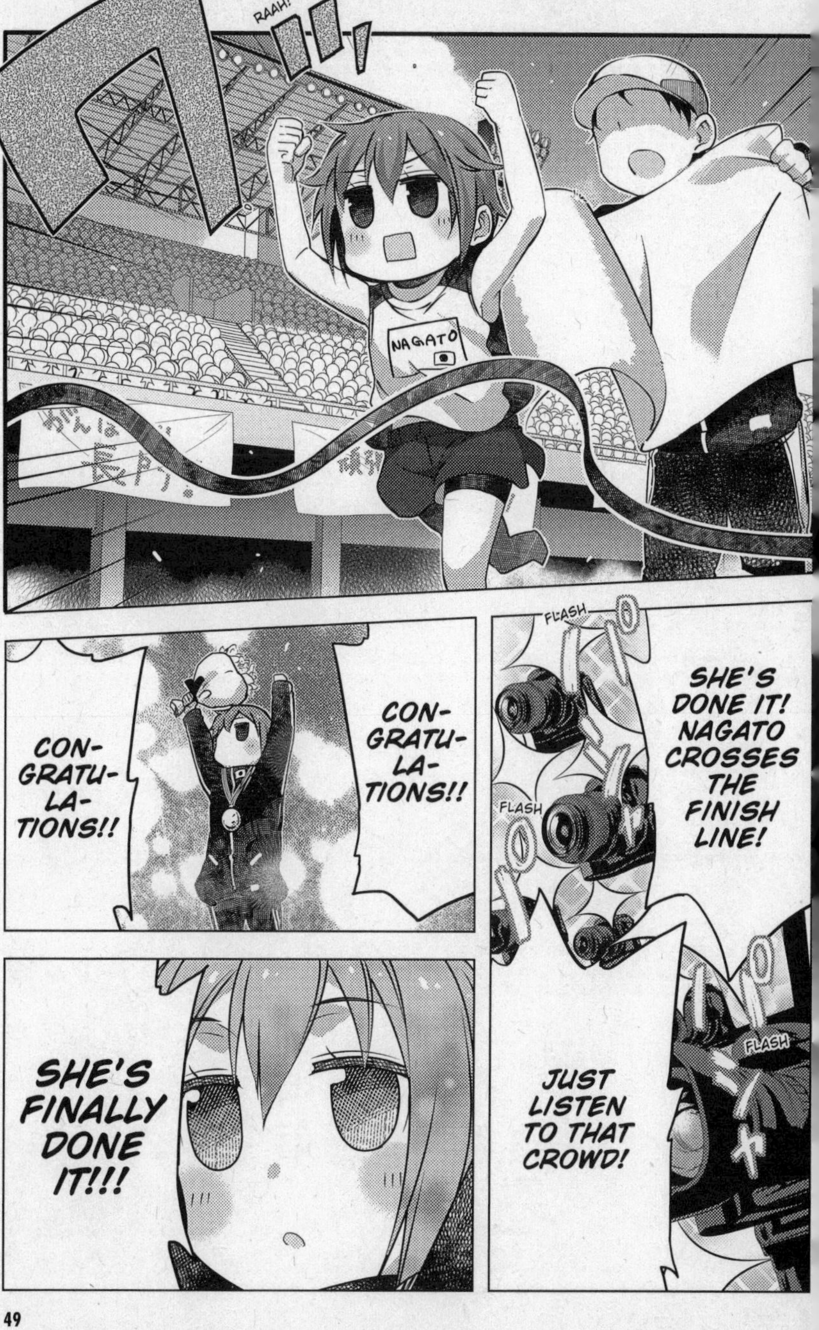
RAAH!
NAGATO
FLASH
SHE'S DONE IT! NAGATO CROSSES THE FINISH LINE!
FLASH
FLASH
JUST LISTEN TO THAT CROWD!
CON-GRATU-LA-TIONS!!
CON-GRATU-LA-TIONS!!
SHE'S FINALLY DONE IT!!!

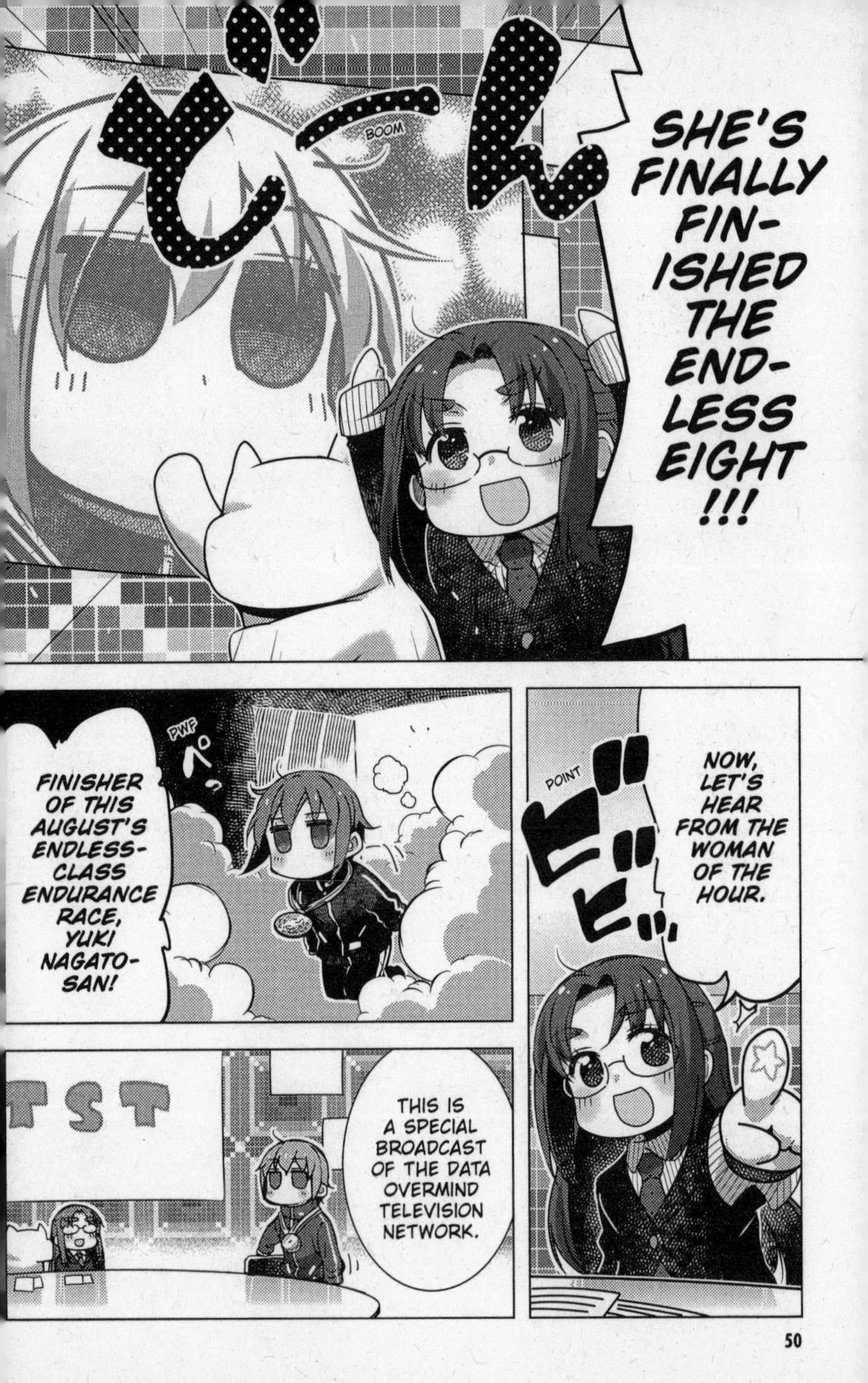
どーん
BOOM
SHE'S FINALLY FIN-ISHED THE END-LESS EIGHT!!!
POINT
NOW, LET'S HEAR FROM THE WOMAN OF THE HOUR.
PWF
FINISHER OF THIS AUGUST'S ENDLESS-CLASS ENDURANCE RACE, YUKI NAGATO-SAN!
TST
THIS IS A SPECIAL BROADCAST OF THE DATA OVERMIND TELEVISION NETWORK.

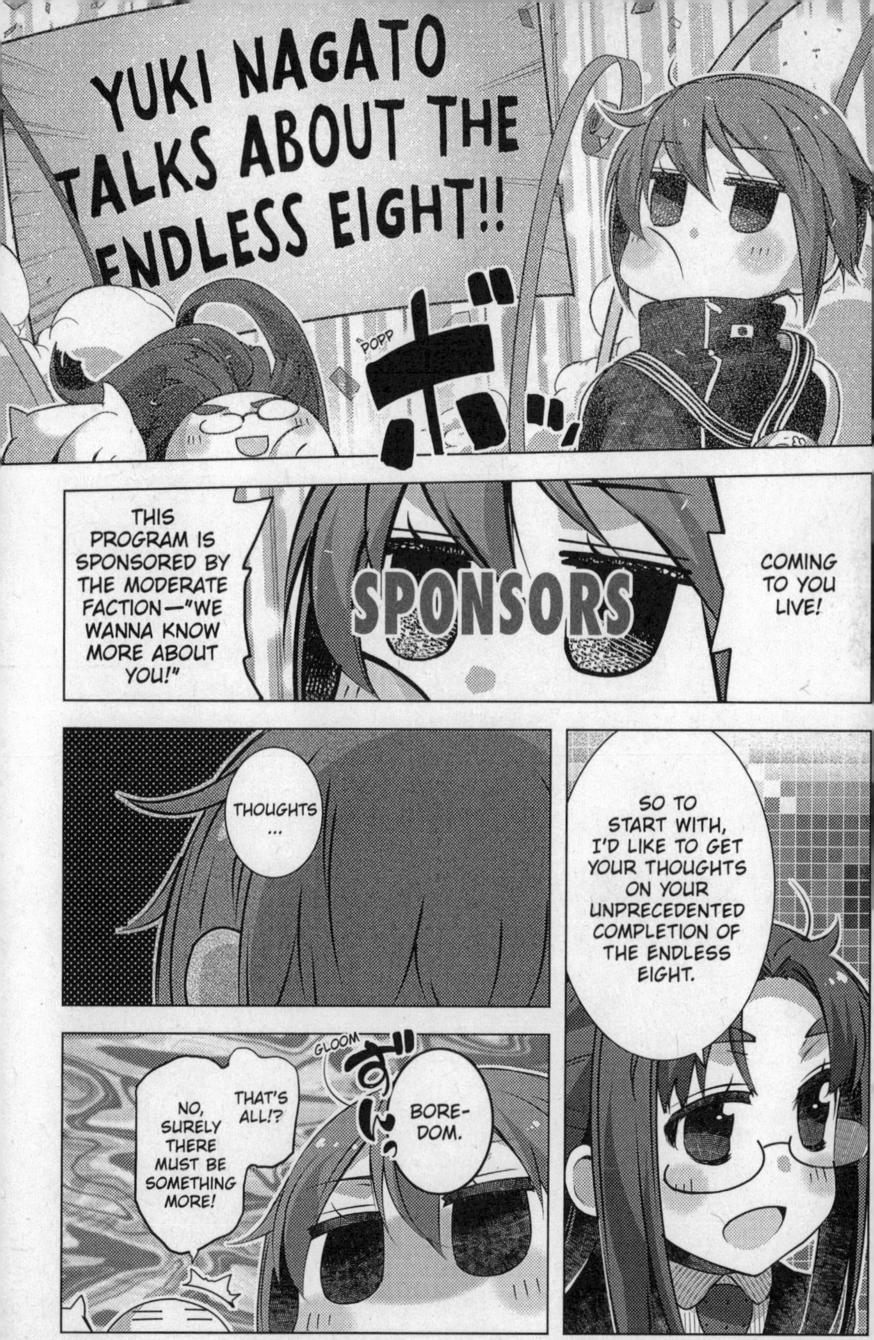
YUKI NAGATO TALKS ABOUT THE ENDLESS EIGHT!!
POPP
COMING TO YOU LIVE!
SPONSORS
THIS PROGRAM IS SPONSORED BY THE MODERATE FACTION—"WE WANNA KNOW MORE ABOUT YOU!"
SO TO START WITH, I'D LIKE TO GET YOUR THOUGHTS ON YOUR UNPRECEDENTED COMPLETION OF THE ENDLESS EIGHT.
THOUGHTS ...
GLOOM
BORE-DOM.
THAT'S ALL!?
NO, SURELY THERE MUST BE SOMETHING MORE!

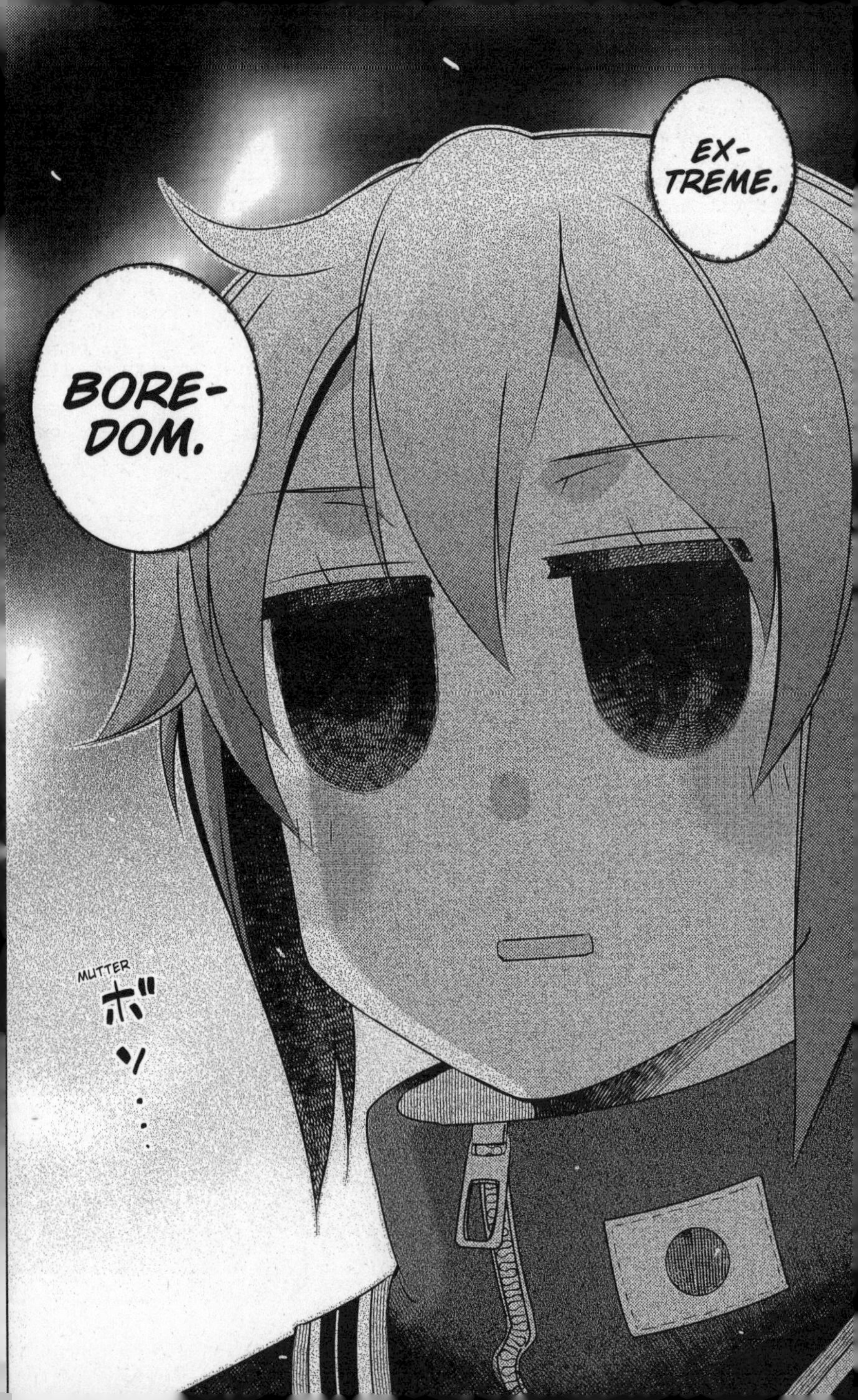
EX-TREME.
BORE-DOM.
MUTTER
ボソ…

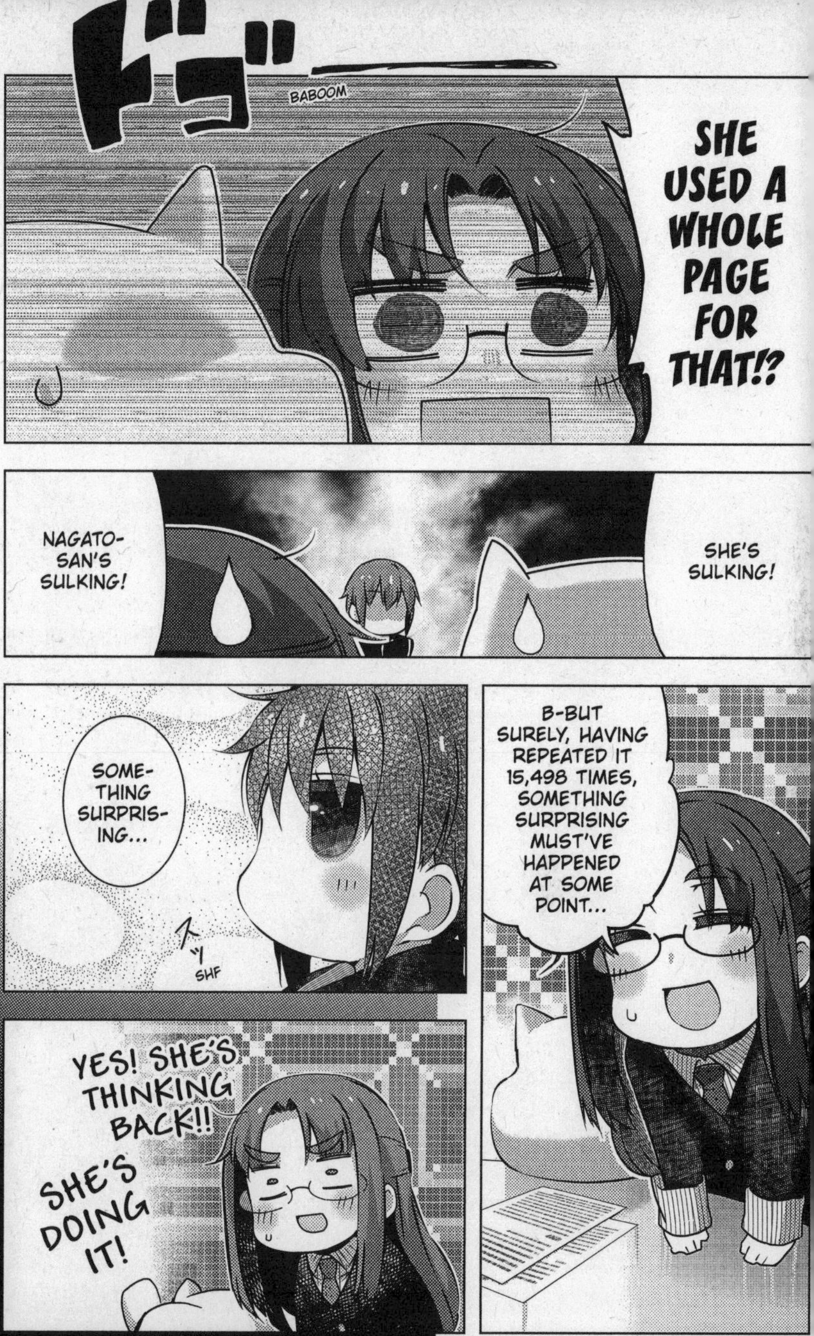
BABOOM
SHE USED A WHOLE PAGE FOR THAT!?
SHE'S SULKING!
NAGATO-SAN'S SULKING!
B-BUT SURELY, HAVING REPEATED IT 15,498 TIMES, SOMETHING SURPRISING MUST'VE HAPPENED AT SOME POINT...
SOME-THING SURPRIS-ING...
SHF
YES! SHE'S THINKING BACK!!
SHE'S DOING IT!

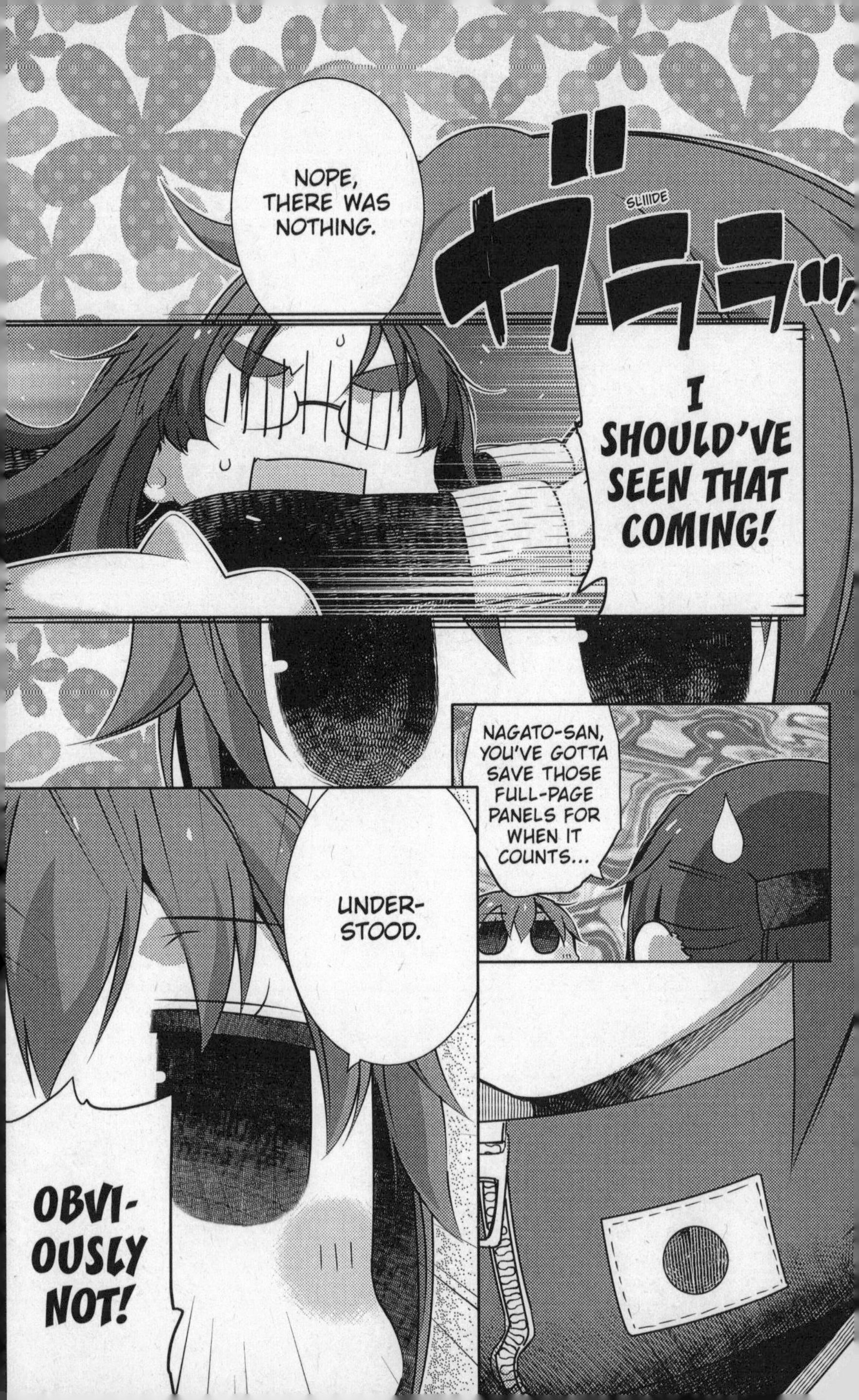
ヴララッ
SLIIIDE
NOPE, THERE WAS NOTHING.
I SHOULD'VE SEEN THAT COMING!
NAGATO-SAN, YOU'VE GOTTA SAVE THOSE FULL-PAGE PANELS FOR WHEN IT COUNTS...
UNDER-STOOD.
OBVI-OUSLY NOT!

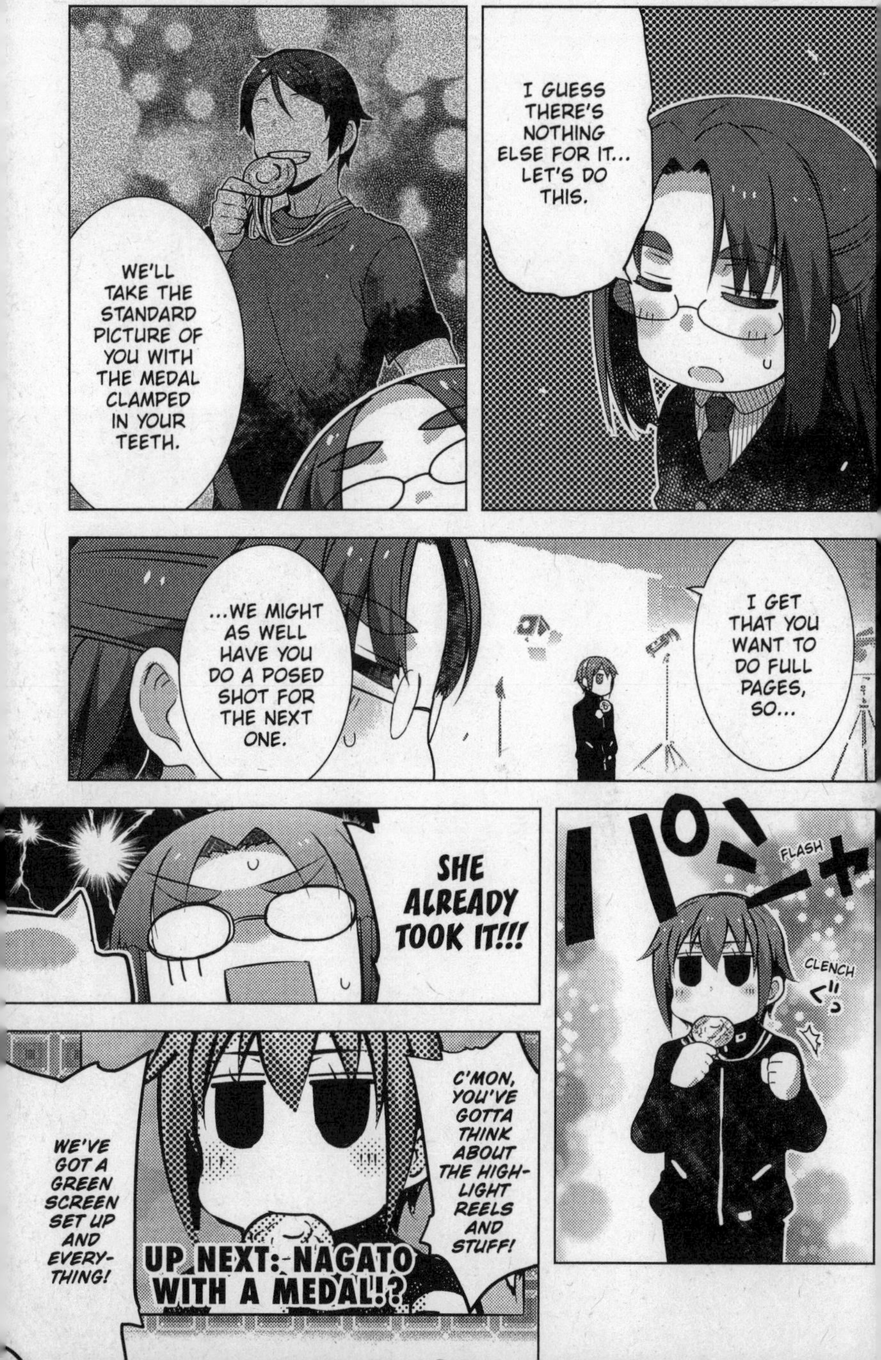
I GUESS THERE'S NOTHING ELSE FOR IT... LET'S DO THIS.
WE'LL TAKE THE STANDARD PICTURE OF YOU WITH THE MEDAL CLAMPED IN YOUR TEETH.
I GET THAT YOU WANT TO DO FULL PAGES, SO...
...WE MIGHT AS WELL HAVE YOU DO A POSED SHOT FOR THE NEXT ONE.
FLASH
CLENCH
SHE ALREADY TOOK IT!!!
C'MON, YOU'VE GOTTA THINK ABOUT THE HIGH-LIGHT REELS AND STUFF!
WE'VE GOT A GREEN SCREEN SET UP AND EVERY-THING!
UP NEXT: NAGATO WITH A MEDAL!?

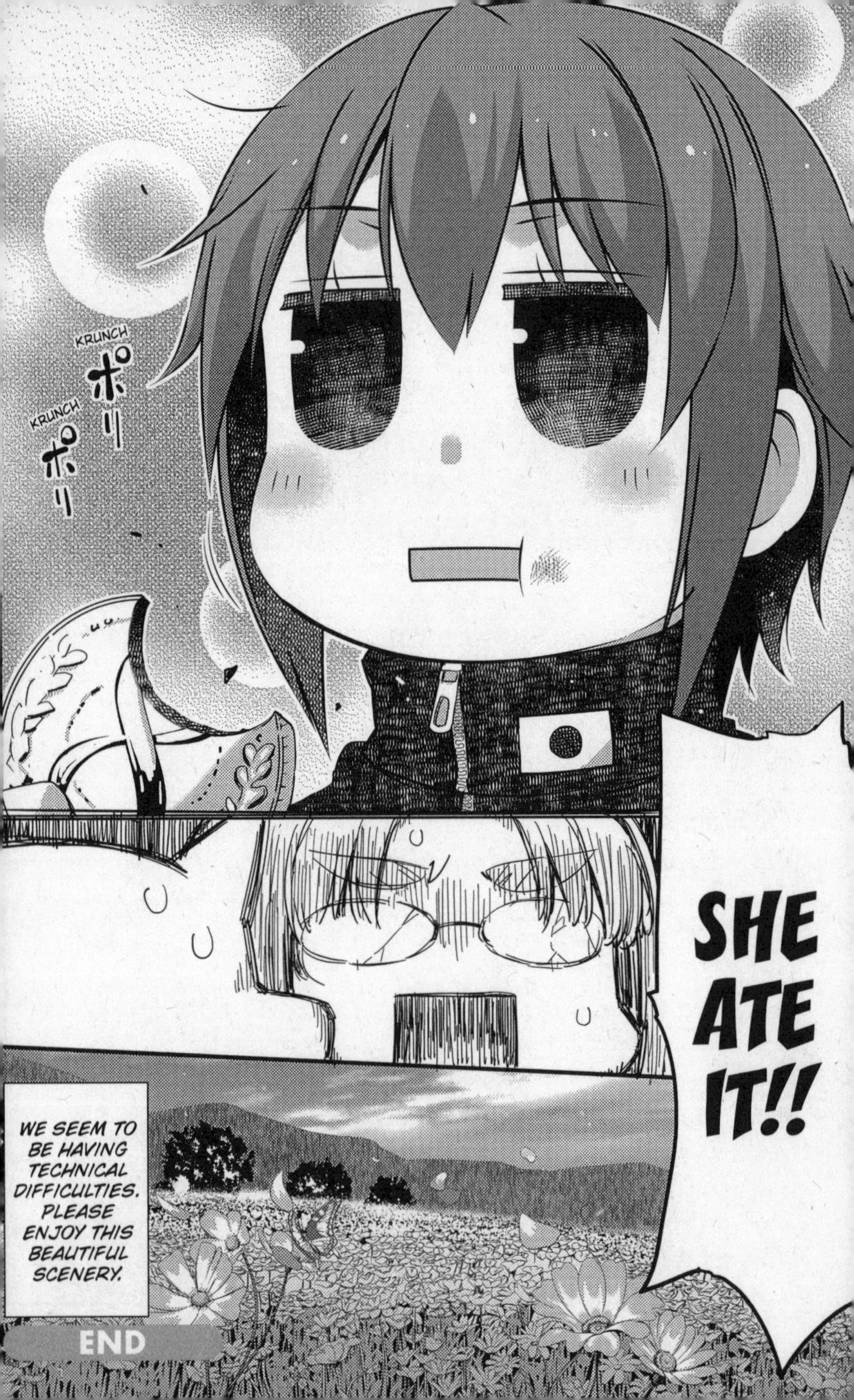
KRUNCH
ポリ
KRUNCH
ポリ
SHE ATE IT!!
WE SEEM TO BE HAVING TECHNICAL DIFFICULTIES. PLEASE ENJOY THIS BEAUTIFUL SCENERY.
END

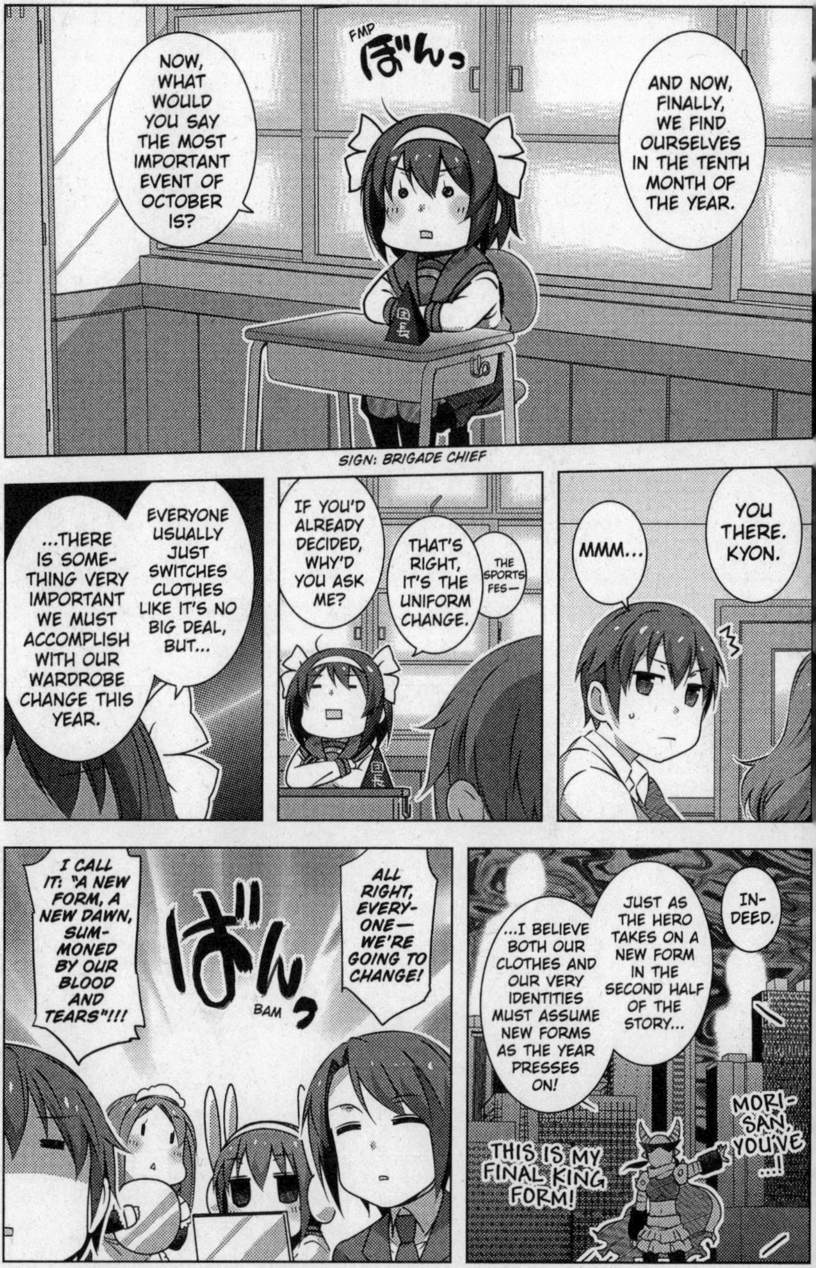
AND NOW, FINALLY, WE FIND OURSELVES IN THE TENTH MONTH OF THE YEAR.
FMP ぼんっ
NOW, WHAT WOULD YOU SAY THE MOST IMPORTANT EVENT OF OCTOBER IS?
YOU THERE. KYON.
MMM...
THE SPORTS FES—
THAT'S RIGHT, IT'S THE UNIFORM CHANGE.
IF YOU'D ALREADY DECIDED, WHY'D YOU ASK ME?
EVERYONE USUALLY JUST SWITCHES CLOTHES LIKE IT'S NO BIG DEAL, BUT...
...THERE IS SOME-THING VERY IMPORTANT WE MUST ACCOMPLISH WITH OUR WARDROBE CHANGE THIS YEAR.
IN-DEED.
JUST AS THE HERO TAKES ON A NEW FORM IN THE SECOND HALF OF THE STORY...
...I BELIEVE BOTH OUR CLOTHES AND OUR VERY IDENTITIES MUST ASSUME NEW FORMS AS THE YEAR PRESSES ON!
MORI-SAN, YOU'VE ...!
THIS IS MY FINAL KING FORM!
ALL RIGHT, EVERY-ONE— WE'RE GOING TO CHANGE!
ばんっ BAM
I CALL IT: "A NEW FORM, A NEW DAWN, SUM-MONED BY OUR BLOOD AND TEARS"!!!

SIGN: BRIGADE CHIEF

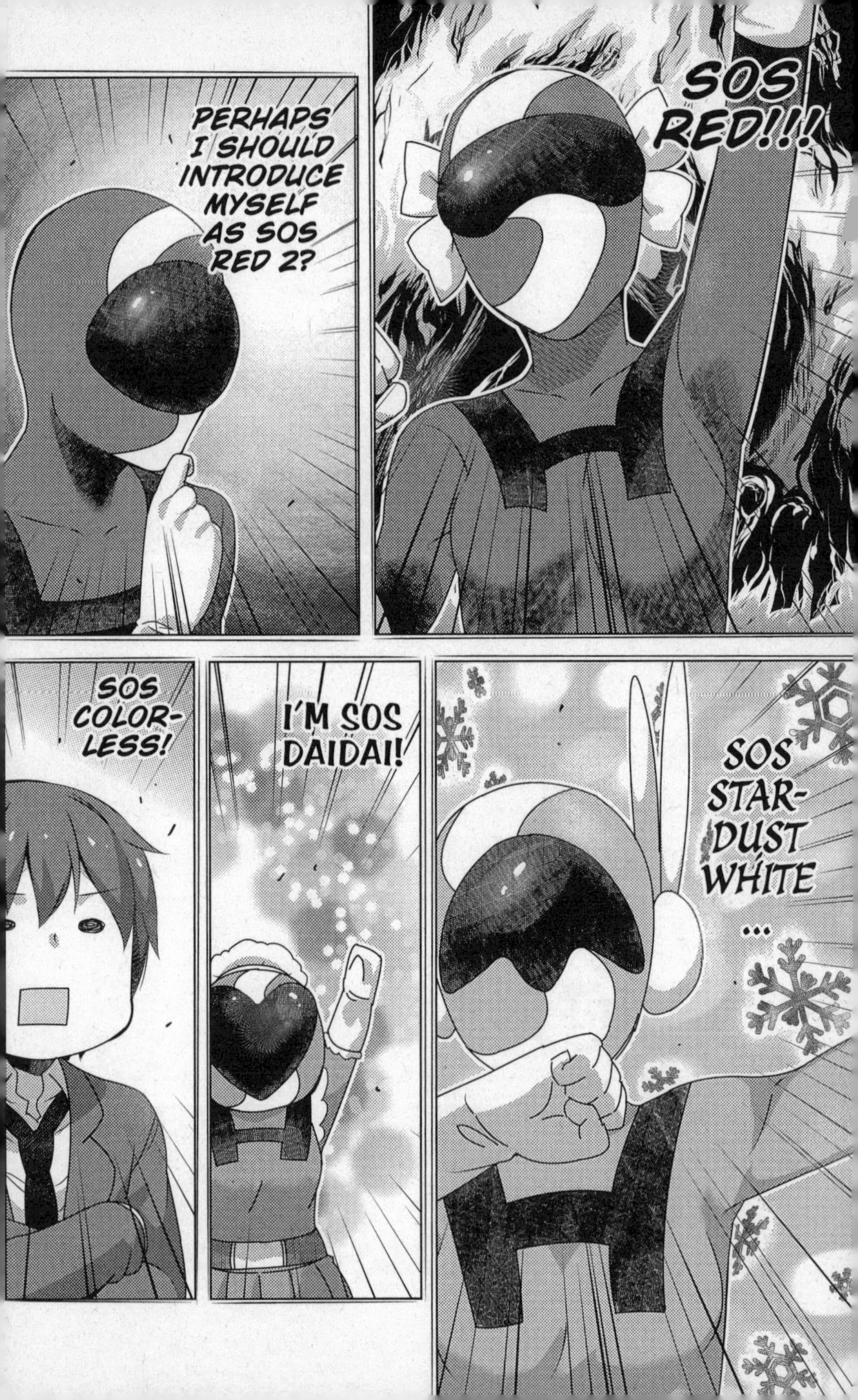
SOS RED!!!
PERHAPS I SHOULD INTRODUCE MYSELF AS SOS RED 2?
SOS STAR-DUST WHITE ...
I'M SOS DAIDAI!
SOS COLOR-LESS!

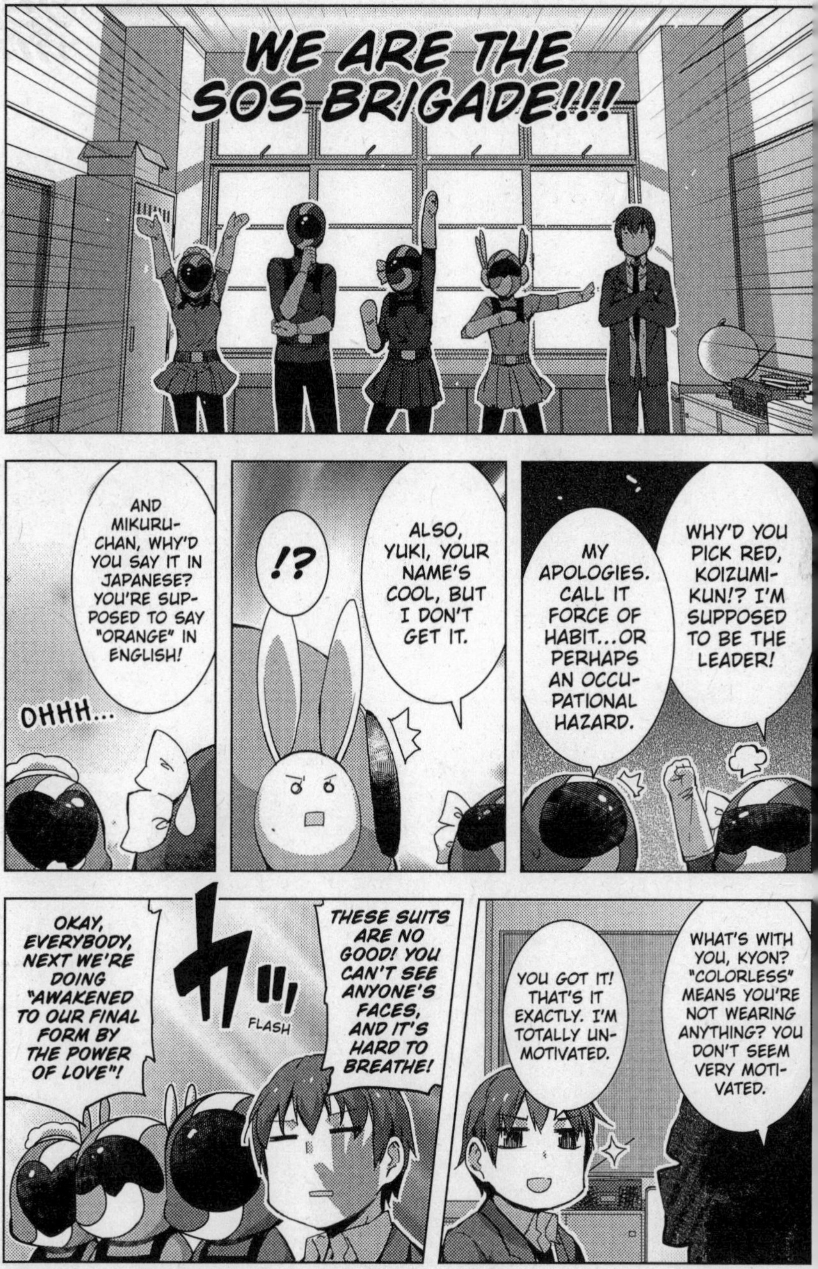
WE ARE THE SOS BRIGADE!!!
WHY'D YOU PICK RED, KOIZUMI-KUN!? I'M SUPPOSED TO BE THE LEADER!
MY APOLOGIES. CALL IT FORCE OF HABIT...OR PERHAPS AN OCCUPATIONAL HAZARD.
ALSO, YUKI, YOUR NAME'S COOL, BUT I DON'T GET IT.
!?
AND MIKURU-CHAN, WHY'D YOU SAY IT IN JAPANESE? YOU'RE SUPPOSED TO SAY "ORANGE" IN ENGLISH!
OHHH...
WHAT'S WITH YOU, KYON? "COLORLESS" MEANS YOU'RE NOT WEARING ANYTHING? YOU DON'T SEEM VERY MOTIVATED.
YOU GOT IT! THAT'S IT EXACTLY. I'M TOTALLY UNMOTIVATED.
THESE SUITS ARE NO GOOD! YOU CAN'T SEE ANYONE'S FACES, AND IT'S HARD TO BREATHE!
FLASH
OKAY, EVERYBODY, NEXT WE'RE DOING "AWAKENED TO OUR FINAL FORM BY THE POWER OF LOVE"!

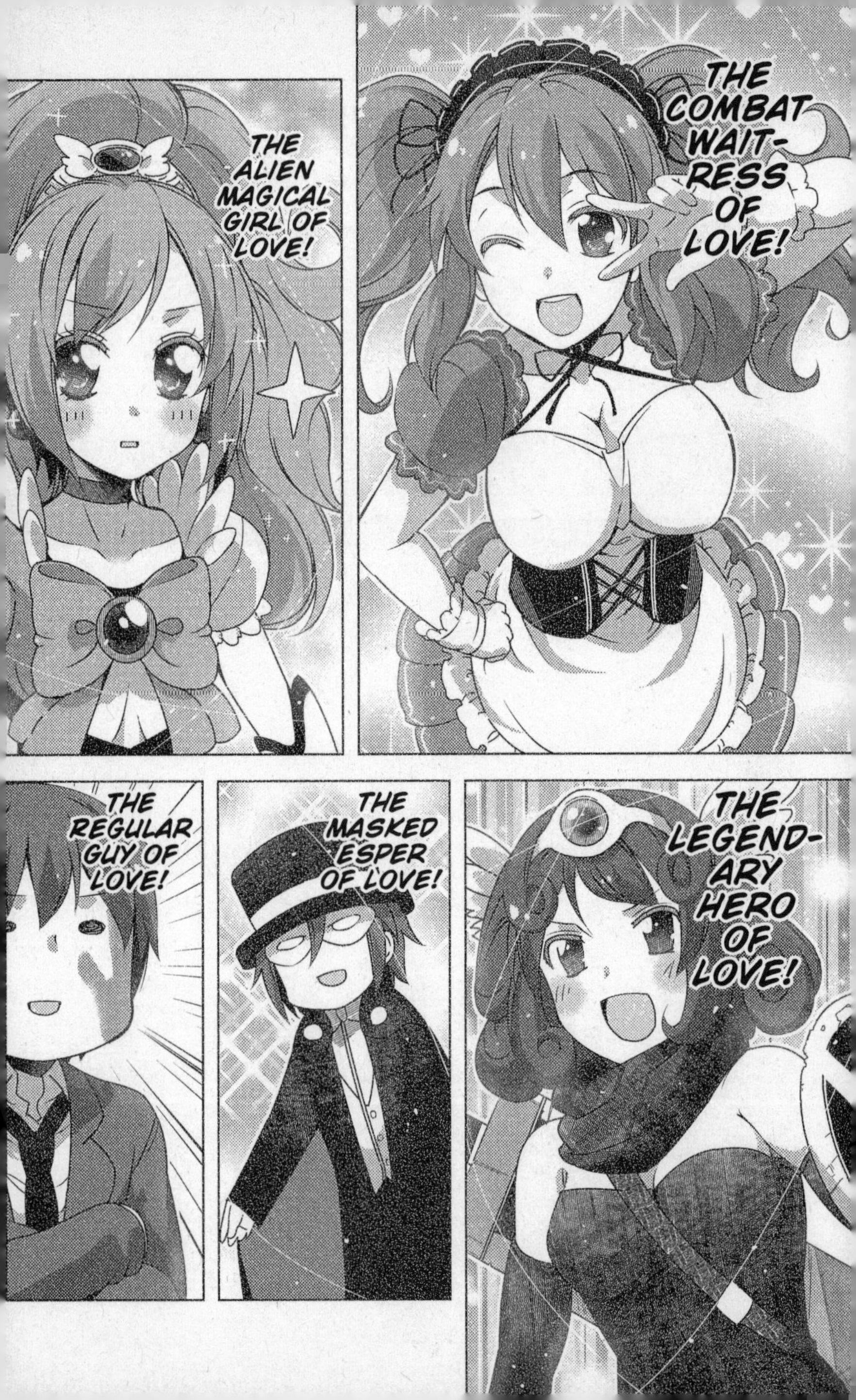
THE COMBAT WAIT-RESS OF LOVE!
THE ALIEN MAGICAL GIRL OF LOVE!
THE LEGEND-ARY HERO OF LOVE!
THE MASKED ESPER OF LOVE!
THE REGULAR GUY OF LOVE!

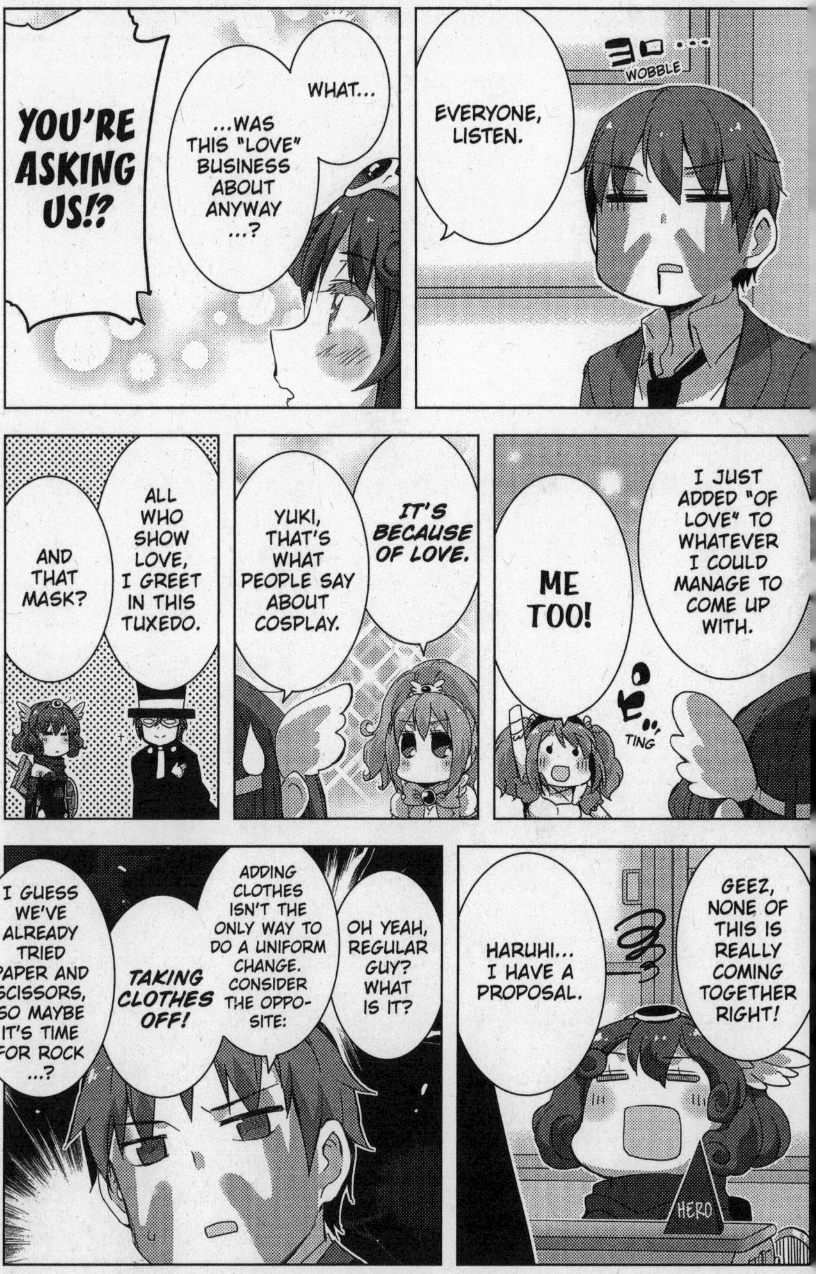
ヨロ…
WOBBLE
EVERYONE, LISTEN.
WHAT…
…WAS THIS "LOVE" BUSINESS ABOUT ANYWAY …?
YOU'RE ASKING US!?
I JUST ADDED "OF LOVE" TO WHATEVER I COULD MANAGE TO COME UP WITH.
ME TOO!
ピ
TING
IT'S BECAUSE OF LOVE.
YUKI, THAT'S WHAT PEOPLE SAY ABOUT COSPLAY.
ALL WHO SHOW LOVE, I GREET IN THIS TUXEDO.
AND THAT MASK?
GEEZ, NONE OF THIS IS REALLY COMING TOGETHER RIGHT!
HARUHI… I HAVE A PROPOSAL.
HERO
OH YEAH, REGULAR GUY? WHAT IS IT?
ADDING CLOTHES ISN'T THE ONLY WAY TO DO A UNIFORM CHANGE. CONSIDER THE OPPO-SITE:
TAKING CLOTHES OFF!
I GUESS WE'VE ALREADY TRIED PAPER AND SCISSORS, SO MAYBE IT'S TIME FOR ROCK …?

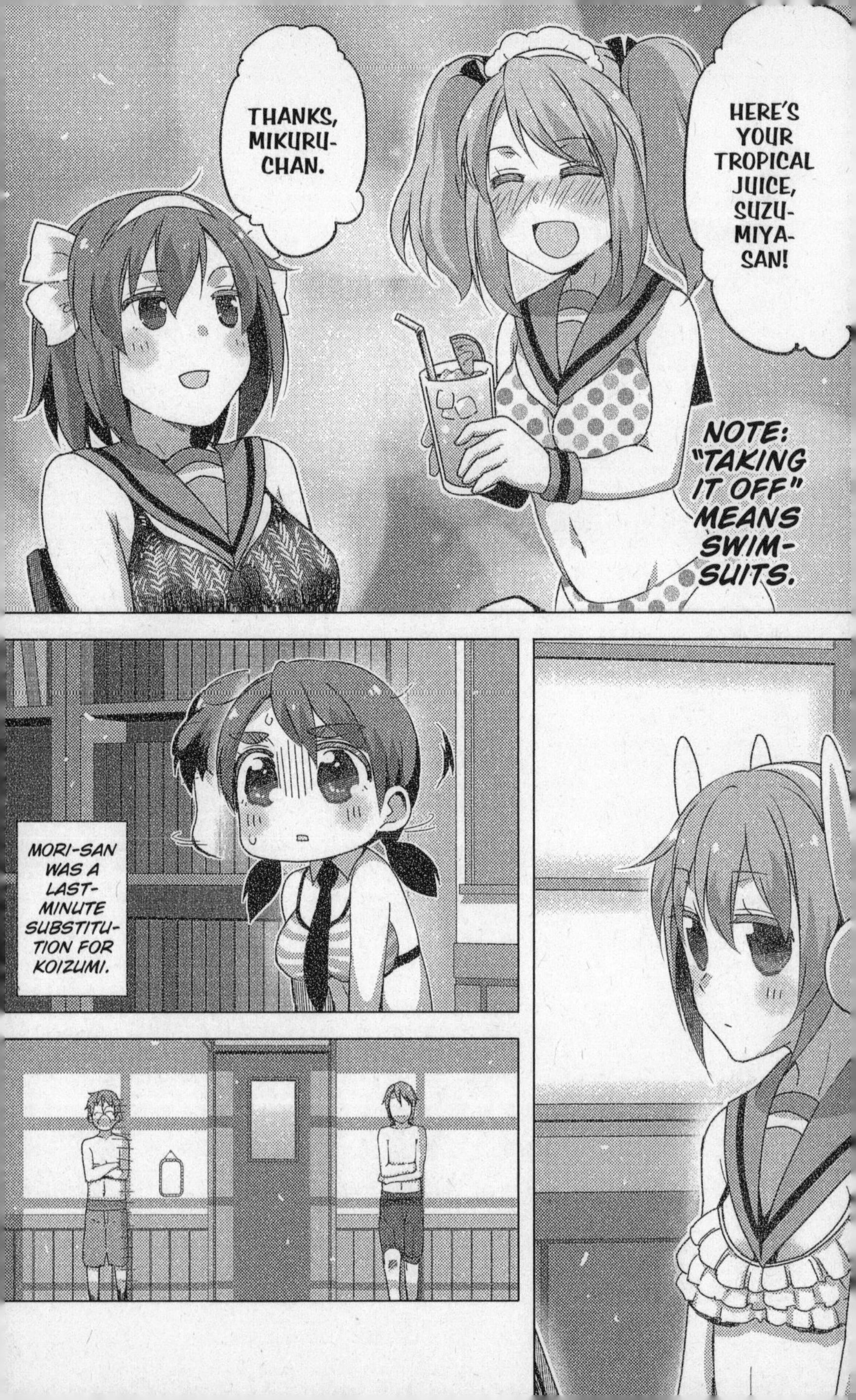
HERE'S YOUR TROPICAL JUICE, SUZU-MIYA-SAN!
THANKS, MIKURU-CHAN.
NOTE: "TAKING IT OFF" MEANS SWIM-SUITS.
MORI-SAN WAS A LAST-MINUTE SUBSTITU-TION FOR KOIZUMI.

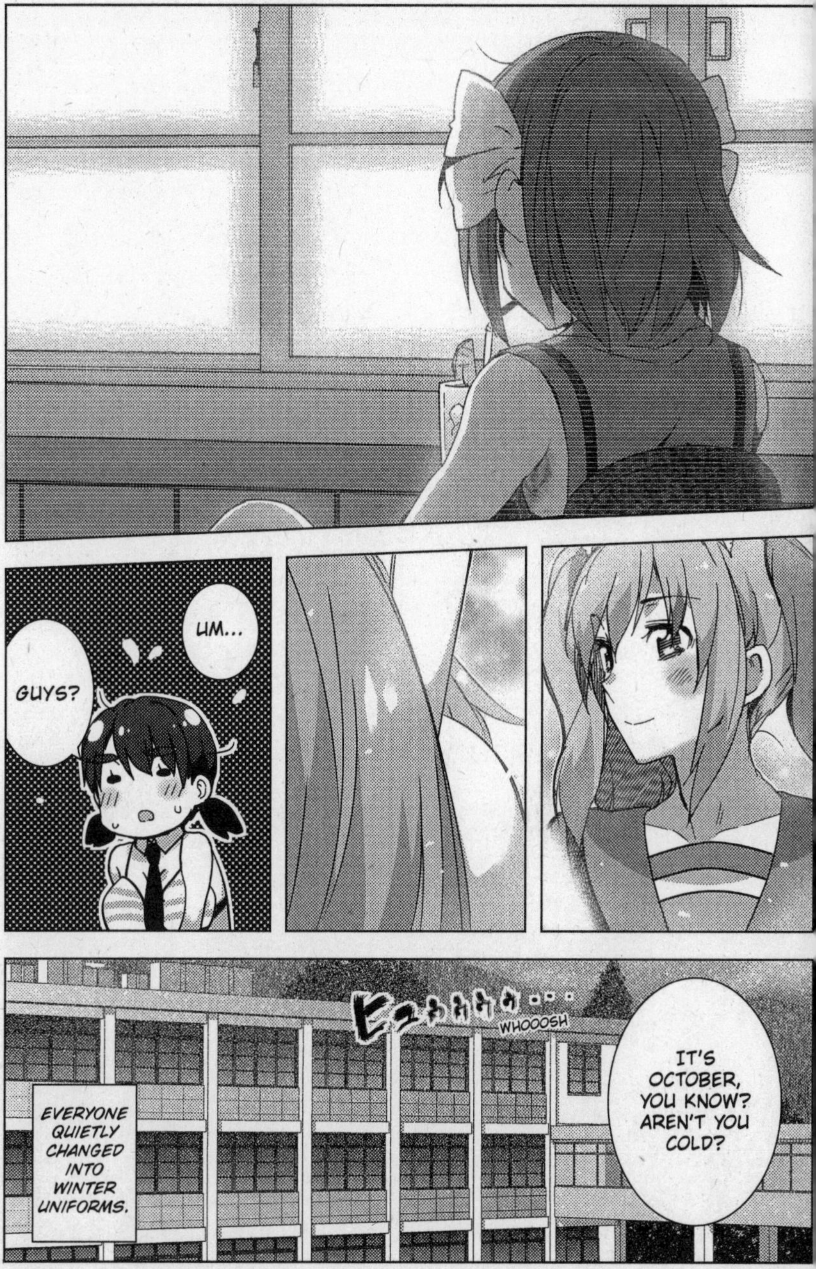
UM...
GUYS?
IT'S OCTOBER, YOU KNOW? AREN'T YOU COLD?
WHOOOSH
EVERYONE QUIETLY CHANGED INTO WINTER UNIFORMS.

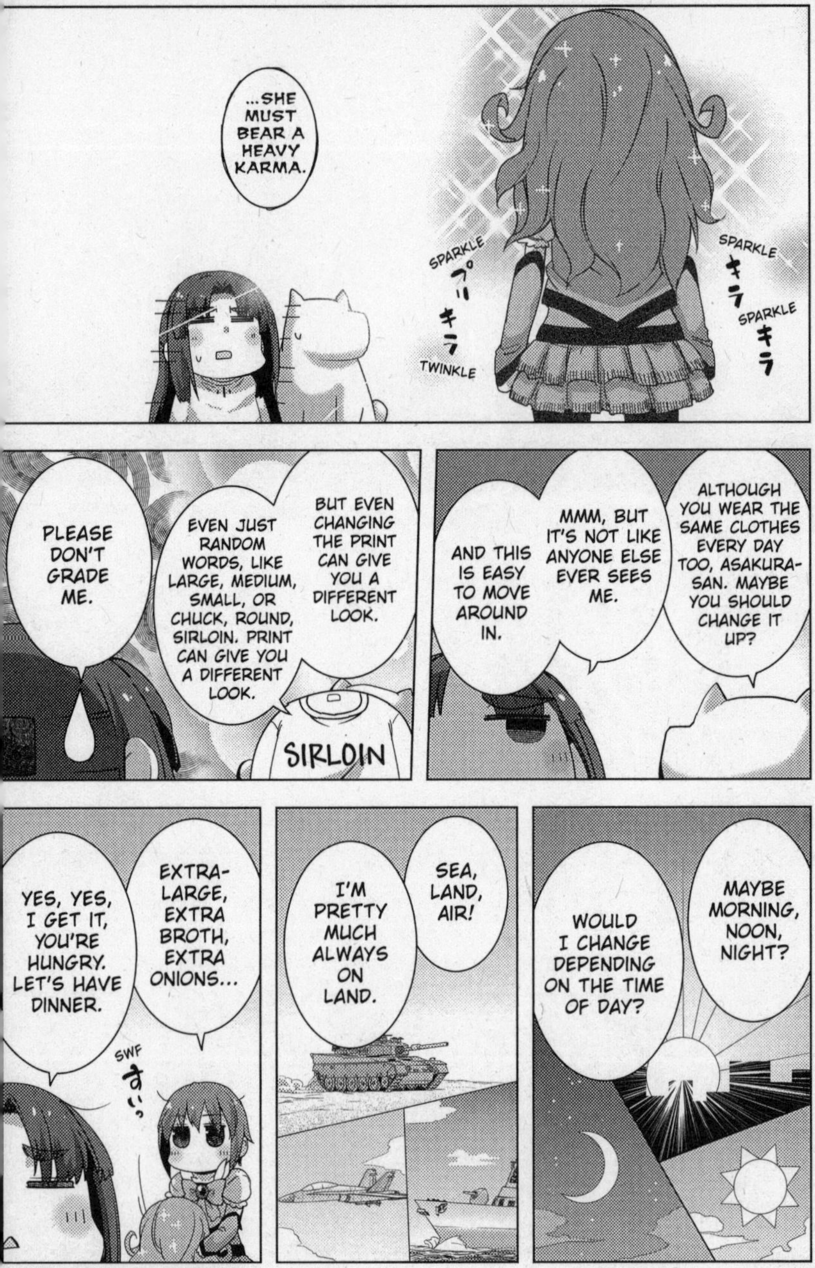
SPARKLE キラ
SPARKLE キラ
SPARKLE キラ TWINKLE
...SHE MUST BEAR A HEAVY KARMA.
ALTHOUGH YOU WEAR THE SAME CLOTHES EVERY DAY TOO, ASAKURA-SAN. MAYBE YOU SHOULD CHANGE IT UP?
MMM, BUT IT'S NOT LIKE ANYONE ELSE EVER SEES ME.
AND THIS IS EASY TO MOVE AROUND IN.
BUT EVEN CHANGING THE PRINT CAN GIVE YOU A DIFFERENT LOOK.
EVEN JUST RANDOM WORDS, LIKE LARGE, MEDIUM, SMALL, OR CHUCK, ROUND, SIRLOIN. PRINT CAN GIVE YOU A DIFFERENT LOOK.
SIRLOIN
PLEASE DON'T GRADE ME.
MAYBE MORNING, NOON, NIGHT?
WOULD I CHANGE DEPENDING ON THE TIME OF DAY?
SEA, LAND, AIR!
I'M PRETTY MUCH ALWAYS ON LAND.
EXTRA-LARGE, EXTRA BROTH, EXTRA ONIONS...
YES, YES, I GET IT, YOU'RE HUNGRY. LET'S HAVE DINNER.
SWF すいっ

END

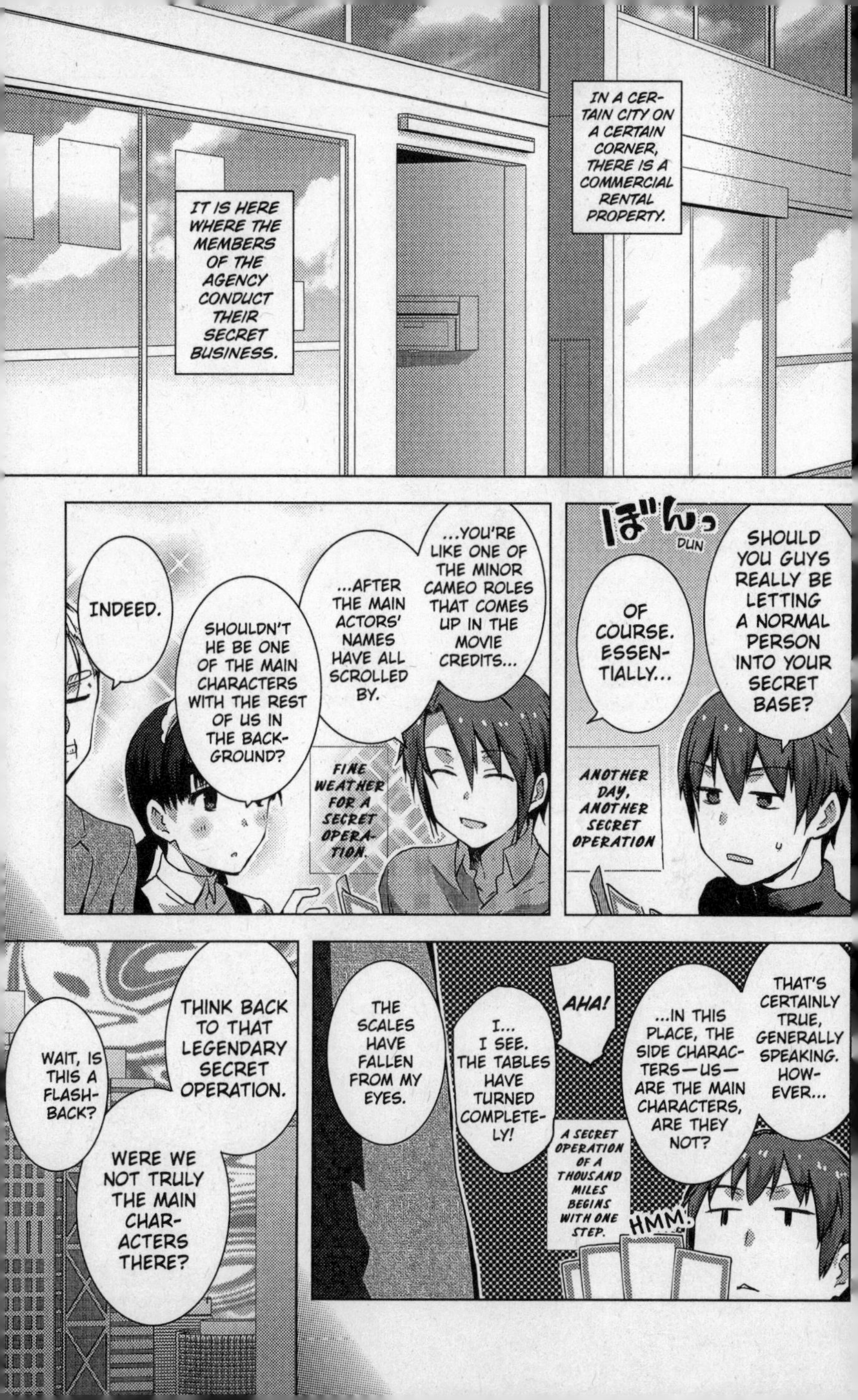
IN A CERTAIN CITY ON A CERTAIN CORNER, THERE IS A COMMERCIAL RENTAL PROPERTY.
IT IS HERE WHERE THE MEMBERS OF THE AGENCY CONDUCT THEIR SECRET BUSINESS.
ぼんっ
DUN
SHOULD YOU GUYS REALLY BE LETTING A NORMAL PERSON INTO YOUR SECRET BASE?
OF COURSE. ESSENTIALLY...
ANOTHER DAY, ANOTHER SECRET OPERATION
...YOU'RE LIKE ONE OF THE MINOR CAMEO ROLES THAT COMES UP IN THE MOVIE CREDITS...
...AFTER THE MAIN ACTORS' NAMES HAVE ALL SCROLLED BY.
SHOULDN'T HE BE ONE OF THE MAIN CHARACTERS WITH THE REST OF US IN THE BACKGROUND?
INDEED.
FINE WEATHER FOR A SECRET OPERATION.
THAT'S CERTAINLY TRUE, GENERALLY SPEAKING. HOWEVER...
...IN THIS PLACE, THE SIDE CHARACTERS—US—ARE THE MAIN CHARACTERS, ARE THEY NOT?
AHA!
I... I SEE. THE TABLES HAVE TURNED COMPLETELY!
THE SCALES HAVE FALLEN FROM MY EYES.
HMM.
A SECRET OPERATION OF A THOUSAND MILES BEGINS WITH ONE STEP.
THINK BACK TO THAT LEGENDARY SECRET OPERATION.
WAIT, IS THIS A FLASHBACK?
WERE WE NOT TRULY THE MAIN CHARACTERS THERE?

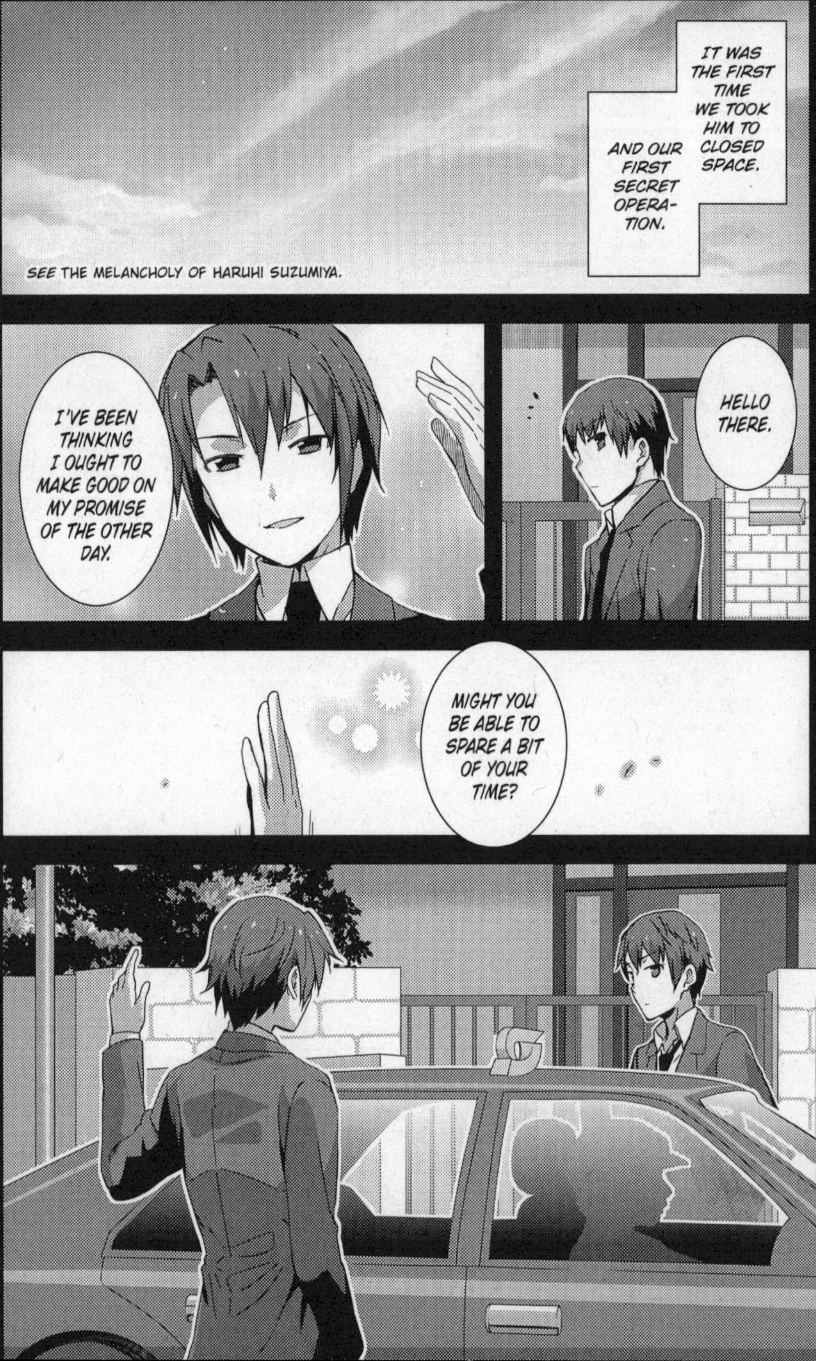
IT WAS THE FIRST TIME WE TOOK HIM TO CLOSED SPACE.
AND OUR FIRST SECRET OPERATION.
SEE THE MELANCHOLY OF HARUHI SUZUMIYA.
HELLO THERE.
I'VE BEEN THINKING I OUGHT TO MAKE GOOD ON MY PROMISE OF THE OTHER DAY.
MIGHT YOU BE ABLE TO SPARE A BIT OF YOUR TIME?

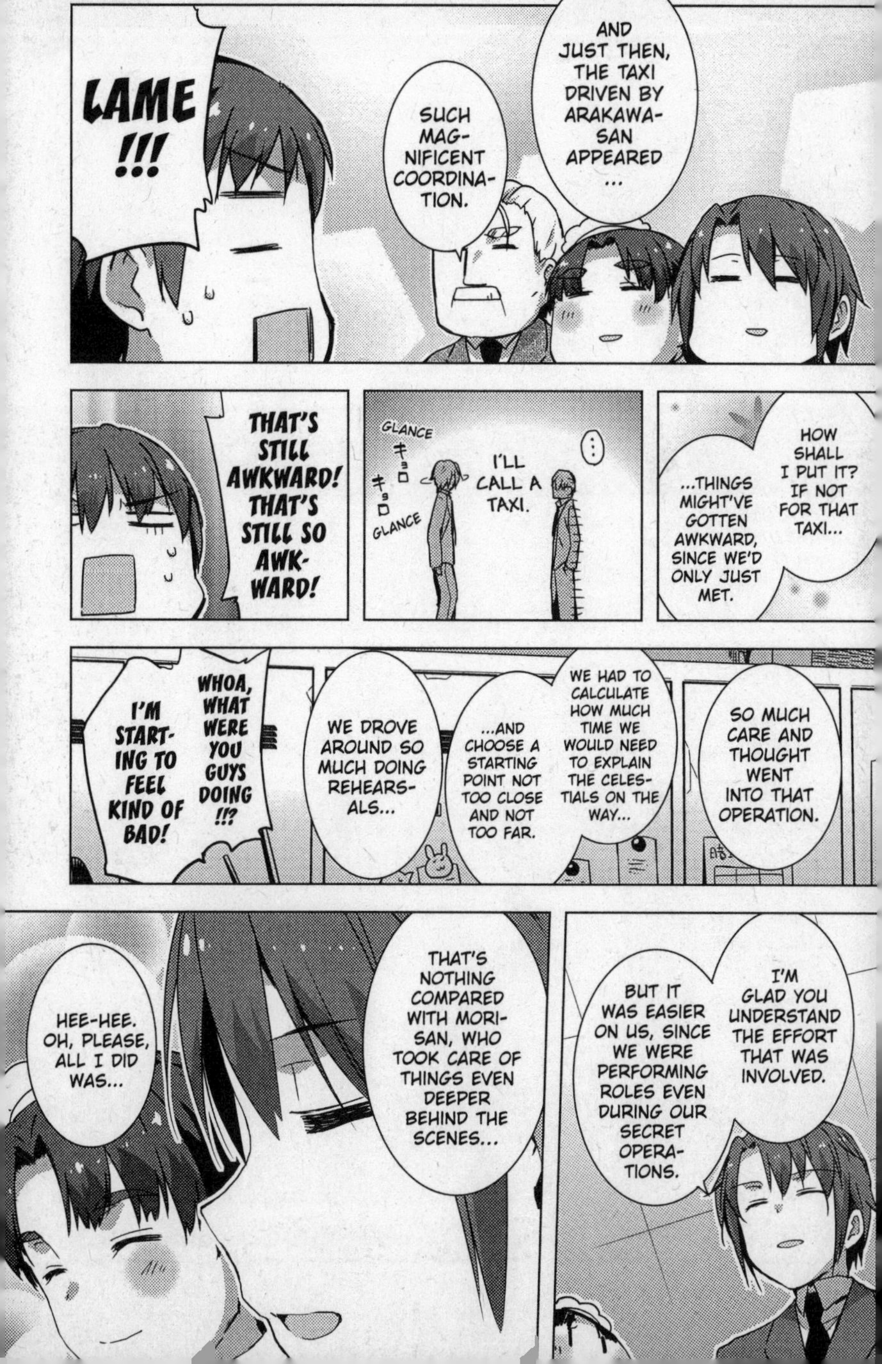
AND JUST THEN, THE TAXI DRIVEN BY ARAKAWA-SAN APPEARED...
SUCH MAGNIFICENT COORDINATION.
LAME!!!
HOW SHALL I PUT IT? IF NOT FOR THAT TAXI...
...THINGS MIGHT'VE GOTTEN AWKWARD, SINCE WE'D ONLY JUST MET.
...
I'LL CALL A TAXI.
キョロ GLANCE
キョロ GLANCE
THAT'S STILL AWKWARD! THAT'S STILL SO AWKWARD!
SO MUCH CARE AND THOUGHT WENT INTO THAT OPERATION.
WE HAD TO CALCULATE HOW MUCH TIME WE WOULD NEED TO EXPLAIN THE CELESTIALS ON THE WAY...
...AND CHOOSE A STARTING POINT NOT TOO CLOSE AND NOT TOO FAR.
WE DROVE AROUND SO MUCH DOING REHEARSALS...
WHOA, WHAT WERE YOU GUYS DOING!!?
I'M STARTING TO FEEL KIND OF BAD!
I'M GLAD YOU UNDERSTAND THE EFFORT THAT WAS INVOLVED.
BUT IT WAS EASIER ON US, SINCE WE WERE PERFORMING ROLES EVEN DURING OUR SECRET OPERATIONS.
THAT'S NOTHING COMPARED WITH MORI-SAN, WHO TOOK CARE OF THINGS EVEN DEEPER BEHIND THE SCENES...
HEE-HEE. OH, PLEASE, ALL I DID WAS...

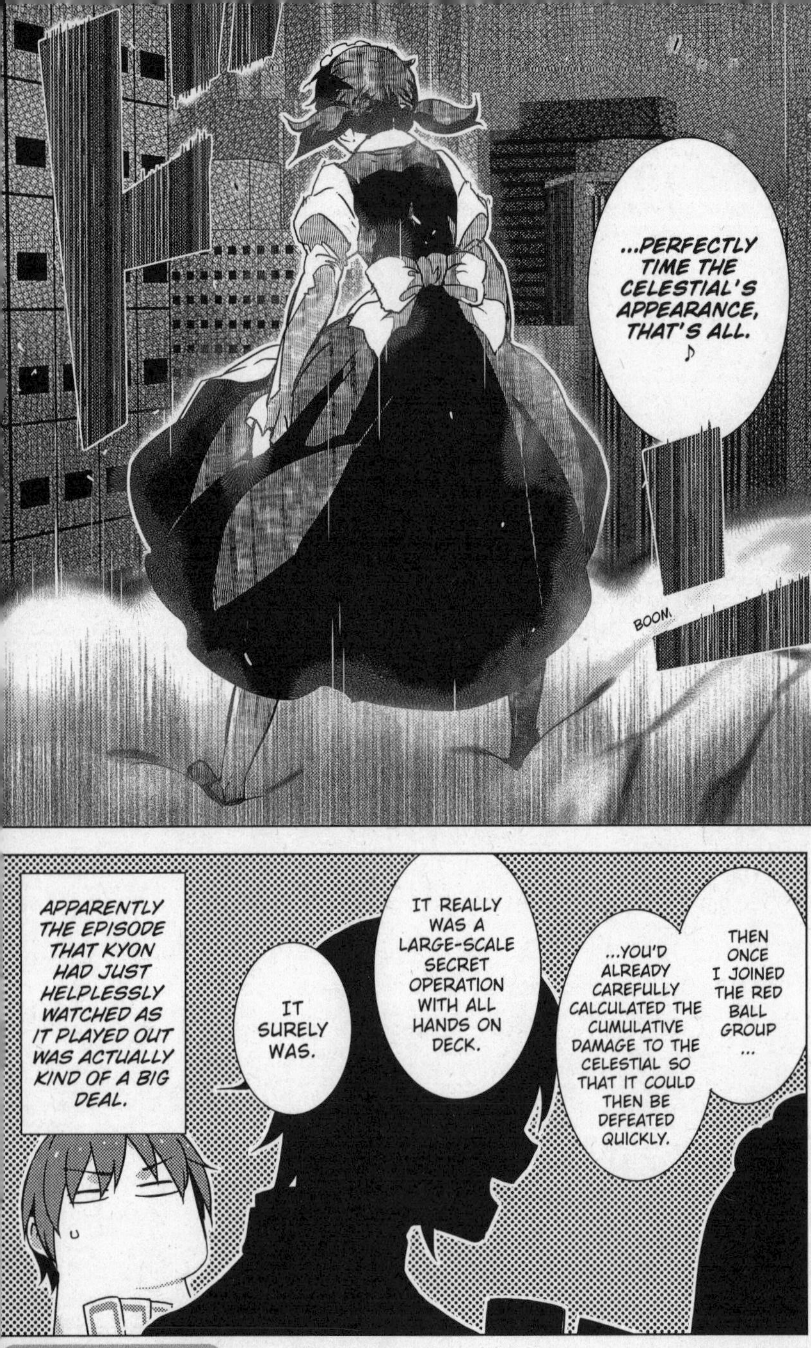
...PERFECTLY TIME THE CELESTIAL'S APPEARANCE, THAT'S ALL. ♪
BOOM
THEN ONCE I JOINED THE RED BALL GROUP ...
...YOU'D ALREADY CAREFULLY CALCULATED THE CUMULATIVE DAMAGE TO THE CELESTIAL SO THAT IT COULD THEN BE DEFEATED QUICKLY.
IT REALLY WAS A LARGE-SCALE SECRET OPERATION WITH ALL HANDS ON DECK.
IT SURELY WAS.
APPARENTLY THE EPISODE THAT KYON HAD JUST HELPLESSLY WATCHED AS IT PLAYED OUT WAS ACTUALLY KIND OF A BIG DEAL.

END

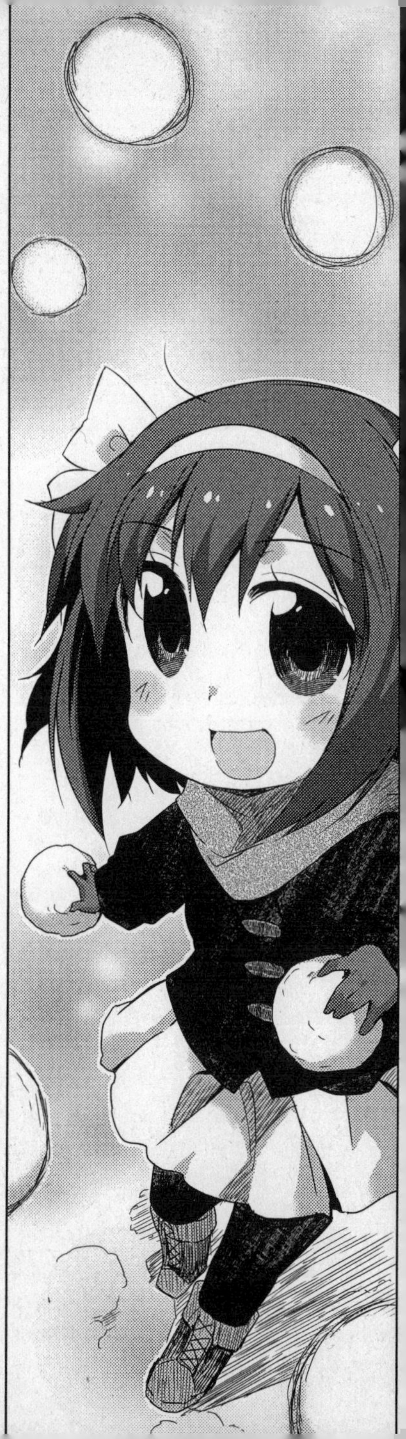

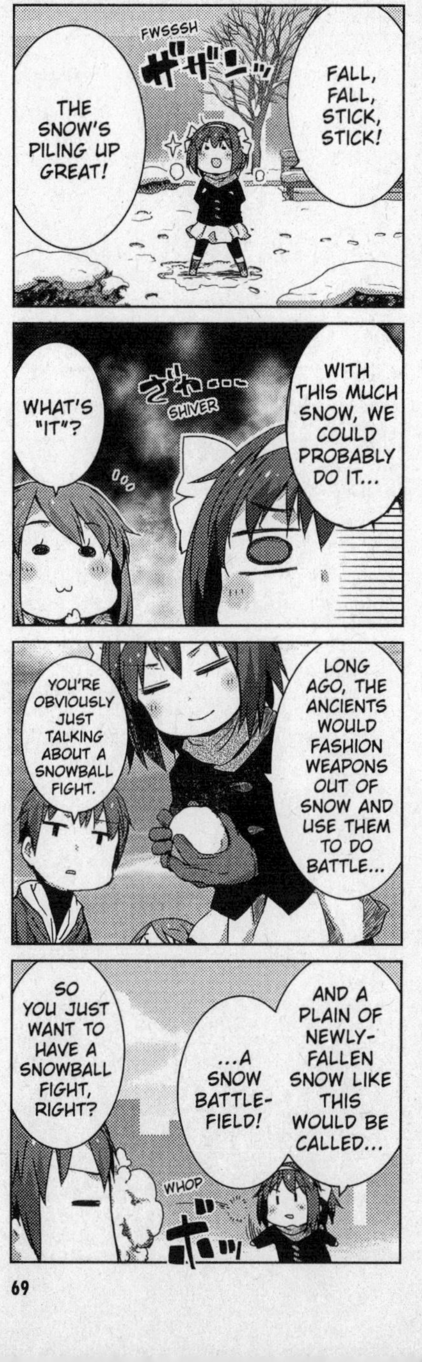
FWSSSH
FALL, FALL, STICK, STICK!
THE SNOW'S PILING UP GREAT!
WITH THIS MUCH SNOW, WE COULD PROBABLY DO IT...
SHIVER
WHAT'S "IT"?
LONG AGO, THE ANCIENTS WOULD FASHION WEAPONS OUT OF SNOW AND USE THEM TO DO BATTLE...
YOU'RE OBVIOUSLY JUST TALKING ABOUT A SNOWBALL FIGHT.
AND A PLAIN OF NEWLY-FALLEN SNOW LIKE THIS WOULD BE CALLED...
...A SNOW BATTLE-FIELD!
SO YOU JUST WANT TO HAVE A SNOWBALL FIGHT, RIGHT?
WHOP

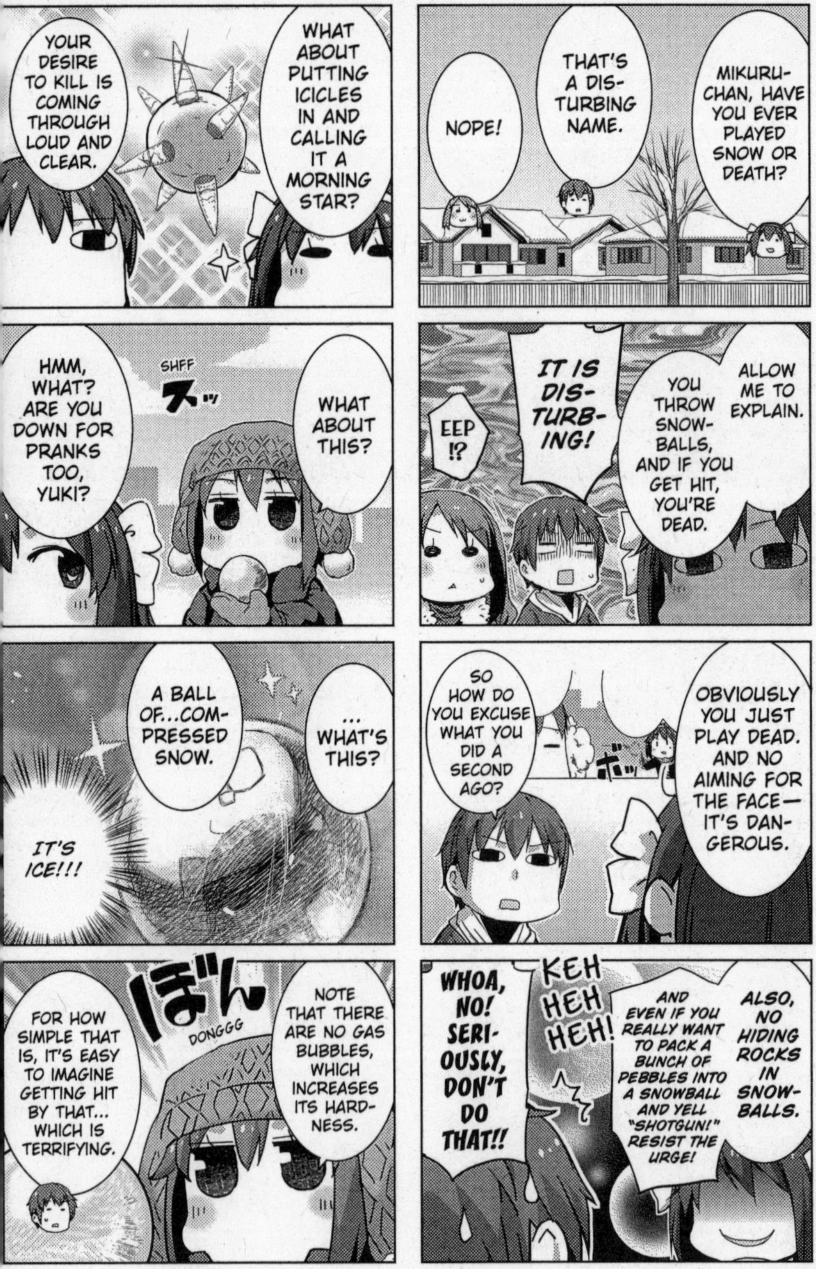
MIKURU-CHAN, HAVE YOU EVER PLAYED SNOW OR DEATH?
THAT'S A DIS-TURBING NAME.
NOPE!
ALLOW ME TO EXPLAIN.
YOU THROW SNOW-BALLS, AND IF YOU GET HIT, YOU'RE DEAD.
IT IS DIS-TURB-ING!
EEP !?
OBVIOUSLY YOU JUST PLAY DEAD. AND NO AIMING FOR THE FACE—IT'S DAN-GEROUS.
SO HOW DO YOU EXCUSE WHAT YOU DID A SECOND AGO?
ALSO, NO HIDING ROCKS IN SNOW-BALLS.
AND EVEN IF YOU REALLY WANT TO PACK A BUNCH OF PEBBLES INTO A SNOWBALL AND YELL "SHOTGUN!" RESIST THE URGE!
KEH HEH HEH!
WHOA, NO! SERI-OUSLY, DON'T DO THAT!!
WHAT ABOUT PUTTING ICICLES IN AND CALLING IT A MORNING STAR?
YOUR DESIRE TO KILL IS COMING THROUGH LOUD AND CLEAR.
WHAT ABOUT THIS?
SHFF
HMM, WHAT? ARE YOU DOWN FOR PRANKS TOO, YUKI?
... WHAT'S THIS?
A BALL OF...COM-PRESSED SNOW.
IT'S ICE!!!
NOTE THAT THERE ARE NO GAS BUBBLES, WHICH INCREASES ITS HARD-NESS.
DONGGG
FOR HOW SIMPLE THAT IS, IT'S EASY TO IMAGINE GETTING HIT BY THAT... WHICH IS TERRIFYING.

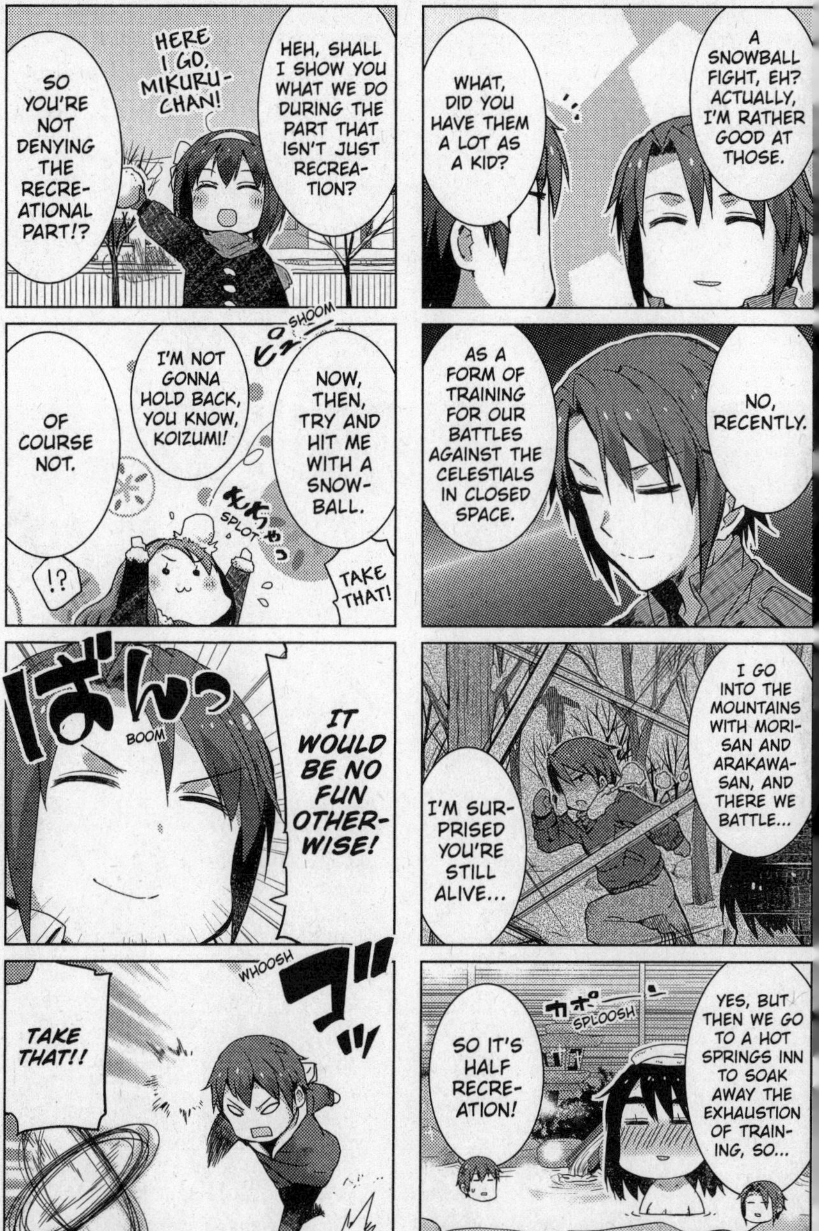
A SNOWBALL FIGHT, EH? ACTUALLY, I'M RATHER GOOD AT THOSE.
WHAT, DID YOU HAVE THEM A LOT AS A KID?
NO, RECENTLY.
AS A FORM OF TRAINING FOR OUR BATTLES AGAINST THE CELESTIALS IN CLOSED SPACE.
I GO INTO THE MOUNTAINS WITH MORI-SAN AND ARAKAWA-SAN, AND THERE WE BATTLE...
I'M SURPRISED YOU'RE STILL ALIVE...
YES, BUT THEN WE GO TO A HOT SPRINGS INN TO SOAK AWAY THE EXHAUSTION OF TRAINING, SO...
カポーン
SPLOOSH
SO IT'S HALF RECREATION!
HEH, SHALL I SHOW YOU WHAT WE DO DURING THE PART THAT ISN'T JUST RECREATION?
HERE I GO, MIKURU-CHAN!
SO YOU'RE NOT DENYING THE RECREATIONAL PART!?
SHOOM
NOW, THEN, TRY AND HIT ME WITH A SNOWBALL.
I'M NOT GONNA HOLD BACK, YOU KNOW, KOIZUMI!
OF COURSE NOT.
TAKE THAT!
SPLOT
!?
IT WOULD BE NO FUN OTHERWISE!
ばんっ
BOOM
ゴッ
WHOOSH
TAKE THAT!!

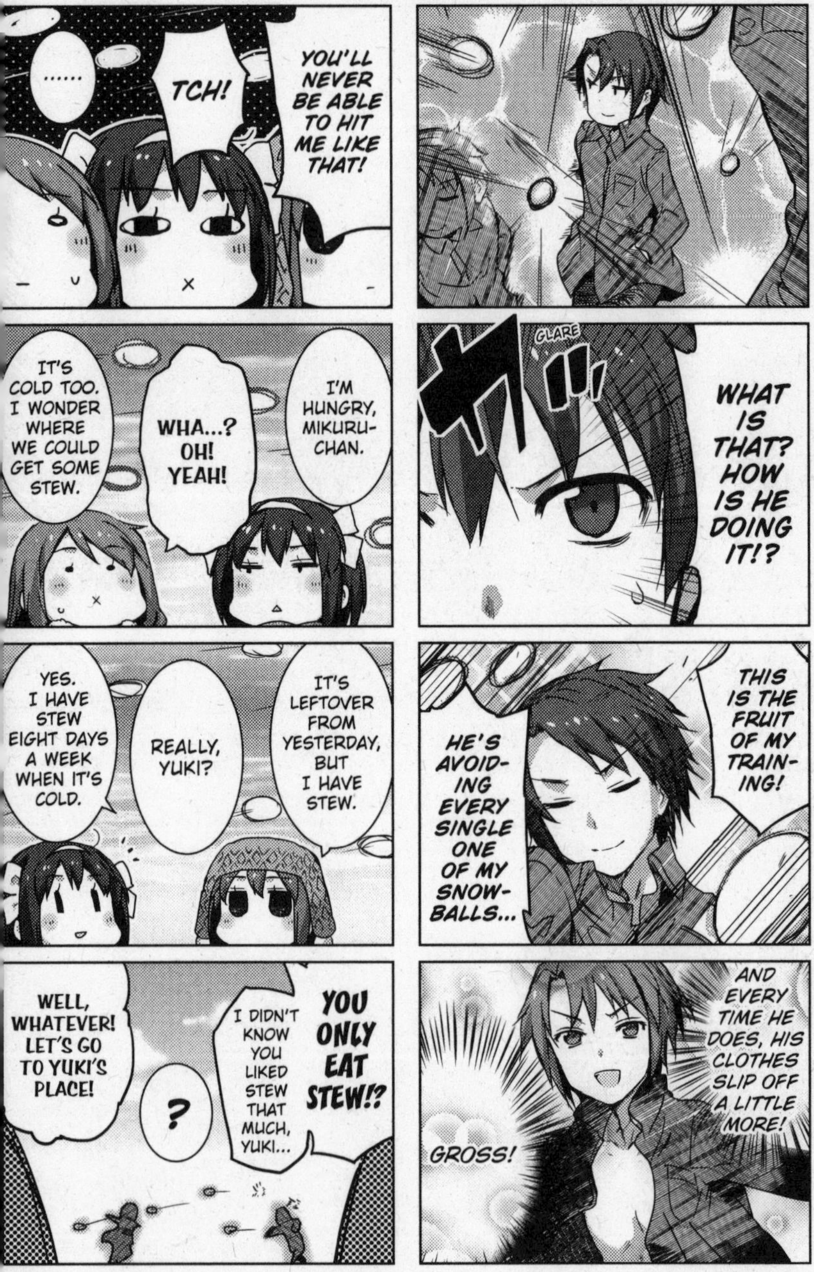
GLARE
WHAT IS THAT? HOW IS HE DOING IT!?
THIS IS THE FRUIT OF MY TRAINING!
HE'S AVOIDING EVERY SINGLE ONE OF MY SNOWBALLS...
AND EVERY TIME HE DOES, HIS CLOTHES SLIP OFF A LITTLE MORE!
GROSS!
YOU'LL NEVER BE ABLE TO HIT ME LIKE THAT!
TCH!
......
I'M HUNGRY, MIKURU-CHAN.
WHA...? OH! YEAH!
IT'S COLD TOO. I WONDER WHERE WE COULD GET SOME STEW.
IT'S LEFTOVER FROM YESTERDAY, BUT I HAVE STEW.
REALLY, YUKI?
YES. I HAVE STEW EIGHT DAYS A WEEK WHEN IT'S COLD.
YOU ONLY EAT STEW!?
I DIDN'T KNOW YOU LIKED STEW THAT MUCH, YUKI...
?
WELL, WHATEVER! LET'S GO TO YUKI'S PLACE!

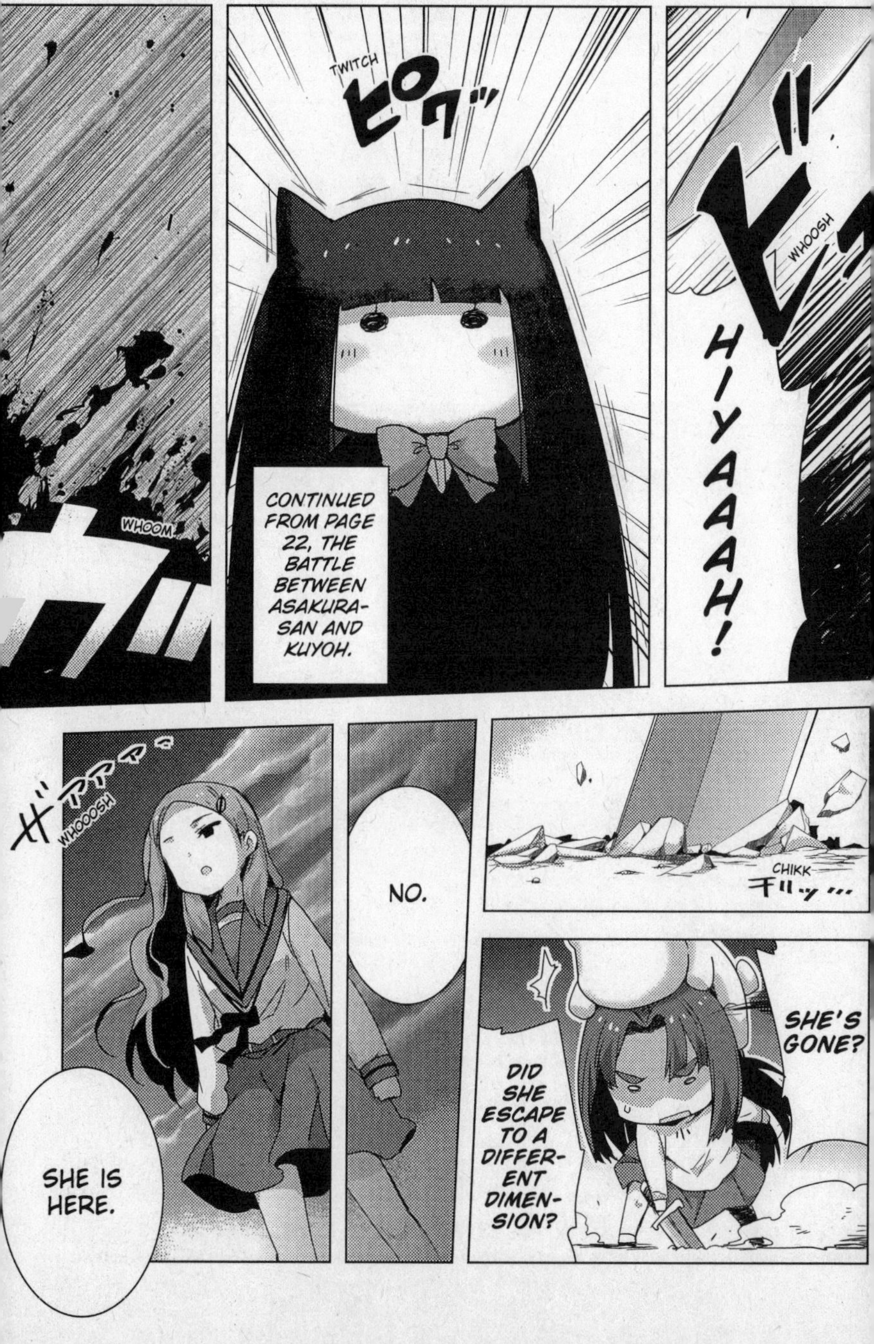
WHOOSH
HIYAAAAH!
TWITCH
CONTINUED FROM PAGE 22, THE BATTLE BETWEEN ASAKURA-SAN AND KUYOH.
WHOOM
CHIKK
SHE'S GONE?
DID SHE ESCAPE TO A DIFFERENT DIMENSION?
NO.
WHOOOSH
SHE IS HERE.

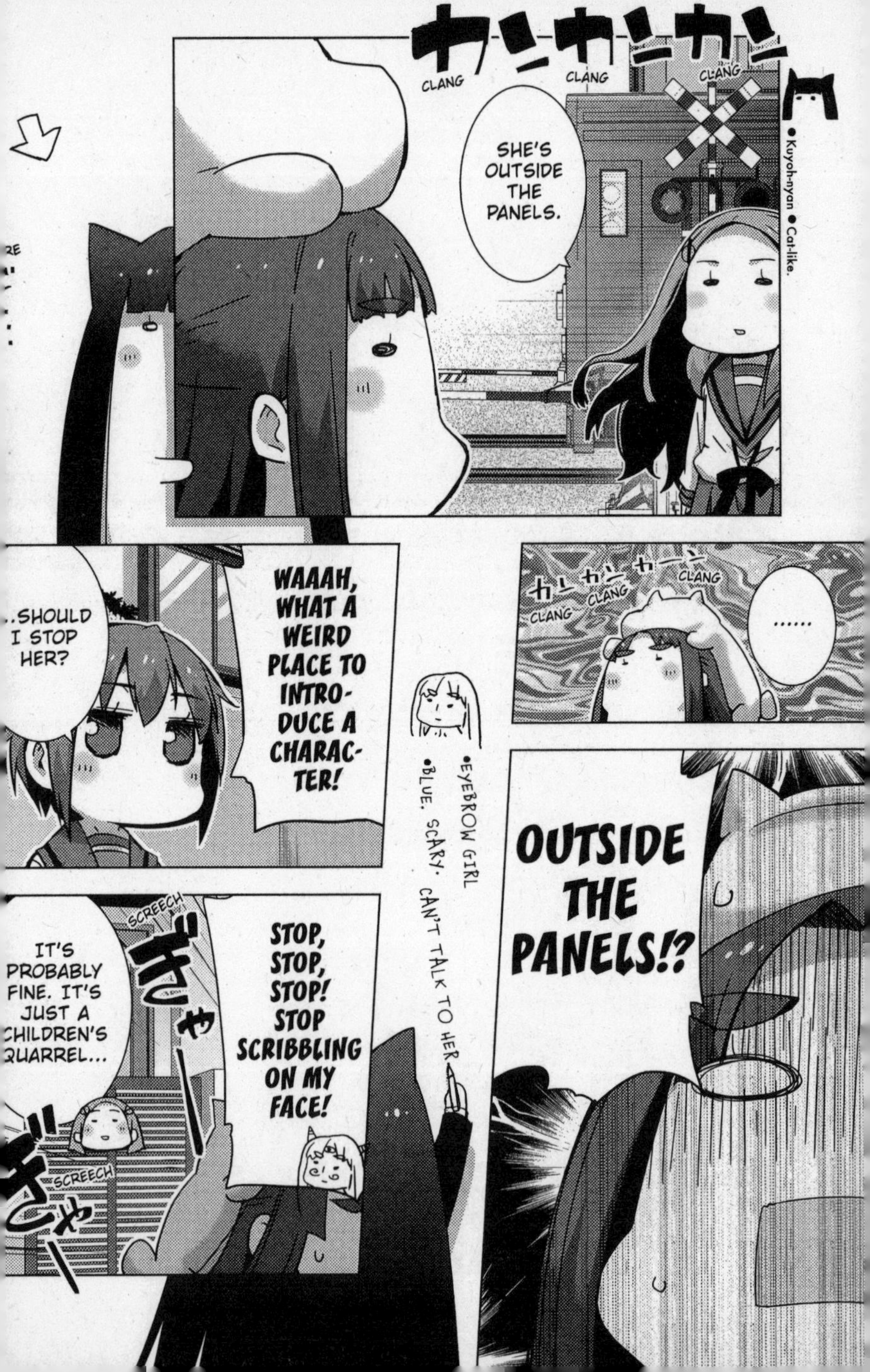
CLANG
CLANG
CLANG
●Kuyoh-nyan ●Cat-like.
SHE'S OUTSIDE THE PANELS.
CLANG
CLANG
CLANG
......
WAAAH, WHAT A WEIRD PLACE TO INTRO-DUCE A CHARAC-TER!
..SHOULD I STOP HER?
●EYEBROW GIRL
●BLUE. SCARY. CAN'T TALK TO HER
OUTSIDE THE PANELS!?
STOP, STOP, STOP! STOP SCRIBBLING ON MY FACE!
SCREECH
IT'S PROBABLY FINE. IT'S JUST A CHILDREN'S QUARREL...
SCREECH

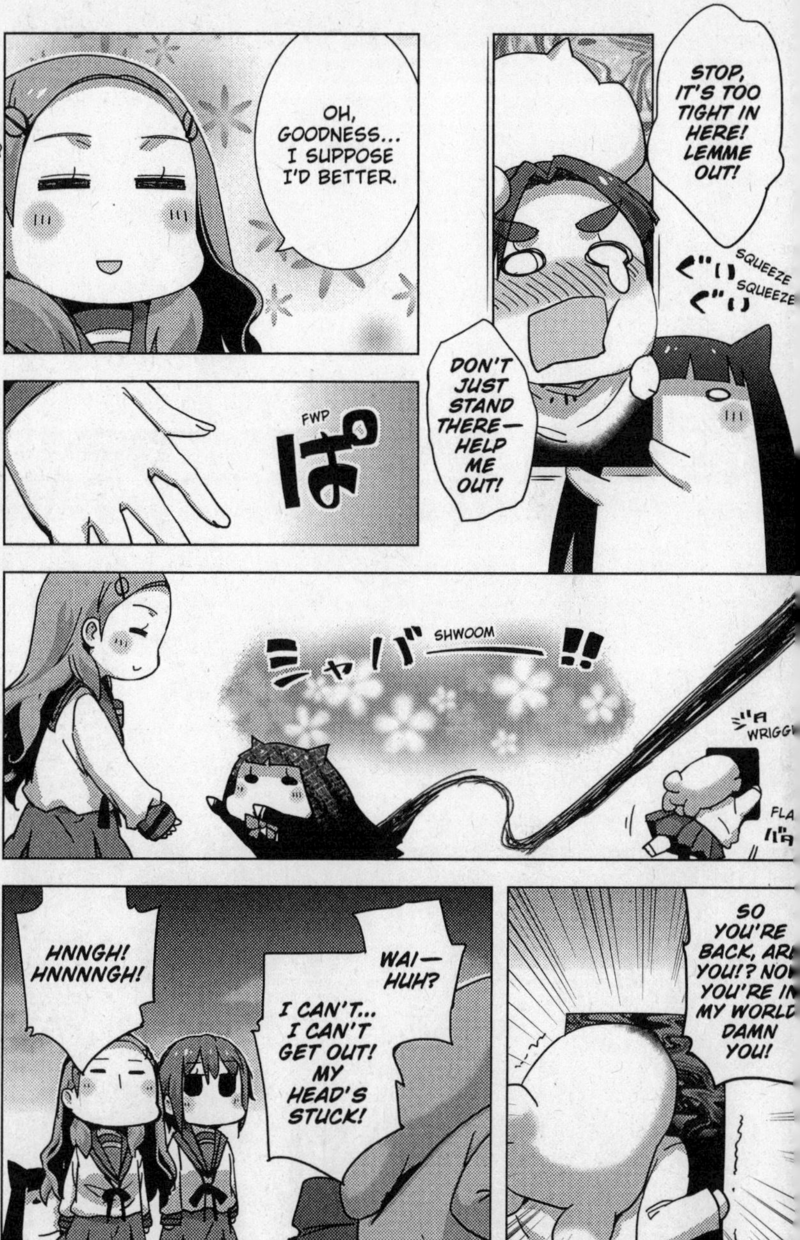
STOP, IT'S TOO TIGHT IN HERE! LEMME OUT!
SQUEEZE
SQUEEZE
DON'T JUST STAND THERE—HELP ME OUT!
OH, GOODNESS... I SUPPOSE I'D BETTER.
FWP
ぱ
SHWOOM
シャバー——!!
WRIGG
FLA
SO YOU'RE BACK, AR YOU!? NO YOU'RE IN MY WORLD DAMN YOU!
WAI— HUH?
I CAN'T... I CAN'T GET OUT! MY HEAD'S STUCK!
HNNGH! HNNNNGH!

●Kimidori-san ●Her hand gives off pheromones that attract Kuyoh (is my guess).

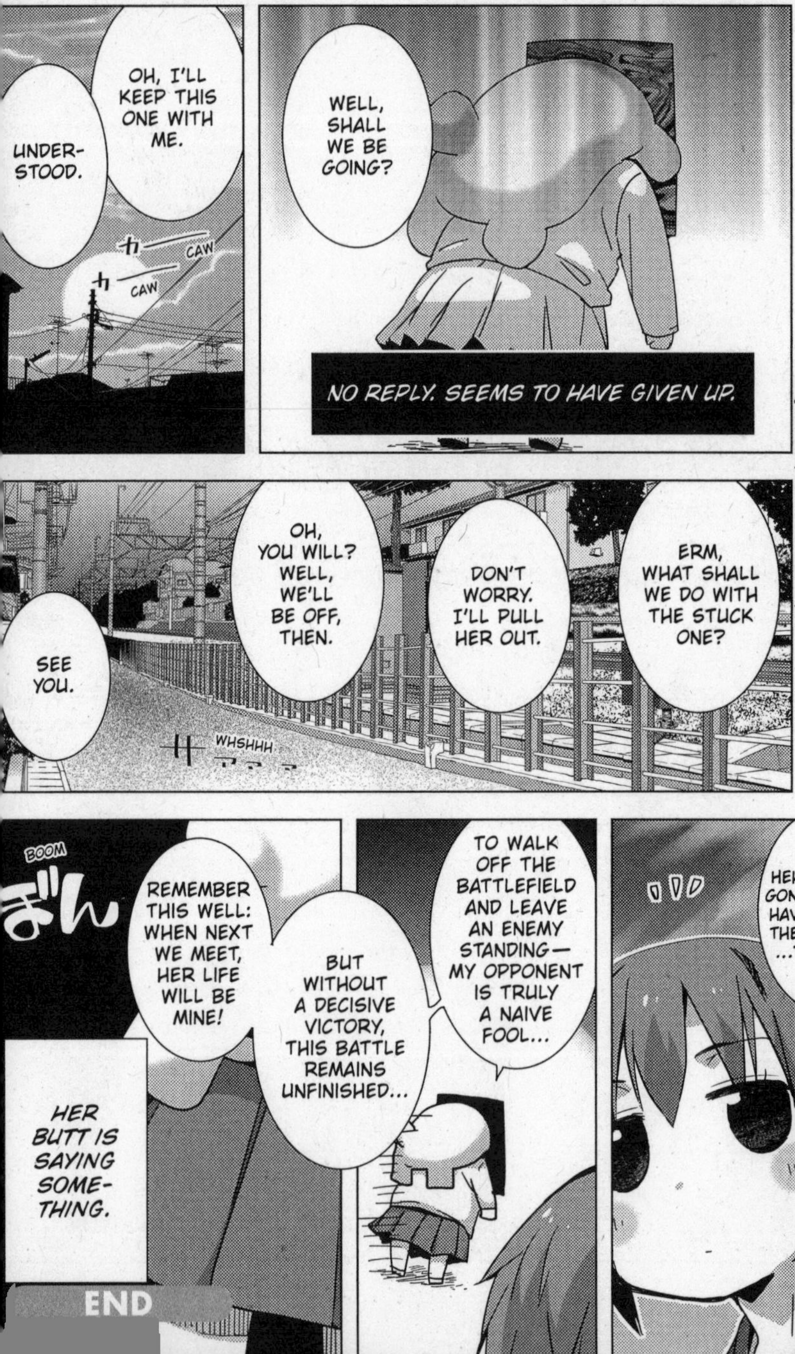
WELL, SHALL WE BE GOING?
NO REPLY. SEEMS TO HAVE GIVEN UP.
OH, I'LL KEEP THIS ONE WITH ME.
UNDER-STOOD.
CAW
CAW
ERM, WHAT SHALL WE DO WITH THE STUCK ONE?
DON'T WORRY. I'LL PULL HER OUT.
OH, YOU WILL? WELL, WE'LL BE OFF, THEN.
SEE YOU.
WHSHHH
HEH, GONE, HAVE THEY...?
TO WALK OFF THE BATTLEFIELD AND LEAVE AN ENEMY STANDING—MY OPPONENT IS TRULY A NAIVE FOOL...
BUT WITHOUT A DECISIVE VICTORY, THIS BATTLE REMAINS UNFINISHED...
REMEMBER THIS WELL: WHEN NEXT WE MEET, HER LIFE WILL BE MINE!
BOOM
ぼん
HER BUTT IS SAYING SOME-THING.
END

●Nagato-san ●Legal guardian of the person stuck between panels.

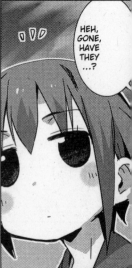

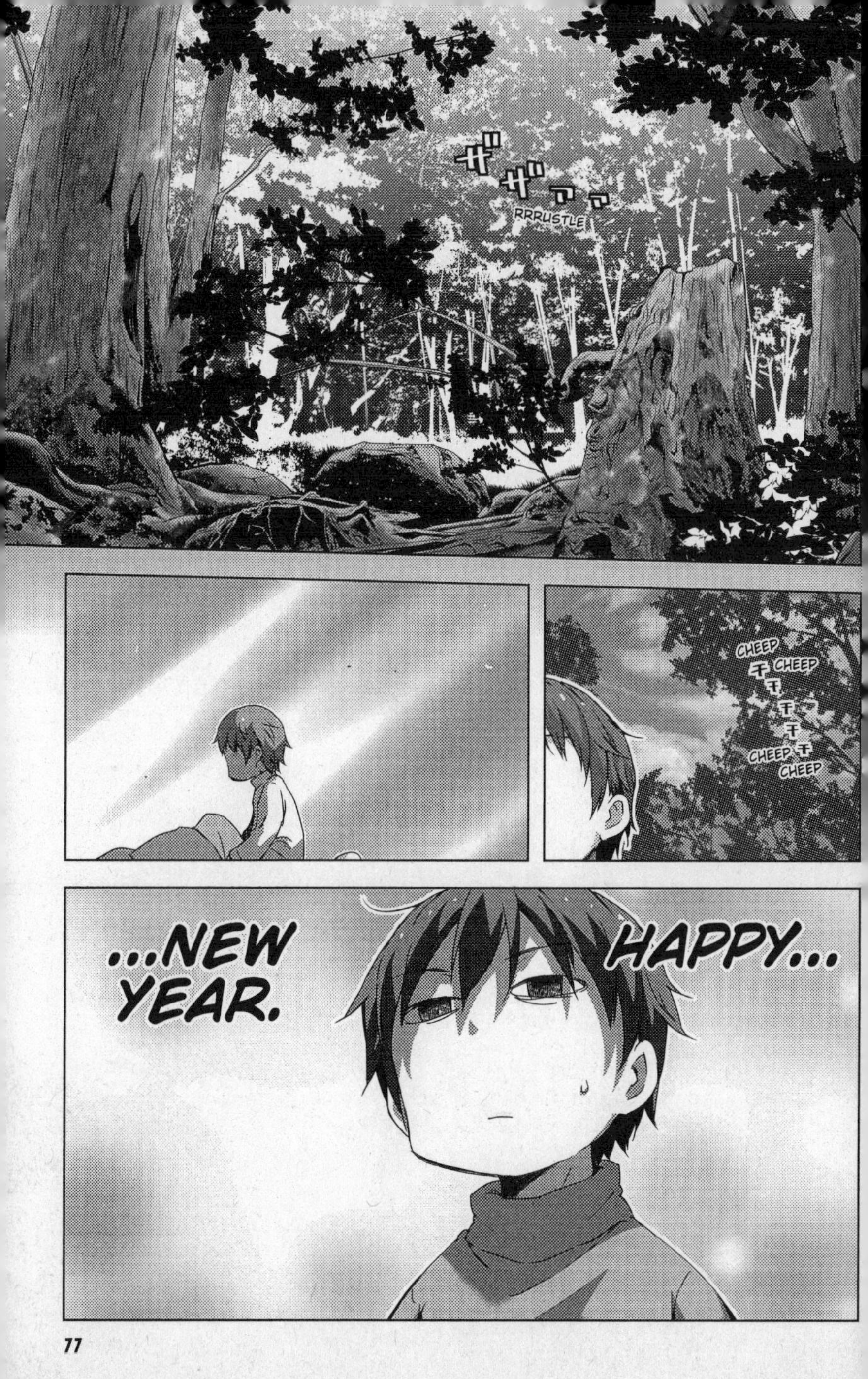
ザザァァ
RRRUSTLE
CHEEP CHEEP
チチチチ
CHEEP チ CHEEP
HAPPY...
...NEW YEAR.

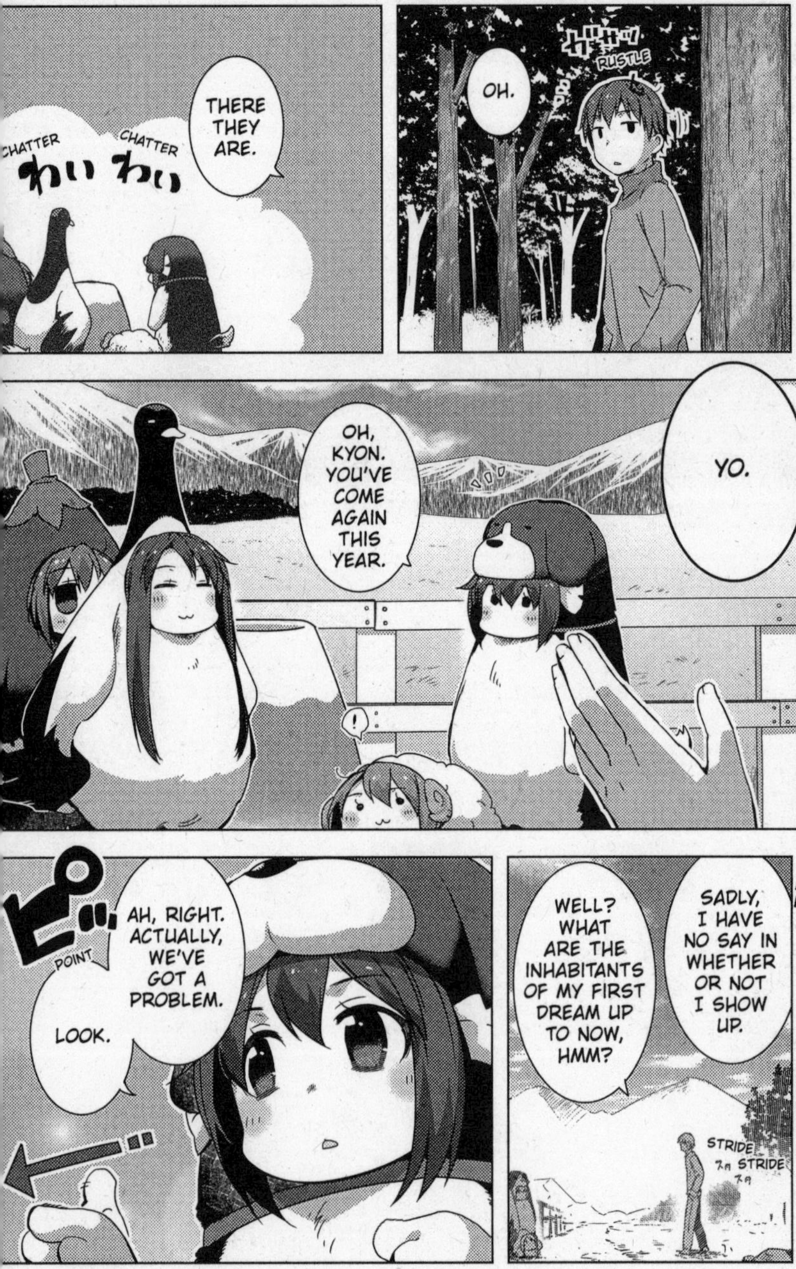

RUSTLE
OH.
THERE THEY ARE.
CHATTER CHATTER
わいわい
YO.
OH, KYON. YOU'VE COME AGAIN THIS YEAR.
!
SADLY, I HAVE NO SAY IN WHETHER OR NOT I SHOW UP.
WELL? WHAT ARE THE INHABITANTS OF MY FIRST DREAM UP TO NOW, HMM?
STRIDE STRIDE
AH, RIGHT. ACTUALLY, WE'VE GOT A PROBLEM.
POINT
LOOK.

●Sheepdog ●A dog that shows up in Kyon's first dream of the new year.

●Mount Fuji ●Lucky omen.

●Crane ●Lucky omen.

●Eggplant ●Lucky omen.

●Sheep ●Emergency rations.

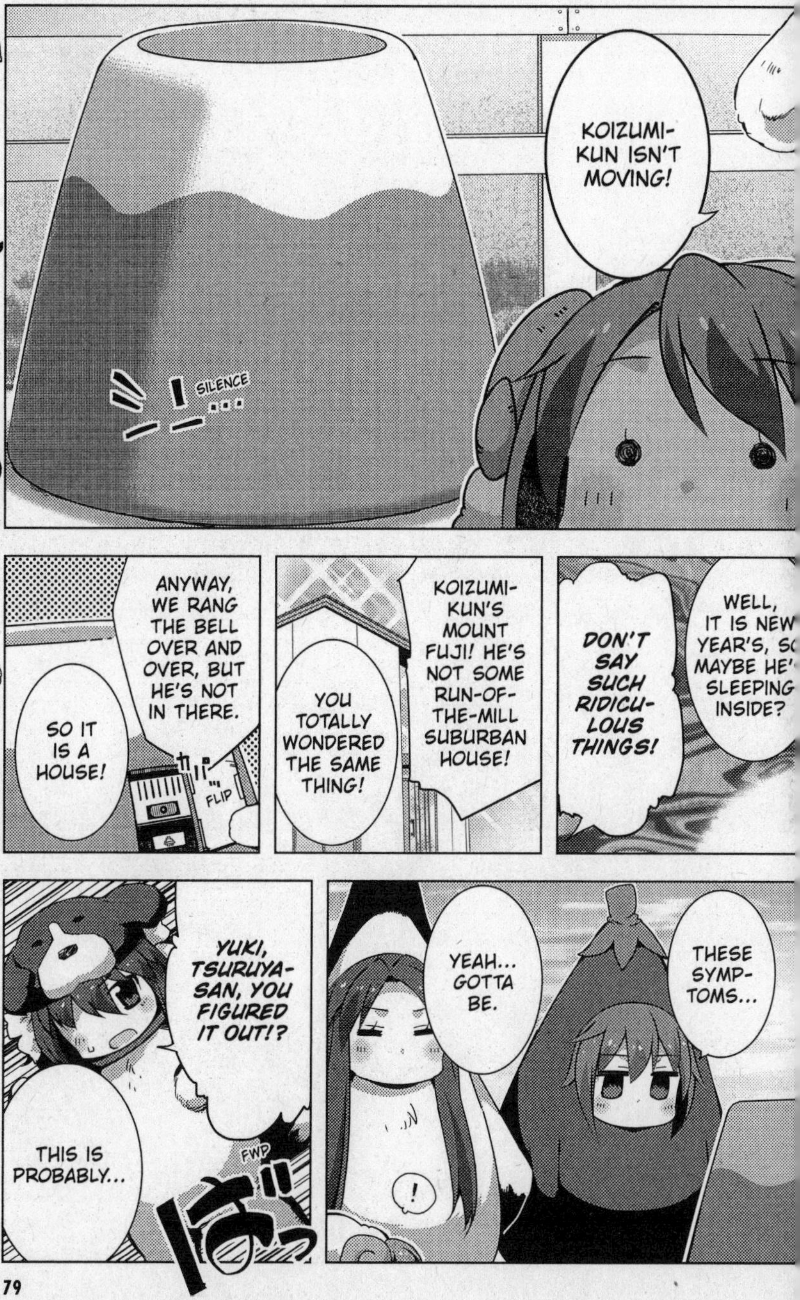
KOIZUMI-KUN ISN'T MOVING!
SILENCE
WELL, IT IS NEW YEAR'S, S MAYBE HE' SLEEPING INSIDE?
DON'T SAY SUCH RIDICULOUS THINGS!
KOIZUMI-KUN'S MOUNT FUJI! HE'S NOT SOME RUN-OF-THE-MILL SUBURBAN HOUSE!
YOU TOTALLY WONDERED THE SAME THING!
ANYWAY, WE RANG THE BELL OVER AND OVER, BUT HE'S NOT IN THERE.
FLIP
SO IT IS A HOUSE!
THESE SYMPTOMS...
YEAH... GOTTA BE.
!
YUKI, TSURUYA-SAN, YOU FIGURED IT OUT!?
FWP
THIS IS PROBABLY...

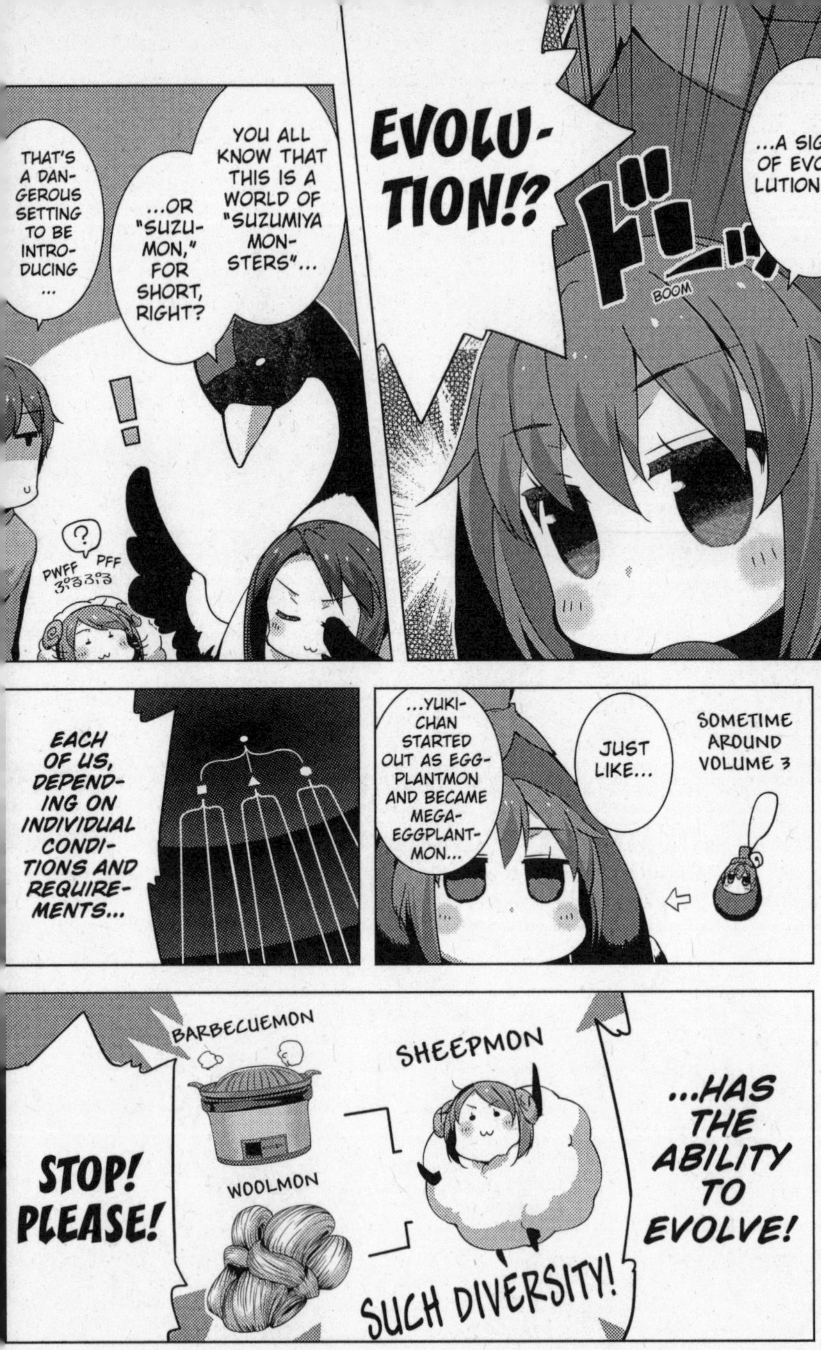

...A SIGN OF EVOLUTION...
ドーン BOOM
EVOLUTION!?
YOU ALL KNOW THAT THIS IS A WORLD OF "SUZUMIYA MONSTERS"...
...OR "SUZUMON," FOR SHORT, RIGHT?
THAT'S A DANGEROUS SETTING TO BE INTRODUCING ...
!
?
PWFF PFF ぷるぷる
SOMETIME AROUND VOLUME 3
JUST LIKE...
...YUKI-CHAN STARTED OUT AS EGGPLANTMON AND BECAME MEGA-EGGPLANTMON...
EACH OF US, DEPENDING ON INDIVIDUAL CONDITIONS AND REQUIREMENTS...
...HAS THE ABILITY TO EVOLVE!
SHEEPMON
BARBECUEMON
WOOLMON
SUCH DIVERSITY!
STOP! PLEASE!

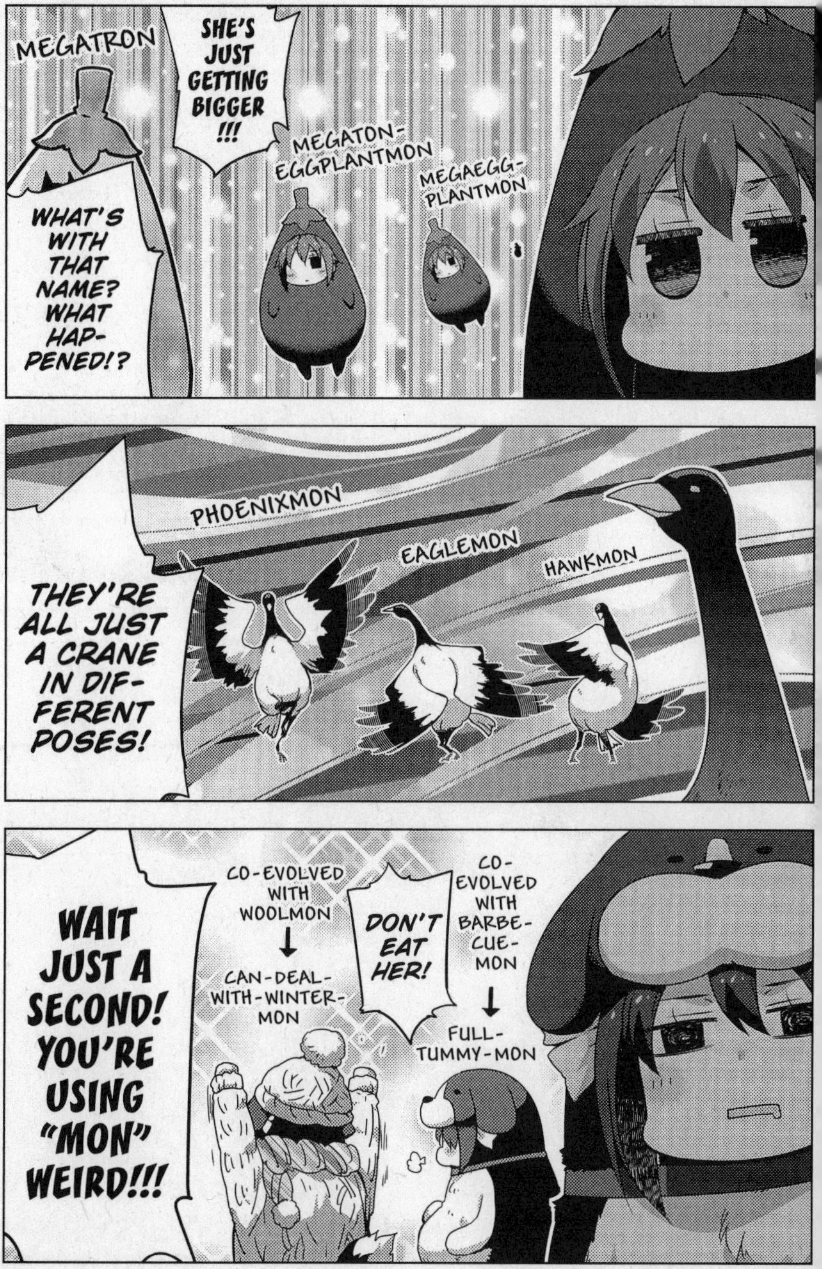

MEGAEGG-PLANTMON
MEGATON-EGGPLANTMON
SHE'S JUST GETTING BIGGER!!!
MEGATRON
WHAT'S WITH THAT NAME? WHAT HAP-PENED!?
HAWKMON
EAGLEMON
PHOENIXMON
THEY'RE ALL JUST A CRANE IN DIF-FERENT POSES!
CO-EVOLVED WITH BARBE-CUE-MON ↓ FULL-TUMMY-MON
DON'T EAT HER!
CO-EVOLVED WITH WOOLMON ↓ CAN-DEAL-WITH-WINTER-MON
WAIT JUST A SECOND! YOU'RE USING "MON" WEIRD!!!

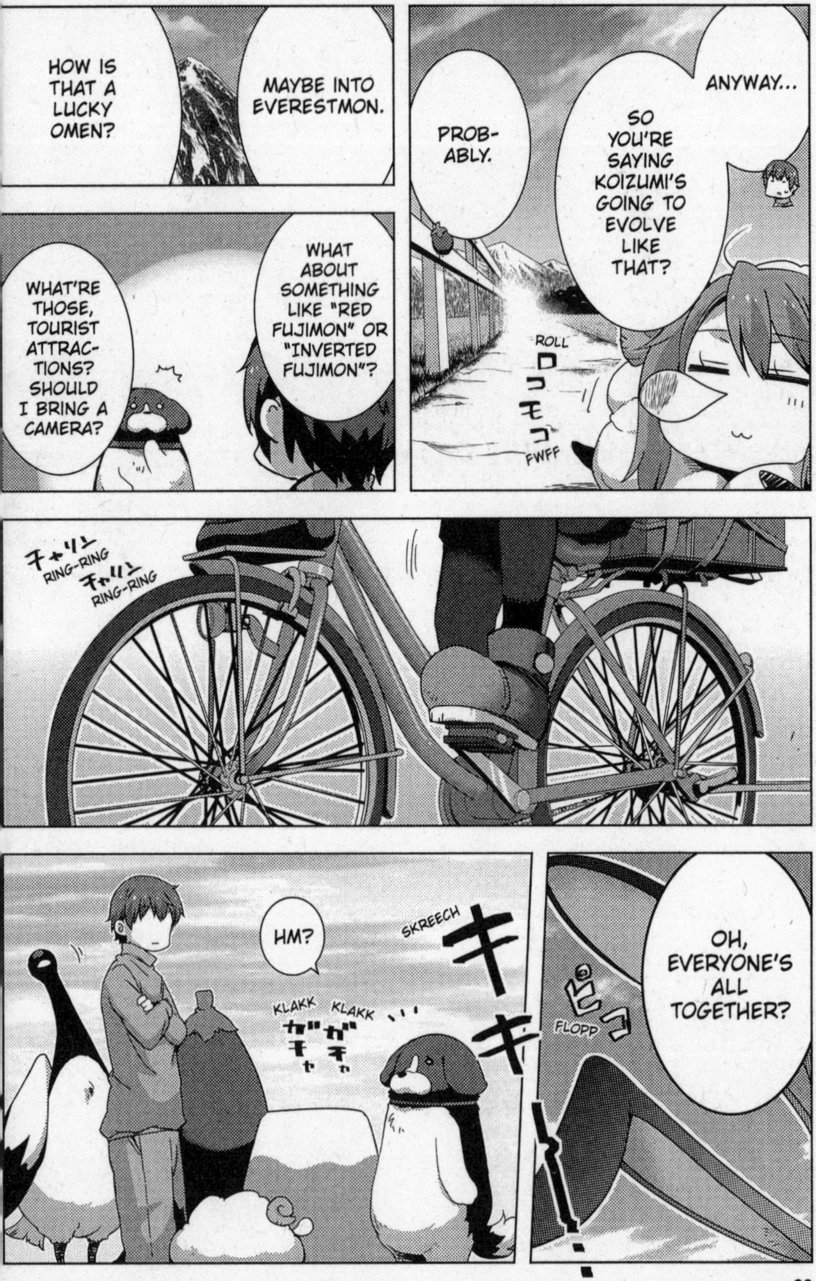
ANYWAY...
SO YOU'RE SAYING KOIZUMI'S GOING TO EVOLVE LIKE THAT?
PROB-ABLY.
ROLL
FWFF
MAYBE INTO EVERESTMON.
HOW IS THAT A LUCKY OMEN?
WHAT ABOUT SOMETHING LIKE "RED FUJIMON" OR "INVERTED FUJIMON"?
WHAT'RE THOSE, TOURIST ATTRAC-TIONS? SHOULD I BRING A CAMERA?
RING-RING
RING-RING
OH, EVERYONE'S ALL TOGETHER?
FLOPP
SKREECH
HM?
KLAKK KLAKK

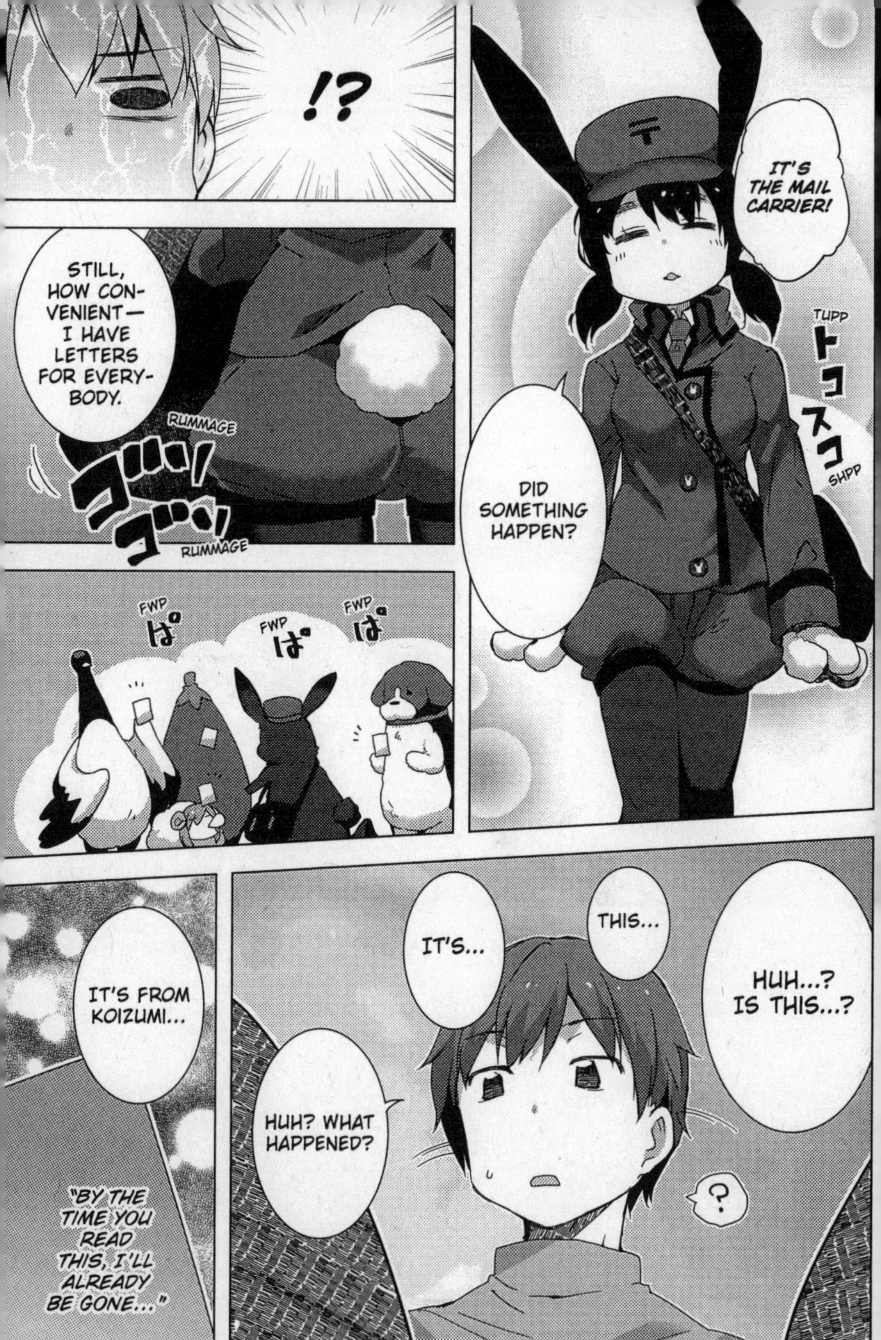

IT'S THE MAIL CARRIER!
TUPP
トコ
スコ
SHPP
DID SOMETHING HAPPEN?
!?
STILL, HOW CON-VENIENT— I HAVE LETTERS FOR EVERY-BODY.
RUMMAGE
RUMMAGE
FWP
ぱ
FWP
ぱ
FWP
ぱ
HUH...? IS THIS...?
THIS...
IT'S...
HUH? WHAT HAPPENED?
?
IT'S FROM KOIZUMI...
"BY THE TIME YOU READ THIS, I'LL ALREADY BE GONE..."

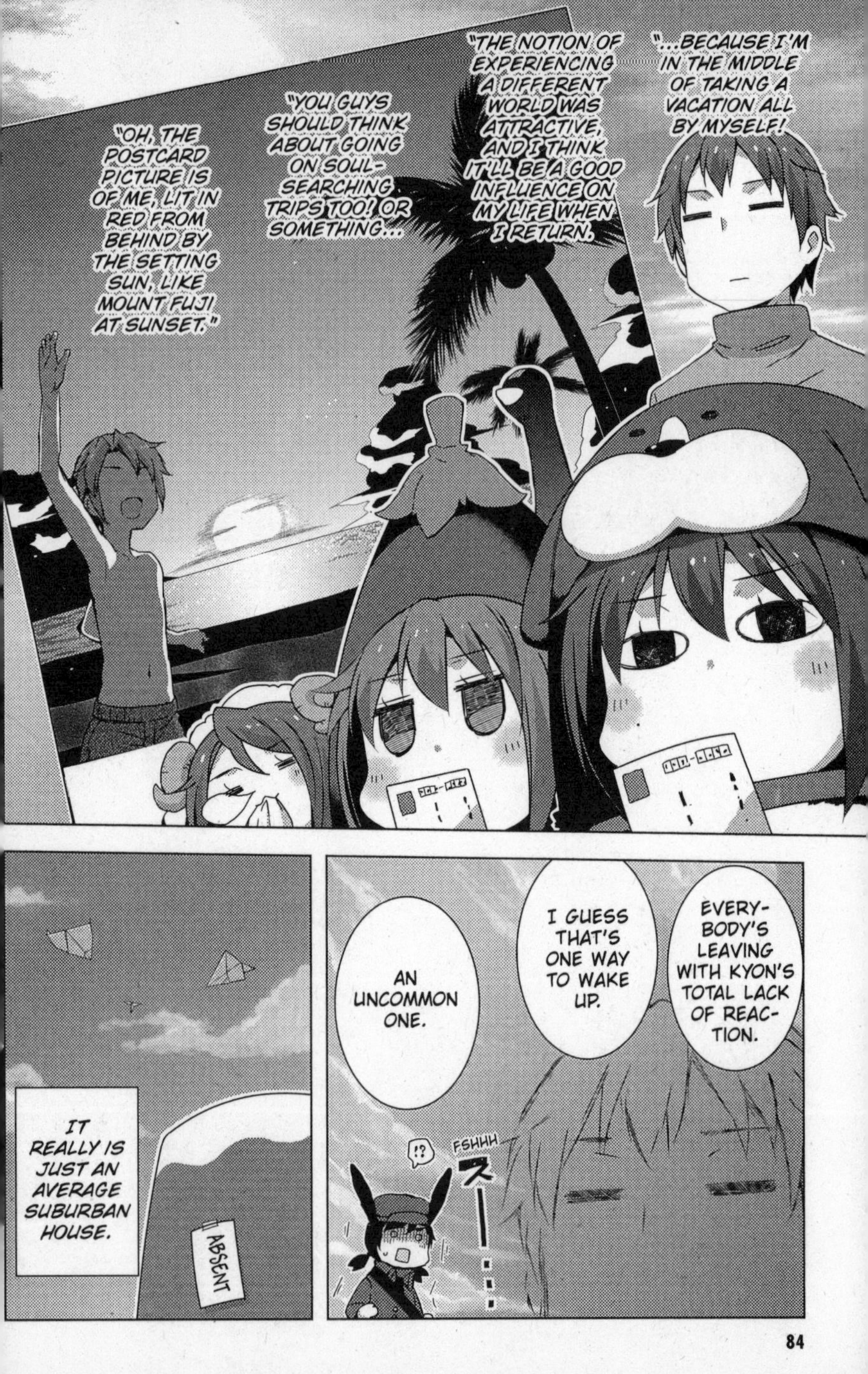
"...BECAUSE I'M IN THE MIDDLE OF TAKING A VACATION ALL BY MYSELF!
"THE NOTION OF EXPERIENCING A DIFFERENT WORLD WAS ATTRACTIVE, AND I THINK IT'LL BE A GOOD INFLUENCE ON MY LIFE WHEN I RETURN.
"YOU GUYS SHOULD THINK ABOUT GOING ON SOUL-SEARCHING TRIPS TOO! OR SOMETHING...
"OH, THE POSTCARD PICTURE IS OF ME, LIT IN RED FROM BEHIND BY THE SETTING SUN, LIKE MOUNT FUJI AT SUNSET."
EVERY-BODY'S LEAVING WITH KYON'S TOTAL LACK OF REAC-TION.
I GUESS THAT'S ONE WAY TO WAKE UP.
AN UNCOMMON ONE.
!?
FSHHH
IT REALLY IS JUST AN AVERAGE SUBURBAN HOUSE.
ABSENT

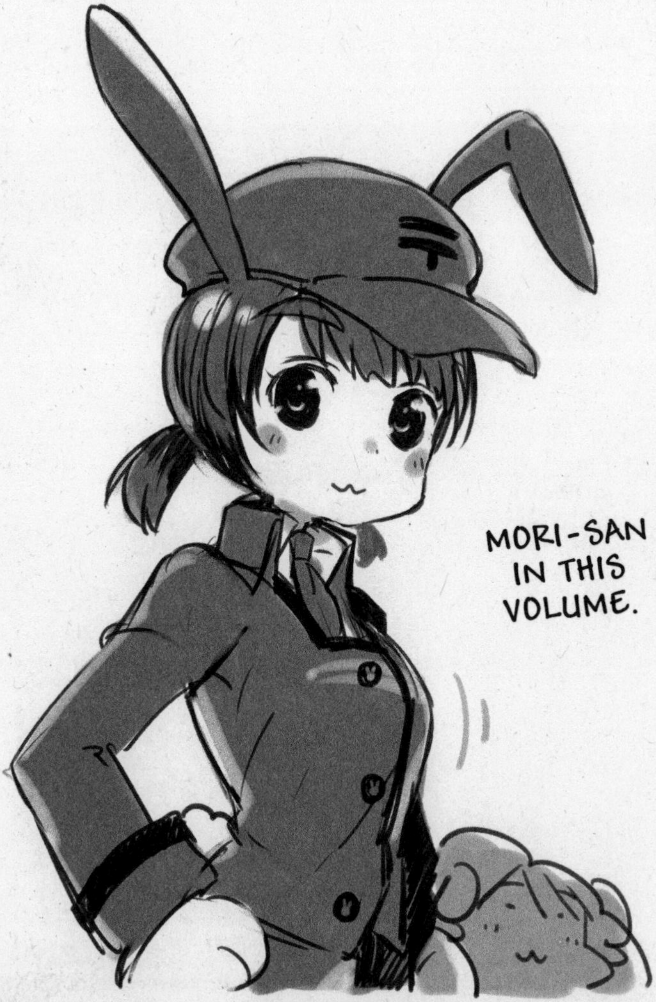
MORI-SAN IN THIS VOLUME.

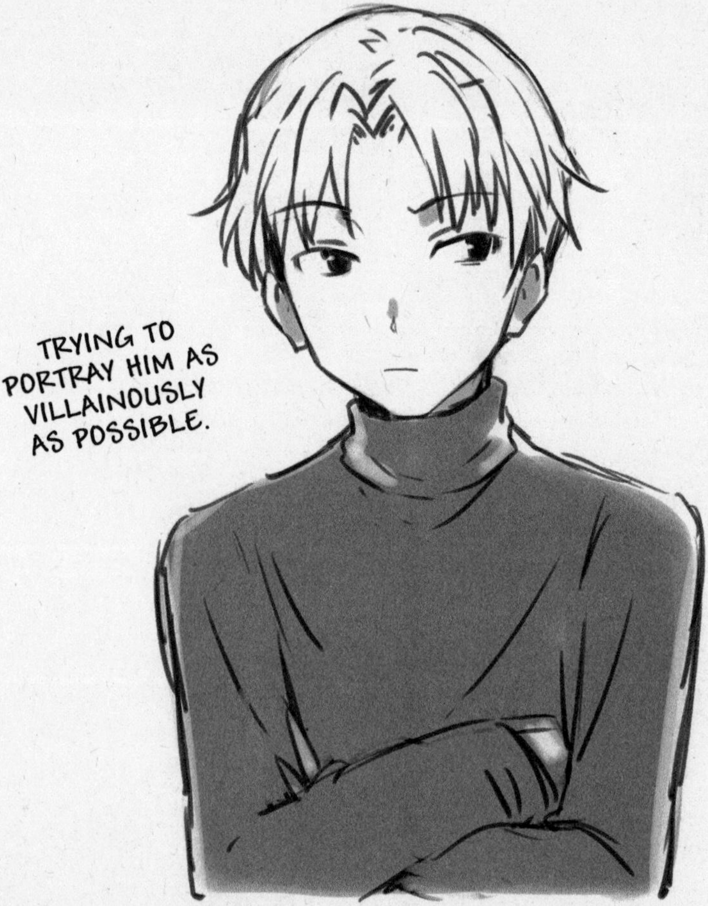
TRYING TO PORTRAY HIM AS VILLAINOUSLY AS POSSIBLE.

FEBRUARY'S USUAL ROUTINE

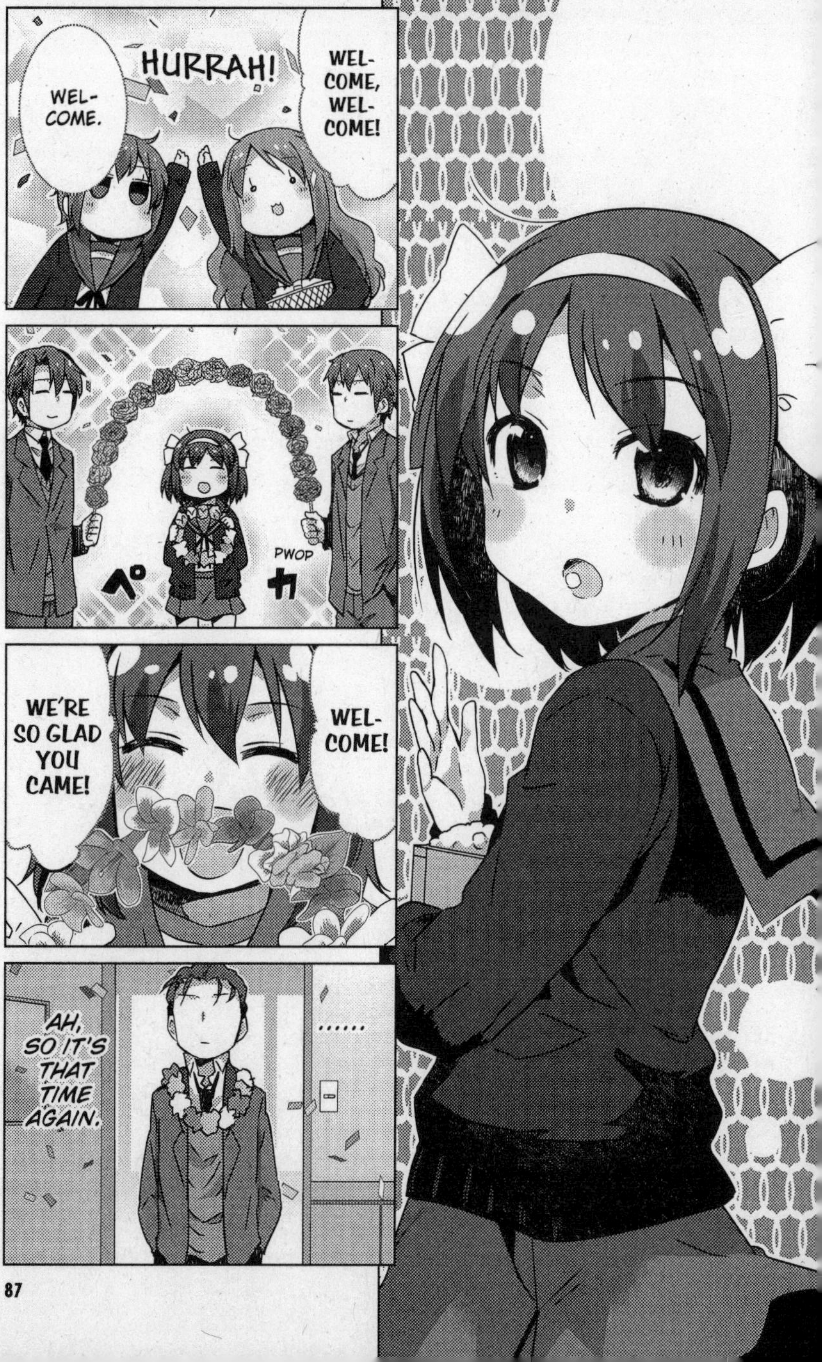
WEL-COME, WEL-COME!
HURRAH!
WEL-COME.
PWOP
カ
ぺ
WEL-COME!
WE'RE SO GLAD YOU CAME!
......
AH, SO IT'S THAT TIME AGAIN.

THE USUAL

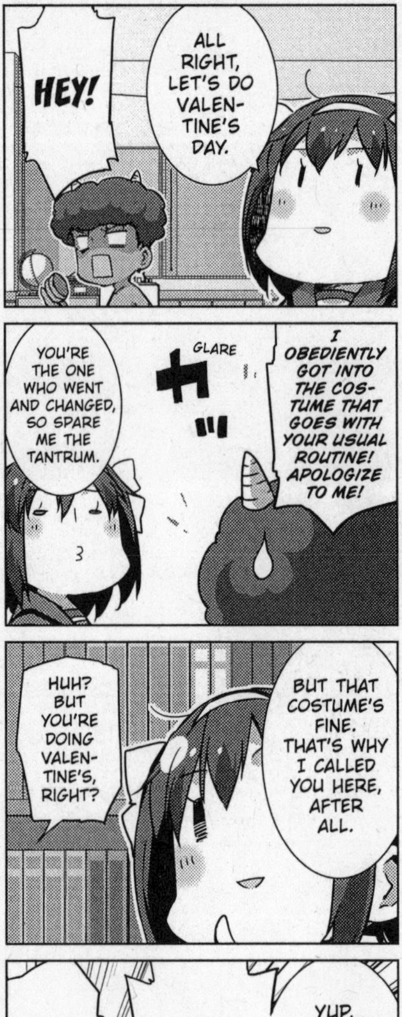
ALL RIGHT, LET'S DO VALEN-TINE'S DAY.
HEY!
I OBEDIENTLY GOT INTO THE COS-TUME THAT GOES WITH YOUR USUAL ROUTINE! APOLOGIZE TO ME!
GLARE
YOU'RE THE ONE WHO WENT AND CHANGED, SO SPARE ME THE TANTRUM.
BUT THAT COSTUME'S FINE. THAT'S WHY I CALLED YOU HERE, AFTER ALL.
HUH? BUT YOU'RE DOING VALEN-TINE'S, RIGHT?
YUP, WE'RE DOING SETSUBUN* AND VALEN-TINE'S AT THE SAME TIME.
SETSU-BALEN-TINE'S !!!
COOL TITLE!

JUST WANTED TO SAY IT ONCE

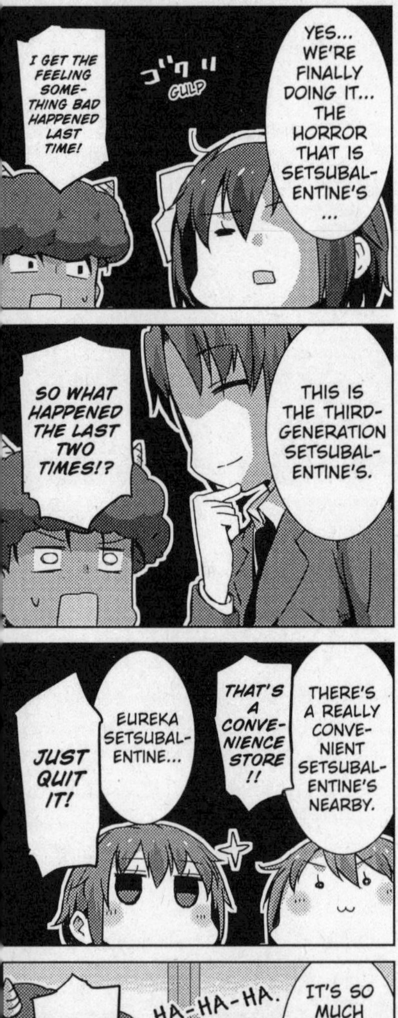
YES... WE'RE FINALLY DOING IT... THE HORROR THAT IS SETSUBAL-ENTINE'S ...
ゴクリ
GULP
I GET THE FEELING SOME-THING BAD HAPPENED LAST TIME!
THIS IS THE THIRD-GENERATION SETSUBAL-ENTINE'S.
SO WHAT HAPPENED THE LAST TWO TIMES!?
THERE'S A REALLY CONVE-NIENT SETSUBAL-ENTINE'S NEARBY.
THAT'S A CONVE-NIENCE STORE !!
EUREKA SETSUBAL-ENTINE...
JUST QUIT IT!
IT'S SO MUCH EASIER ON ME WHEN YOU'RE HERE.
(STRAIGHT MAN.)
HA-HA-HA.
GET TO WORK!

*SETSUBUN IS CONSIDERED THE FIRST HOLIDAY OF SPRING. IN ORDER TO SECURE GOOD FORTUNE FOR THE YEAR, SOMEONE DRESSES UP AS A DEMON WHILE THE REST THROW BEANS AT THEM AND SHOUT "DEMONS OUT, LUCK IN."

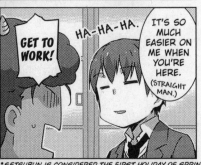

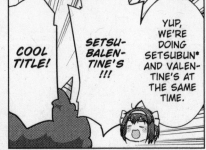

LOCAL SPECIALTY

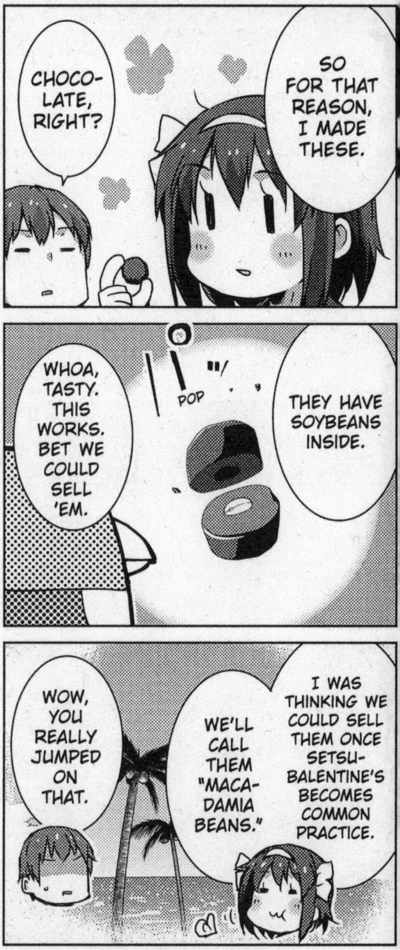

SO FOR THAT REASON, I MADE THESE.
CHOCO-LATE, RIGHT?
THEY HAVE SOYBEANS INSIDE.
POP
WHOA, TASTY. THIS WORKS. BET WE COULD SELL 'EM.
I WAS THINKING WE COULD SELL THEM ONCE SETSU-BALENTINE'S BECOMES COMMON PRACTICE.
WE'LL CALL THEM "MACA-DAMIA BEANS."
WOW, YOU REALLY JUMPED ON THAT.
UH... DO YOU KNOW WHAT "MACADAMIA" MEANS?
DONG
ぼ"んっ
WHO CARES AS LONG AS IT SOUNDS COOL!?

DOING IT

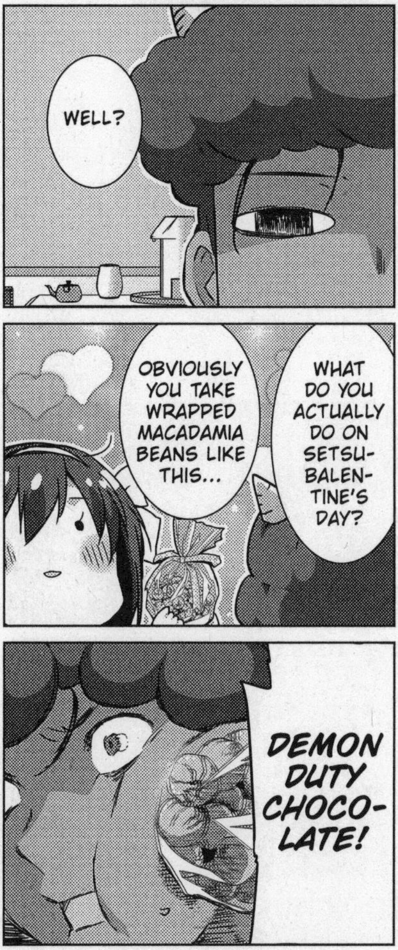

WELL?
WHAT DO YOU ACTUALLY DO ON SETSU-BALEN-TINE'S DAY?
OBVIOUSLY YOU TAKE WRAPPED MACADAMIA BEANS LIKE THIS...
DEMON DUTY CHOCO-LATE!
...YOU SAY, AND THROW 'EM.
WHY, YOU...

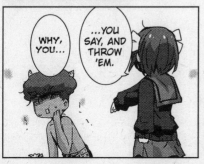

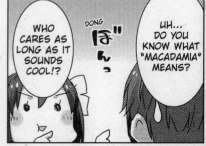

KINDNESS

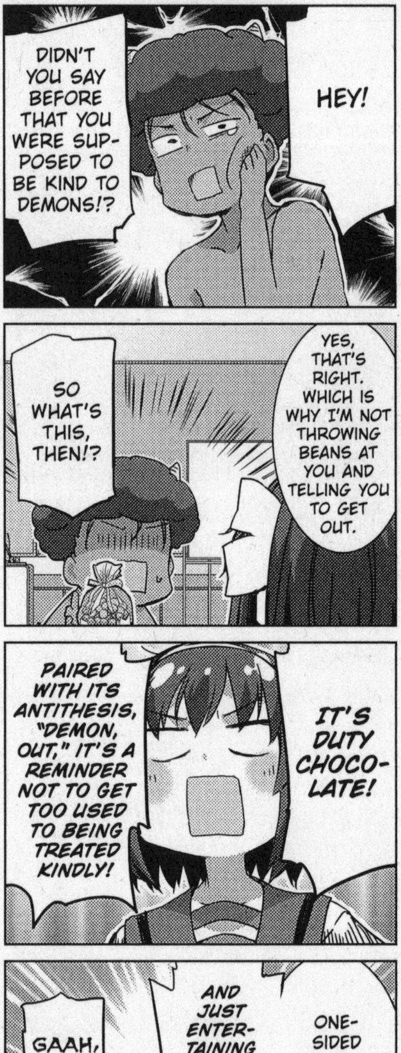
HEY!
DIDN'T YOU SAY BEFORE THAT YOU WERE SUP-POSED TO BE KIND TO DEMONS!?
YES, THAT'S RIGHT. WHICH IS WHY I'M NOT THROWING BEANS AT YOU AND TELLING YOU TO GET OUT.
SO WHAT'S THIS, THEN!?
IT'S DUTY CHOCO-LATE!
PAIRED WITH ITS ANTITHESIS, "DEMON, OUT," IT'S A REMINDER NOT TO GET TOO USED TO BEING TREATED KINDLY!
ONE-SIDED KINDNESS SOMETIMES DRIVES PEOPLE CRAZY!
AND JUST ENTER-TAINING SOMEONE DOESN'T COUNT AS KIND-NESS!!!
GAAH, O-OKAY!!!

HAPPY SETSUBALENTINE'S DAY

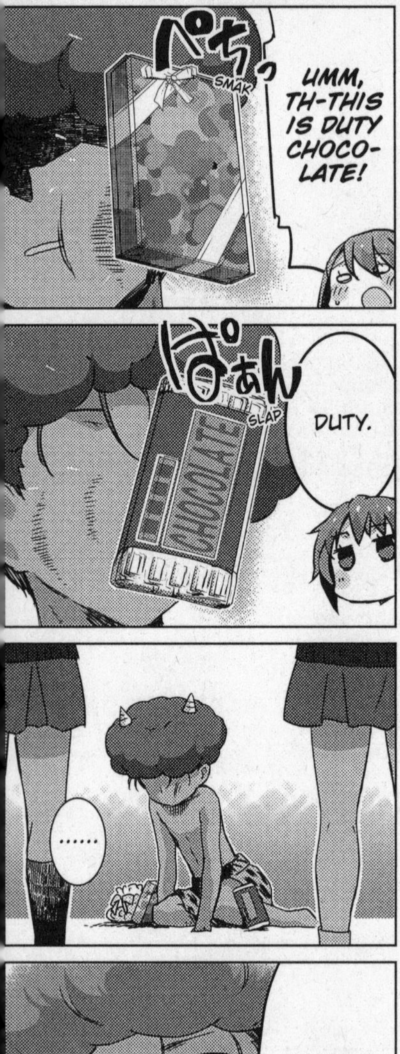
UMM, TH-THIS IS DUTY CHOCO-LATE!
ぺちっ SMAK
DUTY.
ぱぁん SLAP
CHOCOLATE
......
THANK YOU VERY MUCH!
THE DEMON SEEMS TO HAVE UNDER-STOOD SOME-THING.

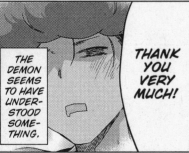

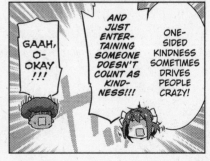

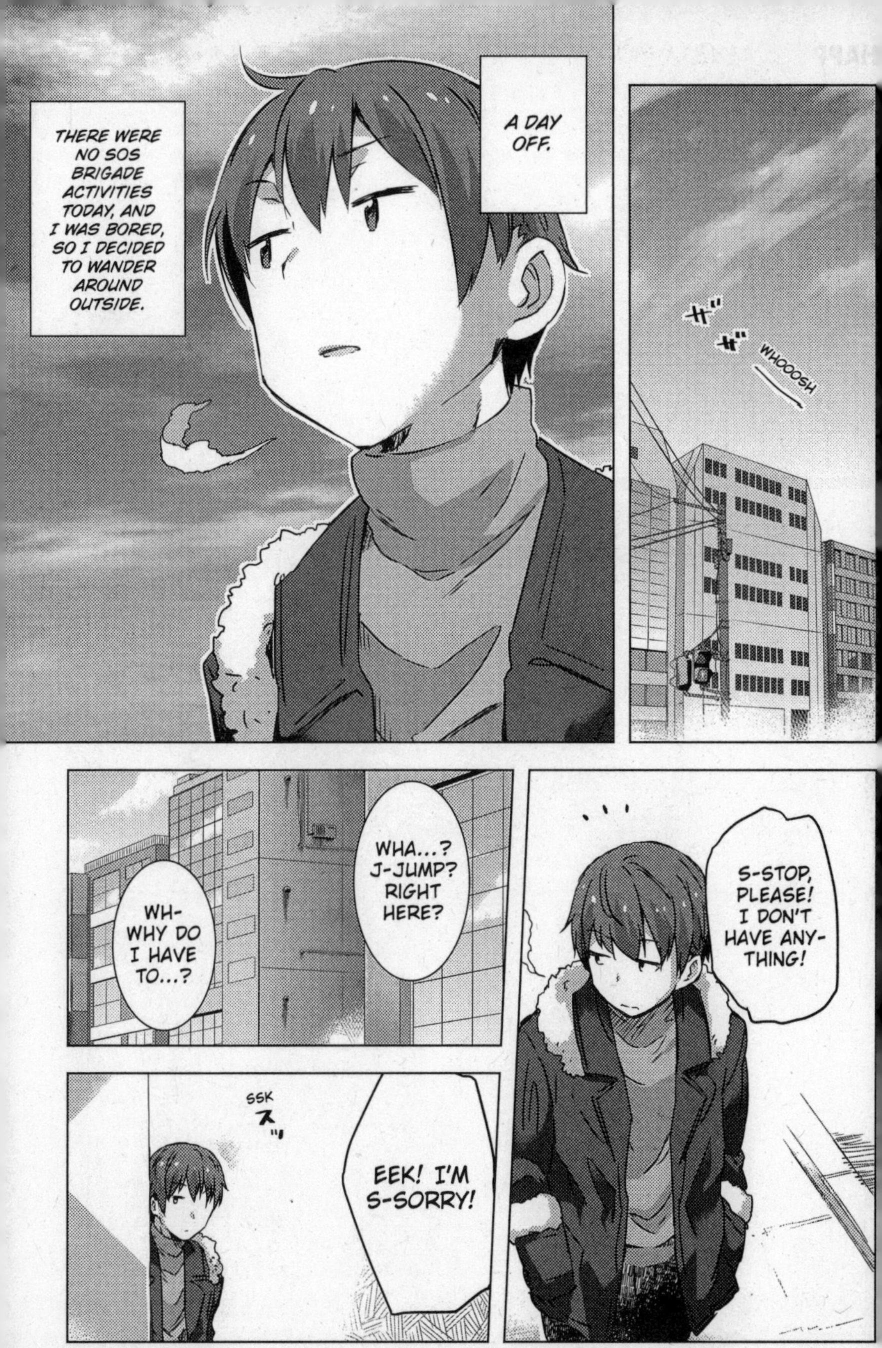
ザ
ザ
WHOOOSH
A DAY OFF.
THERE WERE NO SOS BRIGADE ACTIVITIES TODAY, AND I WAS BORED, SO I DECIDED TO WANDER AROUND OUTSIDE.
S-STOP, PLEASE! I DON'T HAVE ANY-THING!
WHA...? J-JUMP? RIGHT HERE?
WH-WHY DO I HAVE TO...?
EEK! I'M S-SORRY!
SSK
ス

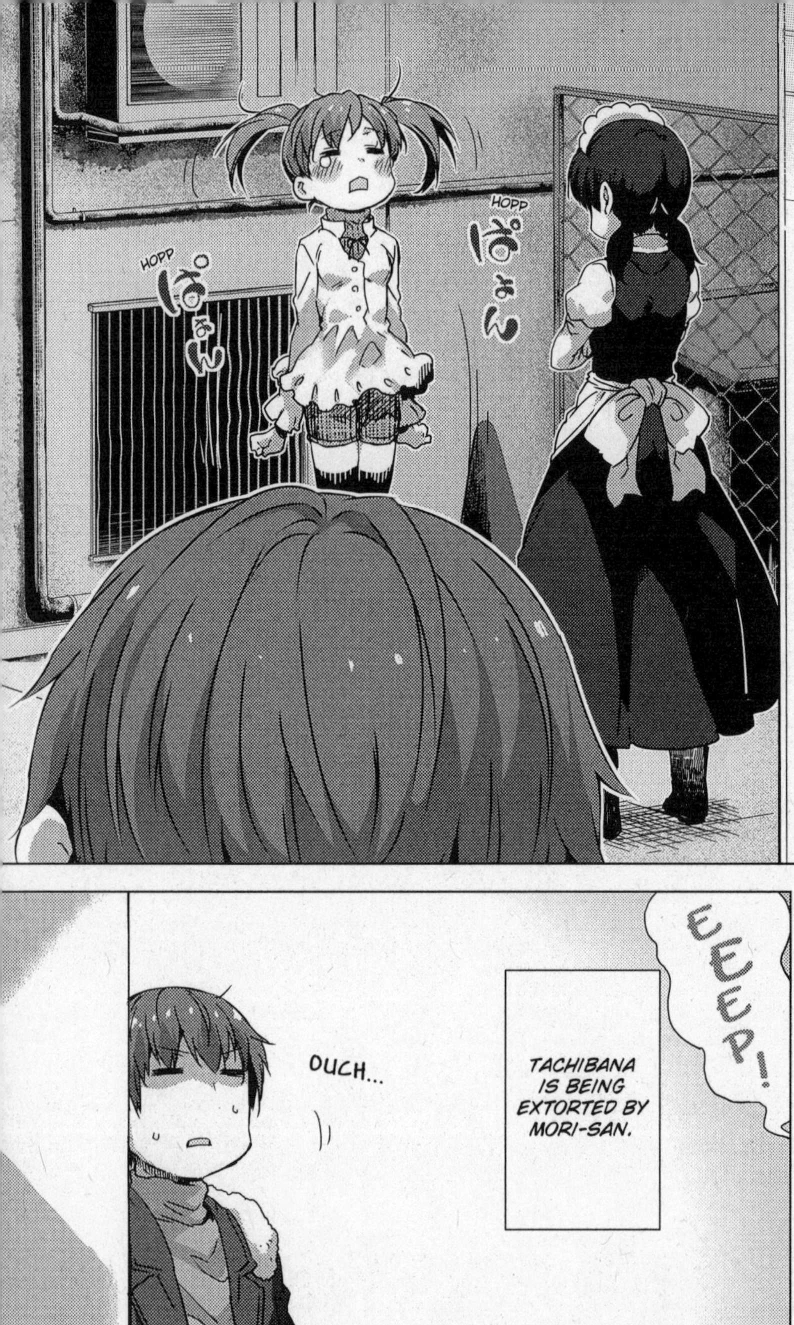
HOPP
ぽよん
HOPP
ぽよん
EEEP!
TACHIBANA IS BEING EXTORTED BY MORI-SAN.
OUCH...

●Tachibana ●A girl from an organization opposing the Agency. Mori-san's enemy!

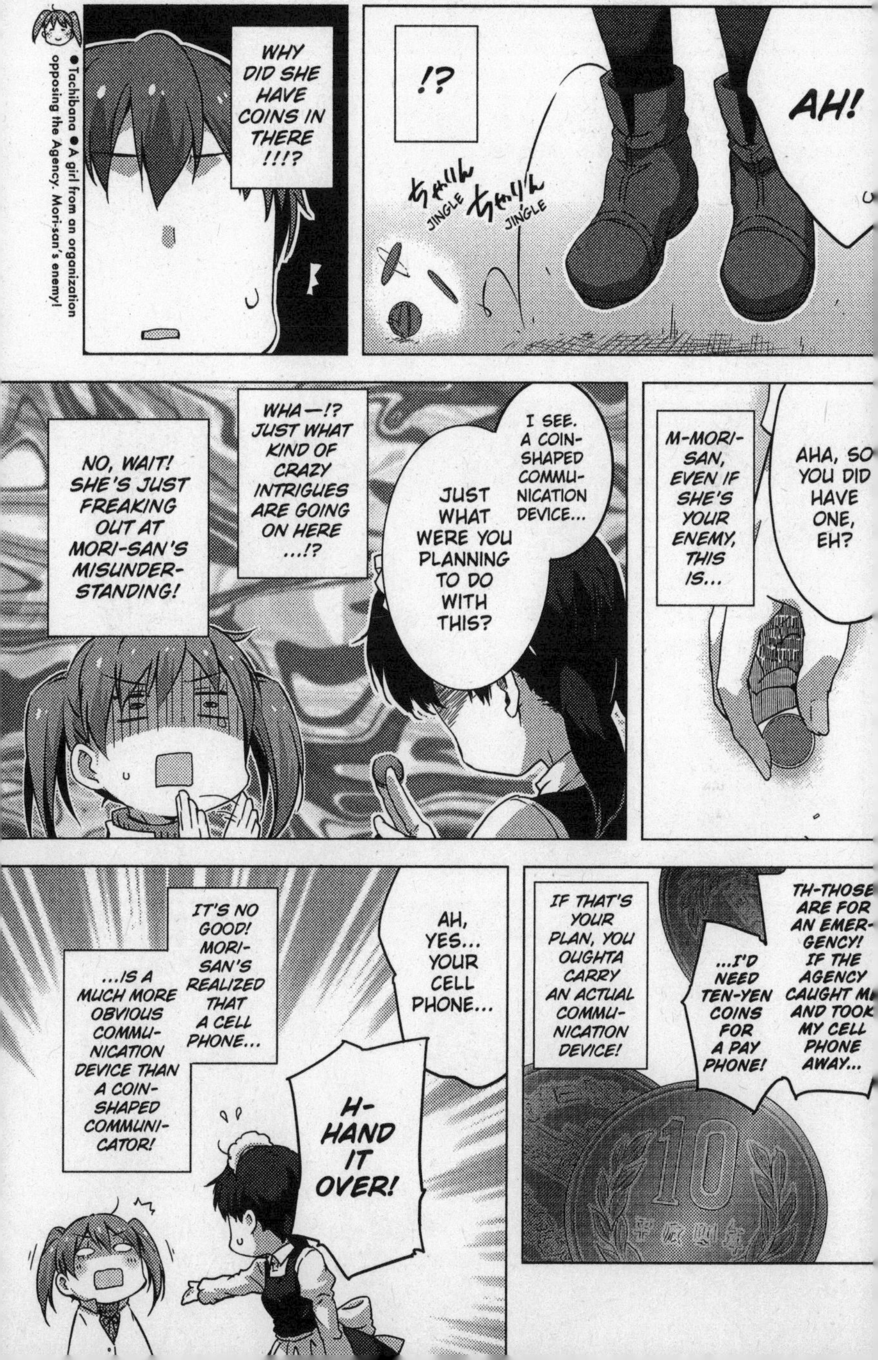
AH!
!?
ちゃりん JINGLE
ちゃりん JINGLE
WHY DID SHE HAVE COINS IN THERE !!!?
AHA, SO YOU DID HAVE ONE, EH?
M-MORI-SAN, EVEN IF SHE'S YOUR ENEMY, THIS IS...
I SEE. A COIN-SHAPED COMMUNICATION DEVICE...
JUST WHAT WERE YOU PLANNING TO DO WITH THIS?
WHA—!? JUST WHAT KIND OF CRAZY INTRIGUES ARE GOING ON HERE ...!?
NO, WAIT! SHE'S JUST FREAKING OUT AT MORI-SAN'S MISUNDERSTANDING!
TH-THOSE ARE FOR AN EMERGENCY! IF THE AGENCY CAUGHT ME AND TOOK MY CELL PHONE AWAY...
...I'D NEED TEN-YEN COINS FOR A PAY PHONE!
IF THAT'S YOUR PLAN, YOU OUGHTA CARRY AN ACTUAL COMMUNICATION DEVICE!
AH, YES... YOUR CELL PHONE...
IT'S NO GOOD! MORI-SAN'S REALIZED THAT A CELL PHONE...
...IS A MUCH MORE OBVIOUS COMMUNICATION DEVICE THAN A COIN-SHAPED COMMUNICATOR!
H-HAND IT OVER!

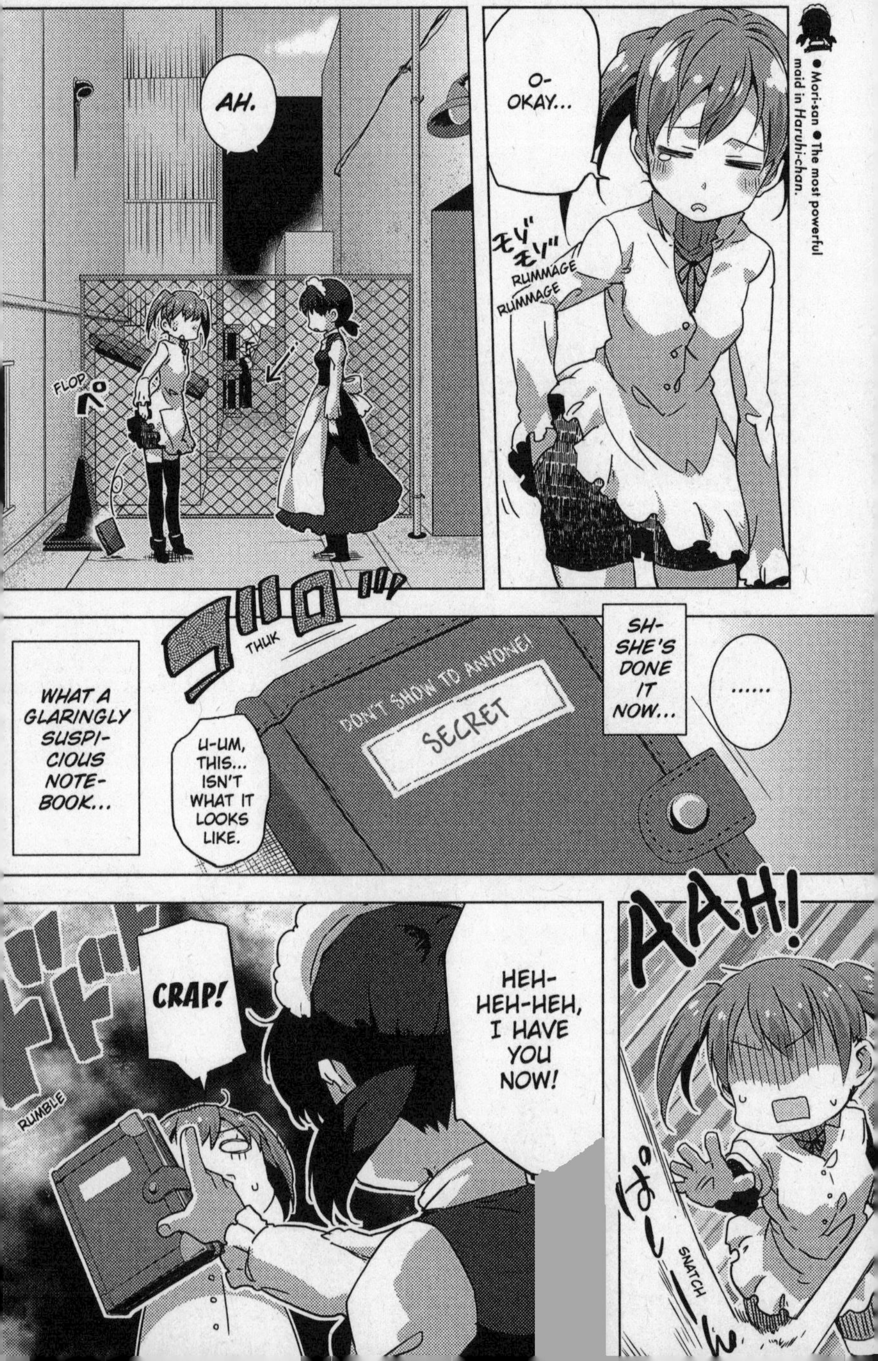
O-OKAY...
モゾモゾ
RUMMAGE RUMMAGE
AH.
FLOP
ペ
......
SH-SHE'S DONE IT NOW...
DON'T SHOW TO ANYONE!
SECRET
THUK
U-UM, THIS... ISN'T WHAT IT LOOKS LIKE.
WHAT A GLARINGLY SUSPICIOUS NOTEBOOK...
AAH!
SNATCH
HEH-HEH-HEH, I HAVE YOU NOW!
CRAP!
RUMBLE

●Mori-san ●The most powerful maid in Haruhi-chan.

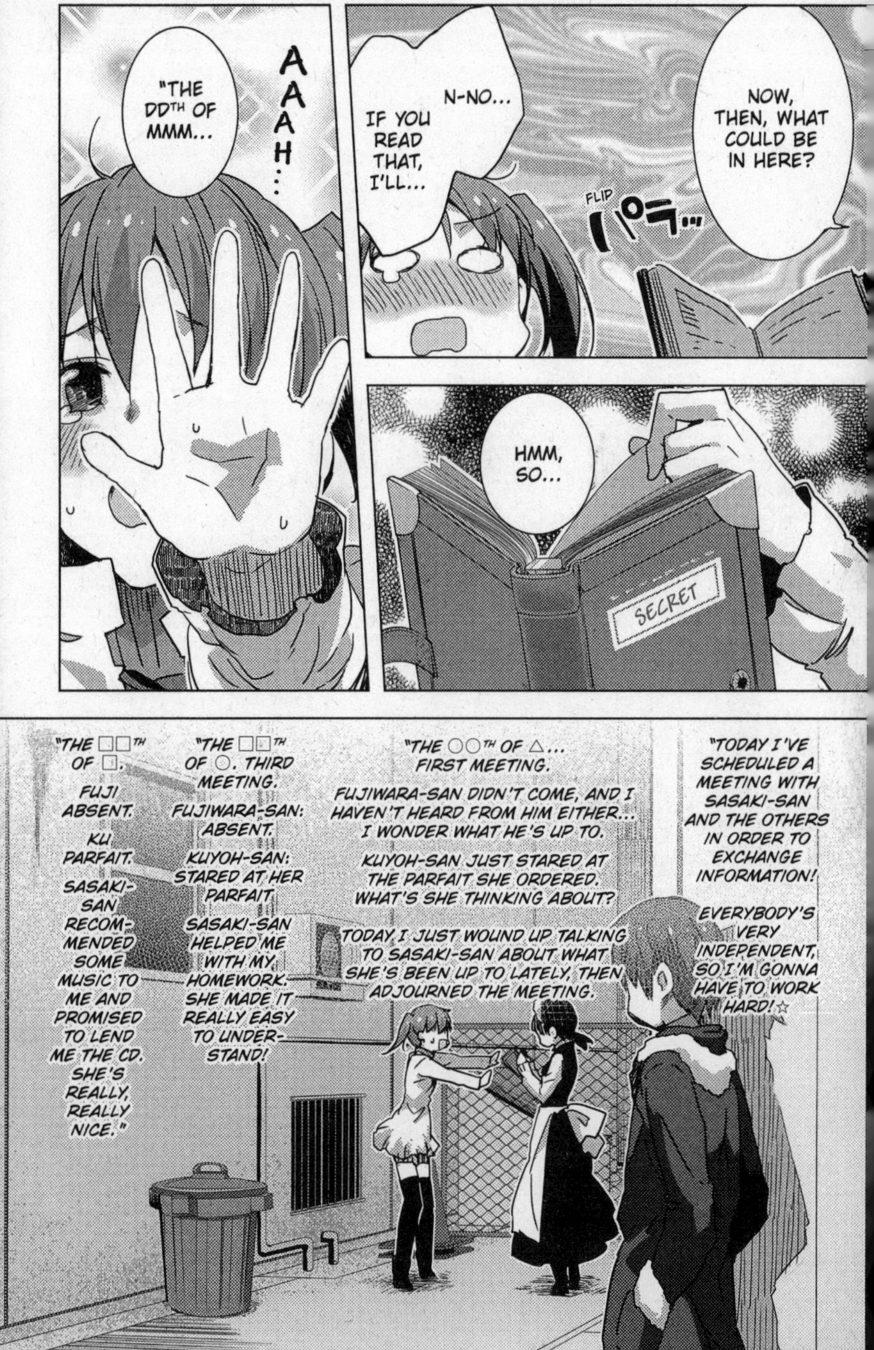
NOW, THEN, WHAT COULD BE IN HERE?
FLIP
パラ…
N-NO…
IF YOU READ THAT, I'LL…
HMM, SO…
"THE DDTH OF MMM…
AAAH…
"TODAY I'VE SCHEDULED A MEETING WITH SASAKI-SAN AND THE OTHERS IN ORDER TO EXCHANGE INFORMATION!
EVERYBODY'S VERY INDEPENDENT, SO I'M GONNA HAVE TO WORK HARD!☆
"THE ○○TH OF △… FIRST MEETING.
FUJIWARA-SAN DIDN'T COME, AND I HAVEN'T HEARD FROM HIM EITHER… I WONDER WHAT HE'S UP TO.
KUYOH-SAN JUST STARED AT THE PARFAIT SHE ORDERED. WHAT'S SHE THINKING ABOUT?
TODAY I JUST WOUND UP TALKING TO SASAKI-SAN ABOUT WHAT SHE'S BEEN UP TO LATELY, THEN ADJOURNED THE MEETING.
"THE □□TH OF ○. THIRD MEETING.
FUJIWARA-SAN: ABSENT.
KUYOH-SAN: STARED AT HER PARFAIT.
SASAKI-SAN HELPED ME WITH MY HOMEWORK. SHE MADE IT REALLY EASY TO UNDERSTAND!
"THE □□TH OF □.
FUJI ABSENT.
KU PARFAIT.
SASAKI-SAN RECOMMENDED SOME MUSIC TO ME AND PROMISED TO LEND ME THE CD. SHE'S REALLY, REALLY NICE."

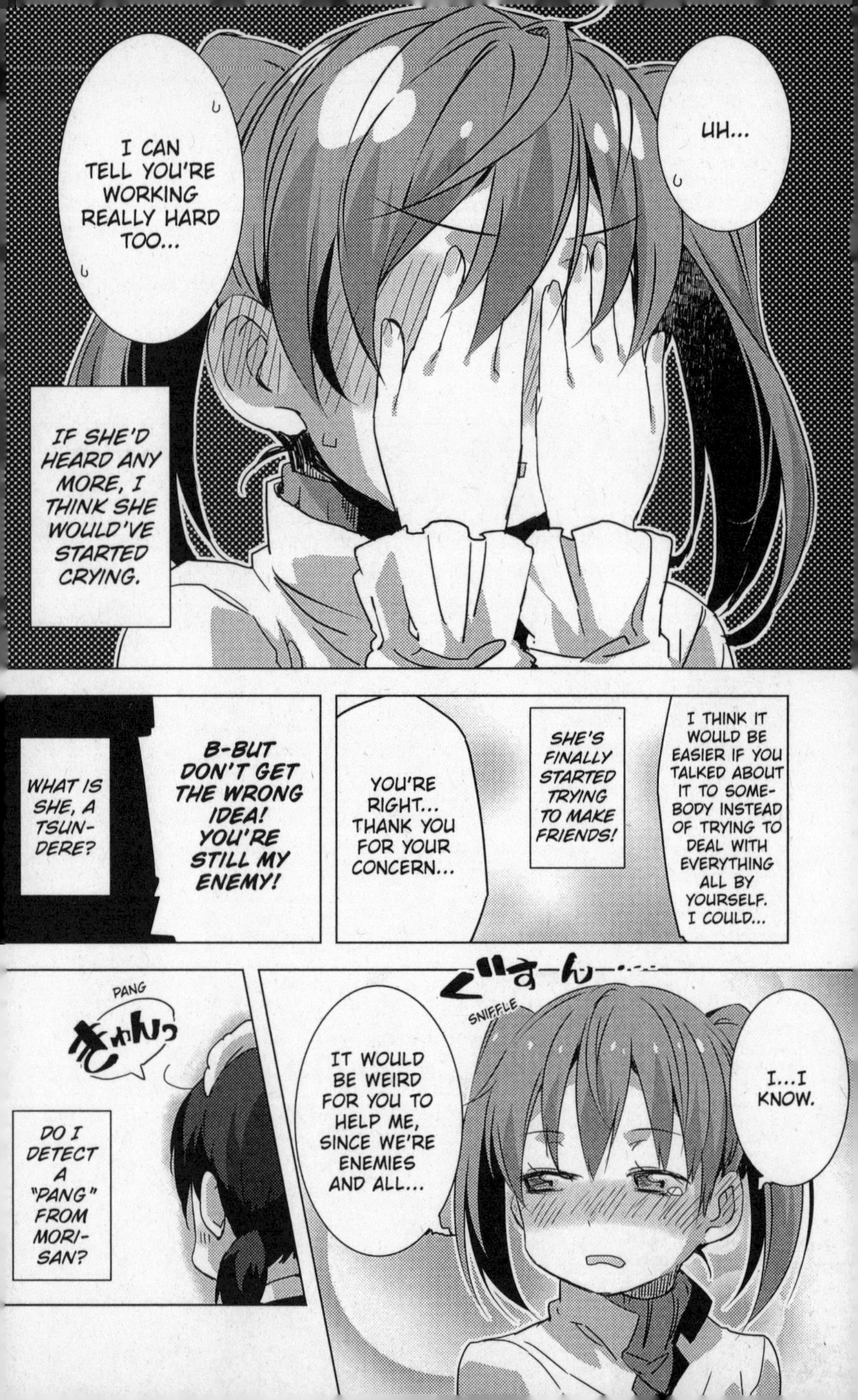
UH...
I CAN TELL YOU'RE WORKING REALLY HARD TOO...
IF SHE'D HEARD ANY MORE, I THINK SHE WOULD'VE STARTED CRYING.
I THINK IT WOULD BE EASIER IF YOU TALKED ABOUT IT TO SOME-BODY INSTEAD OF TRYING TO DEAL WITH EVERYTHING ALL BY YOURSELF. I COULD...
SHE'S FINALLY STARTED TRYING TO MAKE FRIENDS!
YOU'RE RIGHT... THANK YOU FOR YOUR CONCERN...
B-BUT DON'T GET THE WRONG IDEA! YOU'RE STILL MY ENEMY!
WHAT IS SHE, A TSUNDERE?
ぐすん…
SNIFFLE
I...I KNOW.
IT WOULD BE WEIRD FOR YOU TO HELP ME, SINCE WE'RE ENEMIES AND ALL...
きゅんっ
PANG
DO I DETECT A "PANG" FROM MORI-SAN?

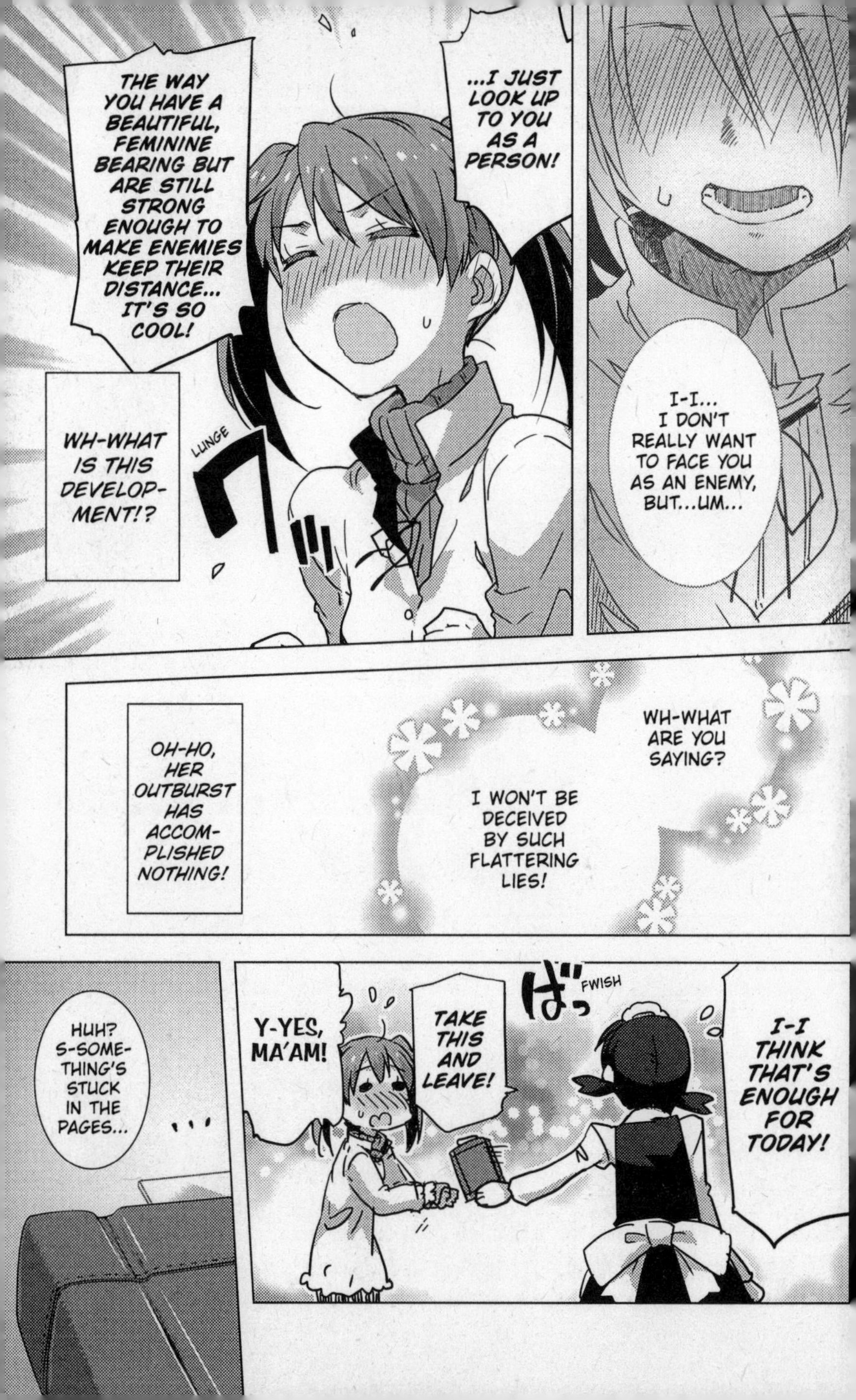
I-I... I DON'T REALLY WANT TO FACE YOU AS AN ENEMY, BUT...UM...
...I JUST LOOK UP TO YOU AS A PERSON!
THE WAY YOU HAVE A BEAUTIFUL, FEMININE BEARING BUT ARE STILL STRONG ENOUGH TO MAKE ENEMIES KEEP THEIR DISTANCE... IT'S SO COOL!
LUNGE
WH-WHAT IS THIS DEVELOP-MENT!?
WH-WHAT ARE YOU SAYING?
I WON'T BE DECEIVED BY SUCH FLATTERING LIES!
OH-HO, HER OUTBURST HAS ACCOM-PLISHED NOTHING!
I-I THINK THAT'S ENOUGH FOR TODAY!
FWISH
TAKE THIS AND LEAVE!
Y-YES, MA'AM!
...
HUH? S-SOME-THING'S STUCK IN THE PAGES...

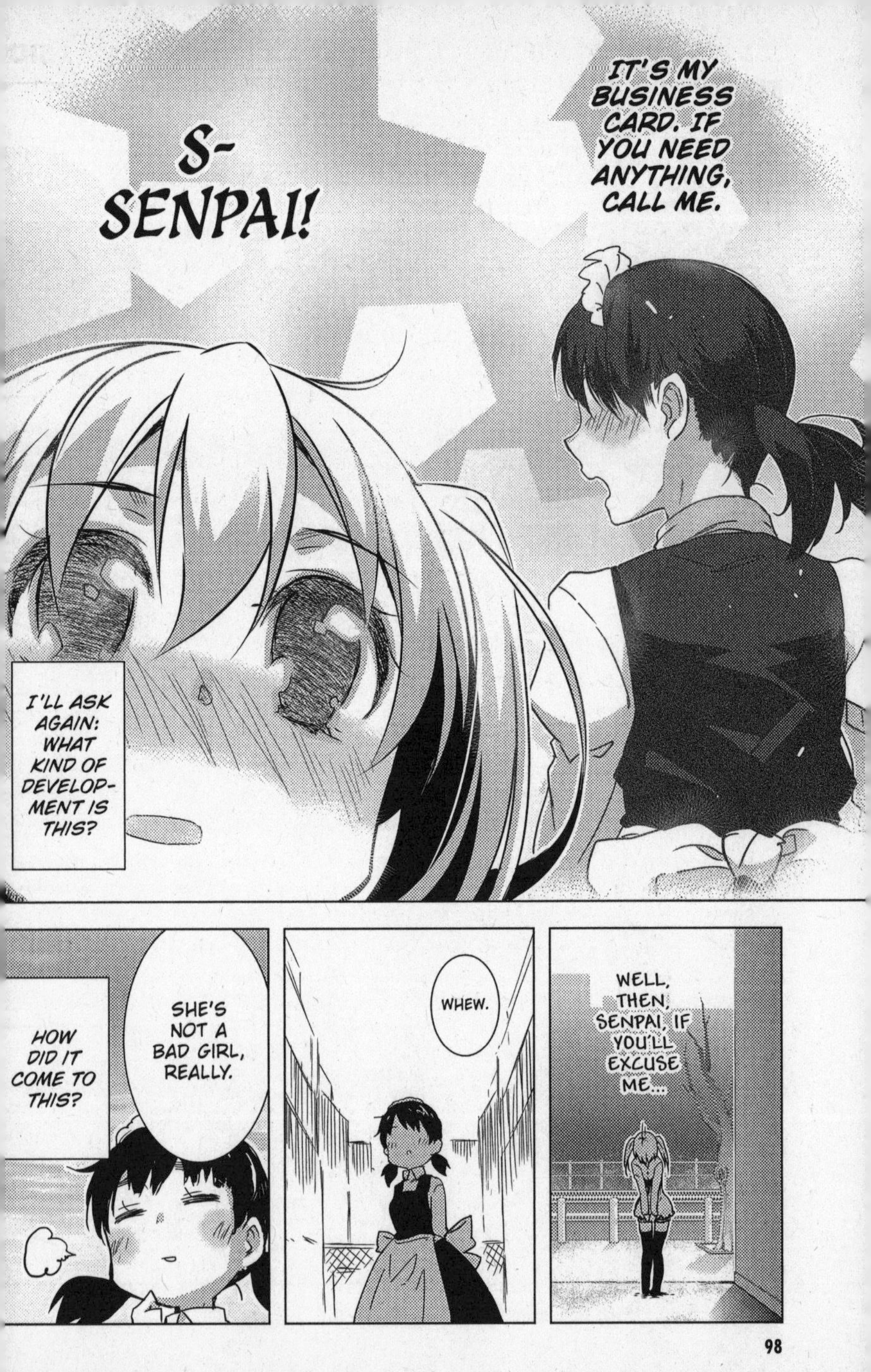
IT'S MY BUSINESS CARD. IF YOU NEED ANYTHING, CALL ME.
S-SENPAI!
I'LL ASK AGAIN: WHAT KIND OF DEVELOPMENT IS THIS?
WELL, THEN, SENPAI, IF YOU'LL EXCUSE ME...
WHEW.
SHE'S NOT A BAD GIRL, REALLY.
HOW DID IT COME TO THIS?

SETSUBUN: SASAKI'S SID

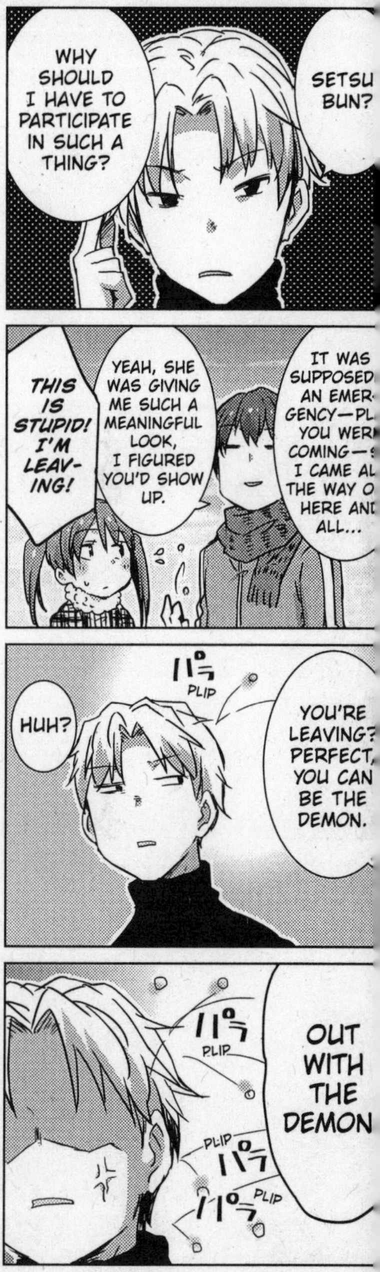
SETSU BUN?
WHY SHOULD I HAVE TO PARTICIPATE IN SUCH A THING?
IT WAS SUPPOSED AN EMER-GENCY—PL YOU WER COMING— I CAME AL THE WAY O HERE AND ALL...
YEAH, SHE WAS GIVING ME SUCH A MEANINGFUL LOOK, I FIGURED YOU'D SHOW UP.
THIS IS STUPID! I'M LEAV-ING!
YOU'RE LEAVING? PERFECT, YOU CAN BE THE DEMON.
パラ PLIP
HUH?
OUT WITH THE DEMON
パラ PLIP
パラ PLIP
パラ PLIP

PROVOCATION

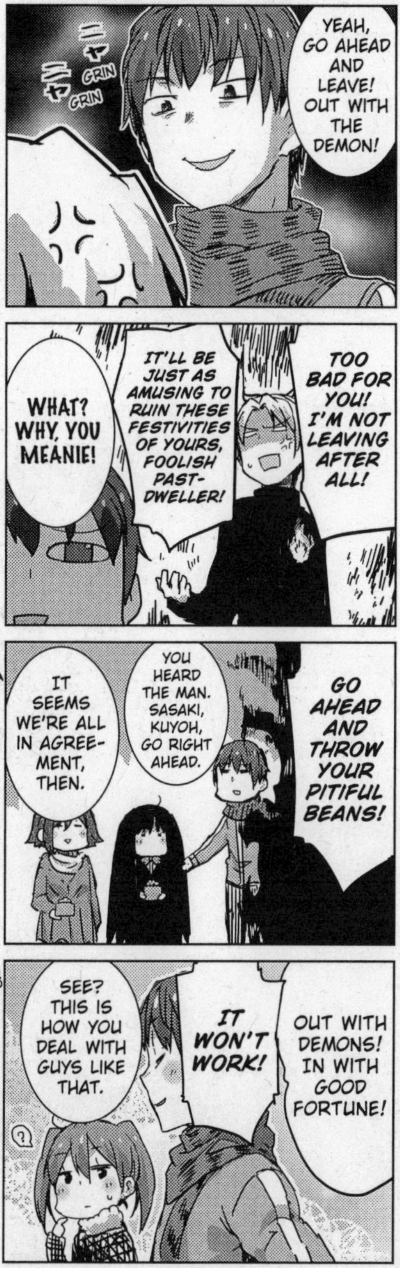
YEAH, GO AHEAD AND LEAVE! OUT WITH THE DEMON!
ニヤ GRIN
ニヤ GRIN
TOO BAD FOR YOU! I'M NOT LEAVING AFTER ALL!
IT'LL BE JUST AS AMUSING TO RUIN THESE FESTIVITIES OF YOURS, FOOLISH PAST-DWELLER!
WHAT? WHY, YOU MEANIE!
GO AHEAD AND THROW YOUR PITIFUL BEANS!
YOU HEARD THE MAN. SASAKI, KUYOH, GO RIGHT AHEAD.
IT SEEMS WE'RE ALL IN AGREEMENT, THEN.
OUT WITH DEMONS! IN WITH GOOD FORTUNE!
IT WON'T WORK!
SEE? THIS IS HOW YOU DEAL WITH GUYS LIKE THAT.
?

●Sasaki ●Tachibana's friend.

●Fujiwara ●Time traveler. Easy to mess with.

BAM, IT'S THE PRESIDENT! CHAPTER 3: "DOKI-DOKI VALENTINE"

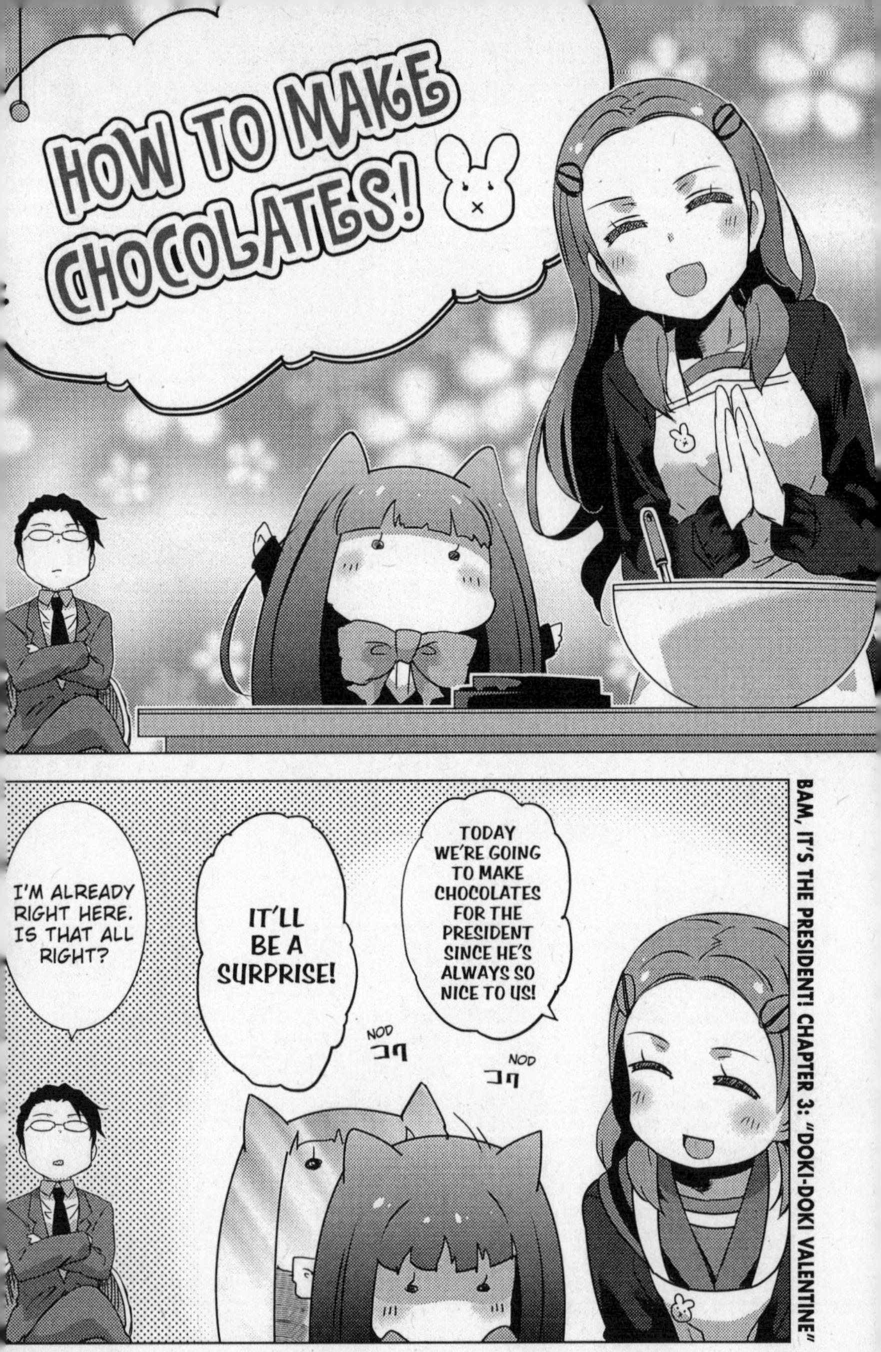
HOW TO MAKE CHOCOLATES!
TODAY WE'RE GOING TO MAKE CHOCOLATES FOR THE PRESIDENT SINCE HE'S ALWAYS SO NICE TO US!
NOD コク
NOD コク
IT'LL BE A SURPRISE!
I'M ALREADY RIGHT HERE. IS THAT ALL RIGHT?

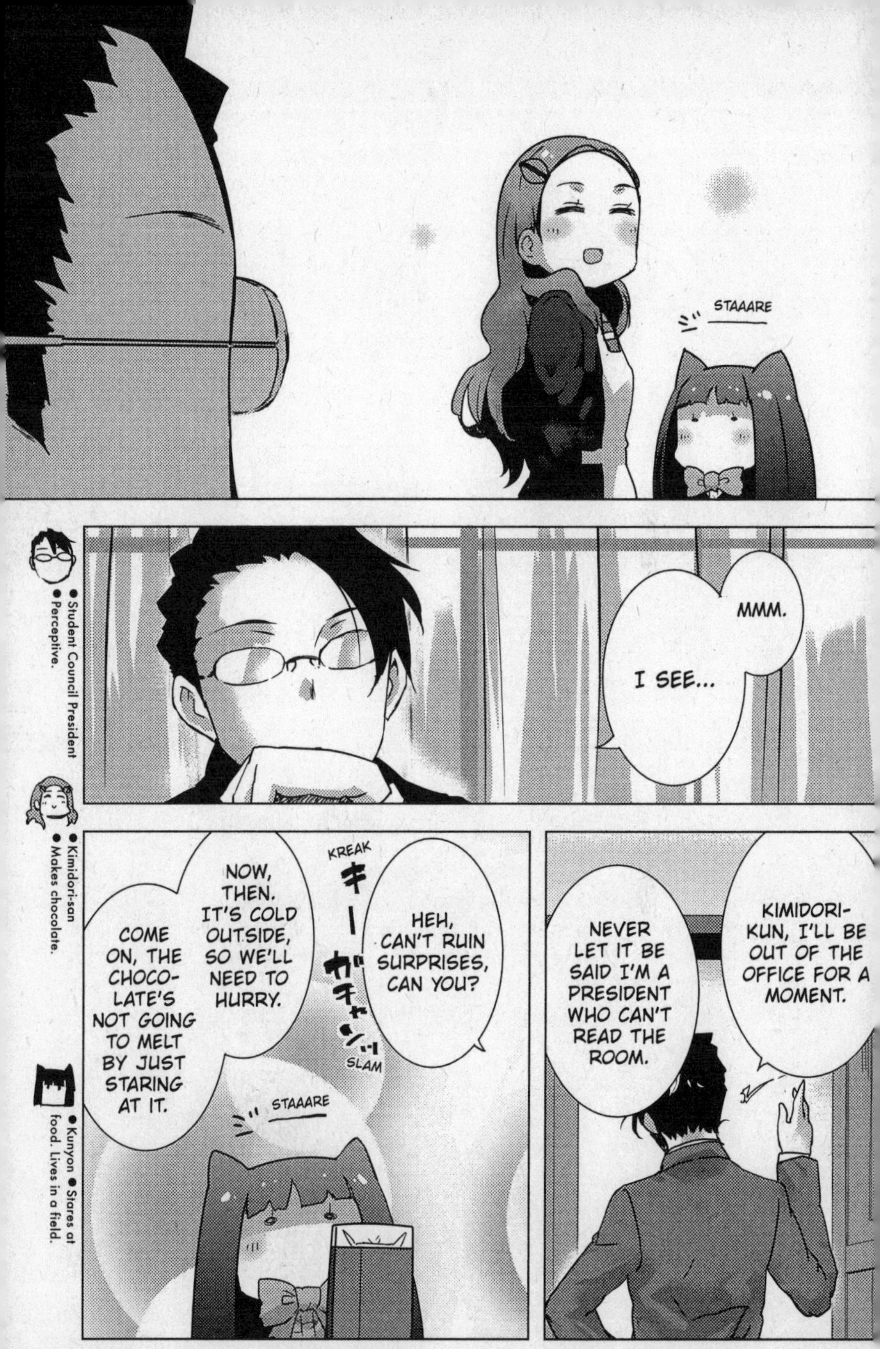
STAAARE
MMM.
I SEE...
KIMIDORI-KUN, I'LL BE OUT OF THE OFFICE FOR A MOMENT.
NEVER LET IT BE SAID I'M A PRESIDENT WHO CAN'T READ THE ROOM.
HEH, CAN'T RUIN SURPRISES, CAN YOU?
KREAK
キーガチャン
SLAM
NOW, THEN. IT'S COLD OUTSIDE, SO WE'LL NEED TO HURRY.
COME ON, THE CHOCO-LATE'S NOT GOING TO MELT BY JUST STARING AT IT.
STAAARE
●Student Council President ●Perceptive.
●Kimidori-san ●Makes chocolate.
●Kunyon ●Stares at food. Lives in a field.

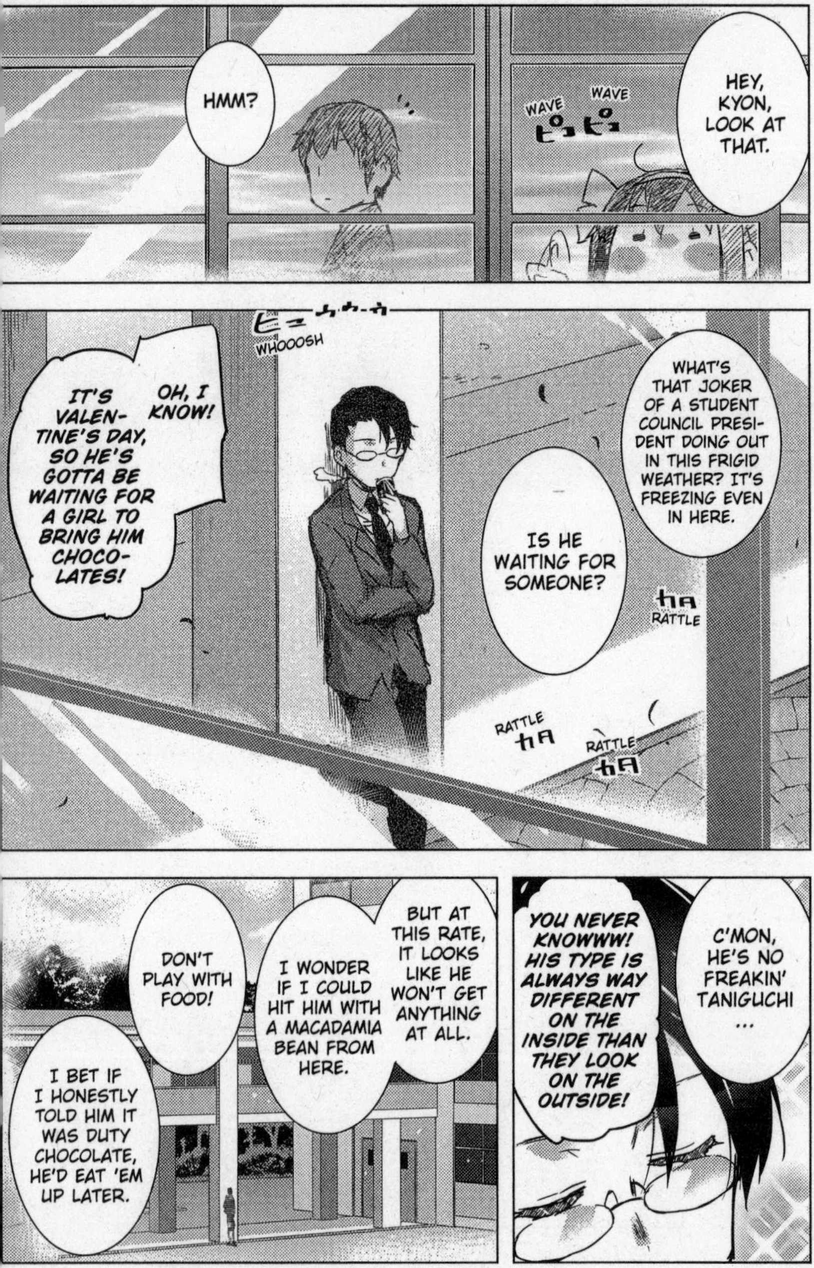
HEY, KYON, LOOK AT THAT.
WAVE WAVE
HMM?
WHAT'S THAT JOKER OF A STUDENT COUNCIL PRESIDENT DOING OUT IN THIS FRIGID WEATHER? IT'S FREEZING EVEN IN HERE.
IS HE WAITING FOR SOMEONE?
RATTLE
RATTLE
RATTLE
WHOOOSH
OH, I KNOW! IT'S VALENTINE'S DAY, SO HE'S GOTTA BE WAITING FOR A GIRL TO BRING HIM CHOCOLATES!
C'MON, HE'S NO FREAKIN' TANIGUCHI ...
YOU NEVER KNOWWW! HIS TYPE IS ALWAYS WAY DIFFERENT ON THE INSIDE THAN THEY LOOK ON THE OUTSIDE!
BUT AT THIS RATE, IT LOOKS LIKE HE WON'T GET ANYTHING AT ALL.
I WONDER IF I COULD HIT HIM WITH A MACADAMIA BEAN FROM HERE.
DON'T PLAY WITH FOOD!
I BET IF I HONESTLY TOLD HIM IT WAS DUTY CHOCOLATE, HE'D EAT 'EM UP LATER.

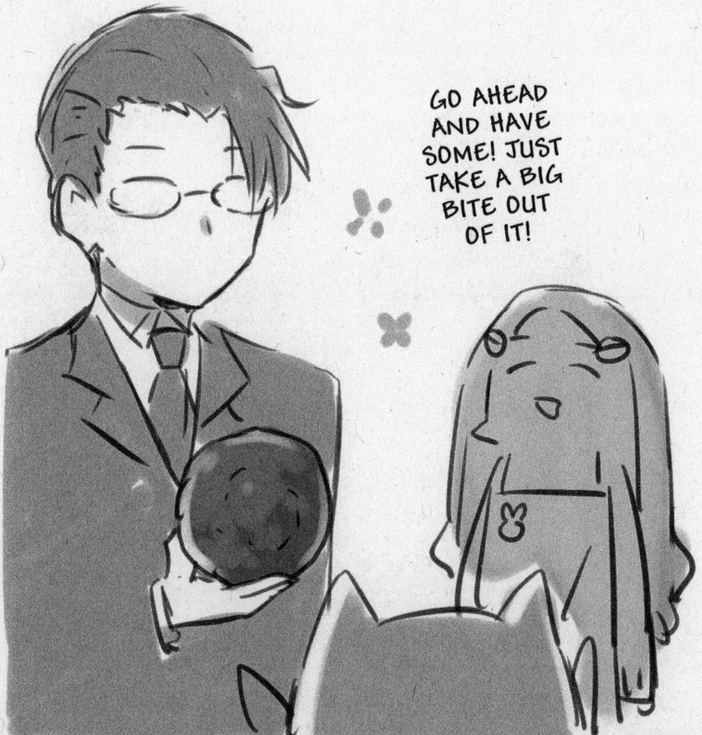
GO AHEAD AND HAVE SOME! JUST TAKE A BIG BITE OUT OF IT!

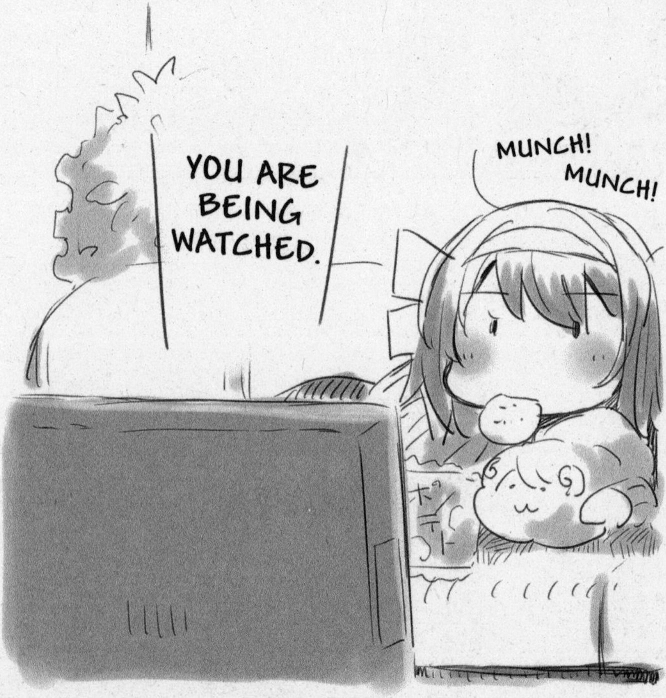
MUNCH! MUNCH!
YOU ARE BEING WATCHED.

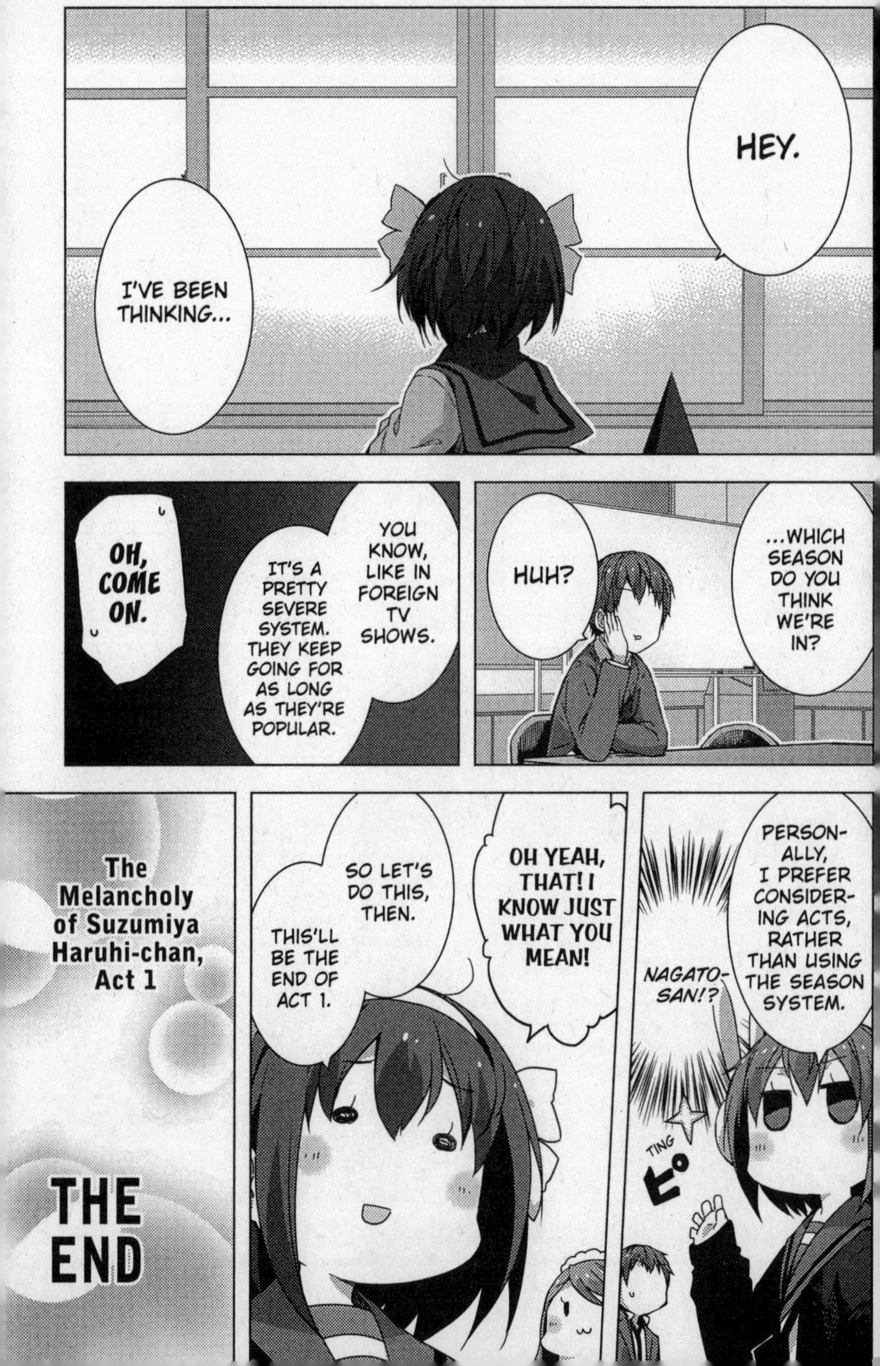
HEY.
I'VE BEEN THINKING...
...WHICH SEASON DO YOU THINK WE'RE IN?
HUH?
YOU KNOW, LIKE IN FOREIGN TV SHOWS.
IT'S A PRETTY SEVERE SYSTEM. THEY KEEP GOING FOR AS LONG AS THEY'RE POPULAR.
OH, COME ON.
PERSON-ALLY, I PREFER CONSIDER-ING ACTS, RATHER THAN USING THE SEASON SYSTEM.
NAGATO-SAN!?
TING
OH YEAH, THAT! I KNOW JUST WHAT YOU MEAN!
SO LET'S DO THIS, THEN.
THIS'LL BE THE END OF ACT 1.
The Melancholy of Suzumiya Haruhi-chan, Act 1
THE END

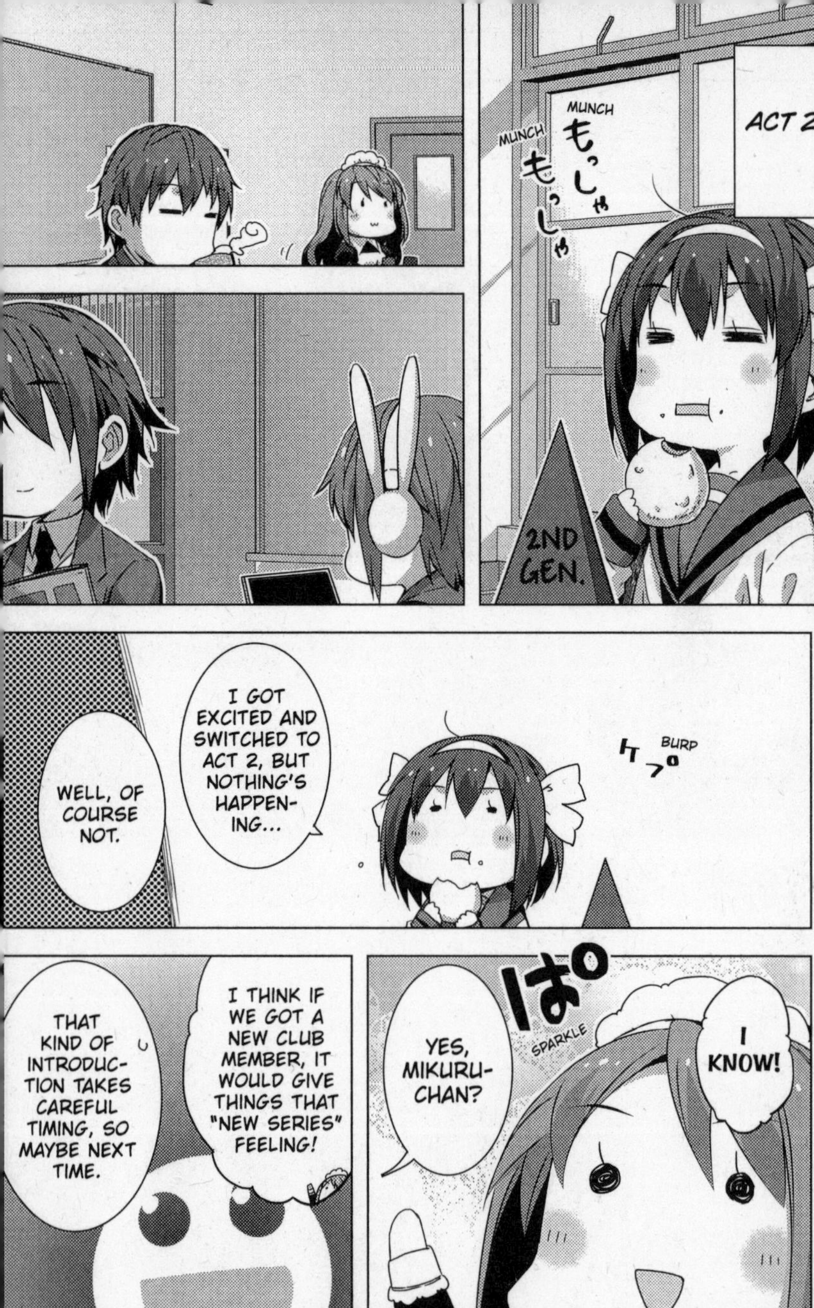
ACT 2.
MUNCH
もっしゃ
MUNCH
もっしゃ
2ND GEN.
ケプ
BURP
I GOT EXCITED AND SWITCHED TO ACT 2, BUT NOTHING'S HAPPEN-ING...
WELL, OF COURSE NOT.
I KNOW!
ぱ
SPARKLE
YES, MIKURU-CHAN?
I THINK IF WE GOT A NEW CLUB MEMBER, IT WOULD GIVE THINGS THAT "NEW SERIES" FEELING!
THAT KIND OF INTRODUC-TION TAKES CAREFUL TIMING, SO MAYBE NEXT TIME.

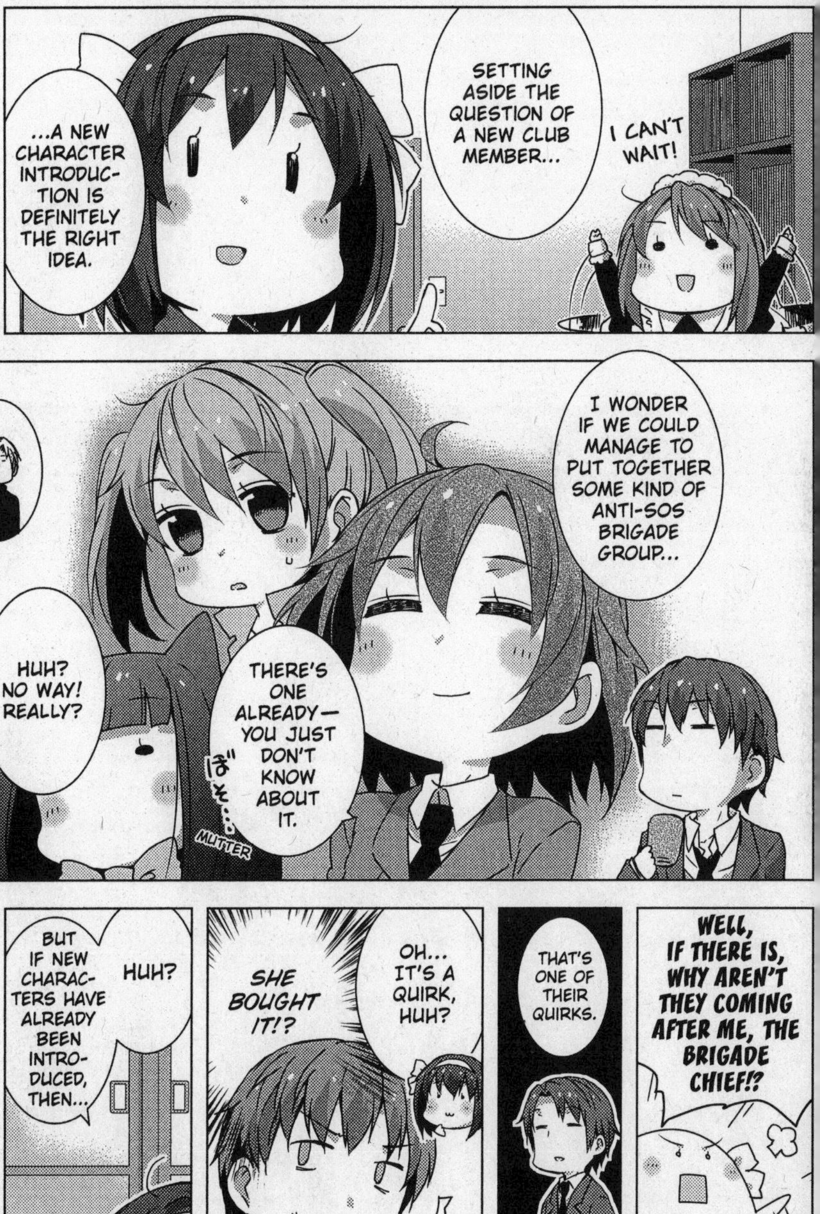
SETTING ASIDE THE QUESTION OF A NEW CLUB MEMBER...
...A NEW CHARACTER INTRODUCTION IS DEFINITELY THE RIGHT IDEA.
I CAN'T WAIT!
I WONDER IF WE COULD MANAGE TO PUT TOGETHER SOME KIND OF ANTI-SOS BRIGADE GROUP...
THERE'S ONE ALREADY—YOU JUST DON'T KNOW ABOUT IT.
ぼそ...
MUTTER
HUH? NO WAY! REALLY?
WELL, IF THERE IS, WHY AREN'T THEY COMING AFTER ME, THE BRIGADE CHIEF!?
THAT'S ONE OF THEIR QUIRKS.
OH... IT'S A QUIRK, HUH?
SHE BOUGHT IT!?
BUT IF NEW CHARACTERS HAVE ALREADY BEEN INTRODUCED, THEN...
HUH?

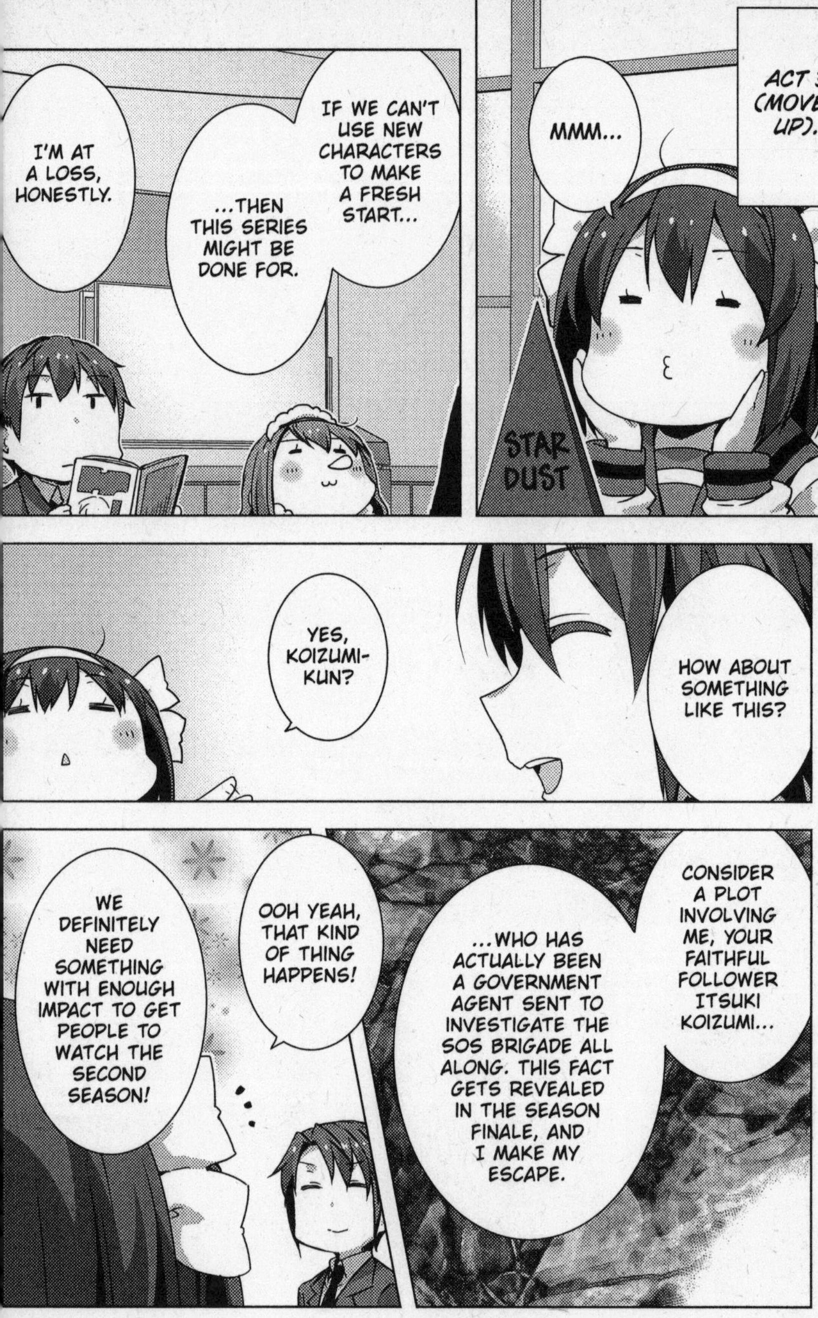
ACT 3 (MOVED UP).
MMM...
STAR DUST
IF WE CAN'T USE NEW CHARACTERS TO MAKE A FRESH START...
...THEN THIS SERIES MIGHT BE DONE FOR.
I'M AT A LOSS, HONESTLY.
HOW ABOUT SOMETHING LIKE THIS?
YES, KOIZUMI-KUN?
CONSIDER A PLOT INVOLVING ME, YOUR FAITHFUL FOLLOWER ITSUKI KOIZUMI...
...WHO HAS ACTUALLY BEEN A GOVERNMENT AGENT SENT TO INVESTIGATE THE SOS BRIGADE ALL ALONG. THIS FACT GETS REVEALED IN THE SEASON FINALE, AND I MAKE MY ESCAPE.
OOH YEAH, THAT KIND OF THING HAPPENS!
WE DEFINITELY NEED SOMETHING WITH ENOUGH IMPACT TO GET PEOPLE TO WATCH THE SECOND SEASON!

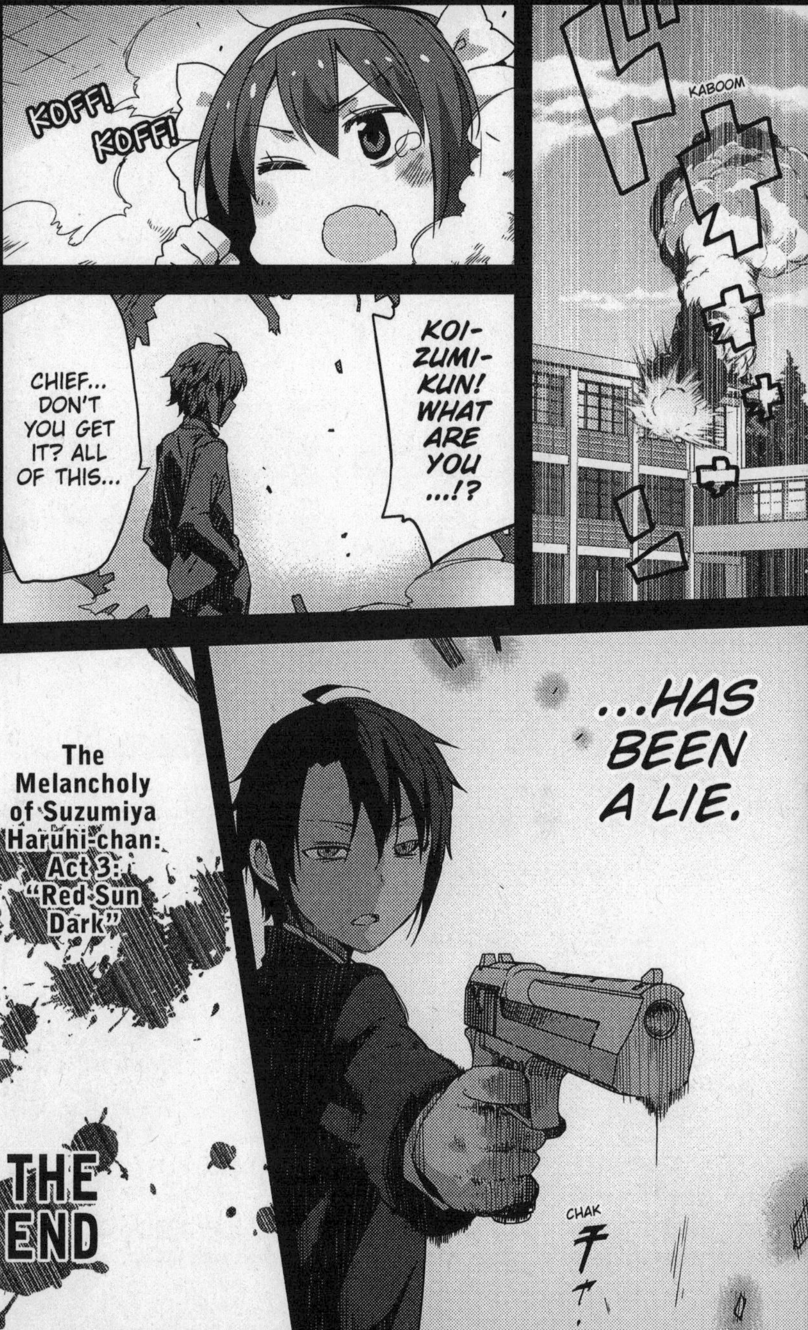
KABOOM
KOFF! KOFF!
KOI-ZUMI-KUN! WHAT ARE YOU ...!?
CHIEF... DON'T YOU GET IT? ALL OF THIS...
...HAS BEEN A LIE.
CHAK
The Melancholy of Suzumiya Haruhi-chan: Act 3: "Red Sun Dark"
THE END

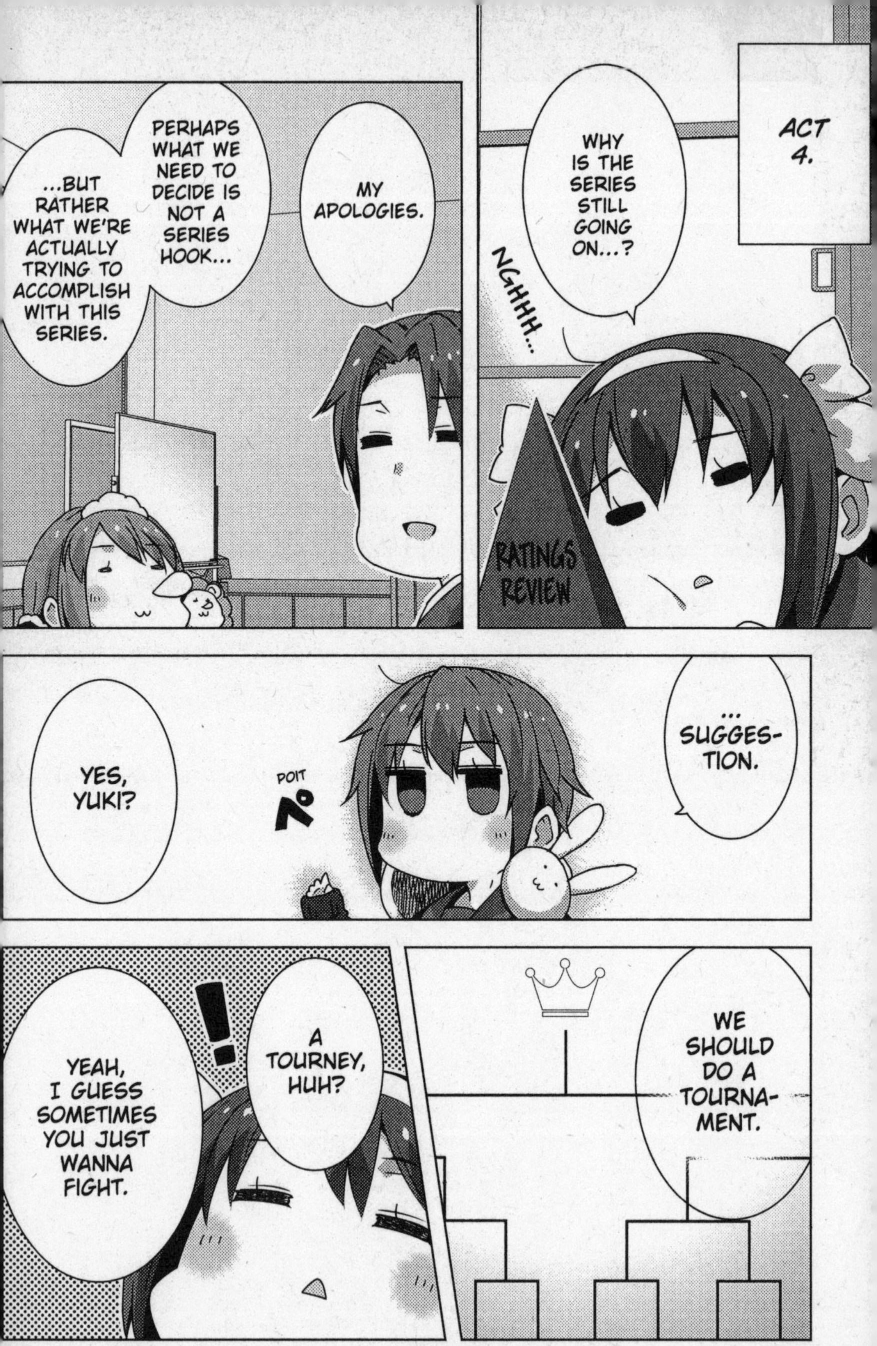
ACT 4.
WHY IS THE SERIES STILL GOING ON...?
NGHHH...
RATINGS REVIEW
MY APOLOGIES.
PERHAPS WHAT WE NEED TO DECIDE IS NOT A SERIES HOOK...
...BUT RATHER WHAT WE'RE ACTUALLY TRYING TO ACCOMPLISH WITH THIS SERIES.
... SUGGES-TION.
POIT
YES, YUKI?
WE SHOULD DO A TOURNA-MENT.
A TOURNEY, HUH?
YEAH, I GUESS SOMETIMES YOU JUST WANNA FIGHT.

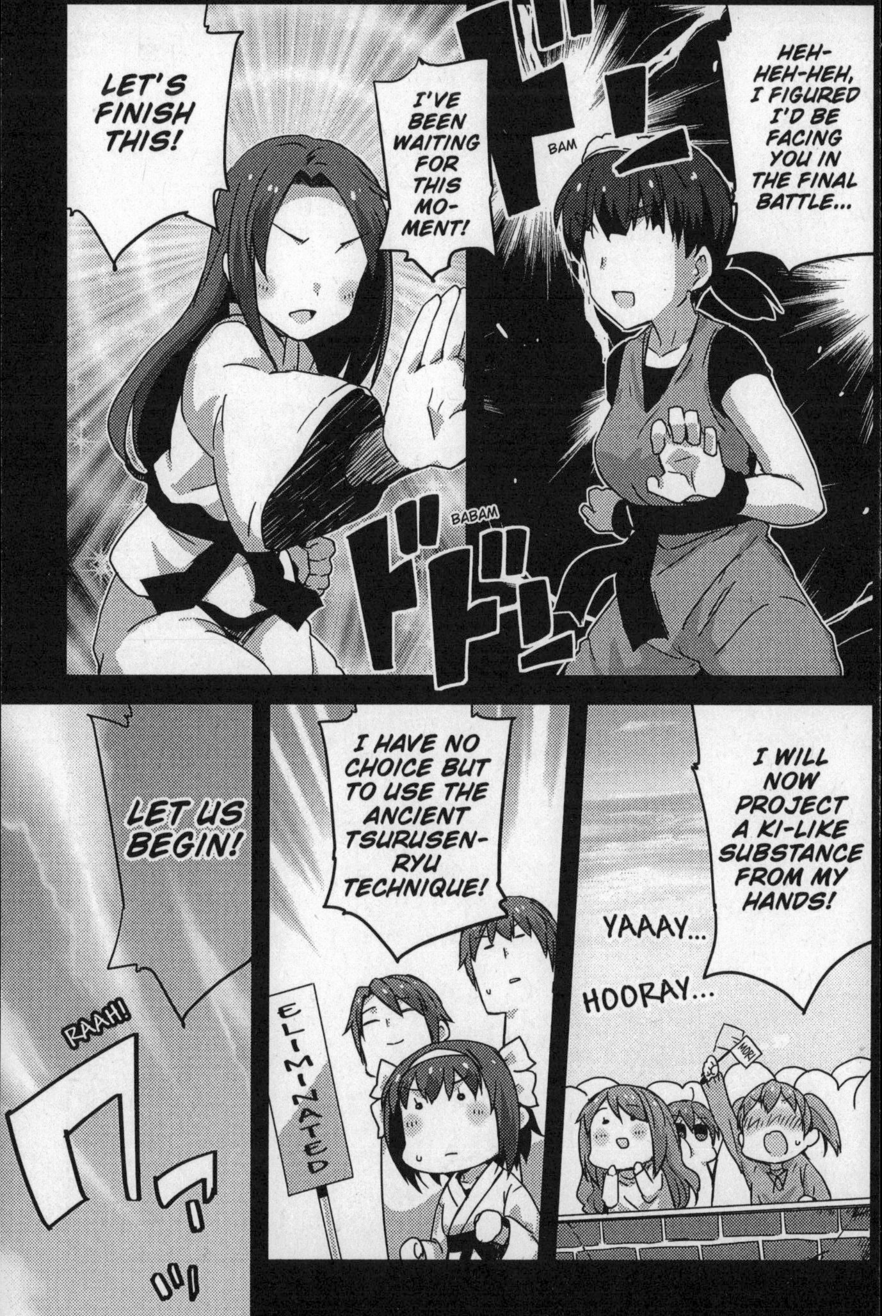
HEH-HEH-HEH, I FIGURED I'D BE FACING YOU IN THE FINAL BATTLE...
BAM
I'VE BEEN WAITING FOR THIS MO-MENT!
LET'S FINISH THIS!
BABAM
I WILL NOW PROJECT A KI-LIKE SUBSTANCE FROM MY HANDS!
YAAAY...
HOORAY...
MORI
I HAVE NO CHOICE BUT TO USE THE ANCIENT TSURUSEN-RYU TECHNIQUE!
ELIMINATED
LET US BEGIN!
RAAH!

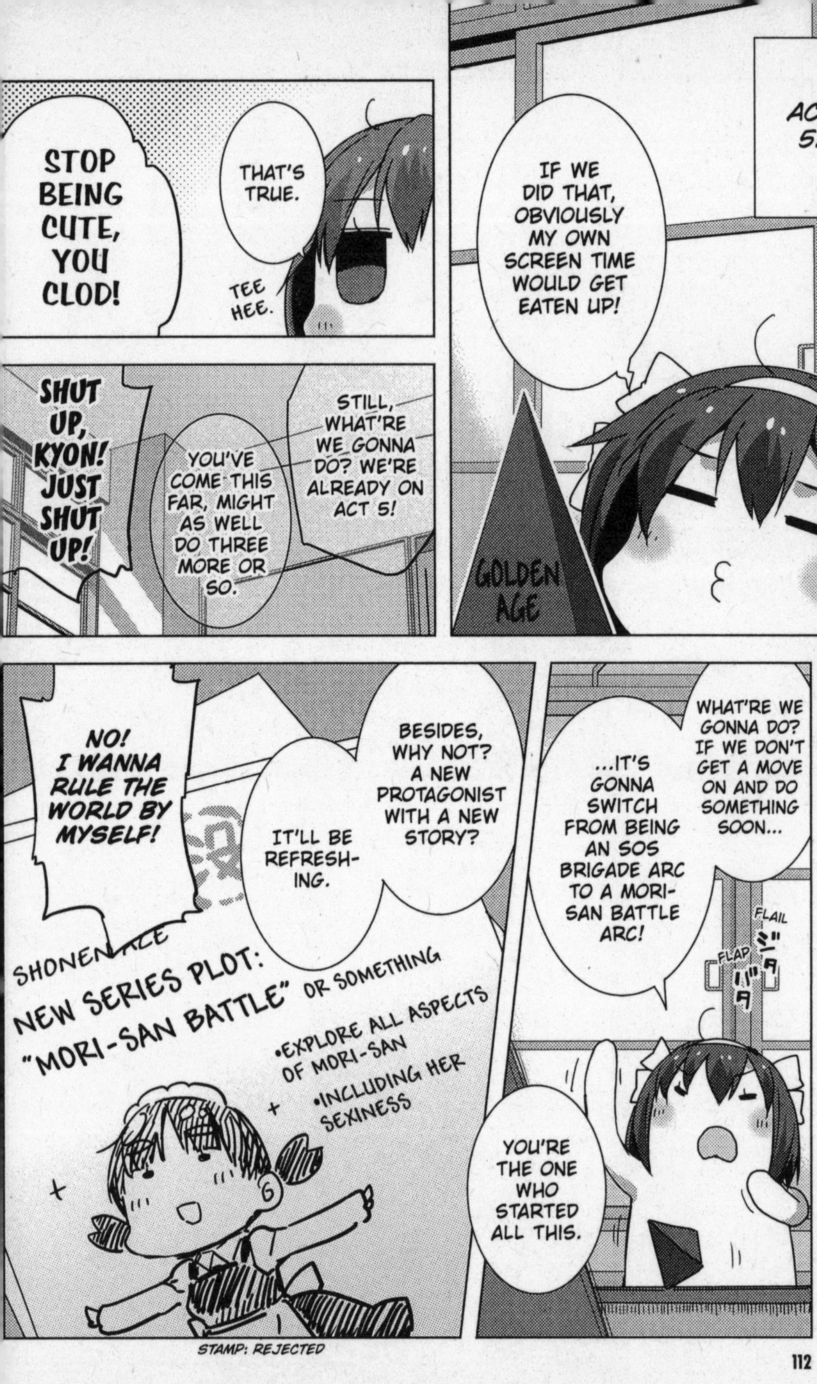
ACT 5.
IF WE DID THAT, OBVIOUSLY MY OWN SCREEN TIME WOULD GET EATEN UP!
GOLDEN AGE
THAT'S TRUE.
TEE HEE.
STOP BEING CUTE, YOU CLOD!
STILL, WHAT'RE WE GONNA DO? WE'RE ALREADY ON ACT 5!
YOU'VE COME THIS FAR, MIGHT AS WELL DO THREE MORE OR SO.
SHUT UP, KYON! JUST SHUT UP!
WHAT'RE WE GONNA DO? IF WE DON'T GET A MOVE ON AND DO SOMETHING SOON...
...IT'S GONNA SWITCH FROM BEING AN SOS BRIGADE ARC TO A MORI-SAN BATTLE ARC!
FLAIL
FLAP
YOU'RE THE ONE WHO STARTED ALL THIS.
BESIDES, WHY NOT? A NEW PROTAGONIST WITH A NEW STORY?
IT'LL BE REFRESHING.
NO! I WANNA RULE THE WORLD BY MYSELF!
SHONEN ACE
NEW SERIES PLOT:
"MORI-SAN BATTLE" OR SOMETHING
•EXPLORE ALL ASPECTS OF MORI-SAN
•INCLUDING HER SEXINESS

STAMP: REJECTED

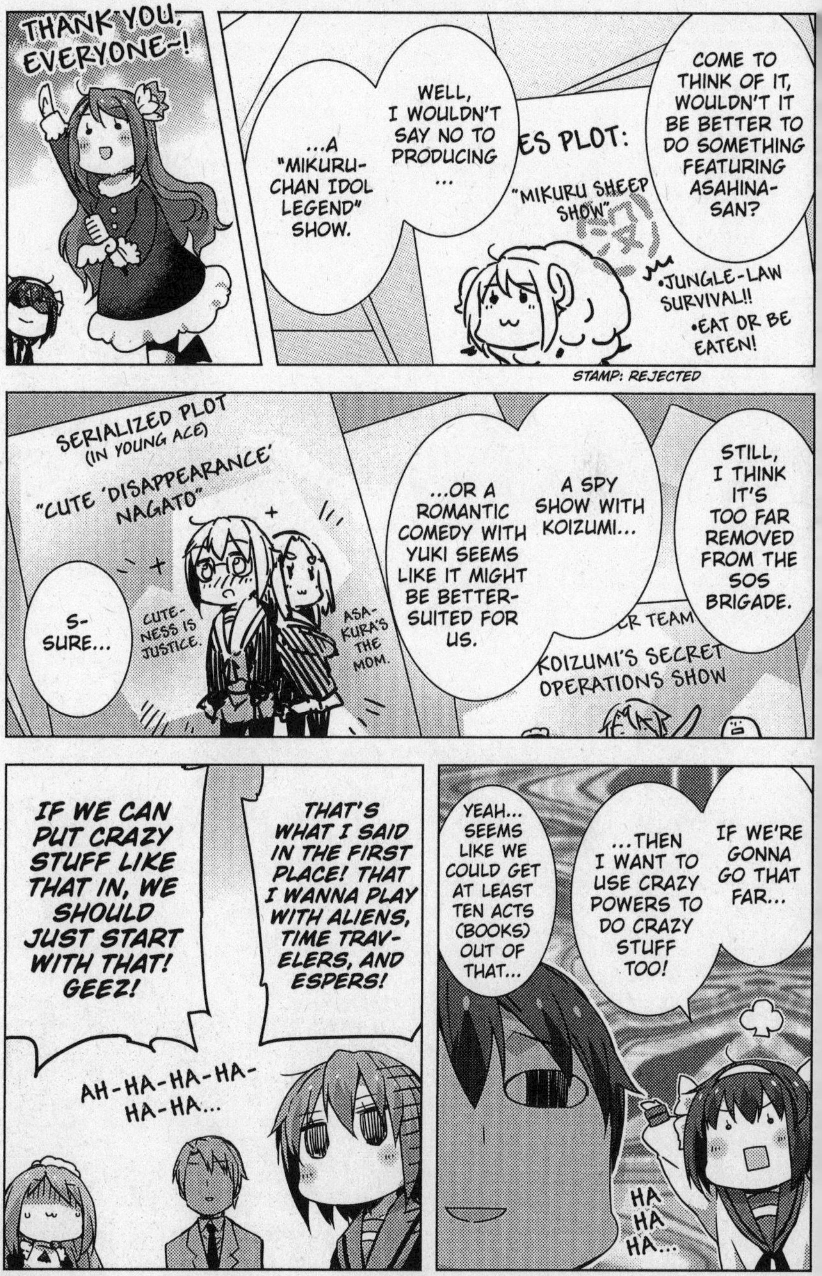
COME TO THINK OF IT, WOULDN'T IT BE BETTER TO DO SOMETHING FEATURING ASAHINA-SAN?
ES PLOT:
"MIKURU SHEEP SHOW"
•JUNGLE-LAW SURVIVAL!!
•EAT OR BE EATEN!
WELL, I WOULDN'T SAY NO TO PRODUCING...
...A "MIKURU-CHAN IDOL LEGEND" SHOW.
THANK YOU, EVERYONE~!
STAMP: REJECTED
STILL, I THINK IT'S TOO FAR REMOVED FROM THE SOS BRIGADE.
A SPY SHOW WITH KOIZUMI...
...OR A ROMANTIC COMEDY WITH YUKI SEEMS LIKE IT MIGHT BE BETTER-SUITED FOR US.
CR TEAM
KOIZUMI'S SECRET OPERATIONS SHOW
SERIALIZED PLOT (IN YOUNG ACE)
"CUTE 'DISAPPEARANCE' NAGATO"
ASA-KURA'S THE MOM.
CUTE-NESS IS JUSTICE.
S-SURE...
IF WE'RE GONNA GO THAT FAR...
...THEN I WANT TO USE CRAZY POWERS TO DO CRAZY STUFF TOO!
YEAH... SEEMS LIKE WE COULD GET AT LEAST TEN ACTS (BOOKS) OUT OF THAT...
HA HA HA...
THAT'S WHAT I SAID IN THE FIRST PLACE! THAT I WANNA PLAY WITH ALIENS, TIME TRAVELERS, AND ESPERS!
IF WE CAN PUT CRAZY STUFF LIKE THAT IN, WE SHOULD JUST START WITH THAT! GEEZ!
AH-HA-HA-HA-HA-HA...

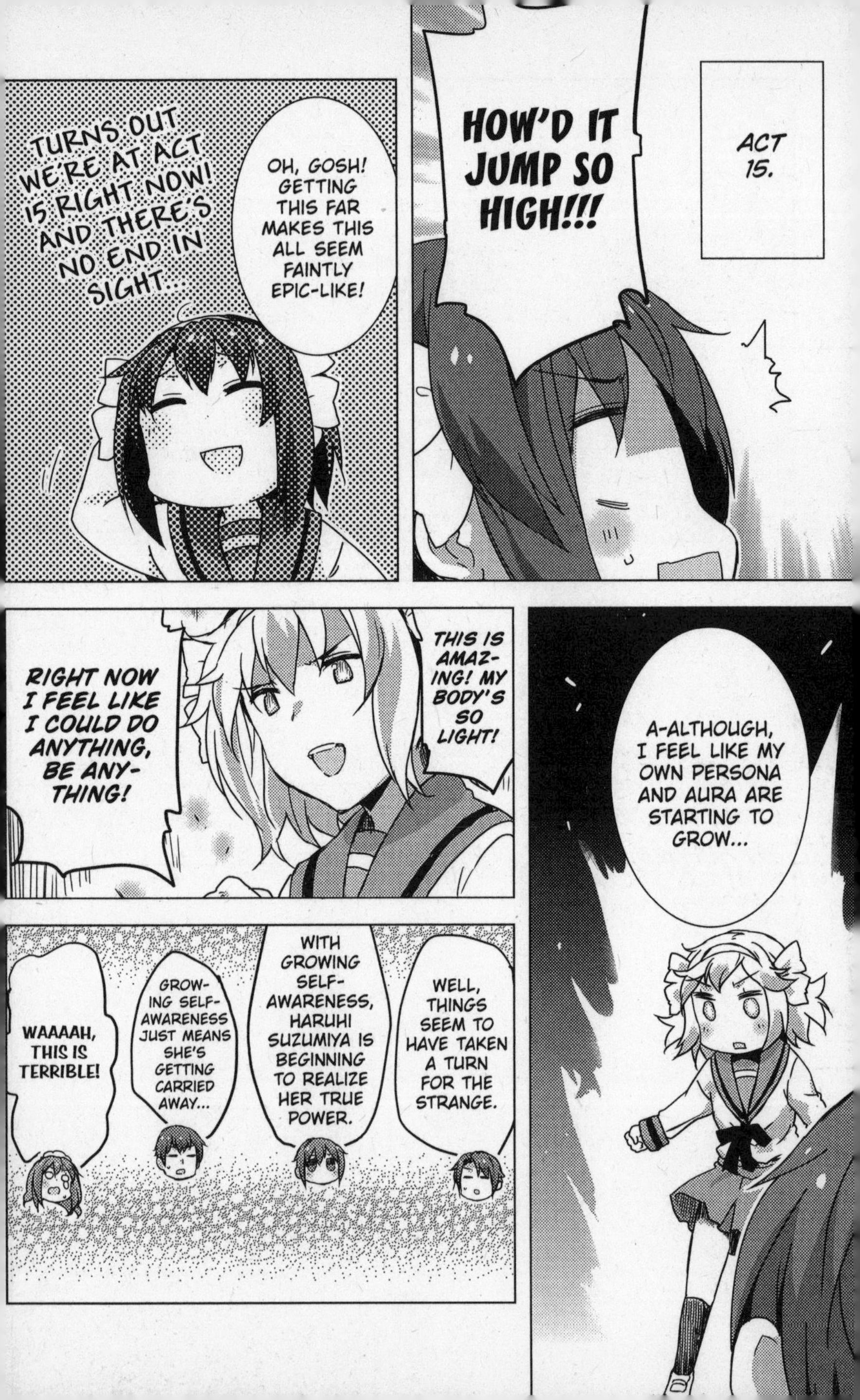
ACT 15.
HOW'D IT JUMP SO HIGH!!!
OH, GOSH! GETTING THIS FAR MAKES THIS ALL SEEM FAINTLY EPIC-LIKE!
TURNS OUT WE'RE AT ACT 15 RIGHT NOW! AND THERE'S NO END IN SIGHT...
A-ALTHOUGH, I FEEL LIKE MY OWN PERSONA AND AURA ARE STARTING TO GROW...
THIS IS AMAZ-ING! MY BODY'S SO LIGHT!
RIGHT NOW I FEEL LIKE I COULD DO ANYTHING, BE ANY-THING!
WELL, THINGS SEEM TO HAVE TAKEN A TURN FOR THE STRANGE.
WITH GROWING SELF-AWARENESS, HARUHI SUZUMIYA IS BEGINNING TO REALIZE HER TRUE POWER.
GROW-ING SELF-AWARENESS JUST MEANS SHE'S GETTING CARRIED AWAY...
WAAAAH, THIS IS TERRIBLE!

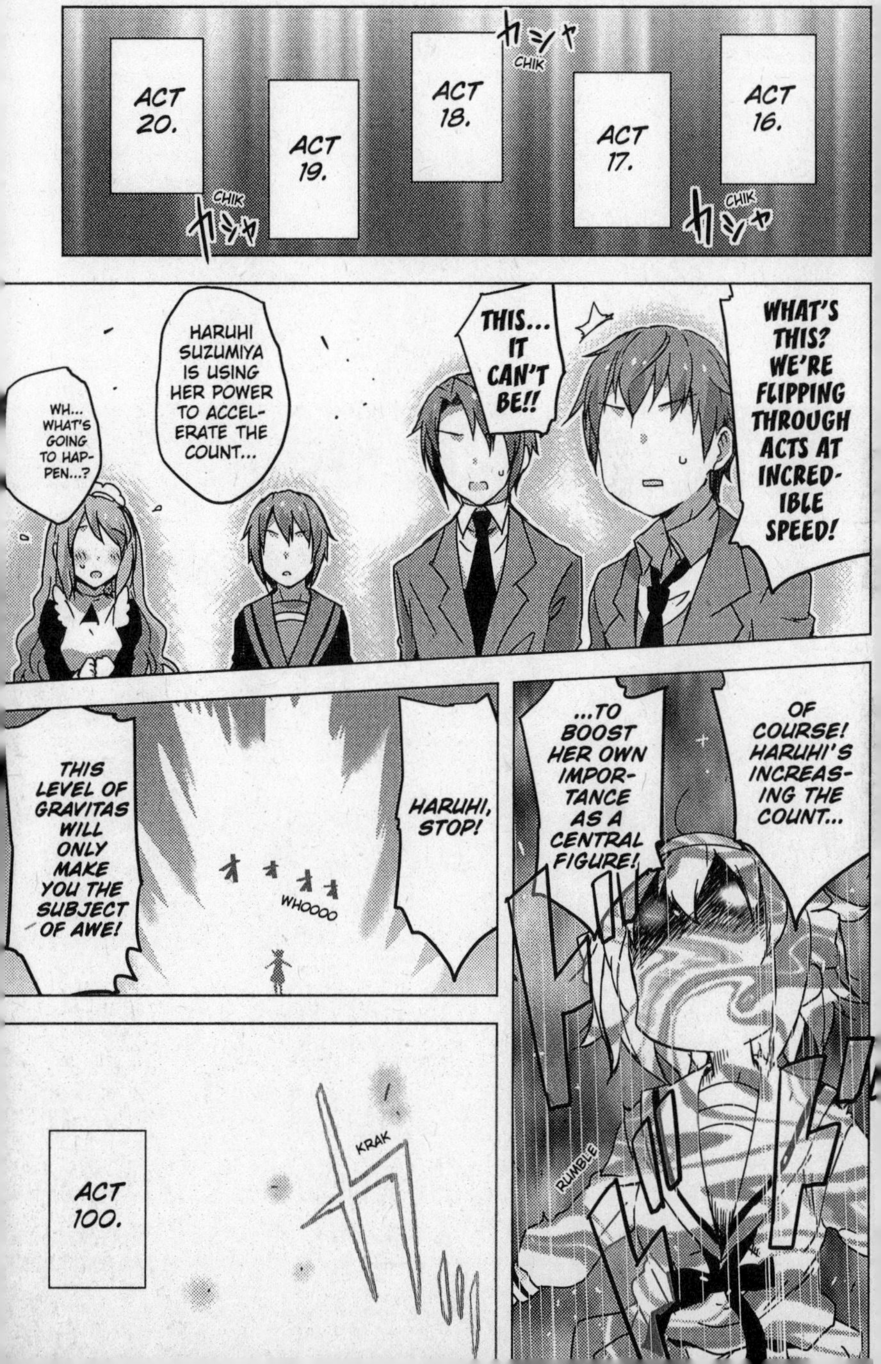
カシャ
CHIK
ACT 16.
ACT 17.
ACT 18.
CHIK
カシャ
ACT 19.
ACT 20.
CHIK
カシャ
WHAT'S THIS? WE'RE FLIPPING THROUGH ACTS AT INCREDIBLE SPEED!
THIS... IT CAN'T BE!!
HARUHI SUZUMIYA IS USING HER POWER TO ACCELERATE THE COUNT...
WH... WHAT'S GOING TO HAPPEN...?
OF COURSE! HARUHI'S INCREASING THE COUNT...
...TO BOOST HER OWN IMPORTANCE AS A CENTRAL FIGURE!
RUMBLE
HARUHI, STOP!
WHOOOO
THIS LEVEL OF GRAVITAS WILL ONLY MAKE YOU THE SUBJECT OF AWE!
KRAK
ACT 100.

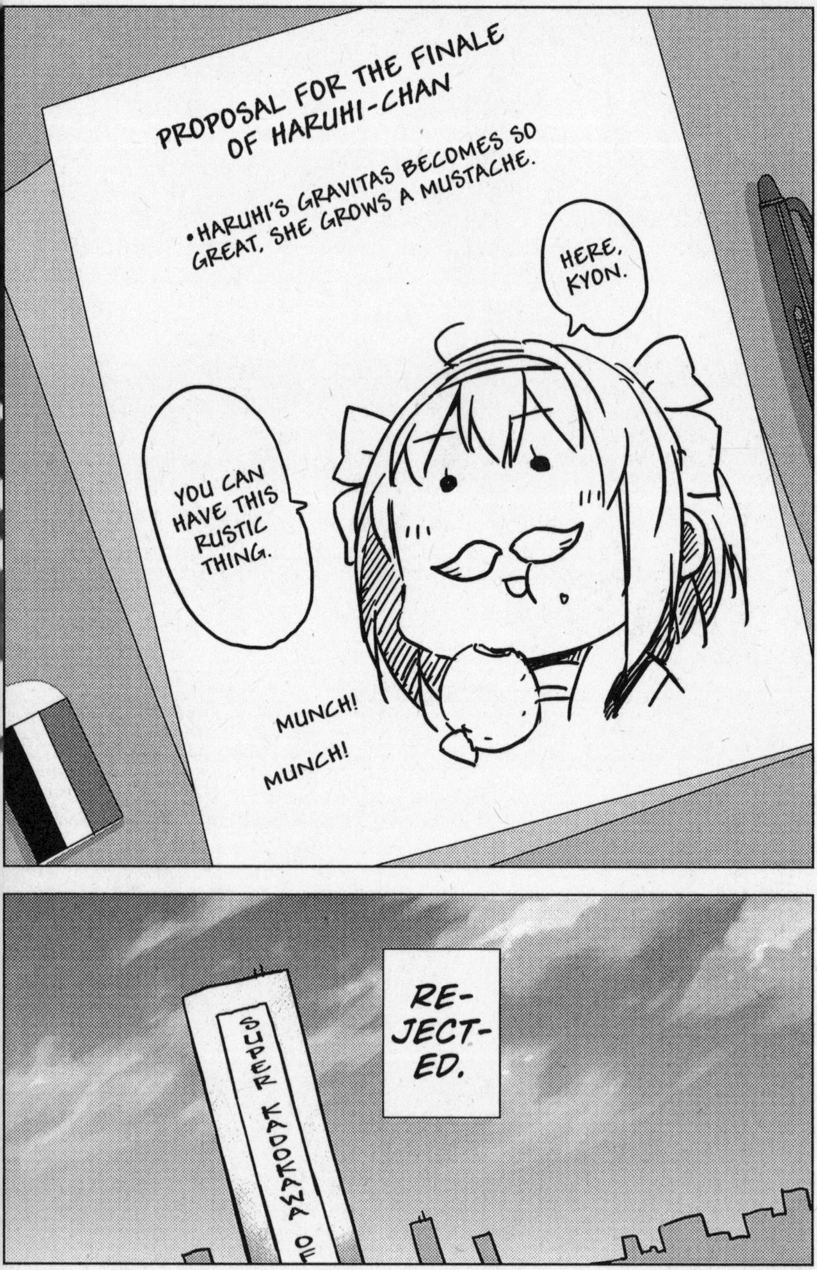
PROPOSAL FOR THE FINALE OF HARUHI-CHAN
•HARUHI'S GRAVITAS BECOMES SO GREAT, SHE GROWS A MUSTACHE.
HERE, KYON.
YOU CAN HAVE THIS RUSTIC THING.
MUNCH! MUNCH!
RE-JECT-ED.
SUPER KADOKAWA OF

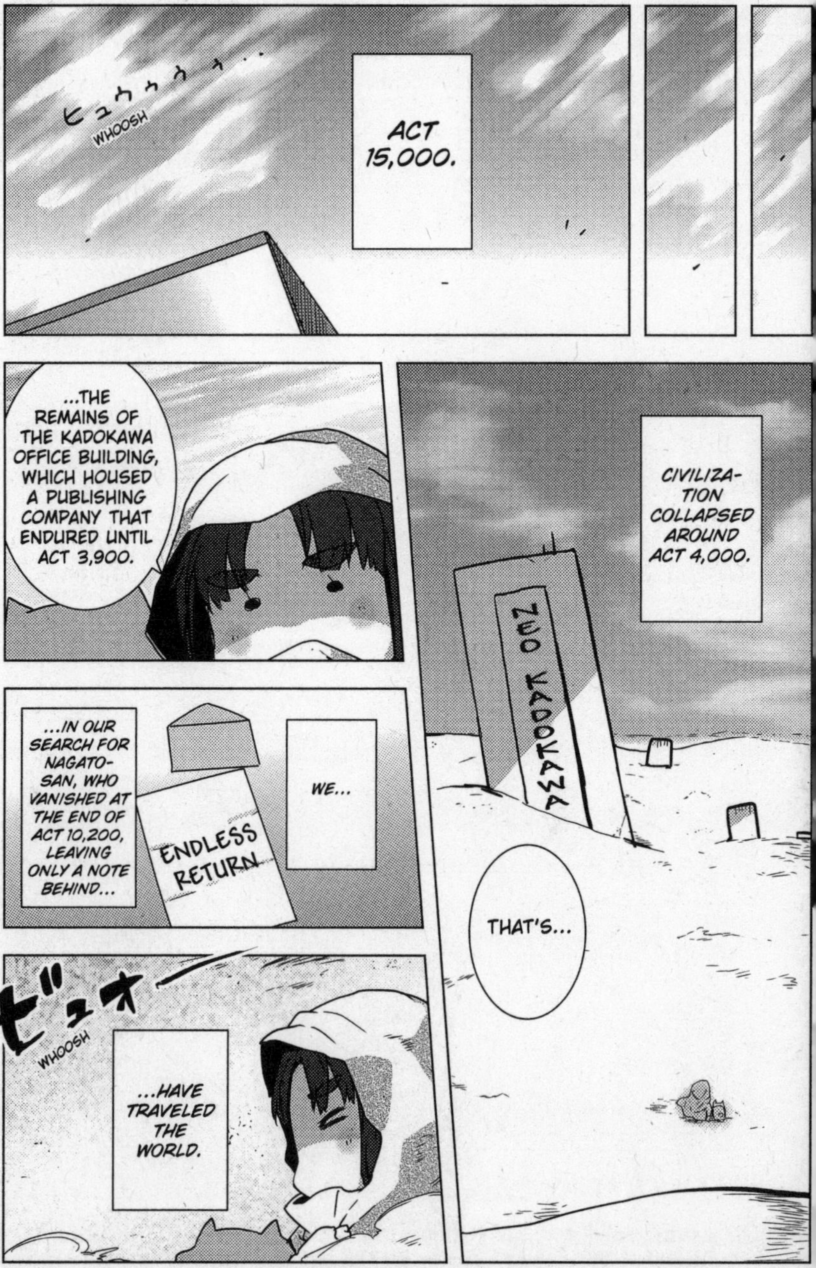
ACT 15,000.
ヒュゥゥゥォ‥
WHOOSH
CIVILIZATION COLLAPSED AROUND ACT 4,000.
NEO KADOKAWA
THAT'S...
...THE REMAINS OF THE KADOKAWA OFFICE BUILDING, WHICH HOUSED A PUBLISHING COMPANY THAT ENDURED UNTIL ACT 3,900.
WE...
...IN OUR SEARCH FOR NAGATO-SAN, WHO VANISHED AT THE END OF ACT 10,200, LEAVING ONLY A NOTE BEHIND...
ENDLESS RETURN
...HAVE TRAVELED THE WORLD.
ビュオ
WHOOSH

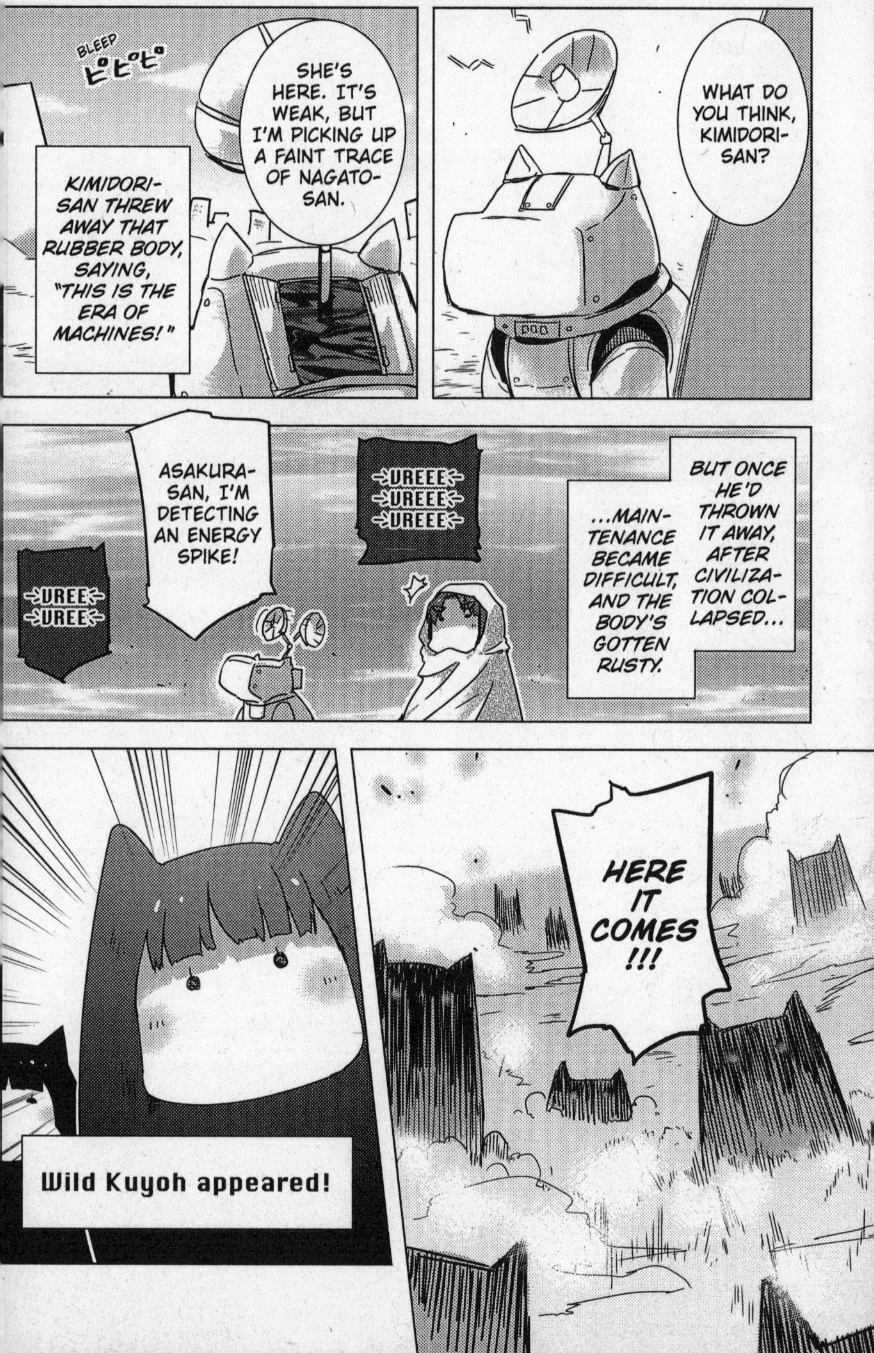
WHAT DO YOU THINK, KIMIDORI-SAN?
SHE'S HERE. IT'S WEAK, BUT I'M PICKING UP A FAINT TRACE OF NAGATO-SAN.
BLEEP
KIMIDORI-SAN THREW AWAY THAT RUBBER BODY, SAYING, "THIS IS THE ERA OF MACHINES!"
BUT ONCE HE'D THROWN IT AWAY, AFTER CIVILIZATION COLLAPSED...
...MAINTENANCE BECAME DIFFICULT, AND THE BODY'S GOTTEN RUSTY.
UREEE UREEE UREEE
ASAKURA-SAN, I'M DETECTING AN ENERGY SPIKE!
UREE UREE
HERE IT COMES!!!
Wild Kuyoh appeared!

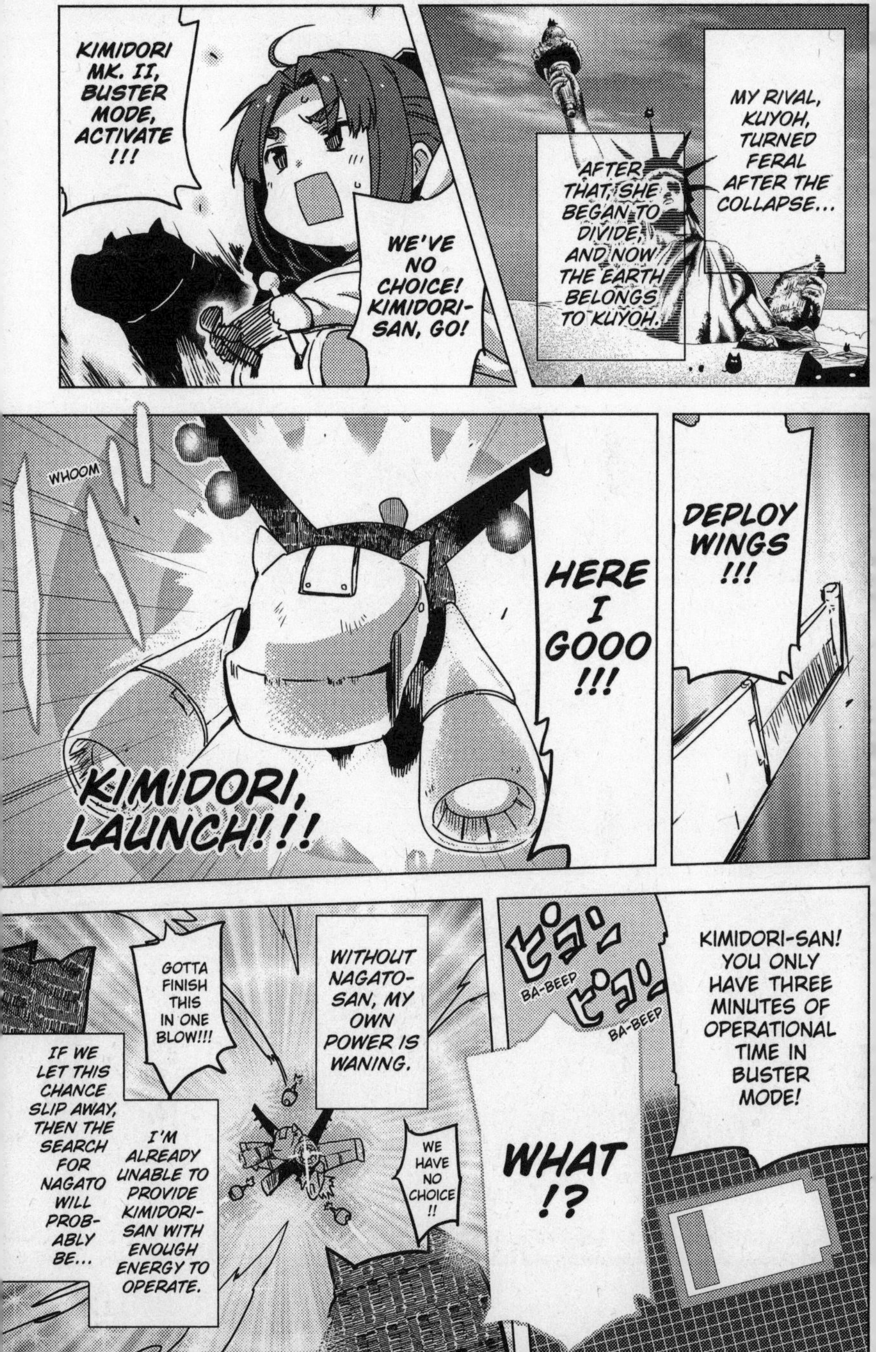
MY RIVAL, KUYOH, TURNED FERAL AFTER THE COLLAPSE...
AFTER THAT, SHE BEGAN TO DIVIDE, AND NOW THE EARTH BELONGS TO KUYOH.
WE'VE NO CHOICE! KIMIDORI-SAN, GO!
KIMIDORI MK. II, BUSTER MODE, ACTIVATE!!!
DEPLOY WINGS!!!
HERE I GOOO!!!
WHOOM
KIMIDORI, LAUNCH!!!
KIMIDORI-SAN! YOU ONLY HAVE THREE MINUTES OF OPERATIONAL TIME IN BUSTER MODE!
ピコン
BA-BEEP
ピコン
BA-BEEP
WHAT!?
WITHOUT NAGATO-SAN, MY OWN POWER IS WANING.
GOTTA FINISH THIS IN ONE BLOW!!!
WE HAVE NO CHOICE!!
I'M ALREADY UNABLE TO PROVIDE KIMIDORI-SAN WITH ENOUGH ENERGY TO OPERATE.
IF WE LET THIS CHANCE SLIP AWAY, THEN THE SEARCH FOR NAGATO WILL PROBABLY BE...

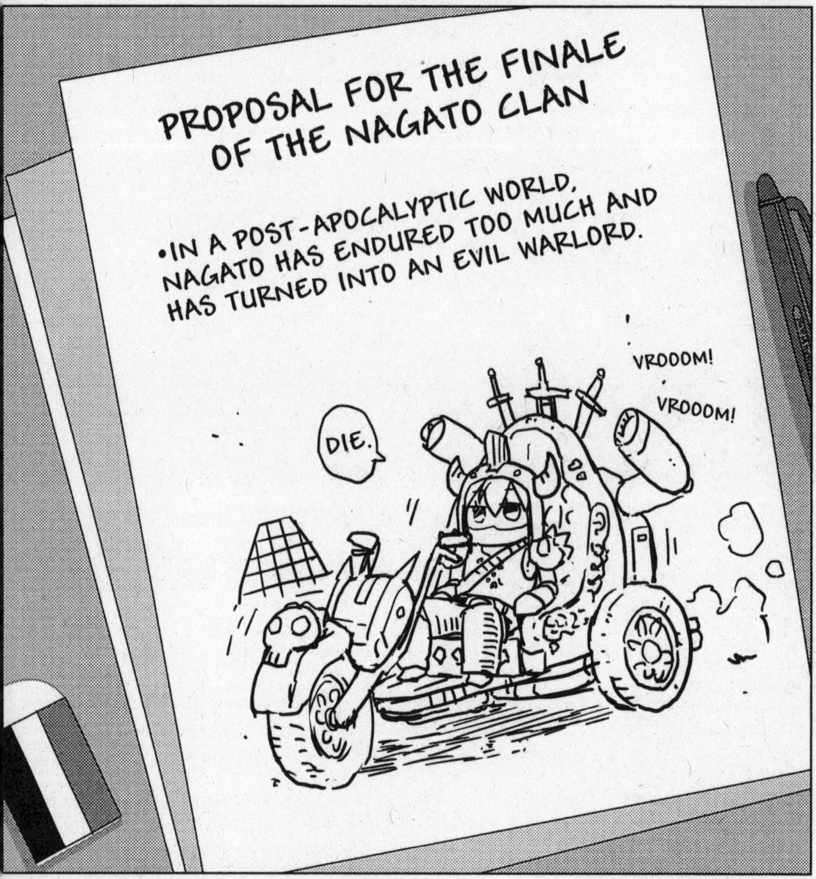
PROPOSAL FOR THE FINALE OF THE NAGATO CLAN
•IN A POST-APOCALYPTIC WORLD, NAGATO HAS ENDURED TOO MUCH AND HAS TURNED INTO AN EVIL WARLORD.
VROOOM!
VROOOM!
DIE.

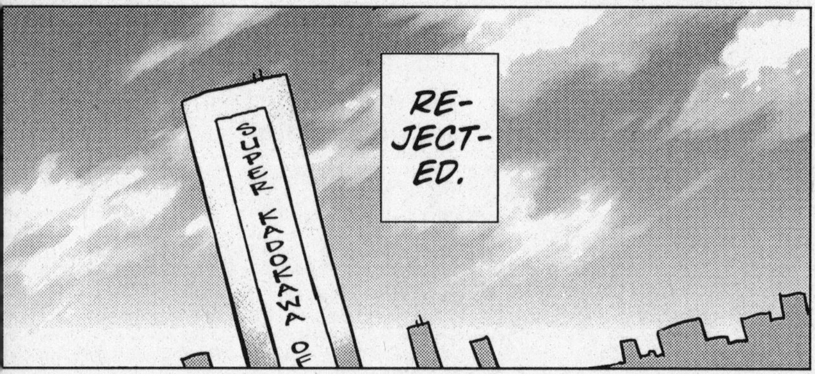
RE-JECT-ED.
SUPER KADOKAWA OF

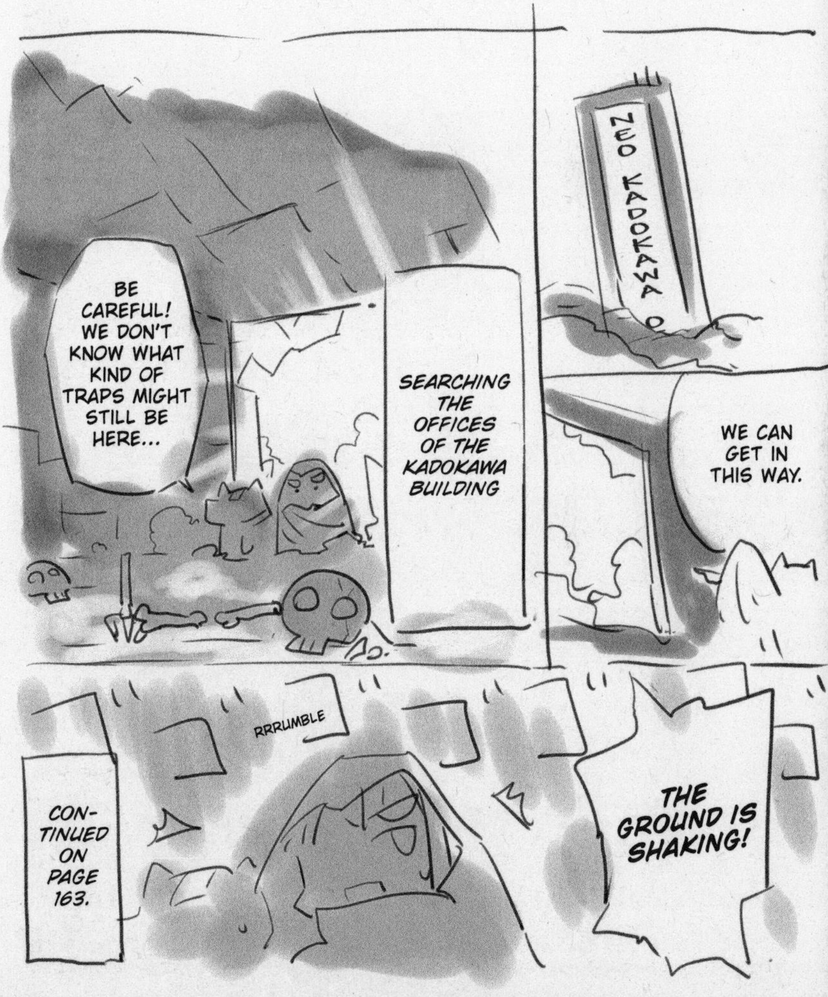
NEO KADOKAWA
WE CAN GET IN THIS WAY.
SEARCHING THE OFFICES OF THE KADOKAWA BUILDING
BE CAREFUL! WE DON'T KNOW WHAT KIND OF TRAPS MIGHT STILL BE HERE...
THE GROUND IS SHAKING!
RRRUMBLE
CON-TINUED ON PAGE 163.

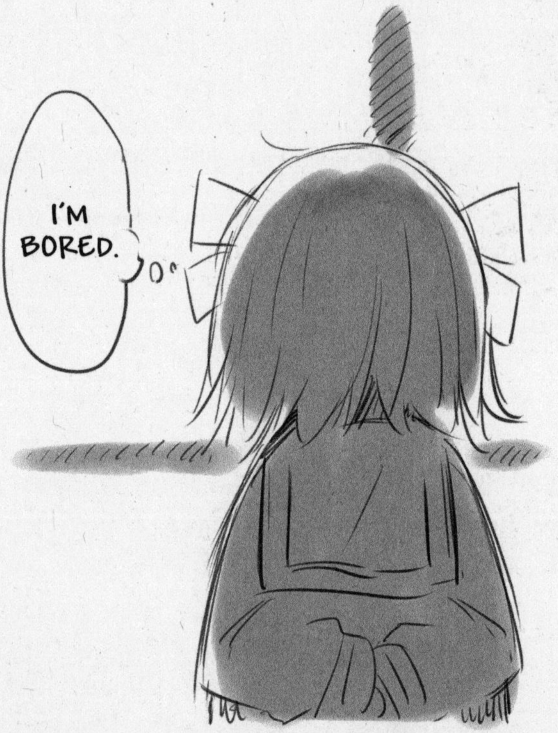
I'M BORED.

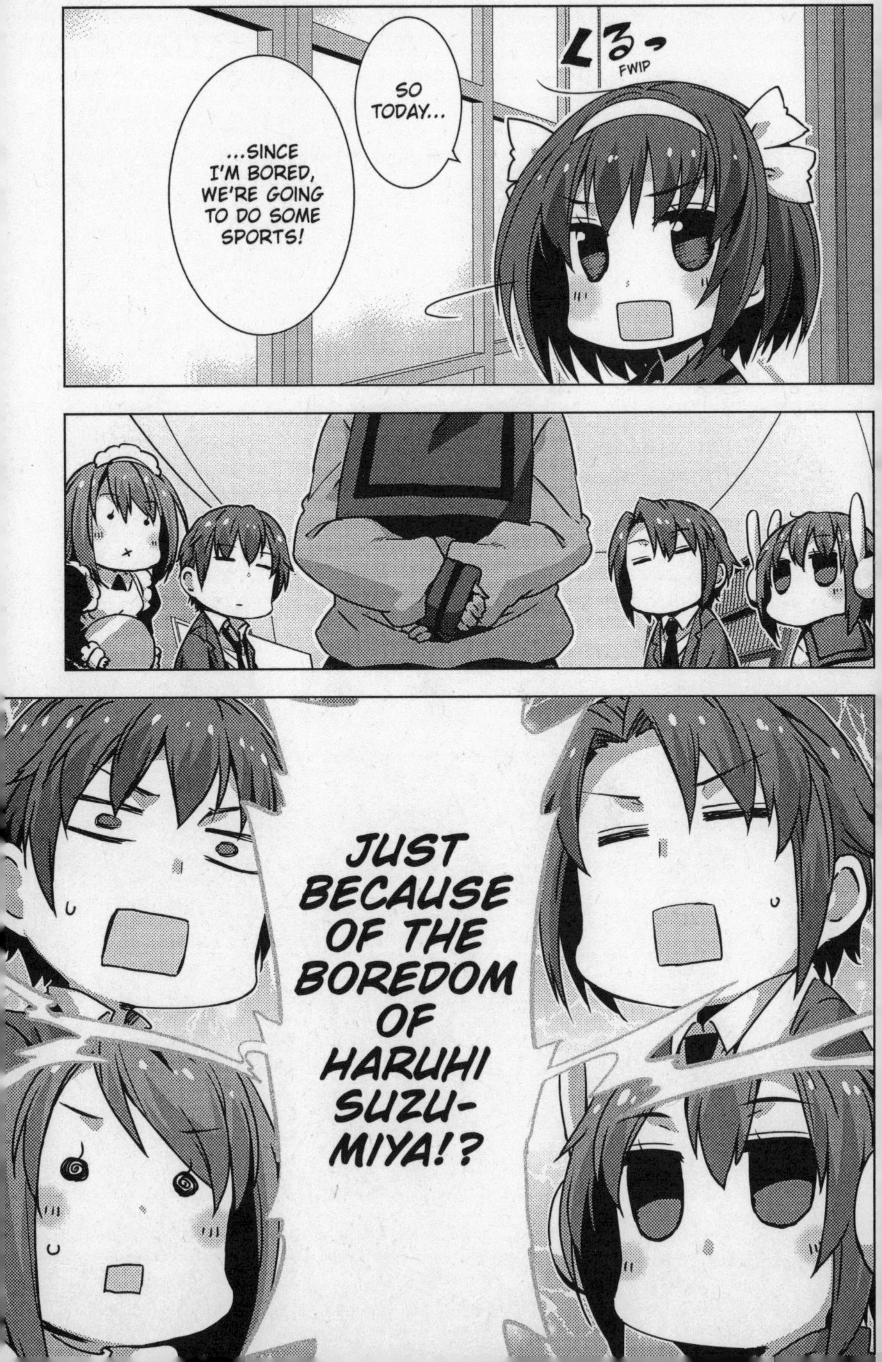

くるっ
FWIP
SO TODAY...
...SINCE I'M BORED, WE'RE GOING TO DO SOME SPORTS!
JUST BECAUSE OF THE BOREDOM OF HARUHI SUZU-MIYA!?

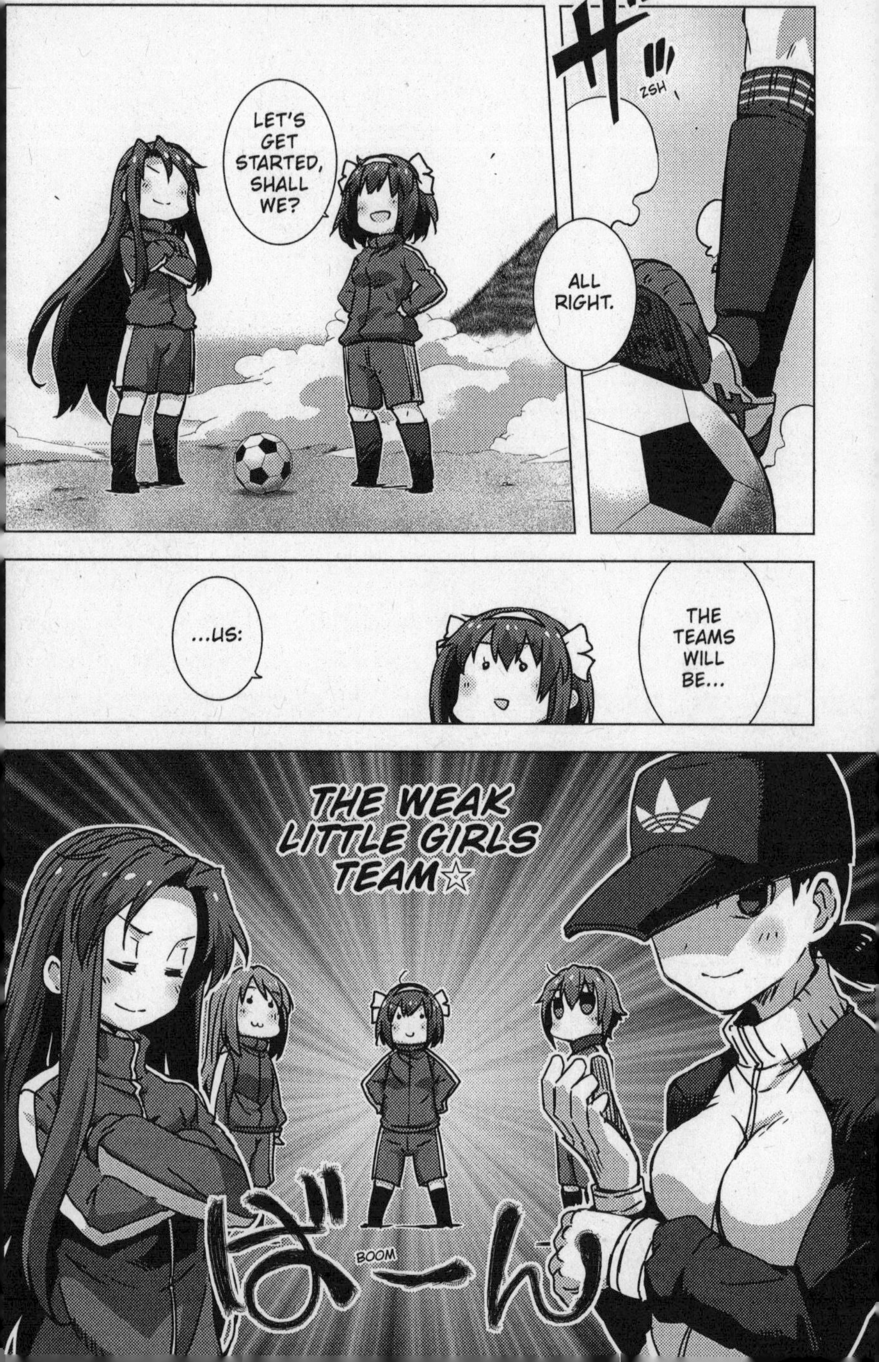
ザ
ZSH
ALL RIGHT.
LET'S GET STARTED, SHALL WE?
THE TEAMS WILL BE...
...US:
THE WEAK LITTLE GIRLS TEAM☆
ばーん
BOOM

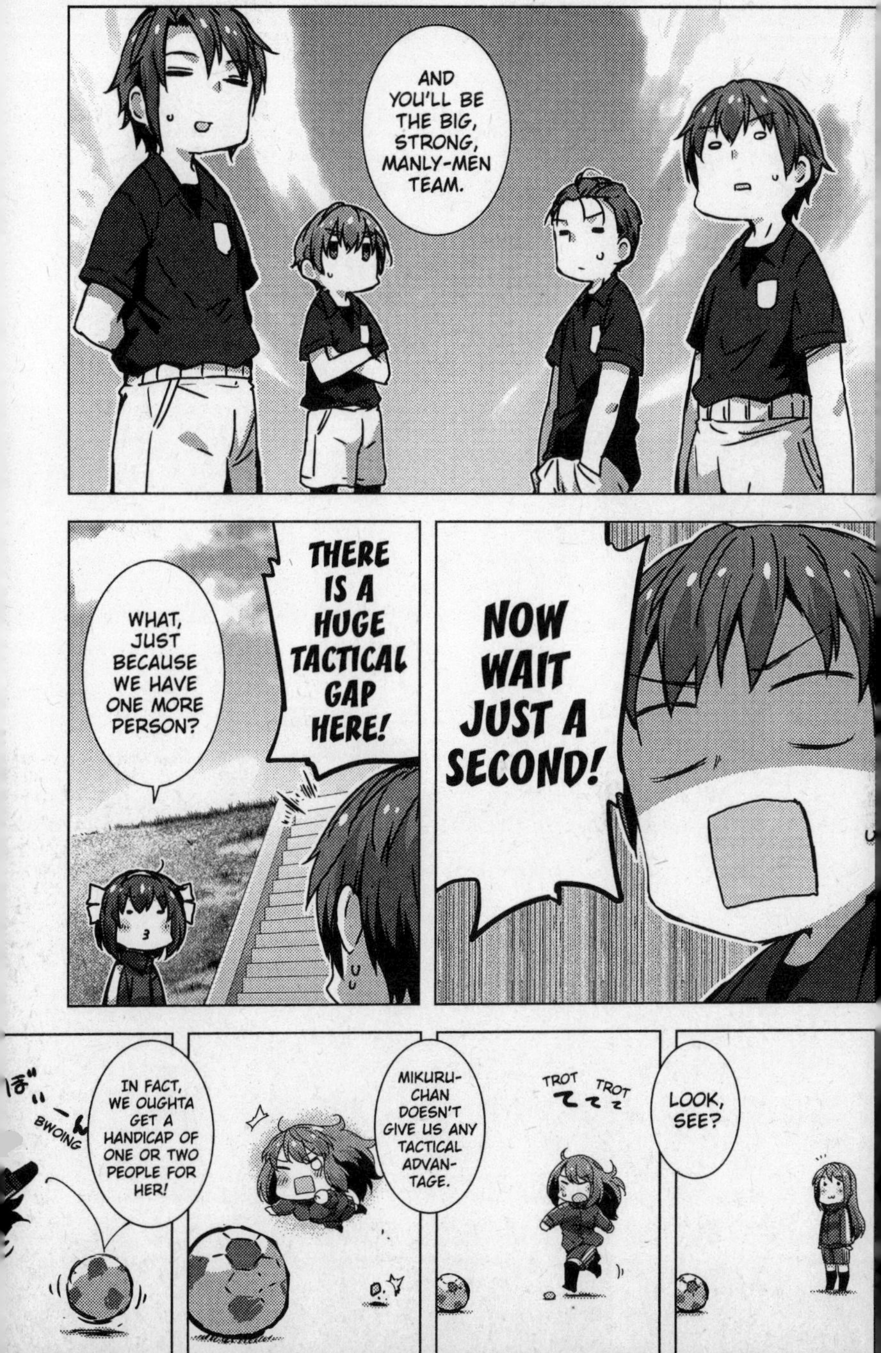
AND YOU'LL BE THE BIG, STRONG, MANLY-MEN TEAM.
NOW WAIT JUST A SECOND!
THERE IS A HUGE TACTICAL GAP HERE!
WHAT, JUST BECAUSE WE HAVE ONE MORE PERSON?
LOOK, SEE?
TROT TROT
MIKURU-CHAN DOESN'T GIVE US ANY TACTICAL ADVANTAGE.
IN FACT, WE OUGHTA GET A HANDICAP OF ONE OR TWO PEOPLE FOR HER!
BWOING

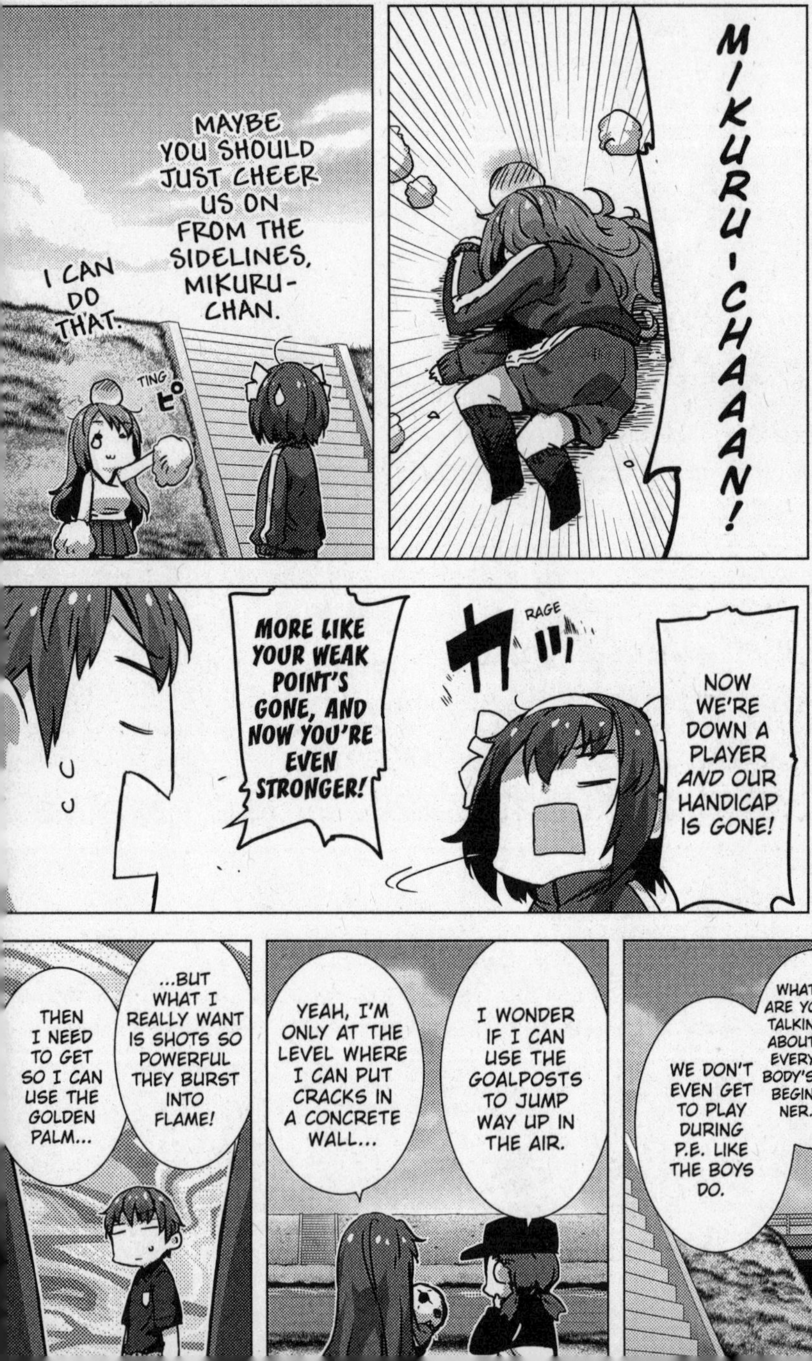
MIKURU-CHAAAAN!
MAYBE YOU SHOULD JUST CHEER US ON FROM THE SIDELINES, MIKURU-CHAN.
I CAN DO THAT.
TING
NOW WE'RE DOWN A PLAYER AND OUR HANDICAP IS GONE!
RAGE
MORE LIKE YOUR WEAK POINT'S GONE, AND NOW YOU'RE EVEN STRONGER!
WHAT ARE YOU TALKING ABOUT? EVERYBODY'S A BEGINNER.
WE DON'T EVEN GET TO PLAY DURING P.E. LIKE THE BOYS DO.
I WONDER IF I CAN USE THE GOALPOSTS TO JUMP WAY UP IN THE AIR.
YEAH, I'M ONLY AT THE LEVEL WHERE I CAN PUT CRACKS IN A CONCRETE WALL...
...BUT WHAT I REALLY WANT IS SHOTS SO POWERFUL THEY BURST INTO FLAME!
THEN I NEED TO GET SO I CAN USE THE GOLDEN PALM...

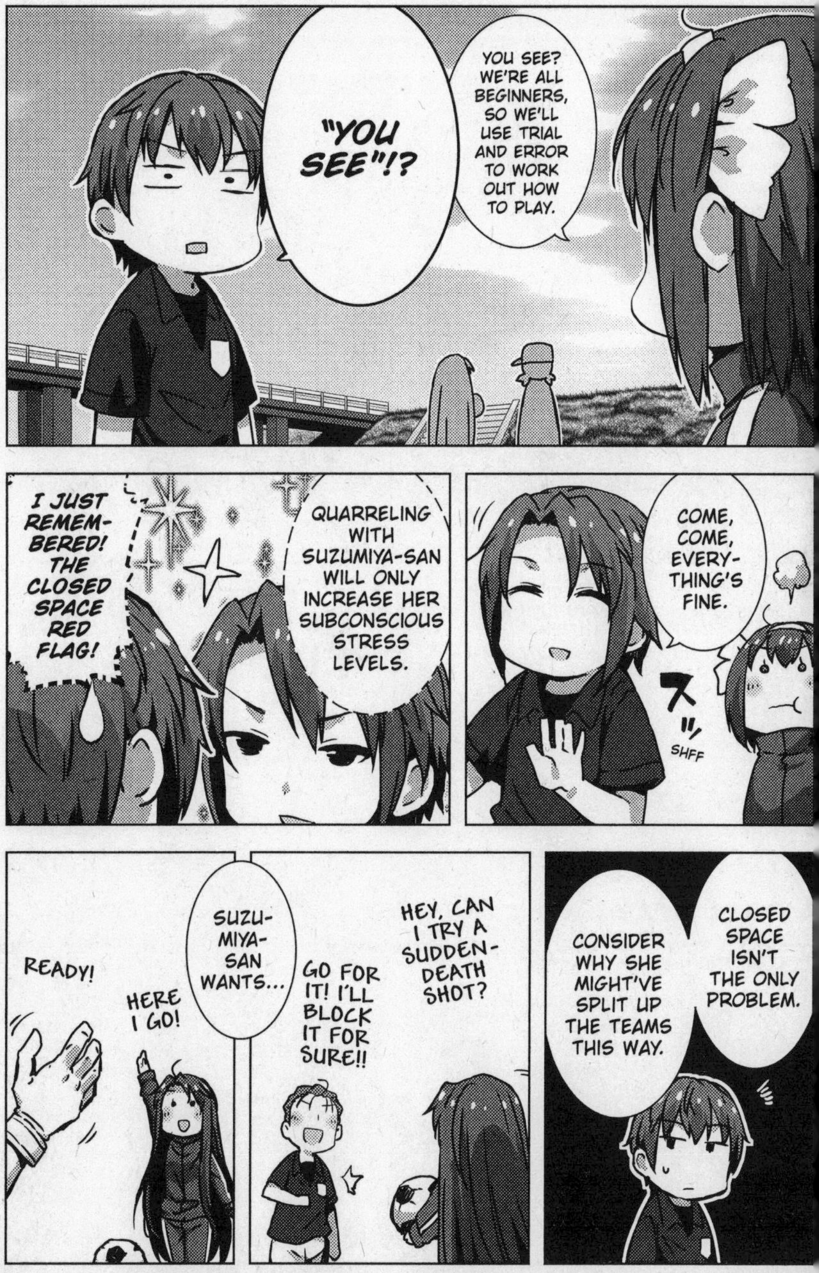
YOU SEE? WE'RE ALL BEGINNERS, SO WE'LL USE TRIAL AND ERROR TO WORK OUT HOW TO PLAY.
"YOU SEE"!?
COME, COME, EVERYTHING'S FINE.
SHFF
QUARRELING WITH SUZUMIYA-SAN WILL ONLY INCREASE HER SUBCONSCIOUS STRESS LEVELS.
I JUST REMEMBERED! THE CLOSED SPACE RED FLAG!
CLOSED SPACE ISN'T THE ONLY PROBLEM.
CONSIDER WHY SHE MIGHT'VE SPLIT UP THE TEAMS THIS WAY.
HEY, CAN I TRY A SUDDEN-DEATH SHOT?
SUZUMIYA-SAN WANTS...
GO FOR IT! I'LL BLOCK IT FOR SURE!!
HERE I GO!
READY!

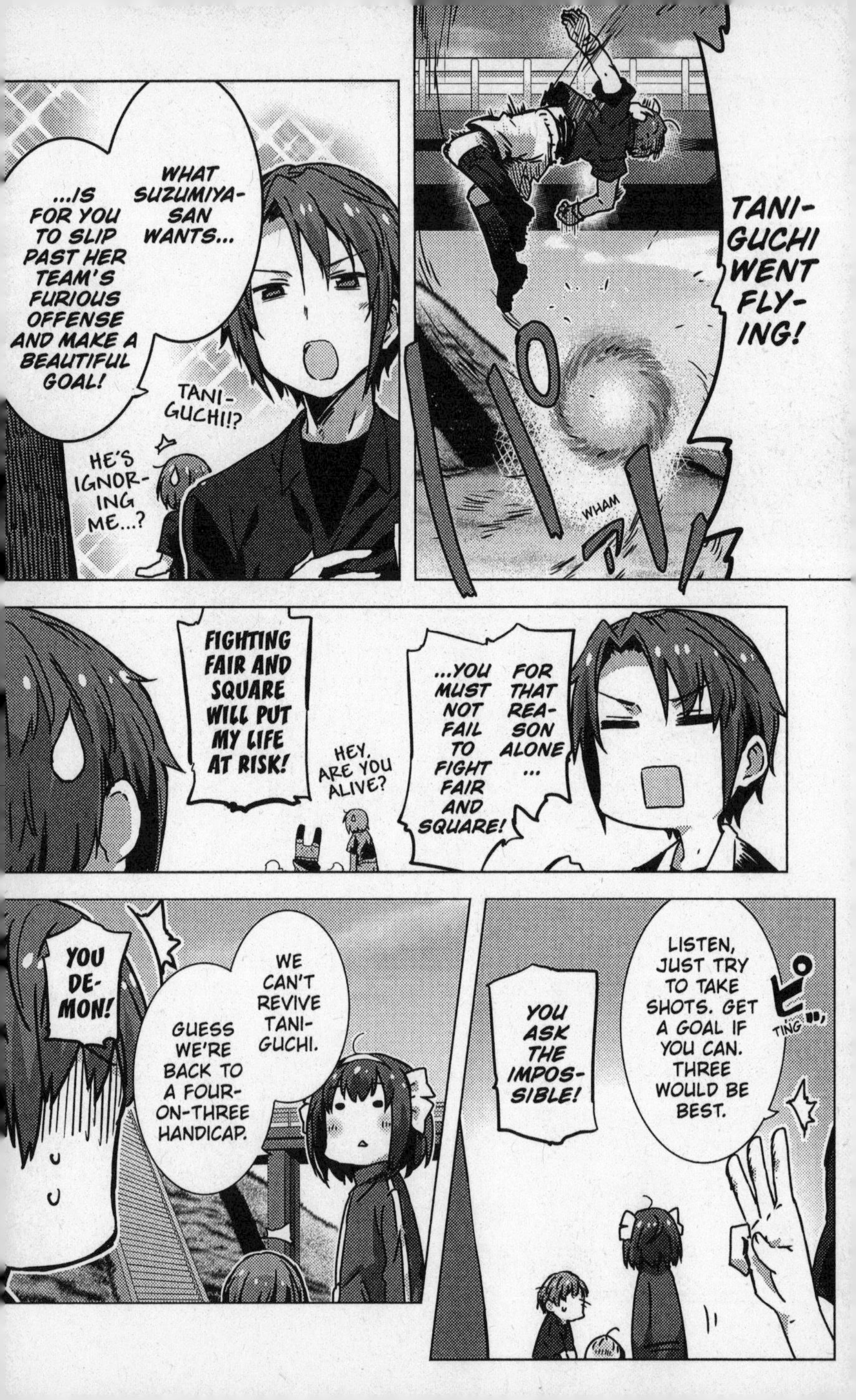
TANI-GUCHI WENT FLY-ING!
WHAM
WHAT SUZUMIYA-SAN WANTS...
...IS FOR YOU TO SLIP PAST HER TEAM'S FURIOUS OFFENSE AND MAKE A BEAUTIFUL GOAL!
TANI-GUCHI!?
HE'S IGNOR-ING ME...?
FOR THAT REA-SON ALONE...
...YOU MUST NOT FAIL TO FIGHT FAIR AND SQUARE!
HEY, ARE YOU ALIVE?
FIGHTING FAIR AND SQUARE WILL PUT MY LIFE AT RISK!
LISTEN, JUST TRY TO TAKE SHOTS. GET A GOAL IF YOU CAN. THREE WOULD BE BEST.
TING
YOU ASK THE IMPOS-SIBLE!
WE CAN'T REVIVE TANI-GUCHI.
GUESS WE'RE BACK TO A FOUR-ON-THREE HANDICAP.
YOU DE-MON!

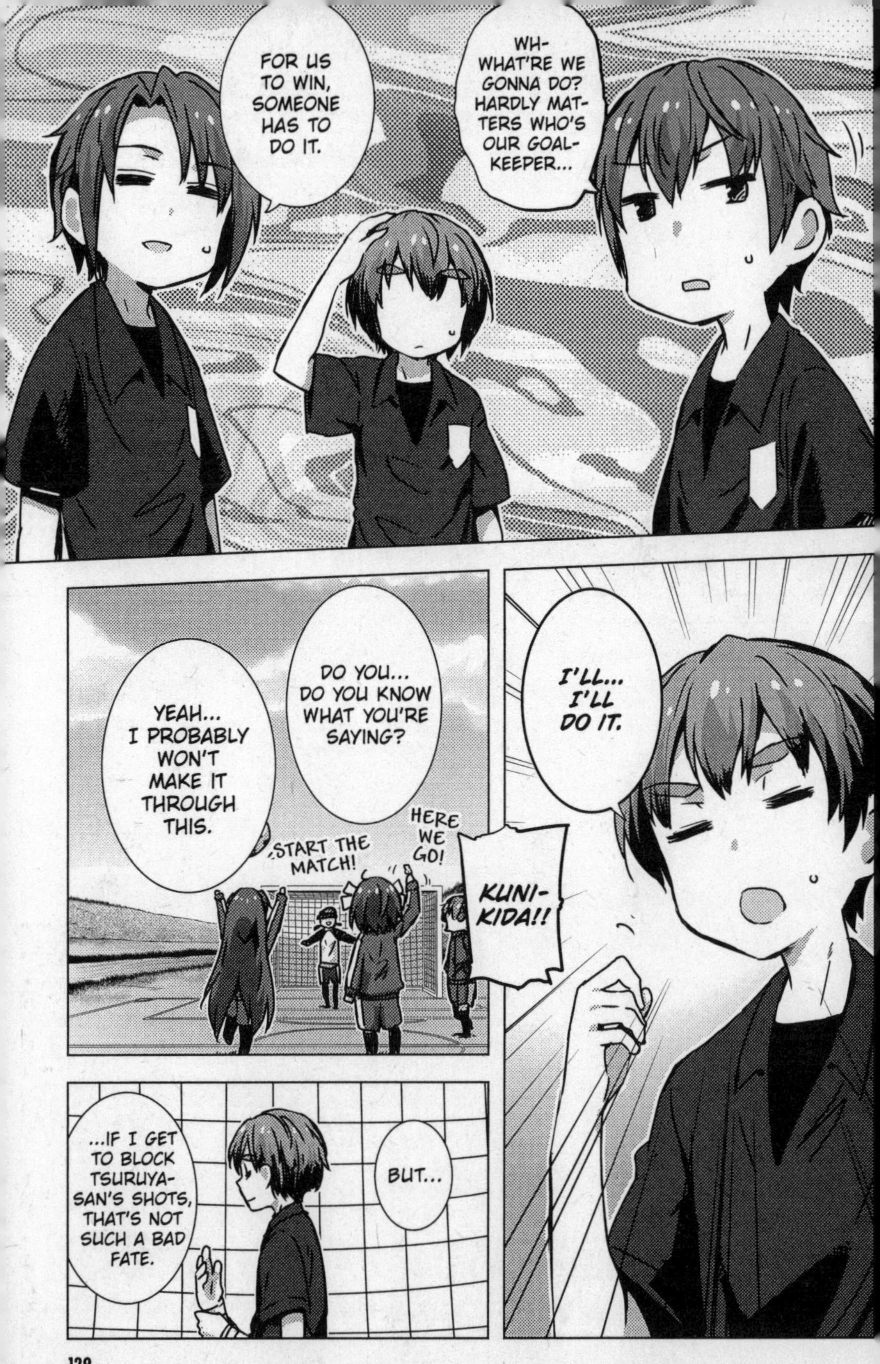
WH- WHAT'RE WE GONNA DO? HARDLY MATTERS WHO'S OUR GOALKEEPER...
FOR US TO WIN, SOMEONE HAS TO DO IT.
I'LL... I'LL DO IT.
KUNI-KIDA!!
DO YOU... DO YOU KNOW WHAT YOU'RE SAYING?
YEAH... I PROBABLY WON'T MAKE IT THROUGH THIS.
HERE WE GO!
START THE MATCH!
BUT...
...IF I GET TO BLOCK TSURUYA-SAN'S SHOTS, THAT'S NOT SUCH A BAD FATE.

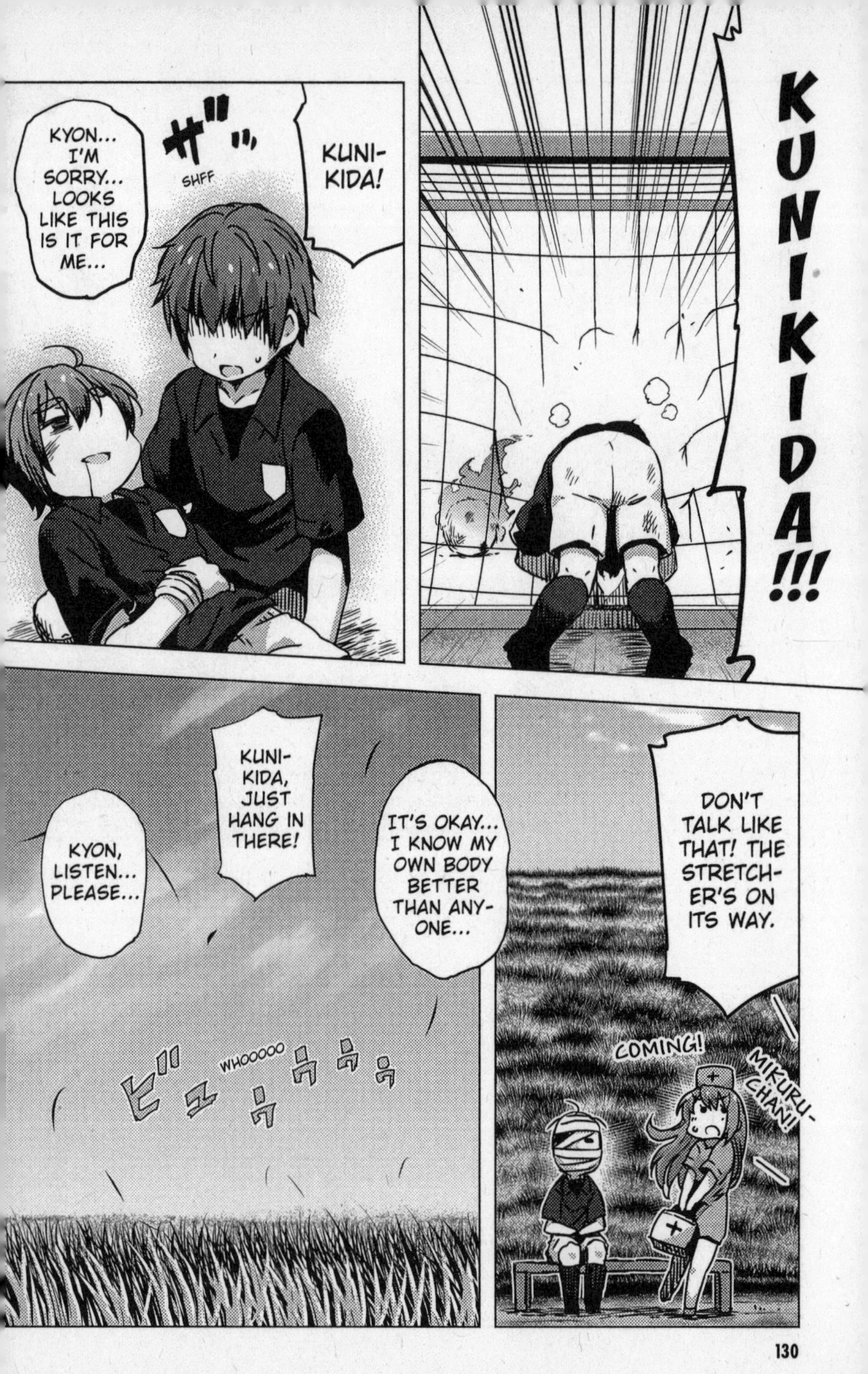
KUNIKIDA!!!
KUNI-KIDA!
SHFF
KYON... I'M SORRY... LOOKS LIKE THIS IS IT FOR ME...
DON'T TALK LIKE THAT! THE STRETCH-ER'S ON ITS WAY.
MIKURU-CHAN!
COMING!
IT'S OKAY... I KNOW MY OWN BODY BETTER THAN ANY-ONE...
KUNI-KIDA, JUST HANG IN THERE!
KYON, LISTEN... PLEASE...
WHOOOOO

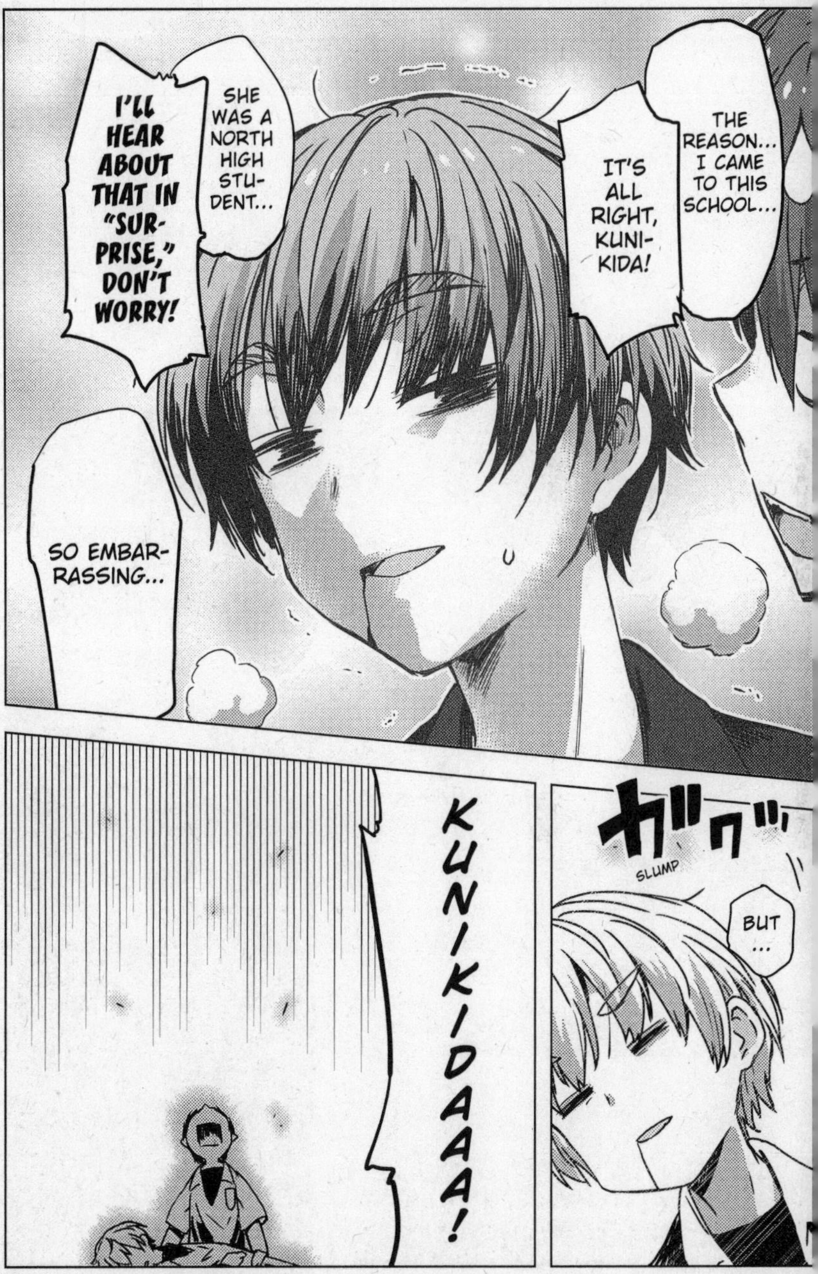
THE REASON... I CAME TO THIS SCHOOL...
IT'S ALL RIGHT, KUNIKIDA!
SHE WAS A NORTH HIGH STUDENT...
I'LL HEAR ABOUT THAT IN "SURPRISE," DON'T WORRY!
SO EMBARRASSING...
ガクッ
SLUMP
BUT...
KUNIKIDAAAA!

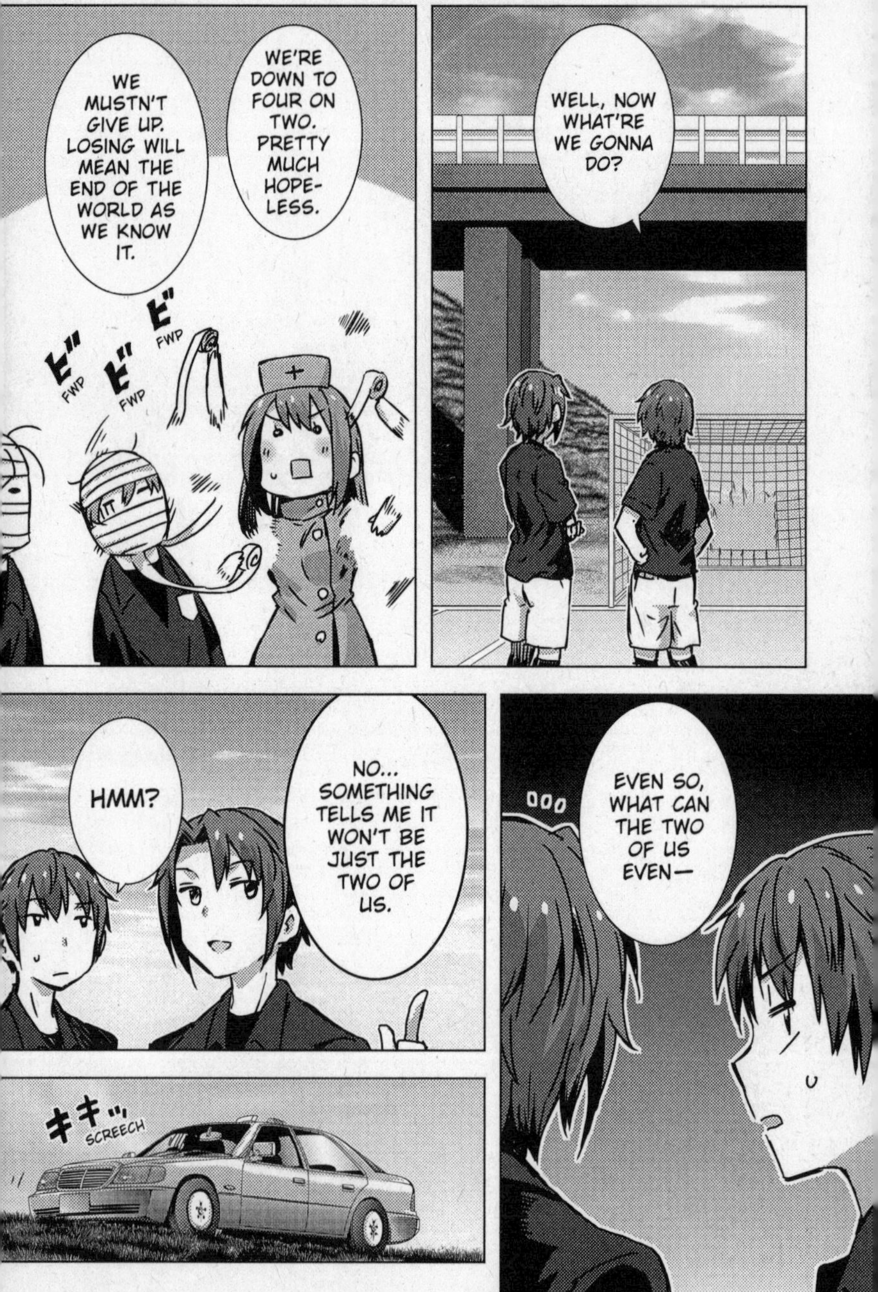
WELL, NOW WHAT'RE WE GONNA DO?
WE'RE DOWN TO FOUR ON TWO. PRETTY MUCH HOPE-LESS.
WE MUSTN'T GIVE UP. LOSING WILL MEAN THE END OF THE WORLD AS WE KNOW IT.
ビ FWP
ビ FWP
ビ FWP
EVEN SO, WHAT CAN THE TWO OF US EVEN—
NO... SOMETHING TELLS ME IT WON'T BE JUST THE TWO OF US.
HMM?
キキッ SCREECH

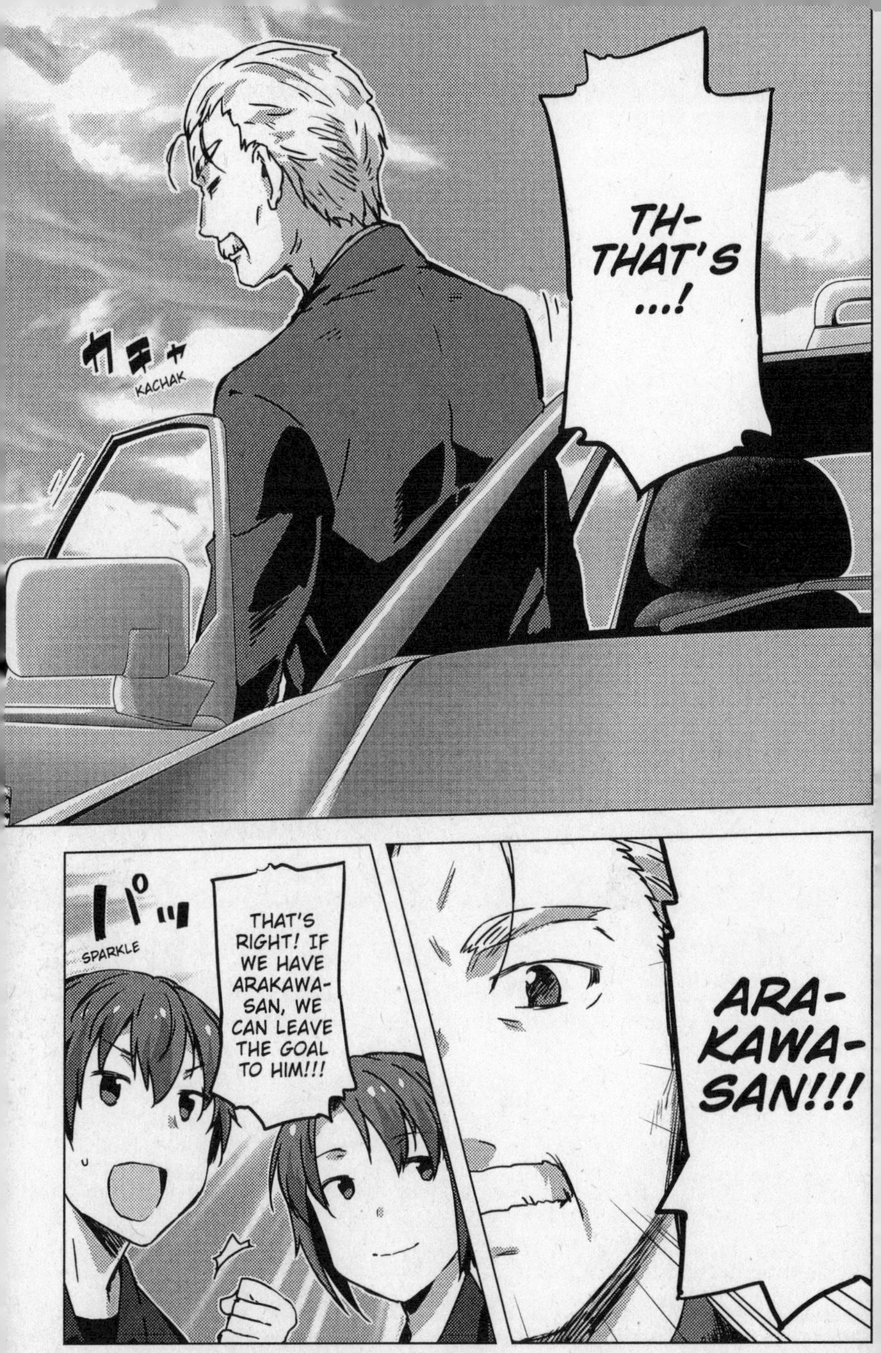
TH- THAT'S ...!
カチャ
KACHAK
ARA- KAWA- SAN!!!
パッ
SPARKLE
THAT'S RIGHT! IF WE HAVE ARAKAWA-SAN, WE CAN LEAVE THE GOAL TO HIM!!!

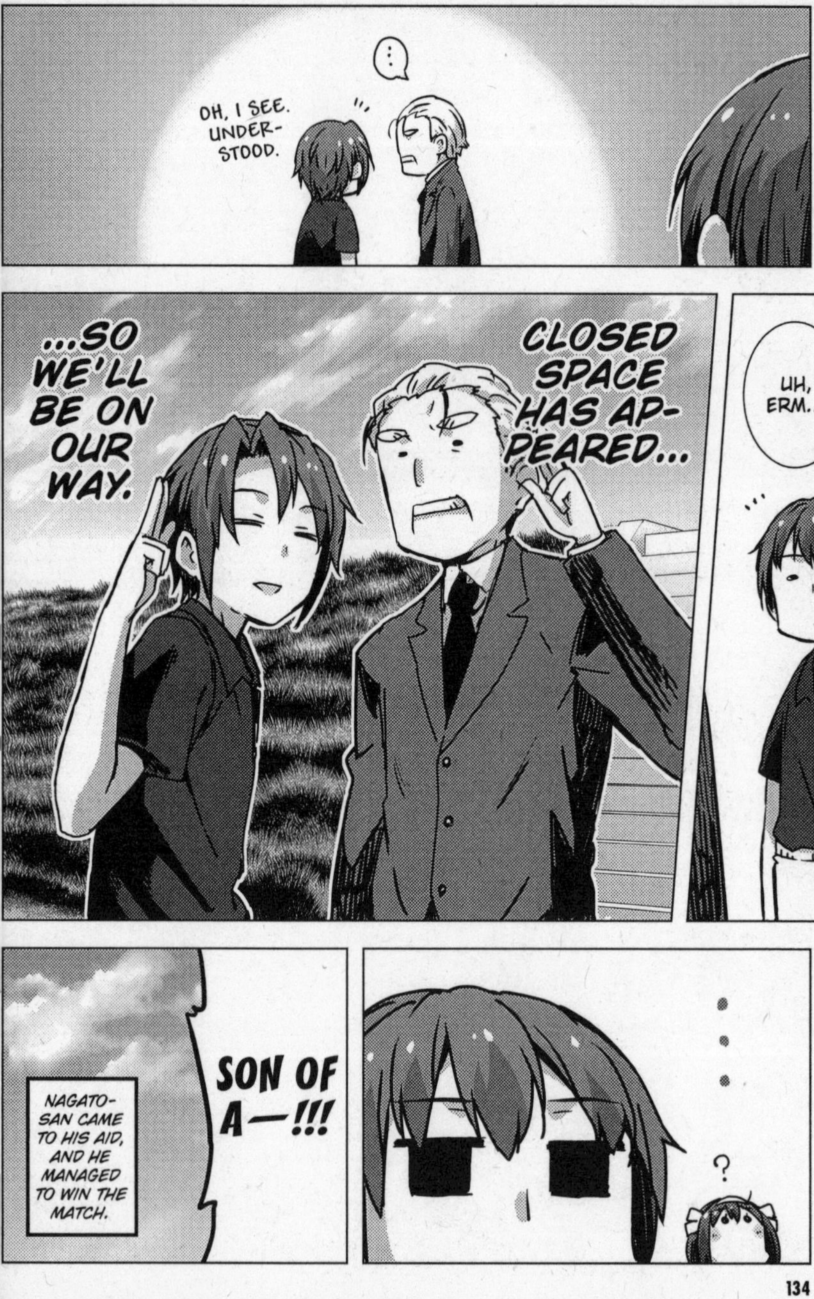
…
OH, I SEE. UNDER-STOOD.
UH, ERM…
CLOSED SPACE HAS AP-PEARED…
…SO WE'LL BE ON OUR WAY.
SON OF A—!!!
NAGATO-SAN CAME TO HIS AID, AND HE MANAGED TO WIN THE MATCH.

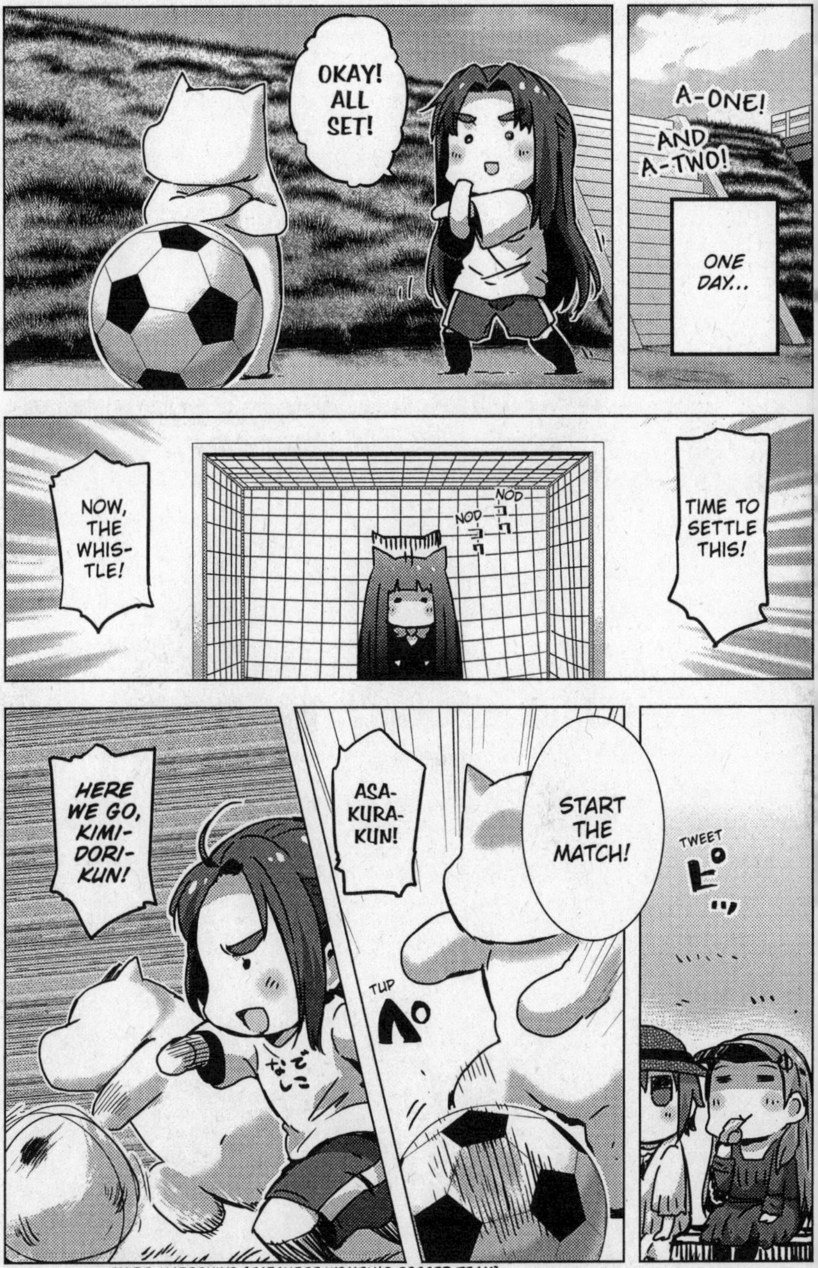
A-ONE!
AND A-TWO!
ONE DAY...
OKAY! ALL SET!
TIME TO SETTLE THIS!
NOD NOD
NOW, THE WHISTLE!
TWEET
START THE MATCH!
ASA-KURA-KUN!
TUP
HERE WE GO, KIMI-DORI-KUN!
なでしこ

SHIRT: NADESHIKO (JAPANESE WOMEN'S SOCCER TEAM)

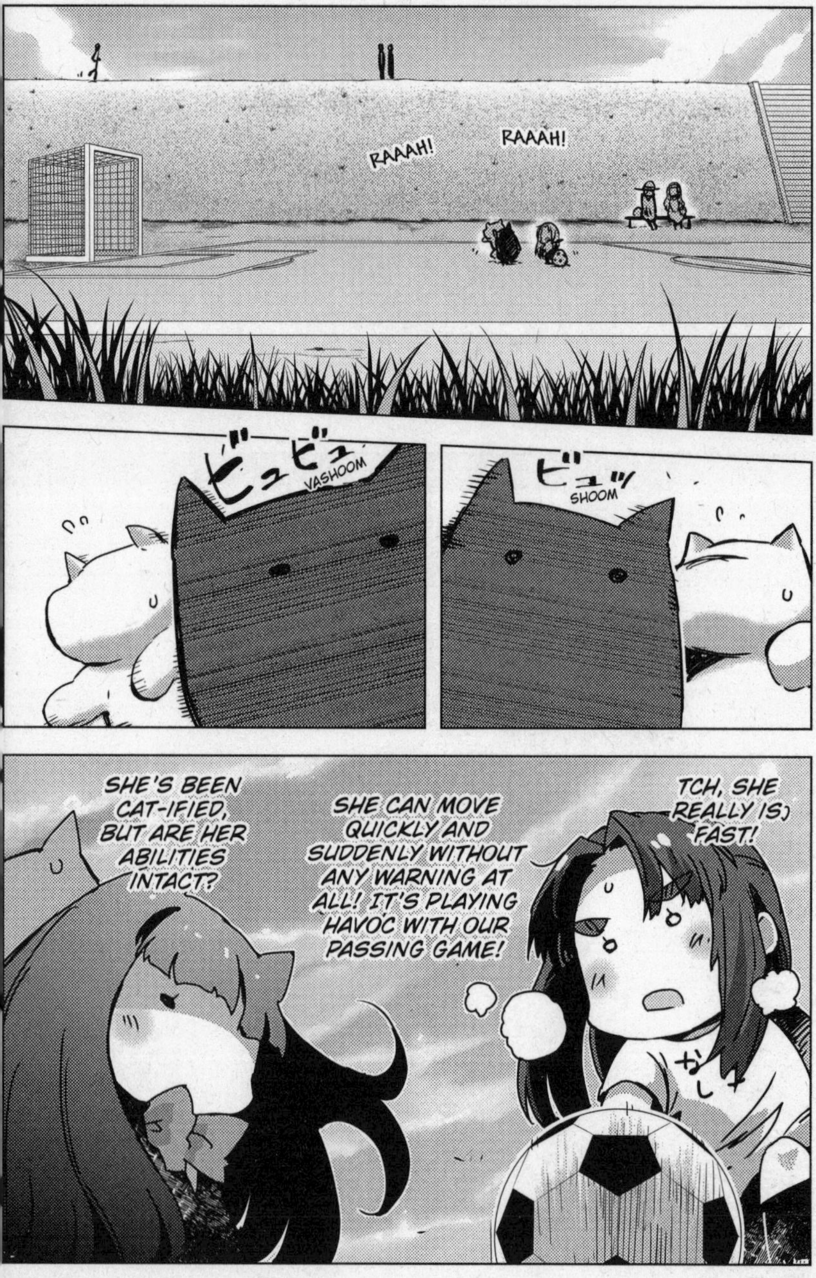
RAAAH!
RAAAH!
ビュッ
SHOOM
ビュビュ
VASHOOM
TCH, SHE REALLY IS FAST!
SHE CAN MOVE QUICKLY AND SUDDENLY WITHOUT ANY WARNING AT ALL! IT'S PLAYING HAVOC WITH OUR PASSING GAME!
SHE'S BEEN CAT-IFIED, BUT ARE HER ABILITIES INTACT?

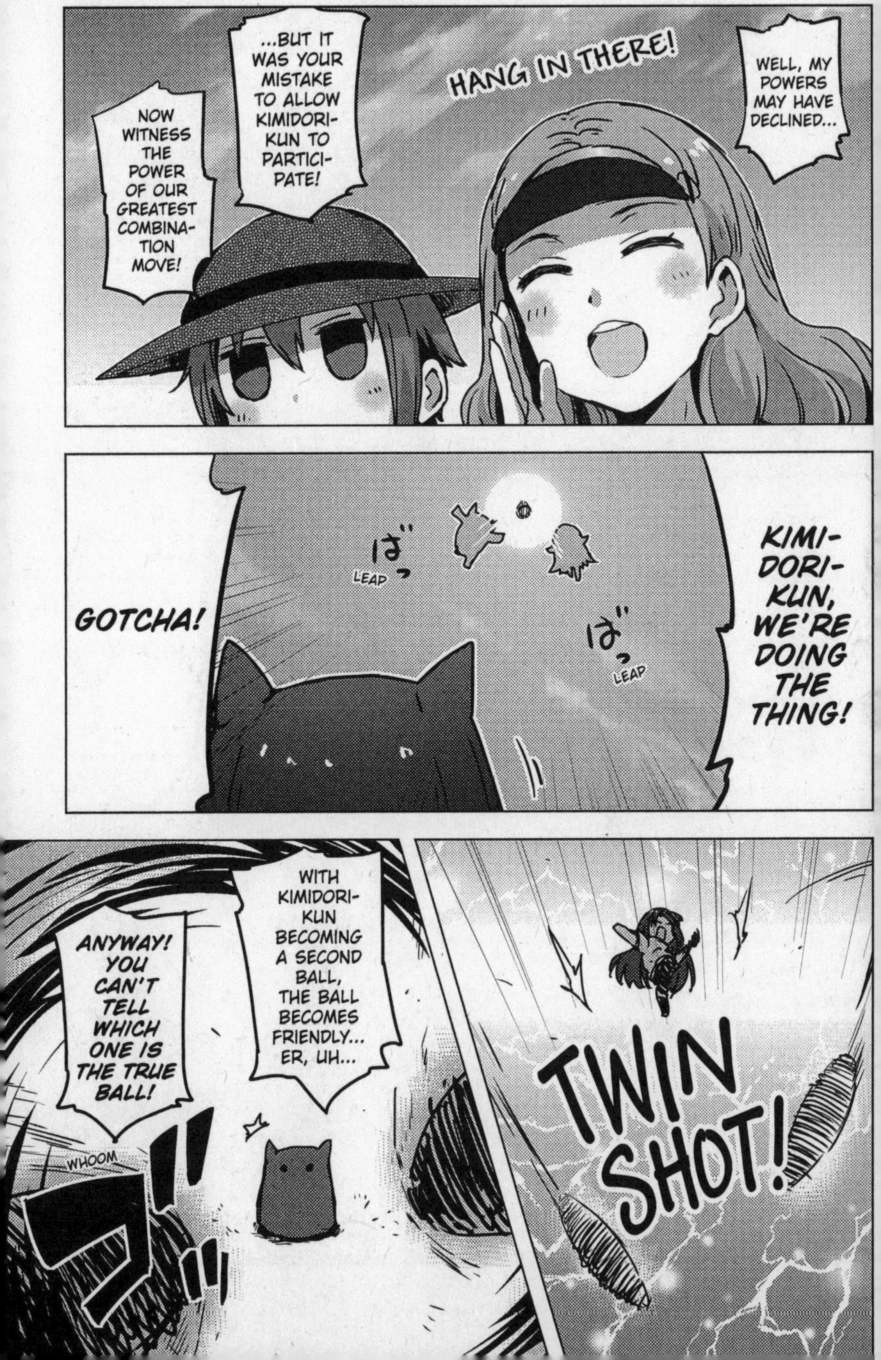
WELL, MY POWERS MAY HAVE DECLINED...
HANG IN THERE!
...BUT IT WAS YOUR MISTAKE TO ALLOW KIMIDORI-KUN TO PARTICIPATE!
NOW WITNESS THE POWER OF OUR GREATEST COMBINATION MOVE!
KIMI-DORI-KUN, WE'RE DOING THE THING!
ばっ LEAP
ばっ LEAP
GOTCHA!
TWIN SHOT!
WITH KIMIDORI-KUN BECOMING A SECOND BALL, THE BALL BECOMES FRIENDLY... ER, UH...
ANYWAY! YOU CAN'T TELL WHICH ONE IS THE TRUE BALL!
WHOOM

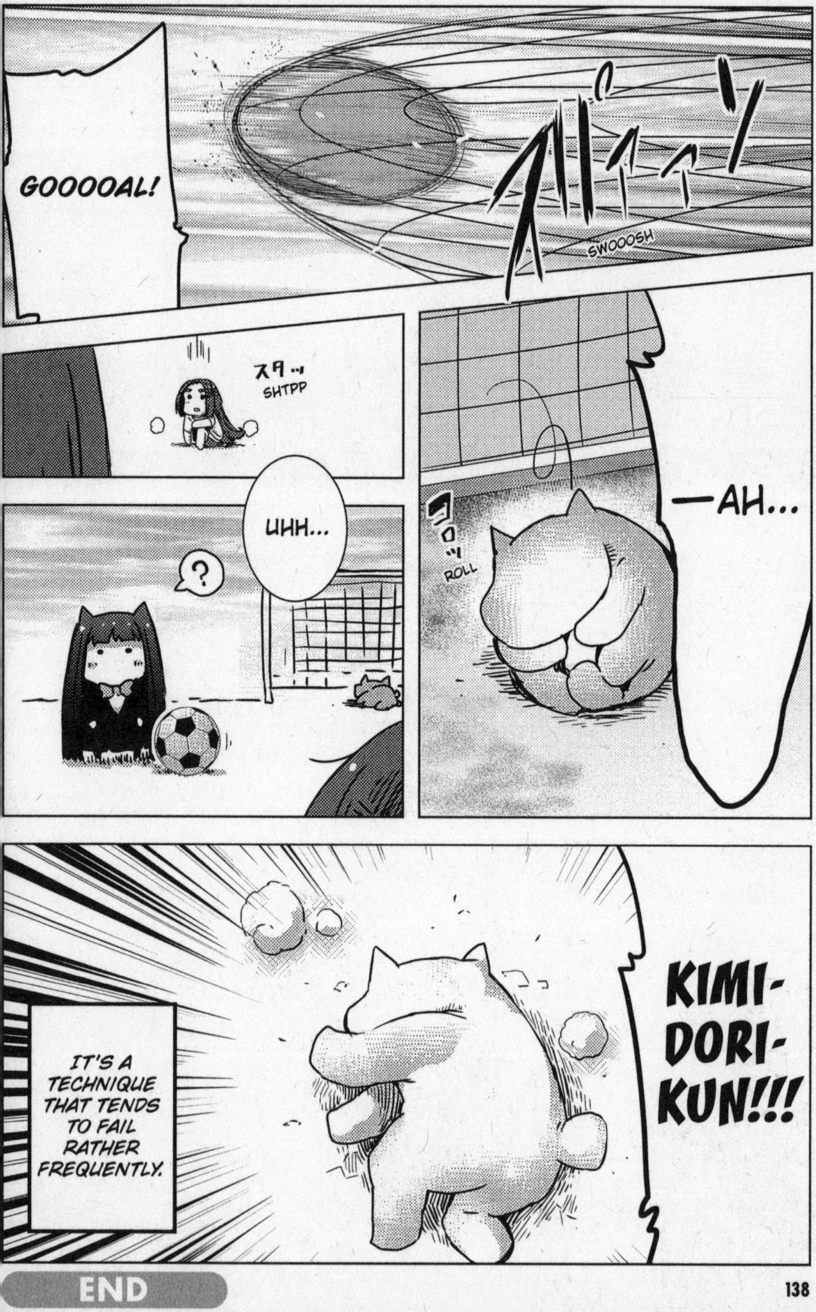
SWOOOSH
GOOOOAL!
—AH...
コロッ
ROLL
スタッ
SHTPP
UHH...
?
KIMI-DORI-KUN!!!
IT'S A TECHNIQUE THAT TENDS TO FAIL RATHER FREQUENTLY.

END

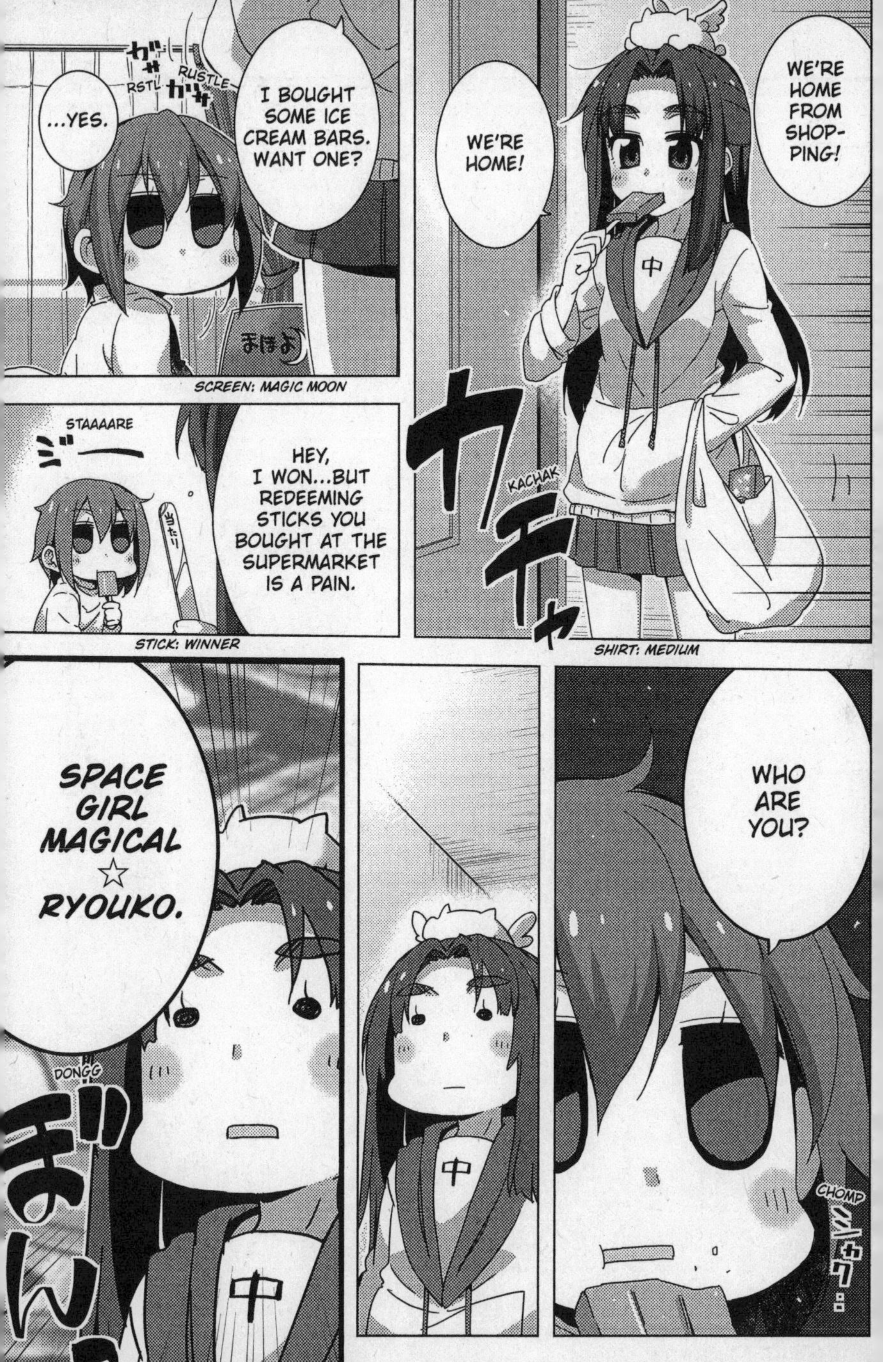
WE'RE HOME FROM SHOP-PING!
WE'RE HOME!
KACHAK
SHIRT: MEDIUM
RUSTLE
RSTL
I BOUGHT SOME ICE CREAM BARS. WANT ONE?
...YES.
SCREEN: MAGIC MOON
STAAAARE
HEY, I WON...BUT REDEEMING STICKS YOU BOUGHT AT THE SUPERMARKET IS A PAIN.
STICK: WINNER
WHO ARE YOU?
CHOMP
SPACE GIRL MAGICAL ☆ RYOUKO.
DONGG

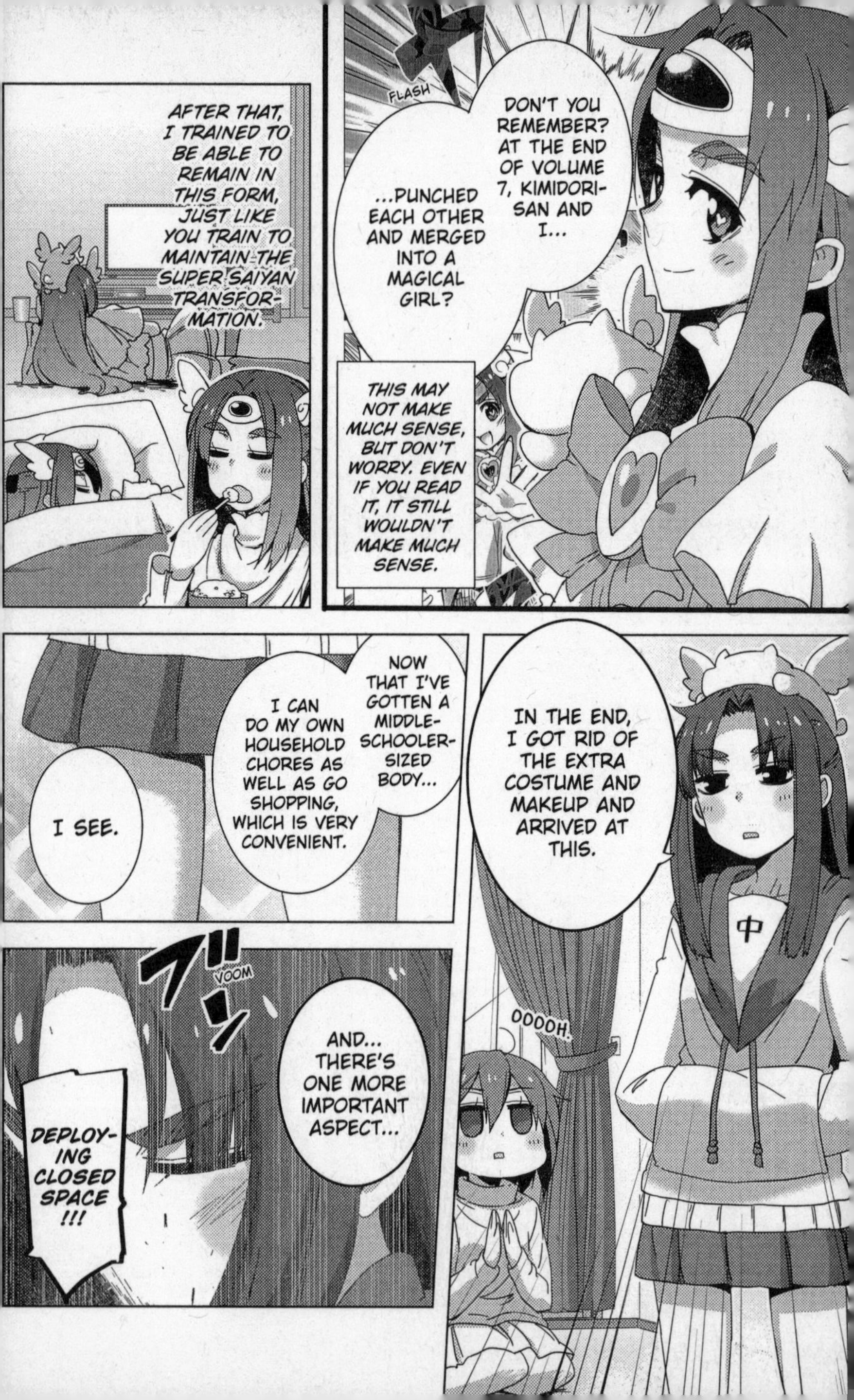
DON'T YOU REMEMBER? AT THE END OF VOLUME 7, KIMIDORI-SAN AND I...
...PUNCHED EACH OTHER AND MERGED INTO A MAGICAL GIRL?
FLASH
THIS MAY NOT MAKE MUCH SENSE, BUT DON'T WORRY. EVEN IF YOU READ IT, IT STILL WOULDN'T MAKE MUCH SENSE.
AFTER THAT, I TRAINED TO BE ABLE TO REMAIN IN THIS FORM, JUST LIKE YOU TRAIN TO MAINTAIN THE SUPER SAIYAN TRANSFORMATION.
IN THE END, I GOT RID OF THE EXTRA COSTUME AND MAKEUP AND ARRIVED AT THIS.
中
OOOOH.
NOW THAT I'VE GOTTEN A MIDDLE-SCHOOLER-SIZED BODY...
I CAN DO MY OWN HOUSEHOLD CHORES AS WELL AS GO SHOPPING, WHICH IS VERY CONVENIENT.
I SEE.
VOOM
AND... THERE'S ONE MORE IMPORTANT ASPECT...
DEPLOYING CLOSED SPACE!!!

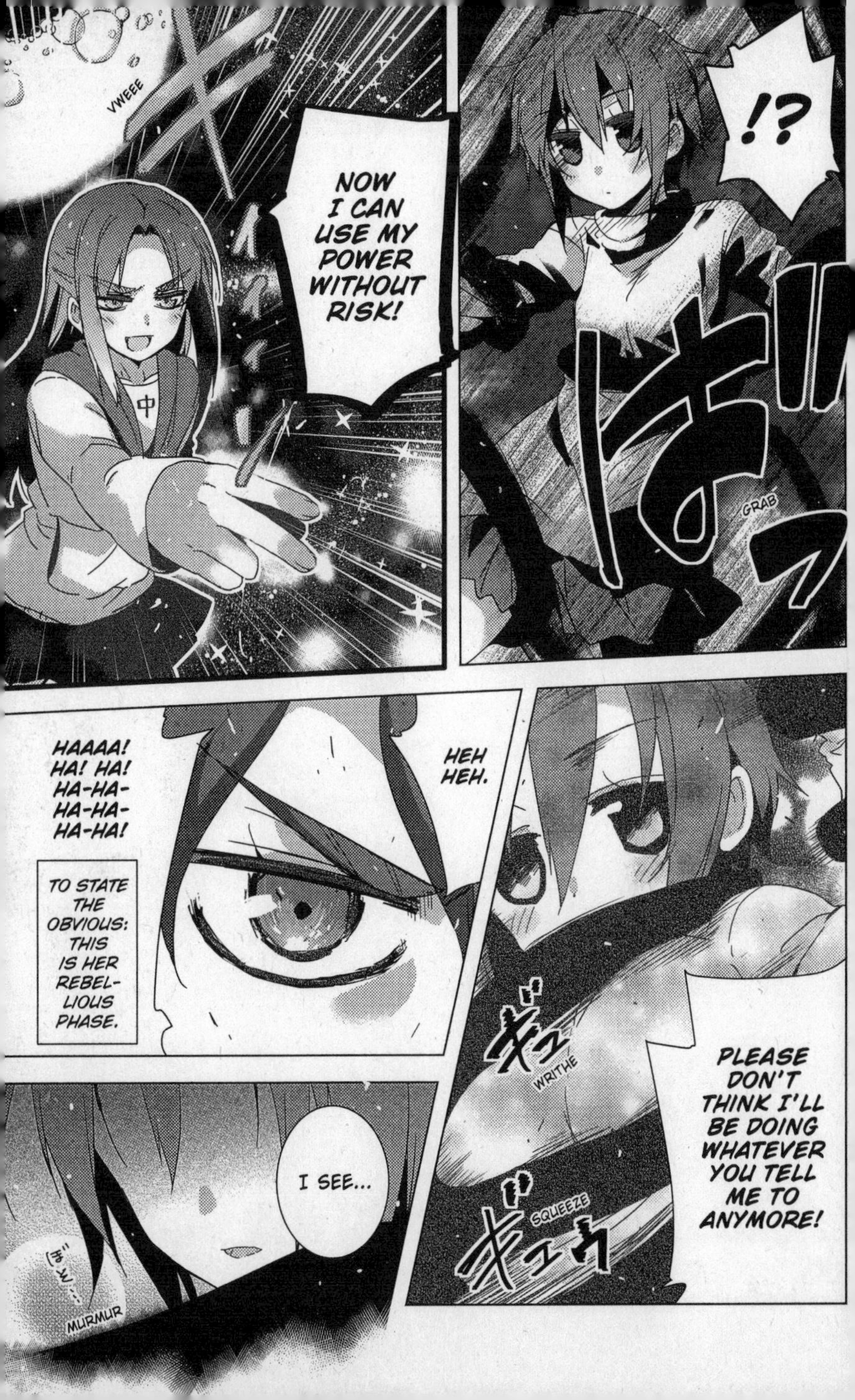
!?
GRAB
VWEEE
NOW I CAN USE MY POWER WITHOUT RISK!
WRITHE
SQUEEZE
PLEASE DON'T THINK I'LL BE DOING WHATEVER YOU TELL ME TO ANYMORE!
HEH HEH.
HAAAA! HA! HA! HA-HA-HA-HA-HA-HA!
TO STATE THE OBVIOUS: THIS IS HER REBELLIOUS PHASE.
I SEE...
MURMUR

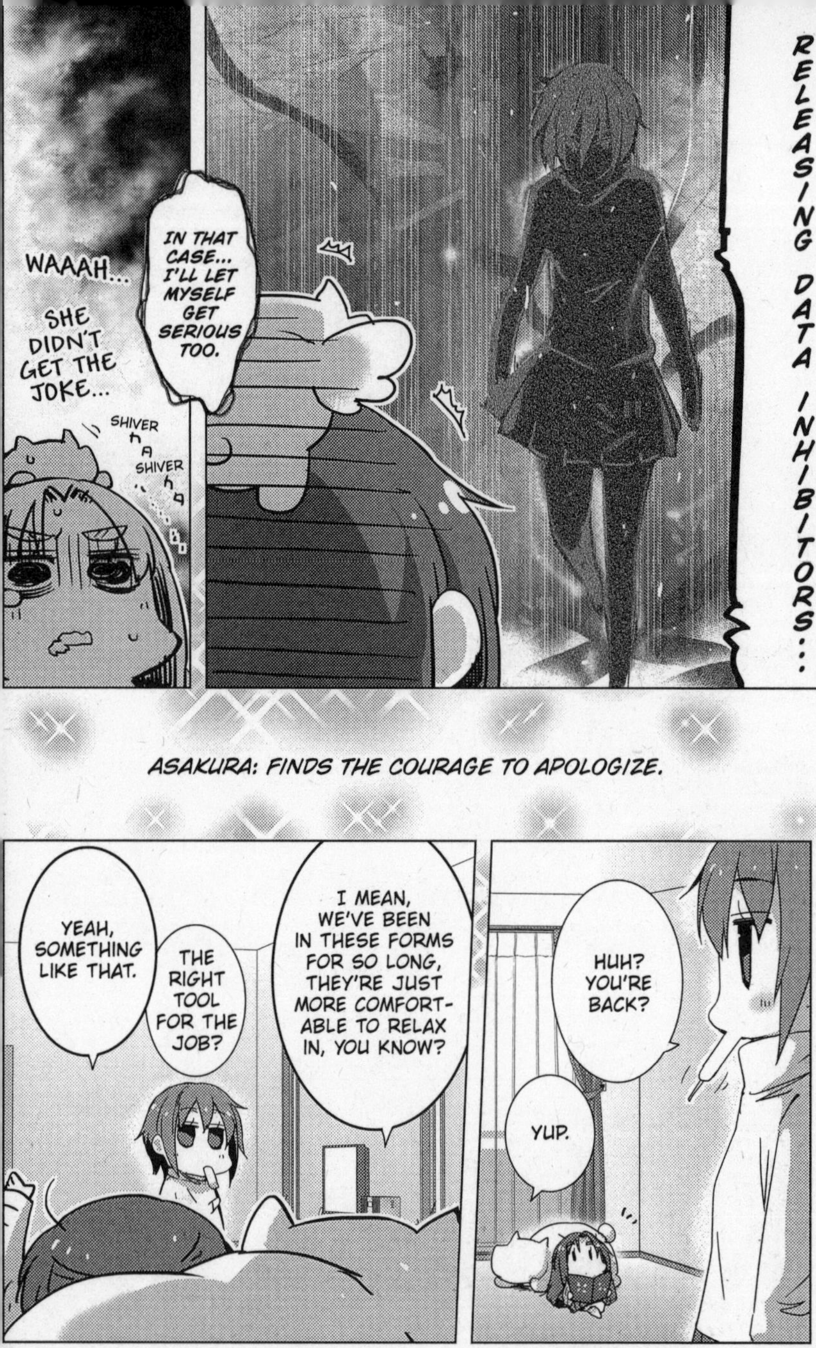
RELEASING DATA INHIBITORS...
IN THAT CASE... I'LL LET MYSELF GET SERIOUS TOO.
WAAAH...
SHE DIDN'T GET THE JOKE...
SHIVER SHIVER
ASAKURA: FINDS THE COURAGE TO APOLOGIZE.
HUH? YOU'RE BACK?
YUP.
I MEAN, WE'VE BEEN IN THESE FORMS FOR SO LONG, THEY'RE JUST MORE COMFORTABLE TO RELAX IN, YOU KNOW?
THE RIGHT TOOL FOR THE JOB?
YEAH, SOMETHING LIKE THAT.

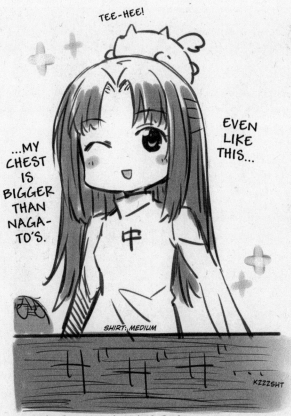

TEE-HEE!
EVEN LIKE THIS...
...MY CHEST IS BIGGER THAN NAGA-TO'S.
SHIRT: MEDIUM
KZZZSHT

← THE FOLLOWING PAGES FIRST APPEARED IN SNEAKER MAGAZINE!

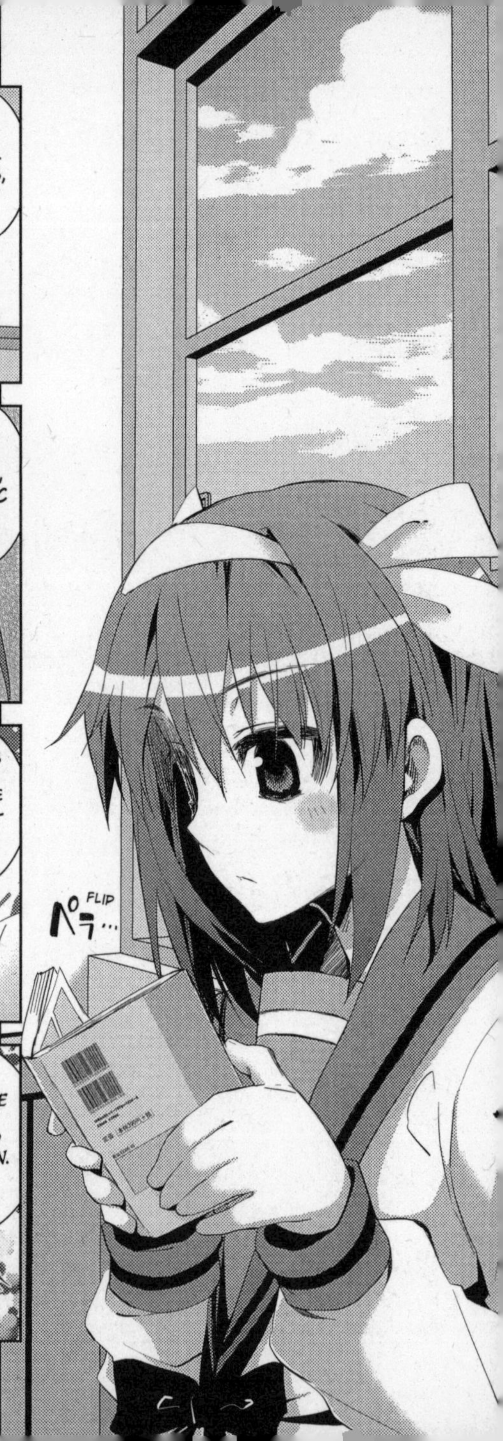
ペラ…
FLIP

LEAP THROUGH TIME

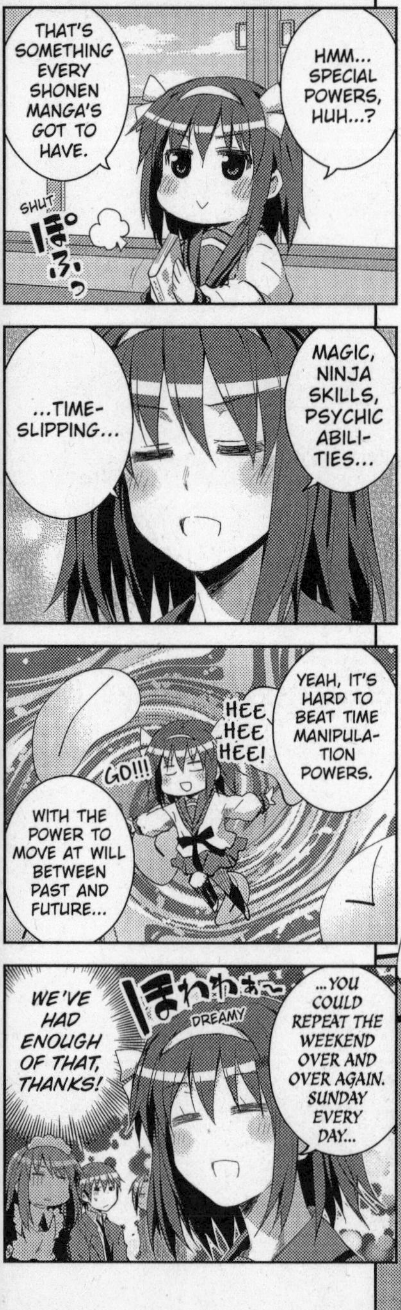
HMM... SPECIAL POWERS, HUH...?
THAT'S SOMETHING EVERY SHONEN MANGA'S GOT TO HAVE.
ぽふっ
SHUT
MAGIC, NINJA SKILLS, PSYCHIC ABILI-TIES...
...TIME-SLIPPING...
YEAH, IT'S HARD TO BEAT TIME MANIPULA-TION POWERS.
HEE HEE HEE!
GO!!!
WITH THE POWER TO MOVE AT WILL BETWEEN PAST AND FUTURE...
...YOU COULD REPEAT THE WEEKEND OVER AND OVER AGAIN. SUNDAY EVERY DAY...
ほわわぁ~
DREAMY
WE'VE HAD ENOUGH OF THAT, THANKS!

TEA GUYS

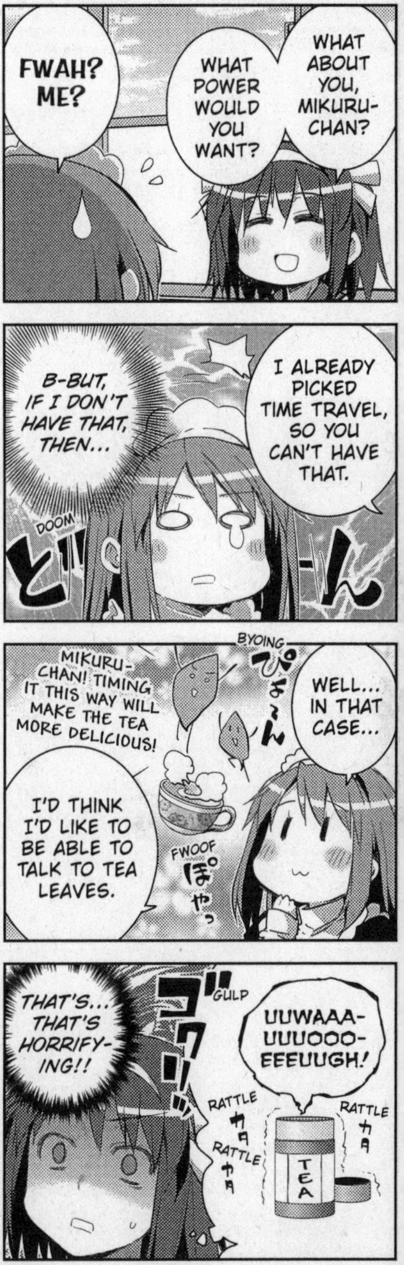
WHAT ABOUT YOU, MIKURU-CHAN?
WHAT POWER WOULD YOU WANT?
FWAH? ME?
I ALREADY PICKED TIME TRAVEL, SO YOU CAN'T HAVE THAT.
B-BUT, IF I DON'T HAVE THAT, THEN...
DOOM
BYOING
ぴょ〜ん
WELL... IN THAT CASE...
MIKURU-CHAN! TIMING IT THIS WAY WILL MAKE THE TEA MORE DELICIOUS!
I'D THINK I'D LIKE TO BE ABLE TO TALK TO TEA LEAVES.
FWOOF
ぽやっ
UUWAAA-UUUOOO-EEEUUGH!
RATTLE
カタ
RATTLE
カタ
RATTLE
カタ
TEA
GULP
ゴクッ
THAT'S... THAT'S HORRIFYING!!

PSYCHO

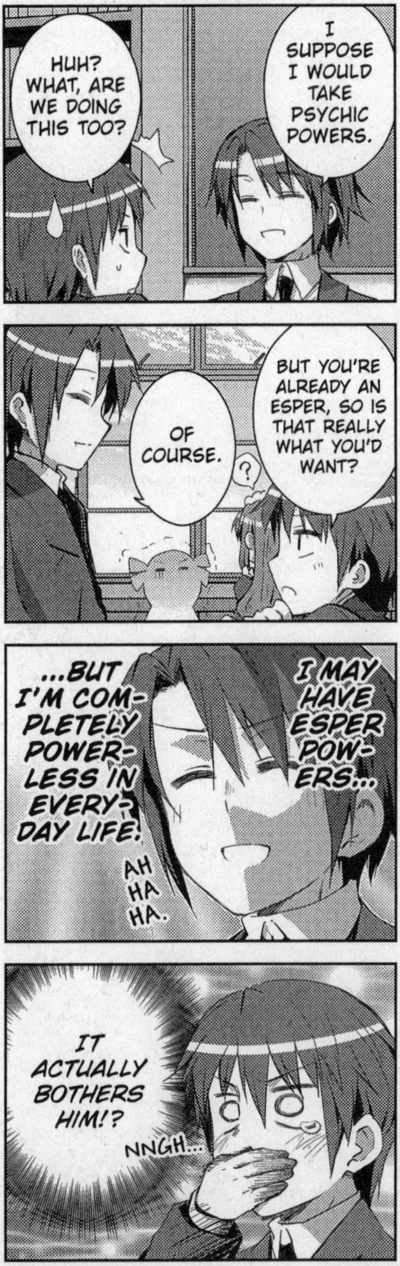
I SUPPOSE I WOULD TAKE PSYCHIC POWERS.
HUH? WHAT, ARE WE DOING THIS TOO?
BUT YOU'RE ALREADY AN ESPER, SO IS THAT REALLY WHAT YOU'D WANT?
OF COURSE.
I MAY HAVE ESPER POWERS...
...BUT I'M COMPLETELY POWERLESS IN EVERYDAY LIFE!
AH HA HA.
IT ACTUALLY BOTHERS HIM!?
NNGH...

PRIVILEGE

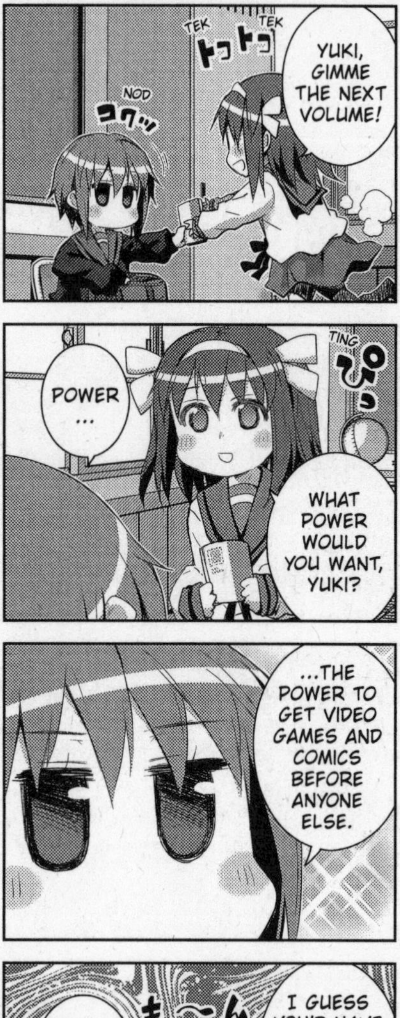
YUKI, GIMME THE NEXT VOLUME!
TEK TEK
NOD
TING
WHAT POWER WOULD YOU WANT, YUKI?
POWER ...
...THE POWER TO GET VIDEO GAMES AND COMICS BEFORE ANYONE ELSE.
I GUESS YOU'D HAVE TO BE A CREATOR OR WORK IN THE BUSI- NESS...
WARRRP
YOU'D HAVE TO BE.

THE STRONGEST

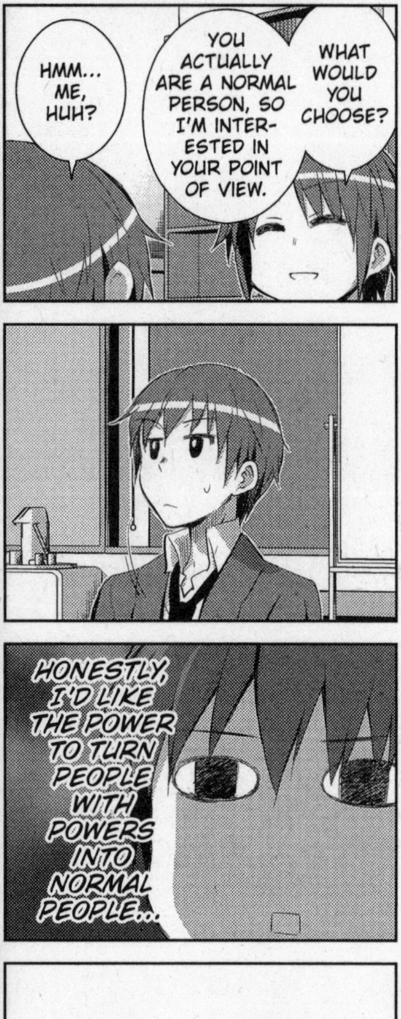
WHAT WOULD YOU CHOOSE?
YOU ACTUALLY ARE A NORMAL PERSON, SO I'M INTER- ESTED IN YOUR POINT OF VIEW.
HMM... ME, HUH?
HONESTLY, I'D LIKE THE POWER TO TURN PEOPLE WITH POWERS INTO NORMAL PEOPLE...

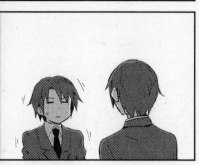

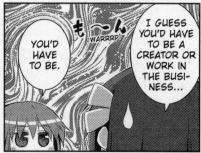

PRACTICAL APPLICATION

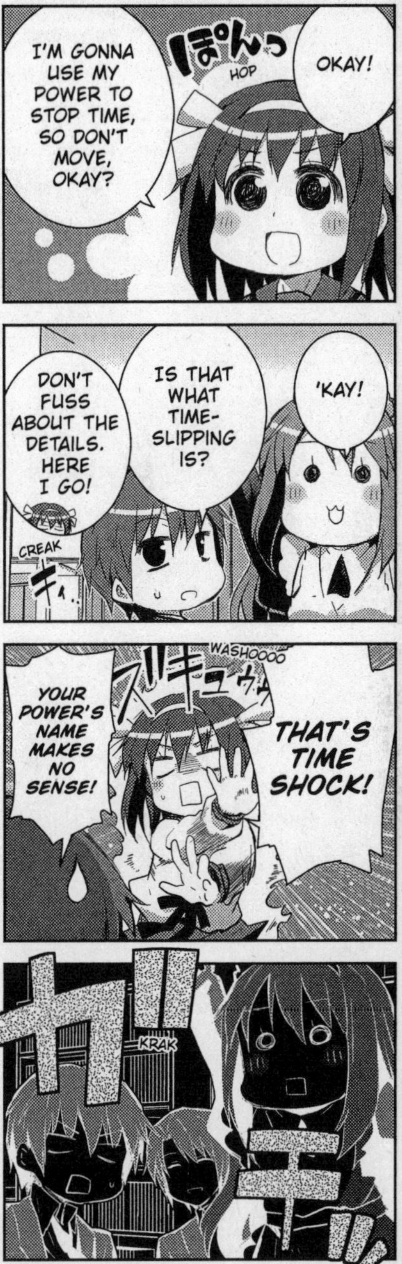
OKAY!
ぽんっ
HOP
I'M GONNA USE MY POWER TO STOP TIME, SO DON'T MOVE, OKAY?
'KAY!
IS THAT WHAT TIME-SLIPPING IS?
DON'T FUSS ABOUT THE DETAILS. HERE I GO!
CREAK
WASHOOOO
THAT'S TIME SHOCK!
YOUR POWER'S NAME MAKES NO SENSE!
KRAK

NATURAL ABILITY

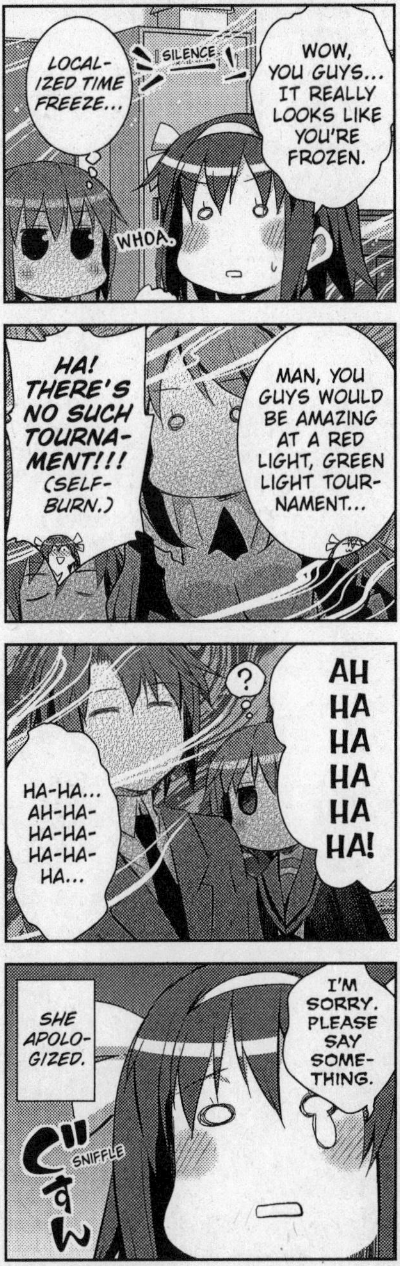
WOW, YOU GUYS... IT REALLY LOOKS LIKE YOU'RE FROZEN.
SILENCE
LOCALIZED TIME FREEZE...
WHOA.
MAN, YOU GUYS WOULD BE AMAZING AT A RED LIGHT, GREEN LIGHT TOURNAMENT...
HA! THERE'S NO SUCH TOURNAMENT!!! (SELF-BURN.)
AH HA HA HA HA HA!
?
HA-HA... AH-HA-HA-HA-HA-HA-HA...
I'M SORRY. PLEASE SAY SOMETHING.
SHE APOLOGIZED.
ぐすん
SNIFFLE

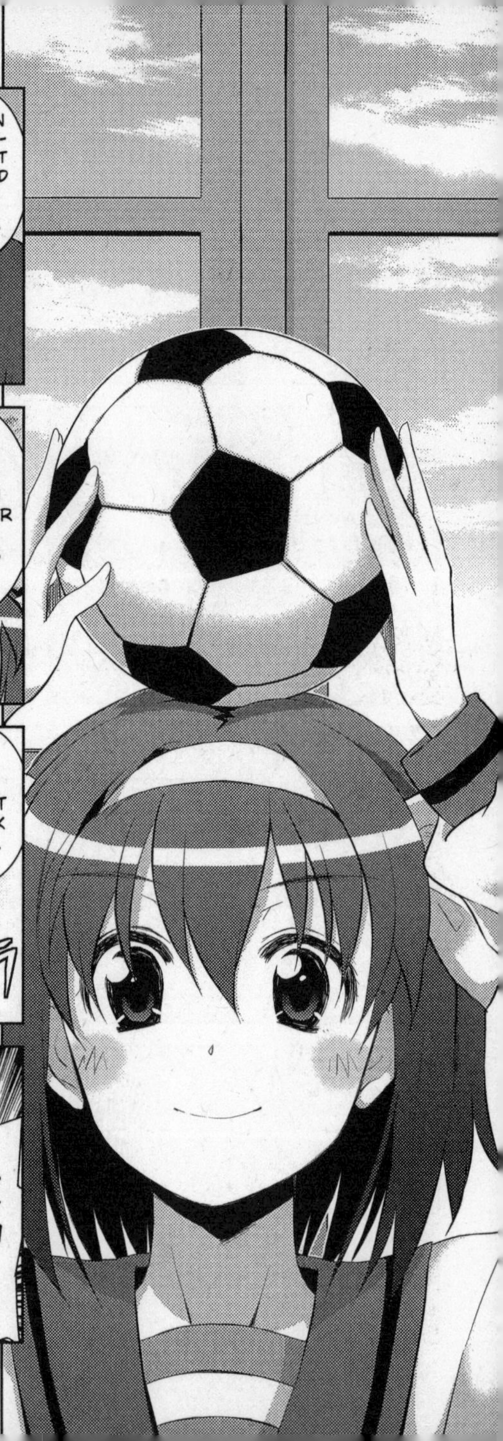

BALL

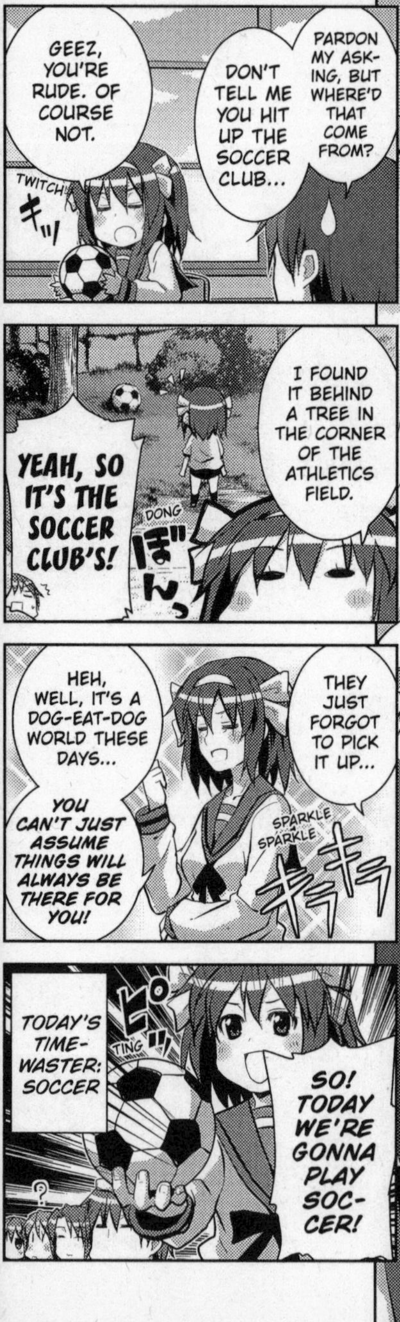
PARDON MY ASK-ING, BUT WHERE'D THAT COME FROM?
DON'T TELL ME YOU HIT UP THE SOCCER CLUB...
GEEZ, YOU'RE RUDE. OF COURSE NOT.
TWITCH
キッ
I FOUND IT BEHIND A TREE IN THE CORNER OF THE ATHLETICS FIELD.
DONG
ぼんっ
YEAH, SO IT'S THE SOCCER CLUB'S!
THEY JUST FORGOT TO PICK IT UP...
SPARKLE SPARKLE
キラキラ
HEH, WELL, IT'S A DOG-EAT-DOG WORLD THESE DAYS...
YOU CAN'T JUST ASSUME THINGS WILL ALWAYS BE THERE FOR YOU!
TODAY'S TIME-WASTER: SOCCER
TING
ピッ!!
SO! TODAY WE'RE GONNA PLAY SOC-CER!

GOAL

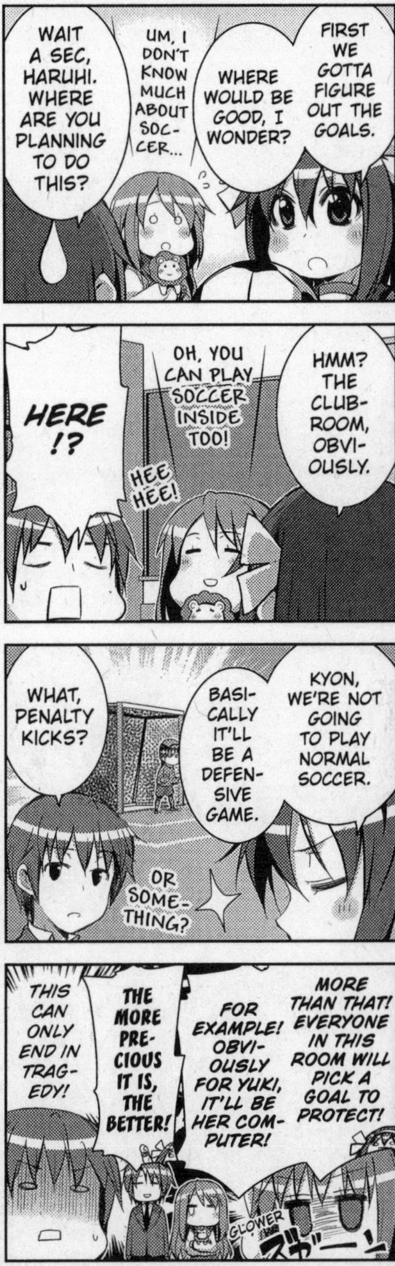

FIRST WE GOTTA FIGURE OUT THE GOALS.
WHERE WOULD BE GOOD, I WONDER?
UM, I DON'T KNOW MUCH ABOUT SOCCER...
WAIT A SEC, HARUHI. WHERE ARE YOU PLANNING TO DO THIS?
HMM? THE CLUBROOM, OBVIOUSLY.
OH, YOU CAN PLAY SOCCER INSIDE TOO!
HEE HEE!
HERE!?
KYON, WE'RE NOT GOING TO PLAY NORMAL SOCCER.
BASICALLY IT'LL BE A DEFENSIVE GAME.
OR SOMETHING?
WHAT, PENALTY KICKS?
MORE THAN THAT! EVERYONE IN THIS ROOM WILL PICK A GOAL TO PROTECT!
FOR EXAMPLE! OBVIOUSLY FOR YUKI, IT'LL BE HER COMPUTER!
THE MORE PRECIOUS IT IS, THE BETTER!
THIS CAN ONLY END IN TRAGEDY!
GLOWER

DECISIONS

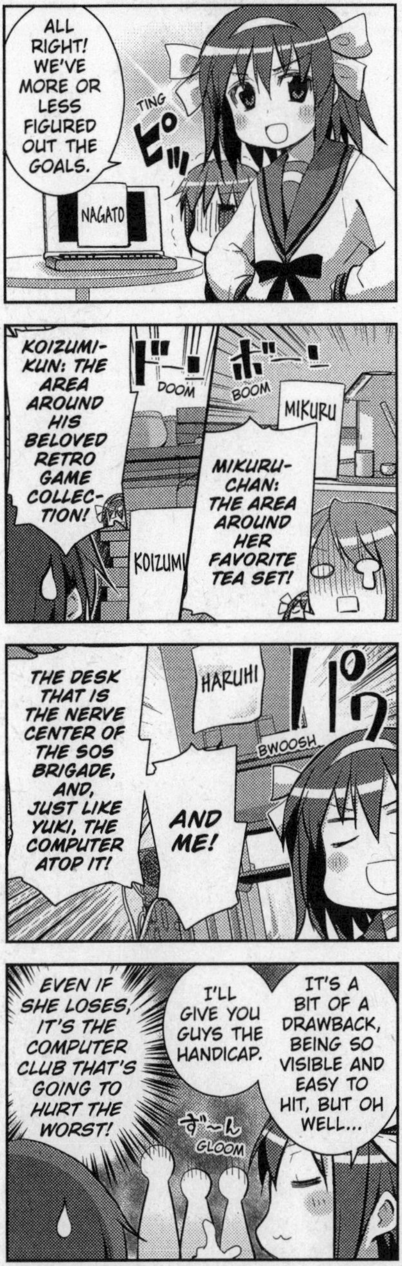

TING
ALL RIGHT! WE'VE MORE OR LESS FIGURED OUT THE GOALS.
NAGATO
MIKURU
BOOM
MIKURU-CHAN: THE AREA AROUND HER FAVORITE TEA SET!
DOOM
KOIZUMI-KUN: THE AREA AROUND HIS BELOVED RETRO GAME COLLECTION!
KOIZUMI
BWOOSH
HARUHI
AND ME!
THE DESK THAT IS THE NERVE CENTER OF THE SOS BRIGADE, AND, JUST LIKE YUKI, THE COMPUTER ATOP IT!
IT'S A BIT OF A DRAWBACK, BEING SO VISIBLE AND EASY TO HIT, BUT OH WELL...
I'LL GIVE YOU GUYS THE HANDICAP.
GLOOM
EVEN IF SHE LOSES, IT'S THE COMPUTER CLUB THAT'S GOING TO HURT THE WORST!

TERRIBLE CONSEQUENCES

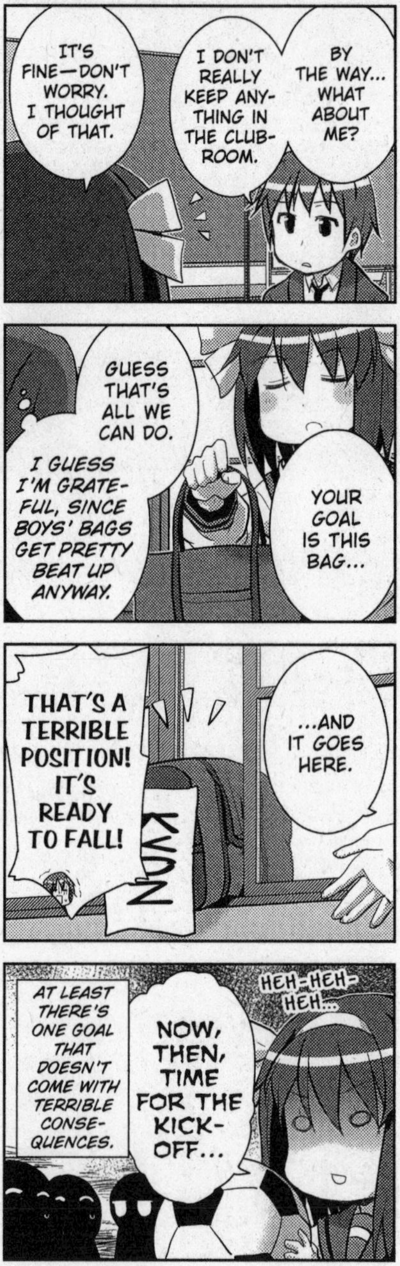
BY THE WAY... WHAT ABOUT ME?
I DON'T REALLY KEEP ANYTHING IN THE CLUBROOM.
IT'S FINE—DON'T WORRY. I THOUGHT OF THAT.
YOUR GOAL IS THIS BAG...
GUESS THAT'S ALL WE CAN DO.
I GUESS I'M GRATEFUL, SINCE BOYS' BAGS GET PRETTY BEAT UP ANYWAY.
...AND IT GOES HERE.
THAT'S A TERRIBLE POSITION! IT'S READY TO FALL!
KYON
HEH-HEH-HEH...
NOW, THEN, TIME FOR THE KICKOFF...
AT LEAST THERE'S ONE GOAL THAT DOESN'T COME WITH TERRIBLE CONSEQUENCES.

KICKOFF

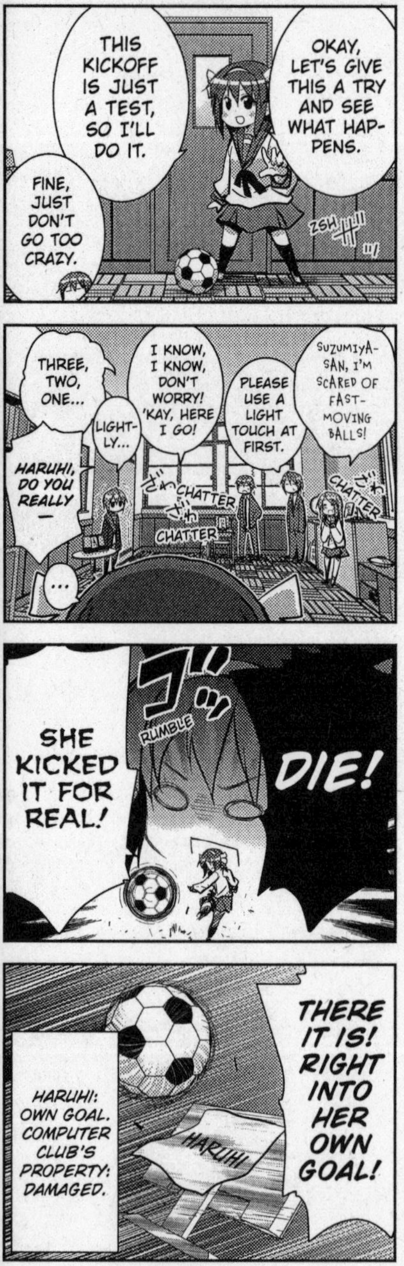
OKAY, LET'S GIVE THIS A TRY AND SEE WHAT HAPPENS.
ZSH
THIS KICKOFF IS JUST A TEST, SO I'LL DO IT.
FINE, JUST DON'T GO TOO CRAZY.
SUZUMIYA-SAN, I'M SCARED OF FAST-MOVING BALLS!
CHATTER
PLEASE USE A LIGHT TOUCH AT FIRST.
I KNOW, I KNOW, DON'T WORRY! 'KAY, HERE I GO!
THREE, TWO, ONE...
LIGHTLY...
CHATTER
CHATTER
HARUHI, DO YOU REALLY—
...
DIE!
RUMBLE
SHE KICKED IT FOR REAL!
THERE IT IS! RIGHT INTO HER OWN GOAL!
HARUHI
HARUHI: OWN GOAL. COMPUTER CLUB'S PROPERTY: DAMAGED.

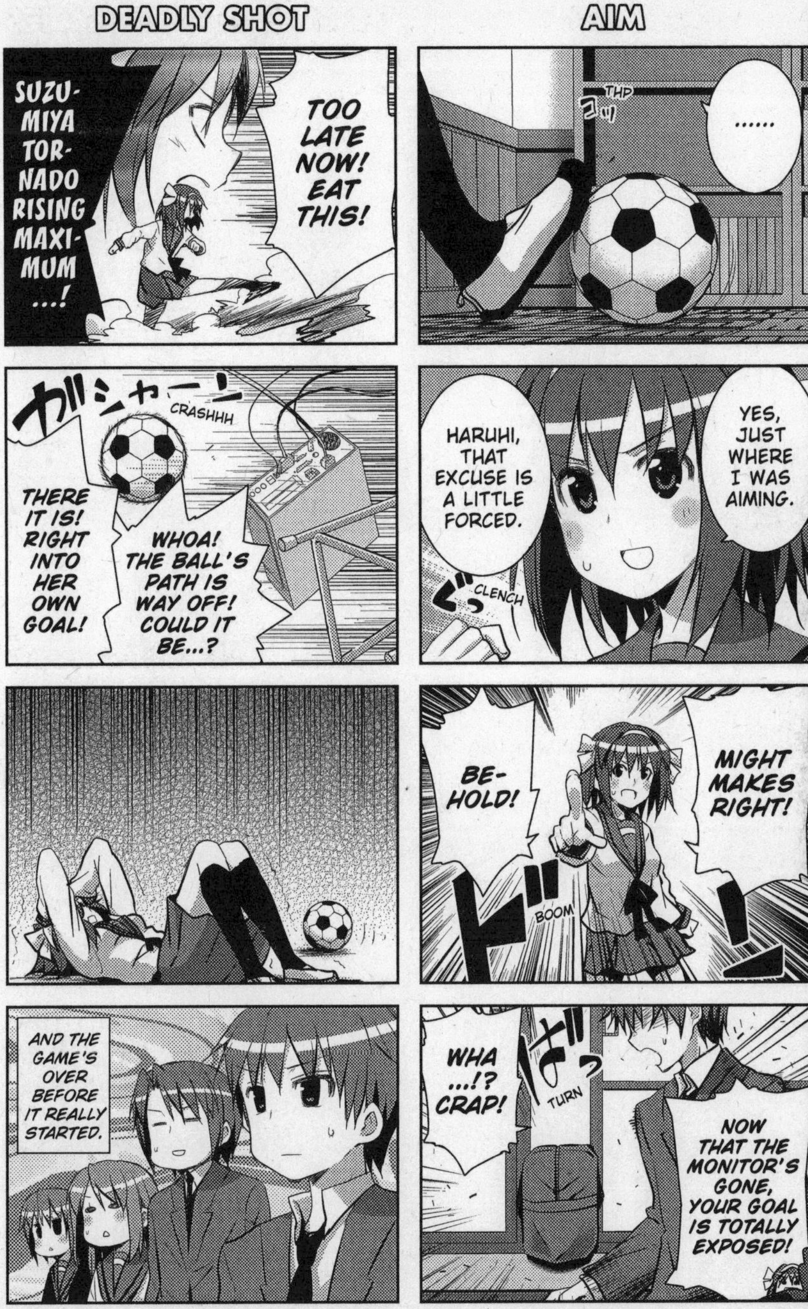
DEADLY SHOT
TOO LATE NOW! EAT THIS!
SUZUMIYA TORNADO RISING MAXIMUM ...!
ガシャーン CRASHHH
WHOA! THE BALL'S PATH IS WAY OFF! COULD IT BE...?
THERE IT IS! RIGHT INTO HER OWN GOAL!
AND THE GAME'S OVER BEFORE IT REALLY STARTED.
AIM
THP コッ
......
YES, JUST WHERE I WAS AIMING.
HARUHI, THAT EXCUSE IS A LITTLE FORCED.
ぐっ CLENCH
MIGHT MAKES RIGHT!
BE-HOLD!
ドン BOOM
ばっ TURN
WHA ...!? CRAP!
NOW THAT THE MONITOR'S GONE, YOUR GOAL IS TOTALLY EXPOSED!

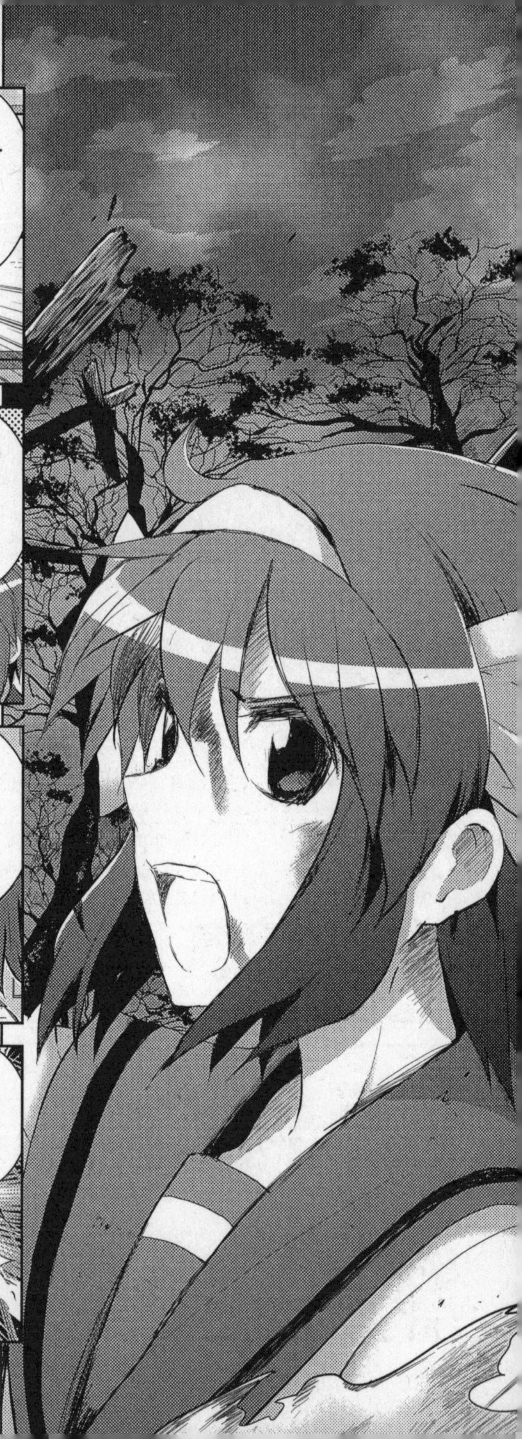

ON BOARD

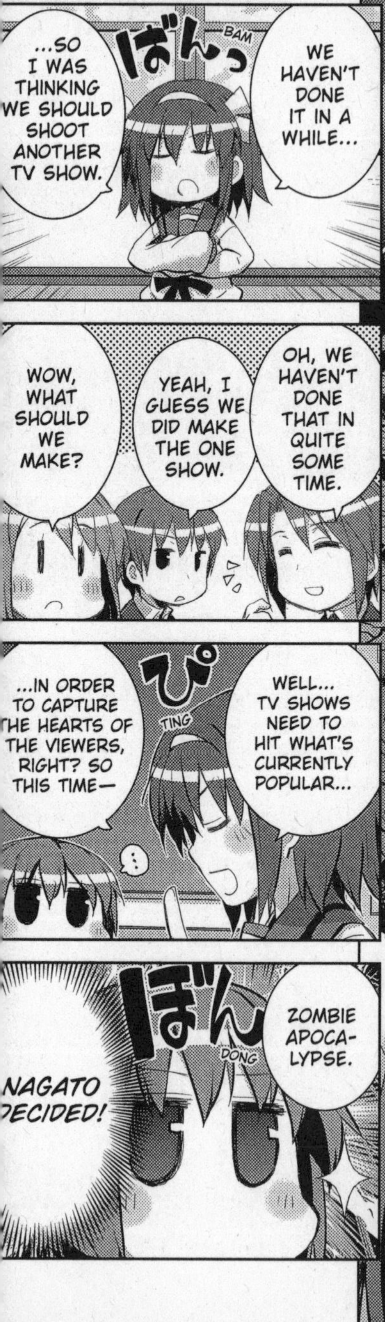

BAM
WE HAVEN'T DONE IT IN A WHILE...
...SO I WAS THINKING WE SHOULD SHOOT ANOTHER TV SHOW.
OH, WE HAVEN'T DONE THAT IN QUITE SOME TIME.
YEAH, I GUESS WE DID MAKE THE ONE SHOW.
WOW, WHAT SHOULD WE MAKE?
TING
WELL... TV SHOWS NEED TO HIT WHAT'S CURRENTLY POPULAR...
...IN ORDER TO CAPTURE THE HEARTS OF THE VIEWERS, RIGHT? SO THIS TIME—
...
ZOMBIE APOCALYPSE.
DONG
NAGATO DECIDED!

EXPLANATION

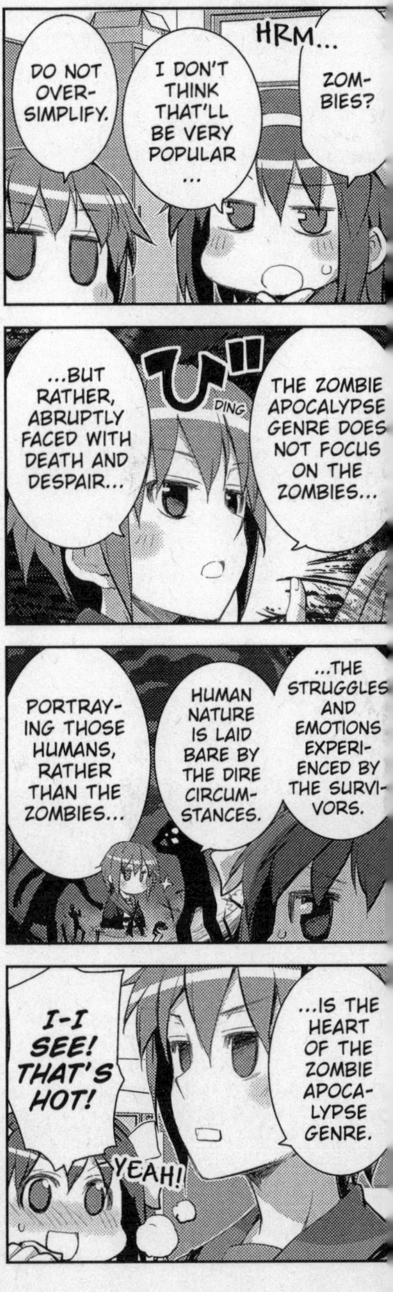
ZOMBIES?
HRM...
I DON'T THINK THAT'LL BE VERY POPULAR...
DO NOT OVERSIMPLIFY.
THE ZOMBIE APOCALYPSE GENRE DOES NOT FOCUS ON THE ZOMBIES...
DING
...BUT RATHER, ABRUPTLY FACED WITH DEATH AND DESPAIR...
...THE STRUGGLES AND EMOTIONS EXPERIENCED BY THE SURVIVORS.
HUMAN NATURE IS LAID BARE BY THE DIRE CIRCUMSTANCES.
PORTRAYING THOSE HUMANS, RATHER THAN THE ZOMBIES...
...IS THE HEART OF THE ZOMBIE APOCALYPSE GENRE.
YEAH!
I-I SEE! THAT'S HOT!

CASTING

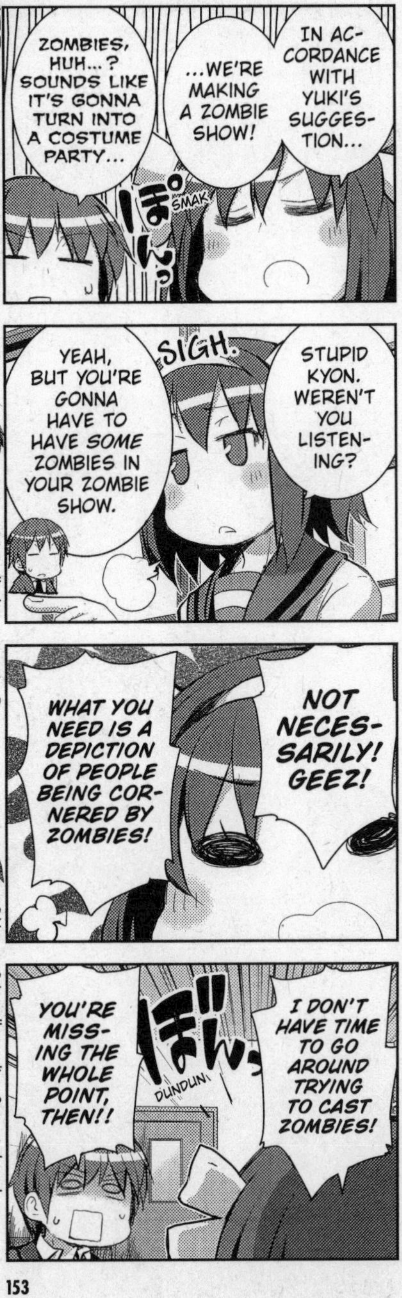
IN ACCORDANCE WITH YUKI'S SUGGESTION...
...WE'RE MAKING A ZOMBIE SHOW!
SMAK
ZOMBIES, HUH...? SOUNDS LIKE IT'S GONNA TURN INTO A COSTUME PARTY...
STUPID KYON. WEREN'T YOU LISTENING?
SIGH.
YEAH, BUT YOU'RE GONNA HAVE TO HAVE SOME ZOMBIES IN YOUR ZOMBIE SHOW.
NOT NECESSARILY! GEEZ!
WHAT YOU NEED IS A DEPICTION OF PEOPLE BEING CORNERED BY ZOMBIES!
I DON'T HAVE TIME TO GO AROUND TRYING TO CAST ZOMBIES!
DUNDUN
YOU'RE MISSING THE WHOLE POINT, THEN!!

●Haruhi-chan ●SOS Brigade Chief. Happened to remember she's been wanting to make a TV show.

●Kyon ●Actually the protagonist. Even zombies flee in the face of his comebacks.

●Nagato ●Actually an alien. Seems to have been influenced by certain video games, anime, and manga.

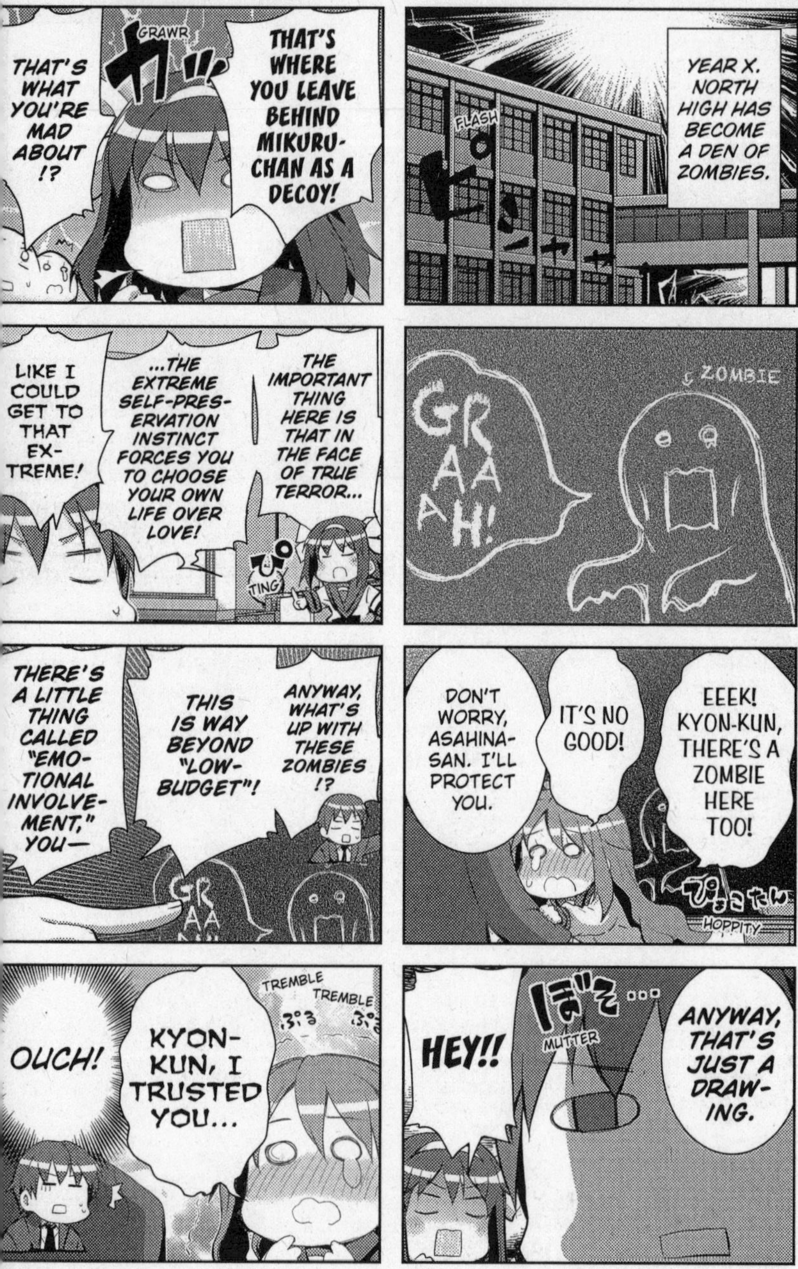

FLASH
YEAR X. NORTH HIGH HAS BECOME A DEN OF ZOMBIES.
GRAAAH!
ZOMBIE
EEEK! KYON-KUN, THERE'S A ZOMBIE HERE TOO!
IT'S NO GOOD!
DON'T WORRY, ASAHINA-SAN. I'LL PROTECT YOU.
HOPPITY
ANYWAY, THAT'S JUST A DRAWING.
MUTTER
HEY!!
THAT'S WHERE YOU LEAVE BEHIND MIKURU-CHAN AS A DECOY!
GRAWR
THAT'S WHAT YOU'RE MAD ABOUT!?
THE IMPORTANT THING HERE IS THAT IN THE FACE OF TRUE TERROR...
...THE EXTREME SELF-PRESERVATION INSTINCT FORCES YOU TO CHOOSE YOUR OWN LIFE OVER LOVE!
TING
LIKE I COULD GET TO THAT EXTREME!
ANYWAY, WHAT'S UP WITH THESE ZOMBIES!?
THIS IS WAY BEYOND "LOW-BUDGET"!
THERE'S A LITTLE THING CALLED "EMOTIONAL INVOLVEMENT," YOU—
TREMBLE TREMBLE
KYON-KUN, I TRUSTED YOU...
OUCH!

●Mikuru-chan ●Actually a time traveler. Her trusting heart is beautiful, a lesson for all of us.

●Koizumi ●Mysterious transfer student and esper. A good guy who prizes going with the flow. Can control red balls.

SETTING DETAILS EPISODE 2

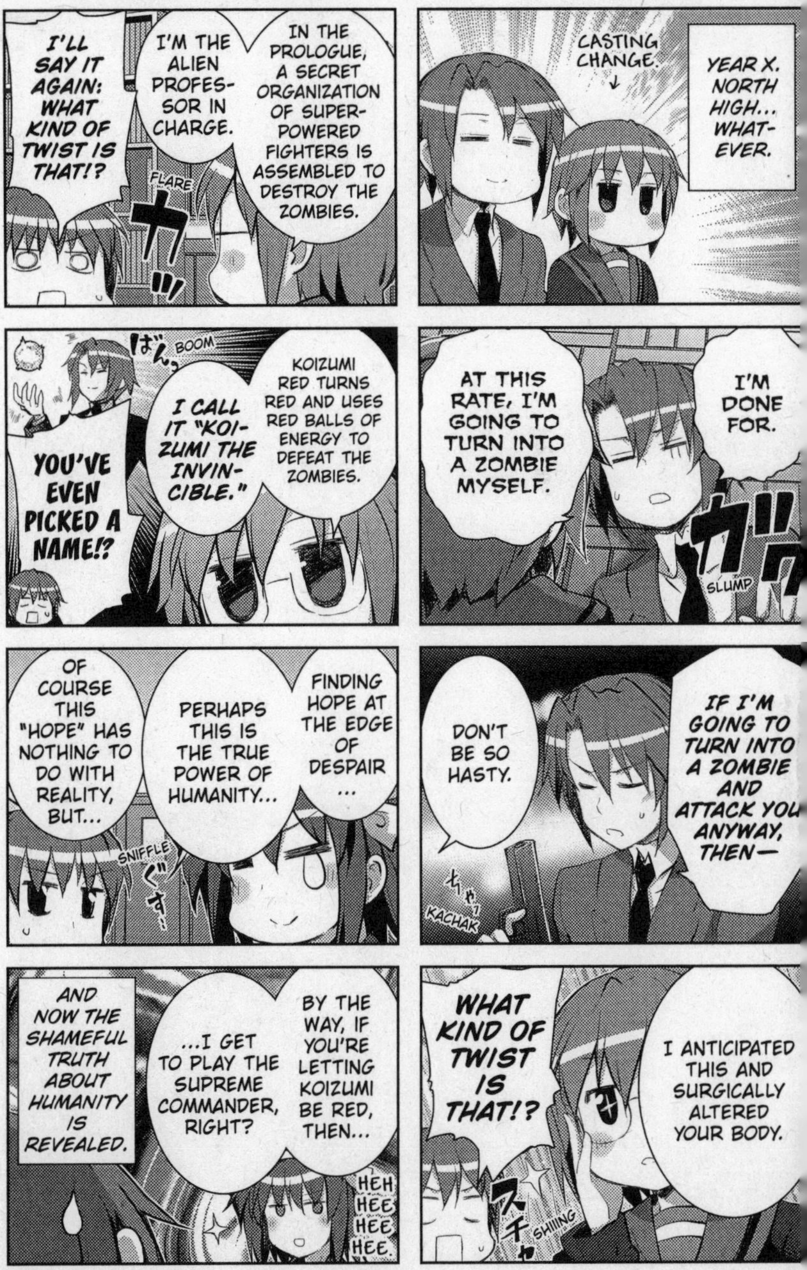

YEAR X. NORTH HIGH... WHATEVER.
CASTING CHANGE.
I'M DONE FOR.
AT THIS RATE, I'M GOING TO TURN INTO A ZOMBIE MYSELF.
SLUMP
IF I'M GOING TO TURN INTO A ZOMBIE AND ATTACK YOU ANYWAY, THEN—
DON'T BE SO HASTY.
KACHAK
I ANTICIPATED THIS AND SURGICALLY ALTERED YOUR BODY.
WHAT KIND OF TWIST IS THAT!?
SHIIING
IN THE PROLOGUE, A SECRET ORGANIZATION OF SUPER-POWERED FIGHTERS IS ASSEMBLED TO DESTROY THE ZOMBIES.
I'M THE ALIEN PROFESSOR IN CHARGE.
I'LL SAY IT AGAIN: WHAT KIND OF TWIST IS THAT!?
FLARE
BOOM
KOIZUMI RED TURNS RED AND USES RED BALLS OF ENERGY TO DEFEAT THE ZOMBIES.
I CALL IT "KOIZUMI THE INVINCIBLE."
YOU'VE EVEN PICKED A NAME!?
FINDING HOPE AT THE EDGE OF DESPAIR...
PERHAPS THIS IS THE TRUE POWER OF HUMANITY...
OF COURSE THIS "HOPE" HAS NOTHING TO DO WITH REALITY, BUT...
SNIFFLE
BY THE WAY, IF YOU'RE LETTING KOIZUMI BE RED, THEN...
...I GET TO PLAY THE SUPREME COMMANDER, RIGHT?
HEH HEE HEE HEE.
AND NOW THE SHAMEFUL TRUTH ABOUT HUMANITY IS REVEALED.

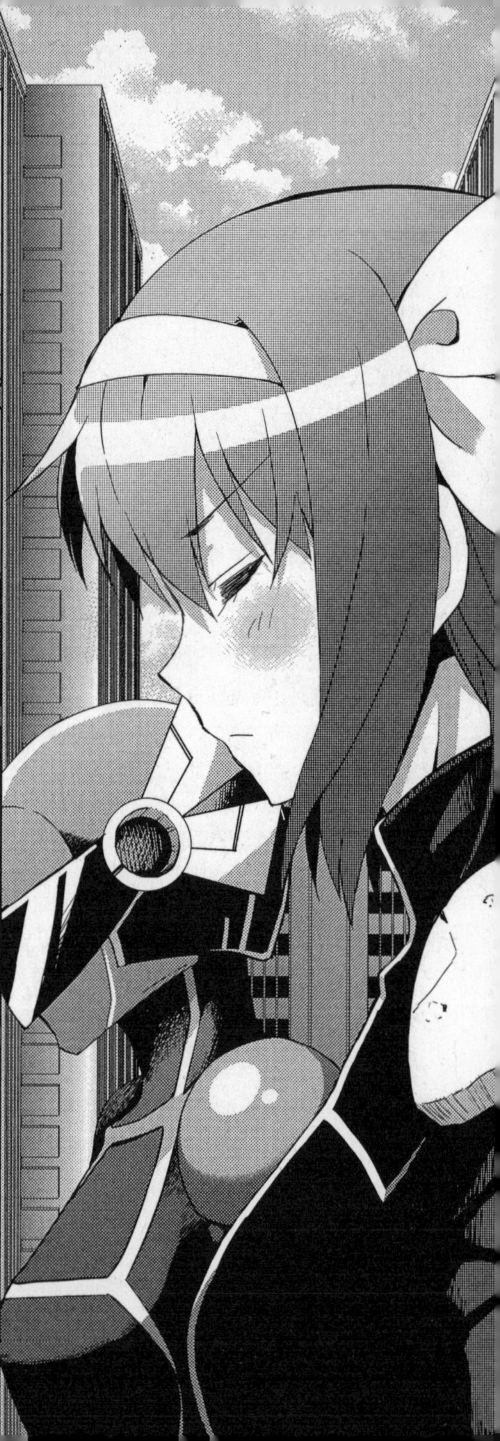

SOS BRIGADE MEETING

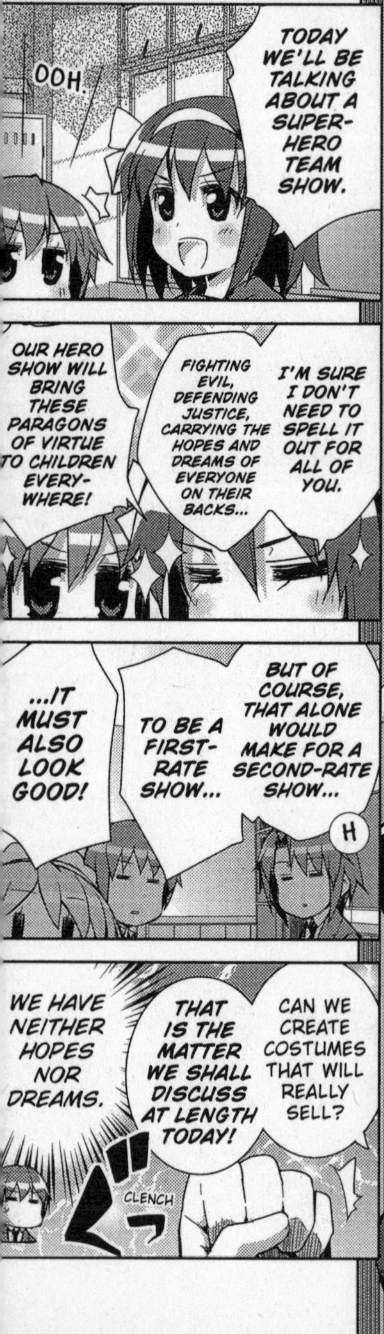
TODAY WE'LL BE TALKING ABOUT A SUPER-HERO TEAM SHOW.
OOH.
I'M SURE I DON'T NEED TO SPELL IT OUT FOR ALL OF YOU.
FIGHTING EVIL, DEFENDING JUSTICE, CARRYING THE HOPES AND DREAMS OF EVERYONE ON THEIR BACKS...
OUR HERO SHOW WILL BRING THESE PARAGONS OF VIRTUE TO CHILDREN EVERY-WHERE!
BUT OF COURSE, THAT ALONE WOULD MAKE FOR A SECOND-RATE SHOW...
H
TO BE A FIRST-RATE SHOW...
...IT MUST ALSO LOOK GOOD!
CAN WE CREATE COSTUMES THAT WILL REALLY SELL?
THAT IS THE MATTER WE SHALL DISCUSS AT LENGTH TODAY!
CLENCH
WE HAVE NEITHER HOPES NOR DREAMS.

NECESSARY ELEMENTS

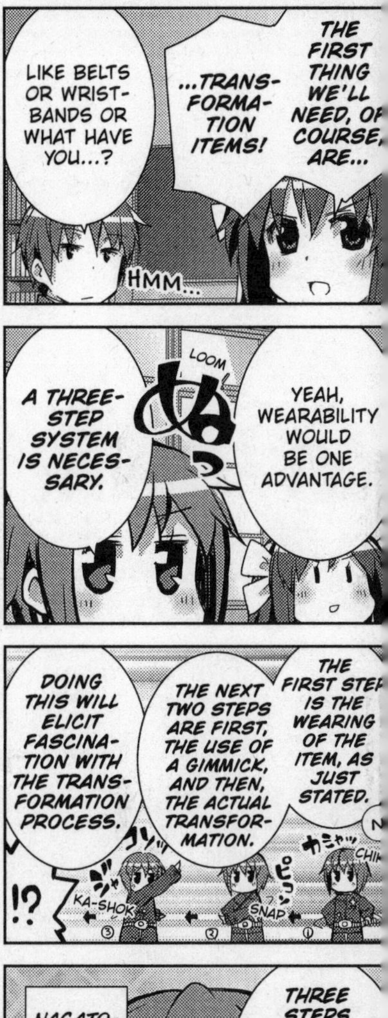
THE FIRST THING WE'LL NEED, OF COURSE, ARE...
...TRANS-FORMA-TION ITEMS!
LIKE BELTS OR WRIST-BANDS OR WHAT HAVE YOU...?
HMM...
YEAH, WEARABILITY WOULD BE ONE ADVANTAGE.
LOOM
A THREE-STEP SYSTEM IS NECES-SARY.
THE FIRST STEF IS THE WEARING OF THE ITEM, AS JUST STATED.
THE NEXT TWO STEPS ARE FIRST, THE USE OF A GIMMICK, AND THEN, THE ACTUAL TRANSFOR-MATION.
DOING THIS WILL ELICIT FASCINA-TION WITH THE TRANS-FORMATION PROCESS.
CHIK
SNAP
KA-SHOK
!?
THREE STEPS ENSURES CHILDREN WIL BE ABLE TO REMEMBER IT WITHOUT IT FEELING TOO DIFFICULT.
NAGATO-SAN, YOU'RE INTENSE !!

TRANSFORMATION BELT

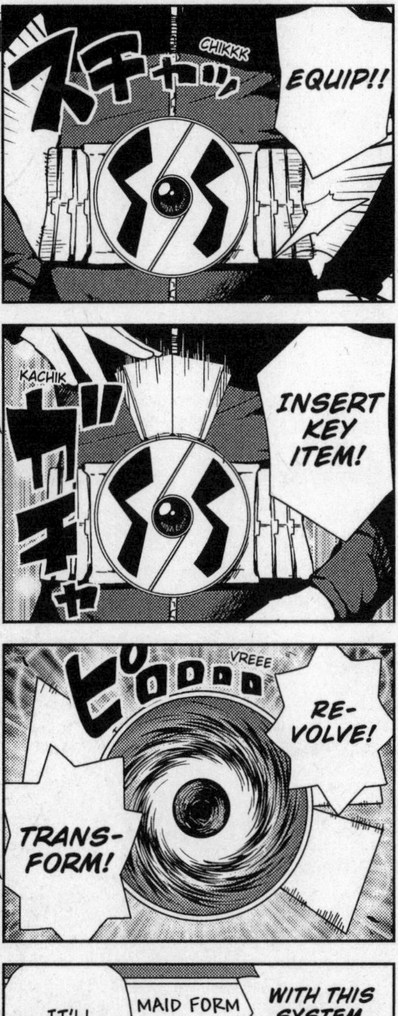
CHIKKK
EQUIP!!
KACHIK
INSERT KEY ITEM!
VREEE
RE-VOLVE!
TRANS-FORM!
WITH THIS SYSTEM, THE TRANS-FORMATION DEPENDS ON THE KEY ITEM YOU USE.
MAID FORM
IT'LL BE LIKE LUGGING AROUND A CHAMPION-SHIP BELT.

●Haruhi-chan ●SOS Brigade Leader. Evidently influenced by superhero team shows.

●Kyon ●Actually the protagonist. Despite being the protagonist, has no heroic attributes.

●Nagato ●Actually an alien. Apparently into sentai shows as well as anime and video games.

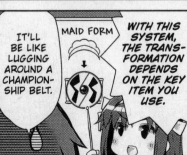

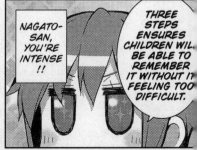

COSTUME

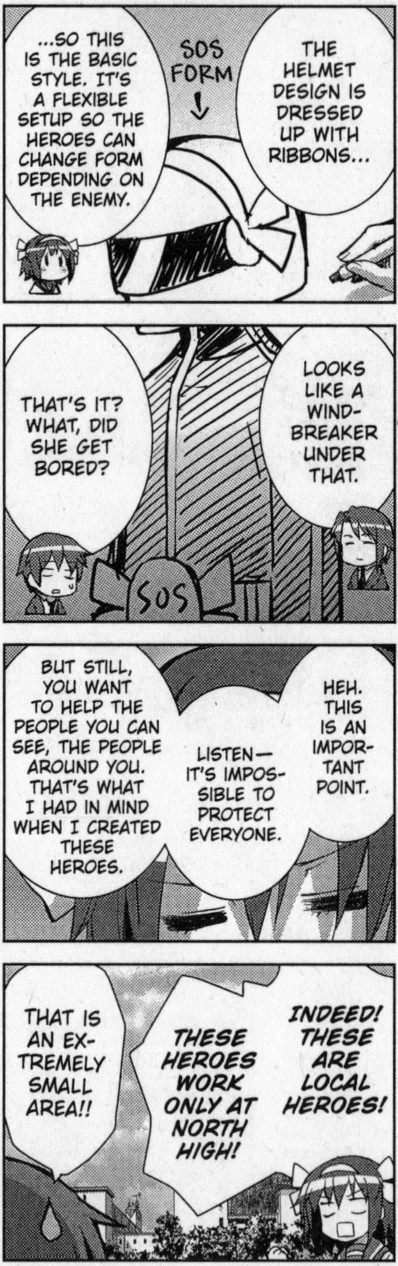
THE HELMET DESIGN IS DRESSED UP WITH RIBBONS...
SOS FORM
...SO THIS IS THE BASIC STYLE. IT'S A FLEXIBLE SETUP SO THE HEROES CAN CHANGE FORM DEPENDING ON THE ENEMY.
LOOKS LIKE A WIND-BREAKER UNDER THAT.
THAT'S IT? WHAT, DID SHE GET BORED?
SOS
HEH. THIS IS AN IMPOR-TANT POINT.
LISTEN— IT'S IMPOS-SIBLE TO PROTECT EVERYONE.
BUT STILL, YOU WANT TO HELP THE PEOPLE YOU CAN SEE, THE PEOPLE AROUND YOU. THAT'S WHAT I HAD IN MIND WHEN I CREATED THESE HEROES.
INDEED! THESE ARE LOCAL HEROES!
THESE HEROES WORK ONLY AT NORTH HIGH!
THAT IS AN EX-TREMELY SMALL AREA!!

● Mikuru-chan ● Actually a time traveler. Doesn't know much about this stuff. A little spacey.

● Koizumi ● Mysterious transfer student and esper. Also the Red guy on the team.

DEADLY WEAPON

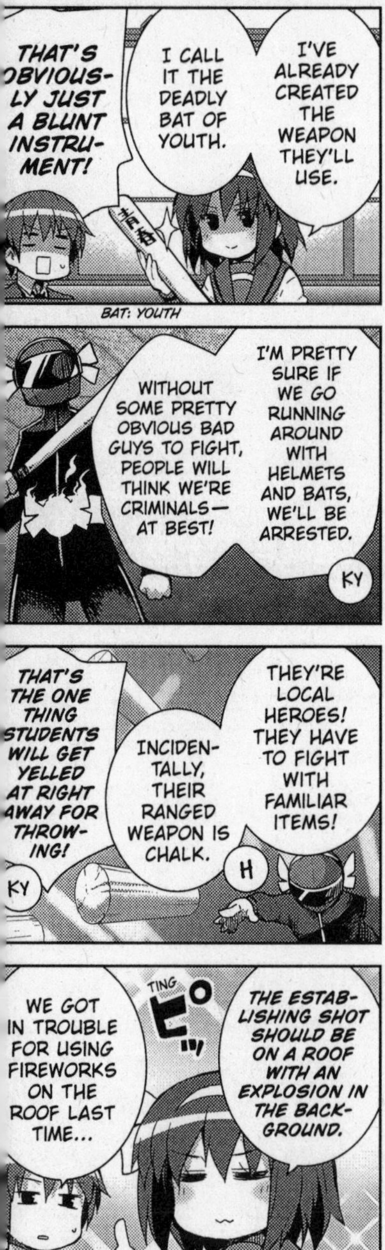
I'VE ALREADY CREATED THE WEAPON THEY'LL USE.
I CALL IT THE DEADLY BAT OF YOUTH.
THAT'S OBVIOUS-LY JUST A BLUNT INSTRU-MENT!
BAT: YOUTH
I'M PRETTY SURE IF WE GO RUNNING AROUND WITH HELMETS AND BATS, WE'LL BE ARRESTED.
WITHOUT SOME PRETTY OBVIOUS BAD GUYS TO FIGHT, PEOPLE WILL THINK WE'RE CRIMINALS— AT BEST!
KY
THEY'RE LOCAL HEROES! THEY HAVE TO FIGHT WITH FAMILIAR ITEMS!
INCIDEN-TALLY, THEIR RANGED WEAPON IS CHALK.
H
THAT'S THE ONE THING STUDENTS WILL GET YELLED AT RIGHT AWAY FOR THROW-ING!
KY
THE ESTAB-LISHING SHOT SHOULD BE ON A ROOF WITH AN EXPLOSION IN THE BACK-GROUND.
TING
WE GOT IN TROUBLE FOR USING FIREWORKS ON THE ROOF LAST TIME...

CASTING

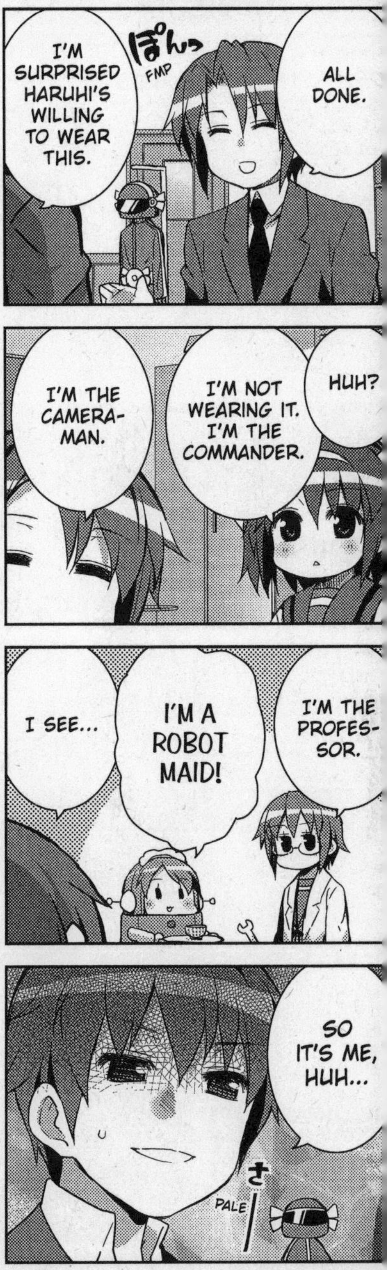
ALL DONE.
ぽんっ
FMP
I'M SURPRISED HARUHI'S WILLING TO WEAR THIS.
HUH?
I'M NOT WEARING IT. I'M THE COMMANDER.
I'M THE CAMERA-MAN.
I'M THE PROFES-SOR.
I'M A ROBOT MAID!
I SEE...
SO IT'S ME, HUH...
さ
PALE

THE SHOW

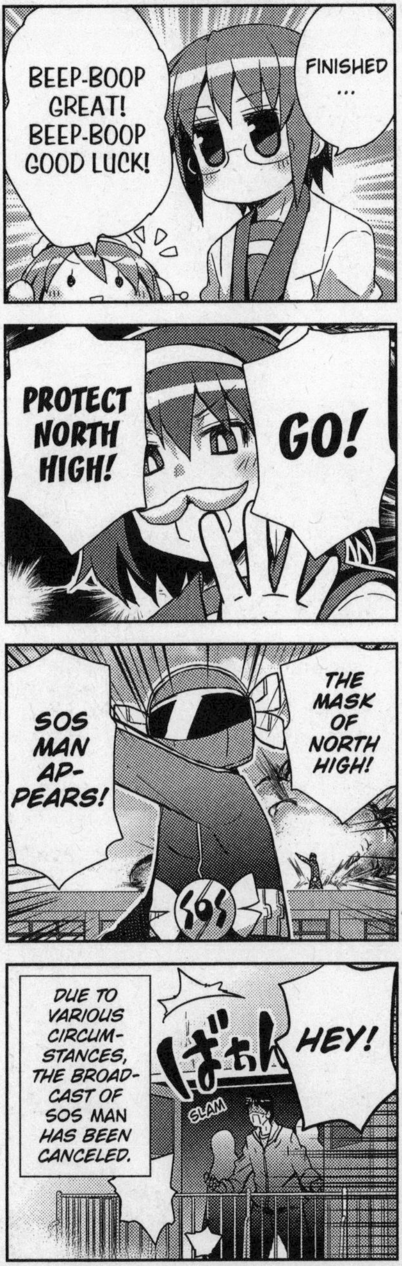
FINISHED ...
BEEP-BOOP GREAT! BEEP-BOOP GOOD LUCK!
GO!
PROTECT NORTH HIGH!
THE MASK OF NORTH HIGH!
SOS MAN AP-PEARS!
HEY!
SLAM
DUE TO VARIOUS CIRCUM-STANCES, THE BROAD-CAST OF SOS MAN HAS BEEN CANCELED.

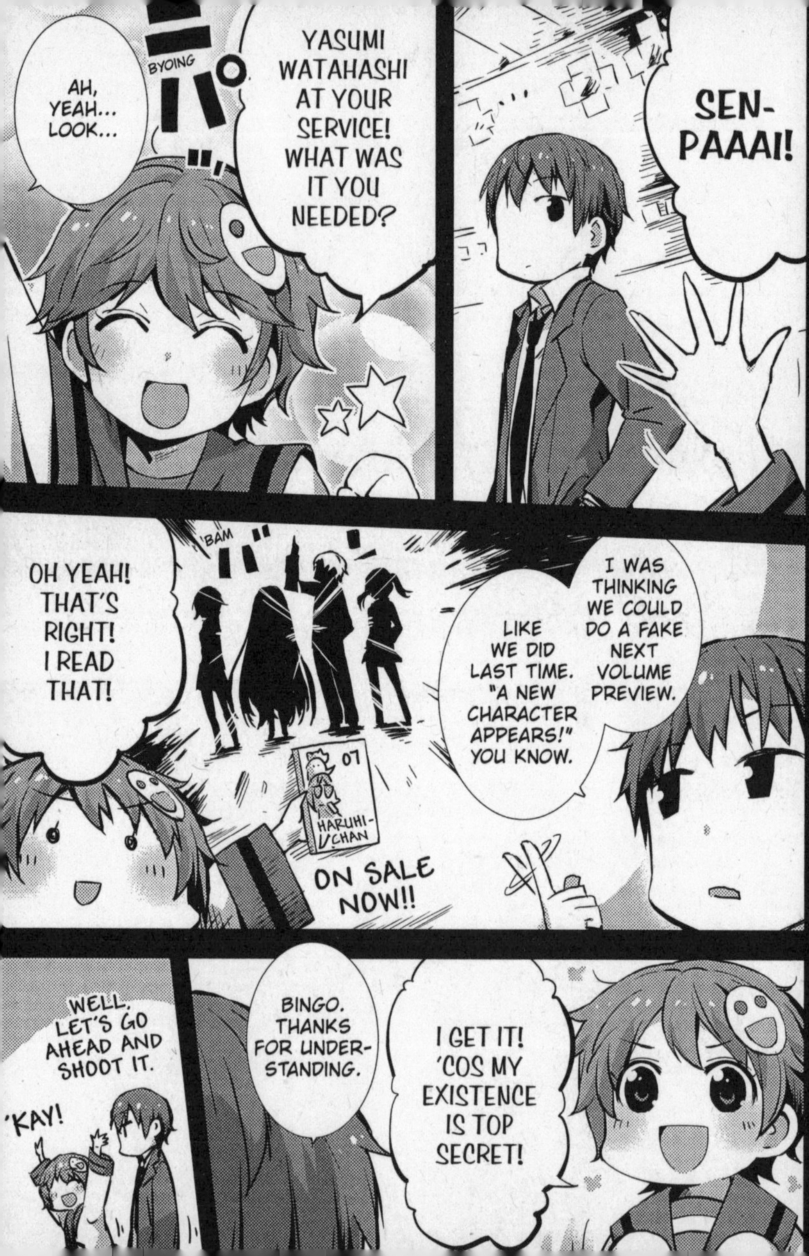
SEN-PAAAI!
BYOING
YASUMI WATAHASHI AT YOUR SERVICE! WHAT WAS IT YOU NEEDED?
AH, YEAH... LOOK...
I WAS THINKING WE COULD DO A FAKE NEXT VOLUME PREVIEW.
LIKE WE DID LAST TIME. "A NEW CHARACTER APPEARS!" YOU KNOW.
BAM
OH YEAH! THAT'S RIGHT! I READ THAT!
07
HARUHI-CHAN
ON SALE NOW!!
I GET IT! 'COS MY EXISTENCE IS TOP SECRET!
BINGO. THANKS FOR UNDERSTANDING.
WELL, LET'S GO AHEAD AND SHOOT IT.
'KAY!

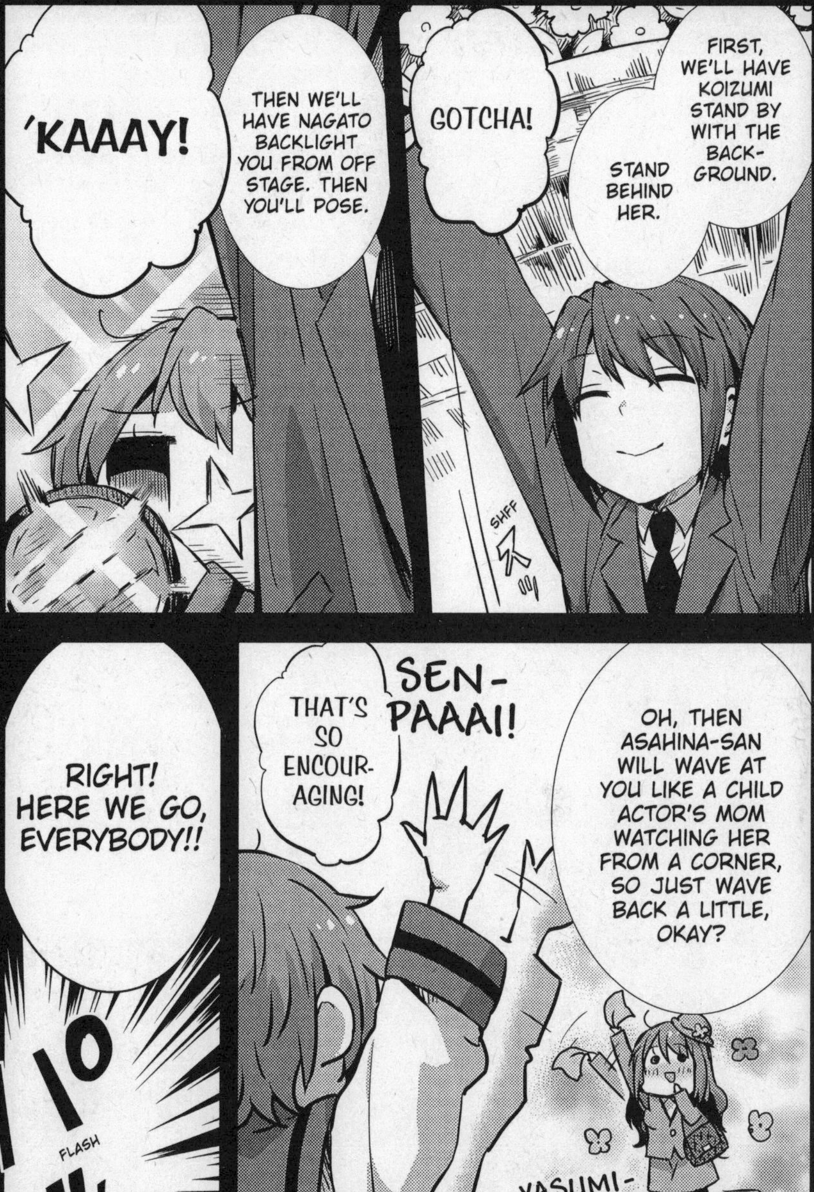
FIRST, WE'LL HAVE KOIZUMI STAND BY WITH THE BACK-GROUND.
STAND BEHIND HER.
GOTCHA!
SHFF
THEN WE'LL HAVE NAGATO BACKLIGHT YOU FROM OFF STAGE. THEN YOU'LL POSE.
'KAAAY!
OH, THEN ASAHINA-SAN WILL WAVE AT YOU LIKE A CHILD ACTOR'S MOM WATCHING HER FROM A CORNER, SO JUST WAVE BACK A LITTLE, OKAY?
SEN-PAAAI!
THAT'S SO ENCOUR-AGING!
YASUMI-CHAAAN!
RIGHT! HERE WE GO, EVERYBODY!!
FLASH

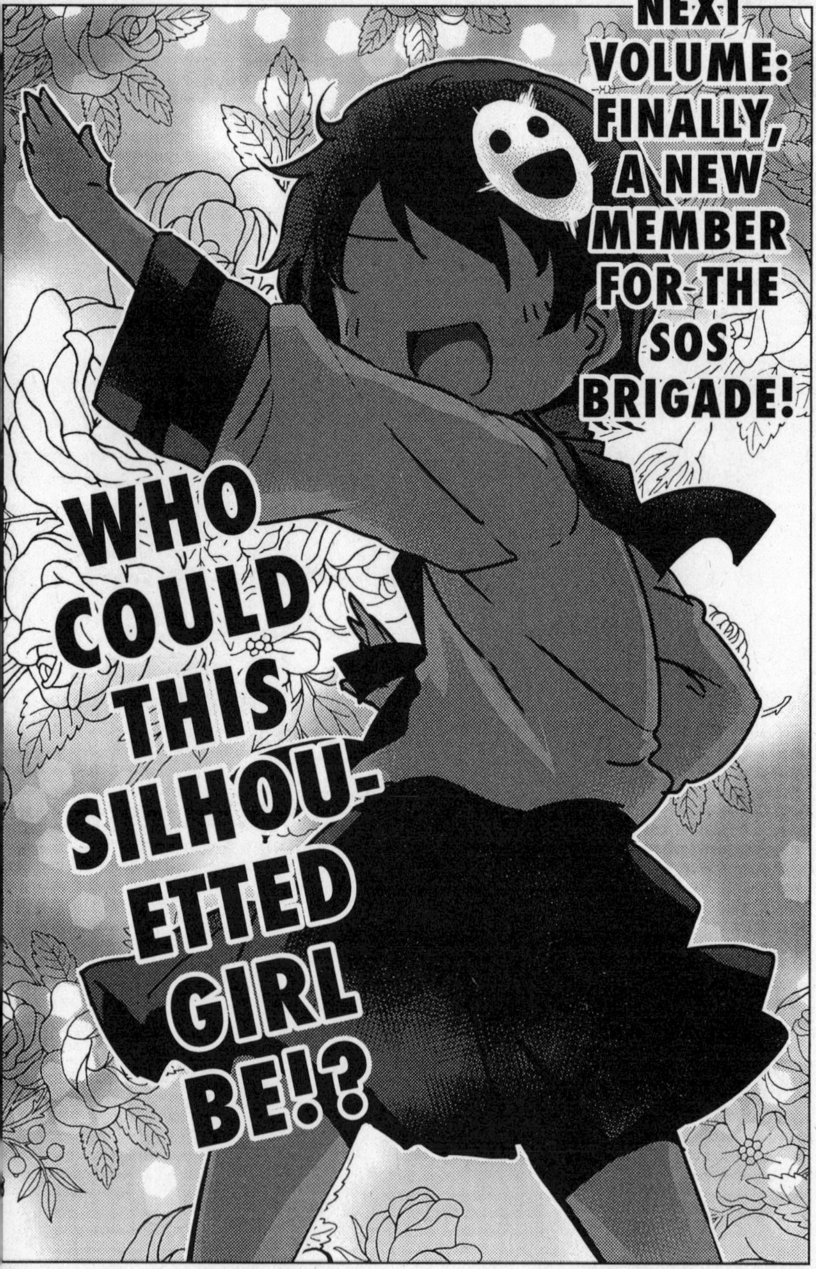
NEXT VOLUME: FINALLY, A NEW MEMBER FOR THE SOS BRIGADE!
WHO COULD THIS SILHOU-ETTED GIRL BE!?

THE MELANCHOLY of SUZUMIYA
HARUHI-CHAN
The Untold Adventures of the SOS Brigade

THE MELANCHOLY OF SUZUMIYA
HARUHI-CHAN
⑧

Original Story: Nagaru Tanigawa
Manga: PUYO
Character Design: Noizi Ito

Translation: Paul Starr
Lettering: Abigail Blackman

The Melancholy of Suzumiya Haruhi-chan Volume 8
© Nagaru TANIGAWA ● Noizi ITO 2013 © PUYO 2013. Edited by KADOKAWA SHOTEN. First published in Japan in 2013 by KADOKAWA CORPORATION, Tokyo. English translation rights arranged with KADOKAWA CORPORATION, Tokyo, through TUTTLE-MORI AGENCY, INC., Tokyo.

English translation © 2014 by Hachette Book Group, Inc.

Yen Press
Hachette Book Group
1290 Avenue of the Americas
New York, NY 10104

www.HachetteBookGroup.com
www.YenPress.com

Yen Press is an imprint of Hachette Book Group, Inc.
The Yen Press name and logo are trademarks of Hachette Book Group, Inc.

First Yen Press Edition: October 2014

ISBN: 978-0-316-33615-4

10 9 8 7 6 5 4 3 2 1

BVG

Printed in the United States of America